MAY 18 2009

W9-ANC-729

GAIA'S GARDEN

GAIA'S GARDEN

A Guide to Home-Scale Permaculture

SECOND EDITION

Toby Hemenway

CHELSEA GREEN PUBLISHING COMPANY

WHITE RIVER JUNCTION, VERMONT

WILLARD LIBRARY, BATTLE CREEK, MI

Copyright © 2000, 2009 by Toby Hemenway

Unless otherwise noted, all photographs copyright © 2009 Toby Hemenway.
Unless otherwise noted, all illustrations copyright © 2009 Elayne Sears.

All rights reserved. No part of this book may be transmitted or reproduced
in any form by any means without permission in writing from the publisher.

Project Manager: Patricia Stone
Developmental Editor: Ben Watson
Copy Editor: Margaret Pinette
Proofreader: Janice Ronish
Designer: Peter Holm, Sterling Hill Productions

Printed in the United States of America
First printing, April 2009
10 9 8 7 6 5 4 3 2 1   09 10 11 12 13

green press INITIATIVE

Chelsea Green Publishing is committed to preserving
ancient forests and natural resources. We elected to
print this title on 20-percent postconsumer recycled
paper, processed chlorine-free. As a result, for this
printing, we have saved:

41 Trees (40' tall and 6-8" diameter)
14,950 Gallons of Wastewater
28 million BTUs Total Energy
2,474 Pounds of Solid Waste
4,560 Pounds of Greenhouse Gases

Chelsea Green Publishing made this paper choice
because we are a member of the Green Press Initiative,
a nonprofit program dedicated to supporting authors,
publishers, and suppliers in their efforts to reduce their
use of fiber obtained from endangered forests. For more
information, visit www.greenpressinitiative.org.

Environmental impact estimates were made using the Environmental
Defense Paper Calculator. For more information visit: www.
papercalculator.org.

Our Commitment to Green Publishing
Chelsea Green sees publishing as a tool for cultural change and ecological stewardship. We strive to align our
book manufacturing practices with our editorial mission and to reduce the impact of our business enterprise
on the environment. We print our books and catalogs on chlorine-free recycled paper, using soy-based inks
whenever possible. This book may cost slightly more because we use recycled paper, and we hope you'll agree
that it's worth it. Chelsea Green is a member of the Green Press Initiative (www.greenpressinitiative.org),
a nonprofit coalition of publishers, manufacturers, and authors working to protect the world's endangered
forests and conserve natural resources.
   Gaia's Garden, Second Edition was printed on Renew Matte, a 20-percent postconsumer recycled paper
supplied by RR Donnelley.

Library of Congress Cataloging-in-Publication Data
Hemenway, Toby, 1952-
  Gaia's garden : a guide to home-scale permaculture / Toby Hemenway. -- 2nd ed.
     p. cm.
  Includes bibliographical references and index.
  ISBN 978-1-60358-029-8
  1. Natural landscaping. 2. Organic gardening. 3. Permaculture. 4. Gaia hypothesis. I. Title.

SB439.H44 2009
635'.048--dc22

                                       2009000785

Chelsea Green Publishing Company
Post Office Box 428
White River Junction, VT 05001
(802) 295-6300
www.chelseagreen.com

For Kiel

And in loving memory of my parents,
Tee and Jackie,
and my sister Leslie

CONTENTS

LIST OF TABLES

PREFACE TO THE SECOND EDITION

When the first edition of *Gaia's Garden* was in press, the staff at Chelsea Green, my agent, and I had animated discussions about whether the word *permaculture* should appear on the cover of the book. Back in 2000, few people had heard the term, and we all had our doubts about using it. Would the word entice potential readers or just baffle them? In the intervening years, *permaculture*, though it hasn't quite become a household word, has popped up in the media, been taught at several dozen universities, and grown a grass-roots network of many thousands of practitioners. Hence, in this edition I felt comfortable with dipping a little deeper into the nature of permaculture. If you still don't know what permaculture is, the first chapter will help explain it.

Although permaculture embraces many disciplines, most people come to it through gardening and their love of plants. Thus, though the permacultural aspects of this book are more overt in this expanded edition, the book remains garden focused rather than a sweeping guide to all aspects of sustainability.

A second change needing some explanation has occurred in the years since the first edition. When I first wrote *Gaia's Garden*, we lived on ten mostly forested acres outside Oakland, Oregon, a village of 850 in very rural Douglas County. This was where I learned the concepts and methods described in the book, and I refer to our Oakland home often. But life is constant change, and many circumstances, including the success of this book, meant that we needed to be nearer to people. We have since moved north by a three-hour drive to Portland, Oregon, and now live on a small urban lot. This forced two changes in the book: The references to our southern Oregon home are now in the past tense, and I have added a chapter on urban permaculture

gardening. The book's focus has always been on the typical North American yard of one-quarter acre or less, but city living and landscaping pose a unique set of challenges and opportunities for ecological gardening in smaller spaces. Since three-quarters of the people on this continent live in metropolitan areas, I wanted to provide all of us, even those with no yard at all, with tools for using our landscapes to reduce our ecological footprint and become more self-reliant, while enhancing habitat for increasingly threatened wildlife.

This book began when I visited a garden that felt unlike any I had seen.

Walking in an ancient forest or snorkeling in a coral reef, I have felt an aliveness, a sense of many interlocking pieces clicking together into a living and dynamic whole. These are places that naturally exude abundance. Sadly, this feeling was lacking in any human-made landscape I had experienced. Natural landscapes seem so rich; they seethe with activity; they hum with life in comparison to our own. Why is it that nature can splash riotous abundance across forest or prairie with careless grace, while we humans struggle to grow a few flowers? Why do our gardens offer so little to the rest of life? Our yards seem so one-dimensional, just simple places that offer a few vegetables or flowers, if that much. Yet nature can do a thousand things at once: feed insects and birds, snakes and deer, and offer them shelter; harvest, store, and purify water; renew and enrich the soil; clean the air and scent it with perfume; and on and on.

Then I encountered a garden that had the vivid aliveness of nature, yet it was packed with fruit and edible greens. Soon I found a few others like it. In these places, using new techniques from permaculture and ecological design and old ones from indigenous people and organic gardening, a growing band of pioneers has created landscapes that feel like nature but provide an abundant home for people as well. These are true backyard ecosystems that were designed with methods and concepts gleaned from nature and that feel as alive as any forest. I wanted to know how to create these places, and I wanted to help others create more. *Gaia's Garden* is the result.

These gardens represent a new landscape, one that provides for people as well as for the rest of nature. You could think of them as "edible landscaping meets wildlife gardening," but they are more than that. These are true backyard ecosystems—not just disconnected fragments—that are as resilient, diverse, productive, and beautiful as those in nature. They are not merely flowery showplaces or ruler-straight arrays of row crops. Yet they also are not the brambly tangles that identify many wildlife gardens. They are places where conscious design has been melded with a respect and understanding of nature's principles. The result is a living and riotously abundant landscape in which all the pieces work together to yield food, flowers, medicinal and edible herbs, even craft supplies and income for the human inhabitants, while providing diverse habitat for helpful insects, birds, and other wildlife. Places where nature does most of the work, but where people are as welcome as the other inhabitants of Earth.

Although this book is about environmentally friendly landscapes, it is not an eco-fanatic's manifesto. It's a book on gardening, full of techniques and garden lore. But between the lines on these pages is a plea for less consumption and more self-reliance. Anyone who would pick up this book is probably familiar with the environmental destruction humans have wrought in the past few decades, so I'm not going to assault my readers with grim statistics. Suffice it to say that we have to do better. This book is an attempt to show one way to proceed. Our home landscapes consume immense amounts of resources—far more water, fertilizer, and pesticides per acre than any industrialized farm. And providing for our needs spurs relentless conversion of wild land into factory farms and industrial forests. Yet our yards, city parks, curbsides, even parking lots and office courtyards could become lush, productive, and attractive landscapes that aid nature while yielding much for us as well, instead of being the grassy voids that they are now. This book shows how to do this, using techniques and examples devised by the pioneers of the sustainable-landscaping movement.

This book is an introduction to ecological and permacultural landscaping. *Gaia's Garden* is not an introductory gardening book—I assume that most of my readers have done a little gardening—but I do attempt to explain some new techniques and concepts well enough for novice gardeners to implement them. Many of the subjects touched on here are large enough to deserve a book of their own, so lamentably I've had to limit how deeply I plunge into some fascinating topics. This may be frustrating to some readers, but I've included an annotated bibliography and a resources section to allow further pursuit of these subjects.

Most plants mentioned in the text are identified by common name to avoid the Latinate bafflement that botanical nomenclature can inflict on many gardeners. For a few unusual or ambiguous species, I've added the botanical name. The various tables and lists of plants are alphabetized by common name, but in those I have included the botanical name as well, as that is the only way to be sure we're all talking about the same species.

With hundreds of thousands of plant species to choose from, these tables cannot hope to be comprehensive lists of all useful plants, but I hope my selections will provide readers with a broad palette from which to choose. To represent the wide variety of geographic regions on this continent, I've also tried to give examples from many areas and for different climates. More Americans now live west of the Mississippi than east of it, and this book reflects that bicoastal reality.

Most of the ideas in this book aren't mine. Many of the techniques shown here have been practiced by indigenous people for millennia or worked out by gardeners of all stripes. They have also been compiled in the ever-broadening array of books on ecological design and permaculture. In this book, I've attempted to synthesize these permacultural ideas with ecologists' growing understanding of what makes nature work. I can claim credit for few of the techniques and concepts described here, merely for the way some of them are presented. And of course, any errors are my own.

Numerous people unselfishly gave me their time, collaboration, hard work, and support. For inspiration, suggestions, and for their development of the ideas of permaculture, my first and biggest thanks go to Bill Mollison and David Holmgren. For touring me through their gardens and for their generosity I thank—in alphabetical order—Earle Barnhart, Douglas Bullock, Joe Bullock, Sam Bullock, Kevin Burkhart, Doug Clayton, Joel Glanzberg, Ben Haggard, Marvin Hegge, the much-missed Simon Henderson, Alan Kapuler, Brad Lancaster, Penny Livingston, Art Ludwig, Vicki Marvick, Anne Nelson, Jerome Osentowski, John Patterson, Barbara Rose, Julia Russell, James Stark, Roxanne Swentzell, Tom Ward, and Mary Zemach. For support and fruitful ideas I thank Peter Bane, Bill Burton, Brock Dolman, Ianto Evans, Heather Flores, Jude Hobbs, Dave Jacke, Keith Johnson, Mark Lakeman, Michael Lockman, Scott Pittman, Bill Roley, Larry and Kathryn Santoyo, Michael Smith, John Valenzuela, and Rick Valley. For assuring me that books were not as hard to write as I feared, a special thanks to Stuart Cowan. To my agent, Natasha Kern, I owe a huge debt for her perseverance, ideas, tenacity, and steadfast confidence and support. Thanks also to my editors, Rachael Cohen and Ben Watson, who have smoothed the text considerably, tidied up my grammatical excesses, and guided me through the labyrinthine process of publication. The staff at Chelsea Green have been a pleasure to collaborate with. And for a thousand graces, large and small, while I twice disappeared into this book, I am grateful to my wife and soulmate, Kiel.

TOBY HEMENWAY

PART ONE

The Garden as Ecosystem

CHAPTER ONE

Introducing the Ecological Garden

The movement toward sustainable landscaping is heating up. Gardeners are increasingly burying their resource-guzzling, zero-habitat lawns under native-plant gardens, wildlife-attracting thickets, and sun-dappled woodlands. It's an encouraging trend, this movement toward more ecologically sound, nature-friendly yards.

Yet not everyone is on board. Some gardeners hesitate to go natural because they can't see where, for example, the orderly rows of a vegetable garden fit into this wilder style. What will happen to those luscious beefsteak tomatoes? Or ornamental plants—does sustainable gardening mean tearing out a treasured cut-flower bed or pulling up grandmother's heirloom roses to make room for a natural-looking landscape?

Nurturing wildlife and preserving native species are admirable goals, but how do *people* fit into these natural landscapes? No gardener wants to feel like a stranger in her own backyard. Gardeners who refuse to be excluded from their own yards, but love nature, have been forced to create fragmented gardens: an orderly vegetable plot here, flower beds there, and a corner for wildlife or a natural landscape. And each of these fragments has its weaknesses. A vegetable garden doesn't offer habitat to native insects, birds, and other wildlife. Quite the contrary—munching bugs and birds are unwelcome visitors. The flower garden, however much pleasure the blooms provide, can't feed the gardener. And a wildlife garden often looks unkempt and provides little for people other than the knowledge that it's good for wild creatures.

This book shows how to integrate these isolated and incomplete pieces into a vigorous, thriving backyard ecosystem that benefits both people and wildlife. These gardens are designed using the same principles that nature uses to create healthy plant communities, so that the different plantings and other elements interconnect and nurture one another.

Ecological gardens meld the best features of wildlife gardens, edible landscapes, and conventional flower and vegetable gardens, but they go beyond simply adding these styles together. They are more than the sum of their parts. An ecological garden feels like a living being, with a character and essence that is unique to each. These gardens are grounded in relatively new concepts such as permaculture and ecological design, but they use time-tested techniques honed to perfection by indigenous people, restoration ecologists, organic farmers, and cutting-edge landscape designers. They combine low environmental impact, low maintenance (once established), and high yields with elegant aesthetics. *Gaia's Garden* provides tools to understand, design, and construct these backyard ecosystems so they will benefit people and the rest of nature as well.

Ecological gardens are filled with beautiful plants that have many uses, providing fruit and vegetables, medicinal and culinary herbs, eye-catching arrays of

Permaculture designer Larry Santoyo of Earthflow Design Works aimed to integrate the greater watershed landscape into this urban Santa Barbara, California, garden. Built at the base of a mountain, the garden was reoriented into terrace beds and pathways that flow along the contour lines to capture precious runoff in the arid climate. An arbor built from locally harvested bamboo frames the view of the neighboring gardens, provides vertical growing area for kiwi vines and wisteria, and creates a zone to rest and relax. Japanese persimmon and citrus trees are mulched with living groundcovers of drought-resistant nasturtium, Mexican primrose *(Oenothera speciosa)*, thyme, and calendula.

colorful blossoms, soil-building mulch, protection from pests, and habitat for wildlife. With thousands of plant species to choose from, we can find plenty that do several of these jobs at once. Multifunctional plants are a hallmark of gardens based on ecological principles: that's how nature works. We can choose food plants that support insects and other wildlife, herbs that break up hardpan, cover crops that are edible, or trees that add nutrients to the soil.

These landscapes can even yield income from edible and medicinal plants, seeds and nursery stock, or dried flowers, and provide construction or craft materials such as lumber, bamboo poles, basket willow, and vegetable dyes. Yet in a garden designed along ecological principles, birds and other animals feel just as welcome in these living landscapes as the gardener. With good design these gardens need only infrequent watering, and the soil renews itself rather than demanding heavy fertilizing. These are living ecosystems, designed using nature's rules and boasting the lushness and resilience of the natural environment.

What Is Permaculture?

I refer often in this book to *permaculture* and *ecological design,* two closely related subjects on which many of the ideas in this book are based. Since permaculture may be an unfamiliar word to some readers, I should do some explaining.

Permaculture uses a set of principles and practices to design sustainable human settlements. The word, a contraction of both "permanent culture" and "permanent agriculture," was coined by two Australians. The first was Bill Mollison, a charismatic and iconoclastic one-time forester, schoolteacher, trapper, field naturalist, and author of the dense and encyclopedic bible of the field, *Permaculture: A Designer's Manual.* The other is David Holmgren, one of the first of Bill's many students, who has brilliantly expanded permaculture's scope.

Mollison says the original idea for permaculture came to him in 1959 when he was observing marsupials browsing in Tasmanian rain forests. Inspired and awed by the life-giving abundance and rich interconnectedness of this ecosystem, he jotted in his diary, "I believe that we could build systems that would function as well as this one does." In the 1970s he and Holmgren, using what they had observed in nature and in indigenous cultures, began to identify the principles that made those systems so rich and sustainable. Their hope was to apply these principles to designing ecologically sound, productive landscapes. They reasoned that if life had been thriving on Earth for over three billion years, if indigenous peoples had been living relatively harmoniously in their environments for millennia, then life and indigenous cultures must have figured out some things about sustainability. David's undergraduate thesis, which he and Bill revised and expanded, evolved into the groundbreaking book *Permaculture One.*

Permaculture began, then, as a set of tools for designing landscapes that are modeled after nature, yet include humans, and this book—once we get the definition of permaculture out of the way—will focus on the landscape-design aspect of permaculture. But Mollison, Holmgren, and those who came after them quickly realized that even if we learn to create farms, gardens, and landscapes that mimic nature, a sustainable land use that is embedded in an unsustainable society won't prevent our tenure on this planet from being short, increasingly impoverished, or both. However, it turns out that permaculture's principles—since they are grounded in nature's wisdom—have breathtaking scope, far beyond permaculture's origins in agriculture. Permaculture has been used to design buildings, energy and wastewater systems, villages, and even less tangible structures such as school curricula, businesses, community groups, and decision-making processes.

How does permaculture do this?

Though on one level permaculture practitioners design with organisms, buildings, and those less tangibles that we refer to as invisible structures, they focus less on the objects themselves than on the careful design of relationships among them—interconnections—that will create a healthy, sustainable whole. These relationships are what turn a collection of unrelated parts into a functioning system, whether it's a backyard, a community, or an ecosystem.

If this still seems a mite theoretical, here is a more down-to-earth definition of permaculture. If we think of practices like organic gardening, recycling, natural building, renewable energy, and even consensus decision-making and social-justice efforts as tools for sustainability, then permaculture is the toolbox that helps us organize and decide when and how to use those tools. Permaculture is not a discipline in itself but rather a design approach based on connecting different disciplines, strategies, and techniques. It, like nature, uses and melds the best features of whatever is available to it. Some people new to this approach think of permaculture as a set of techniques. Although there are certain methods that are used often because they illustrate permaculture principles beautifully, such as herb spirals and keyhole beds (which you'll see in the following pages), there are few, if any, techniques that belong only to permaculture. Permaculturists employ techniques from a broad range of disciplines, but these tools are selected and applied according to how well they allow permaculture's principles to be applied, not because a particular method is "how we do it in permaculture."

In a culture that focuses on things rather than on relationships, permaculture's emphasis on connections instead of "stuff" can make it tricky to explain. Some beginning permaculturists have annoyed advocates of various sustainable practices by saying "permaculture includes organic gardening (or solar energy, or natural building)." But rather than absorbing those disciplines or considering them as part of (and thus smaller than) it, permaculture shows us where and how to apply these important ideas. It is a linking science.

The aim of permaculture is to design ecologically sound, economically prosperous human communities. It is guided by a set of ethics: caring for Earth, caring for people, and reinvesting the surplus that this care will create. From these ethics stem a set of design guidelines or principles, described in many places and in slightly varying forms. The list below is the version I use, compiled with the aid of many permaculture teachers and flowing from the work of Mollison, Holmgren, and their coauthors.

Permaculture Principles

A. Core Principles for Ecological Design

1. Observe. Use protracted and thoughtful observation rather than prolonged and thoughtless action. Observe the site and its elements in all seasons. Design for specific sites, clients, and cultures.
2. Connect. Use relative location, that is, place the elements of your design in ways that create useful relationships and time-saving connections among all parts. The number of connections among elements creates a healthy, diverse ecosystem, not the number of elements.
3. Catch and store energy and materials. Identify, collect, and hold useful flows. Every cycle is an opportunity for yield, every gradient (in slope, charge, temperature, and the like) can produce energy. Reinvesting resources builds capacity to capture yet more resources.
4. Each element performs multiple functions. Choose and place each element in a design to perform as many functions as possible. Beneficial connections between diverse components create a stable whole. Stack elements in both space and time.
5. Each function is supported by multiple elements. Use multiple methods to achieve important functions and to create synergies. Redundancy protects when one or more elements fail.
6. Make the least change for the greatest effect. Understand the system you are working with well enough to find its "leverage points" and intervene there, where the least work accomplishes the most change.
7. Use small-scale, intensive systems. Start at your doorstep with the smallest systems that will do the job and build on your successes. Grow by "chunking"—that is, developing a small system or

Gardens that *Really* Work with Nature

Ecology, Mr. Webster tells us, is "concerned with the interrelationship of organisms and their environments." I call these gardens *ecological* because they connect one organism—people—to their environment, because they link the many pieces of a garden together, and because they can play a role in preserving healthy ecosystems.

Ecological gardens also blend many garden styles together, which gives the gardener enough leeway to emphasize the qualities—food, flowers, herbs, crafts, and so on—he or she likes most. Some ecological gardening finds its roots in edible landscaping, which, in a creative melding, frees food plants from their vegetable-patch prison and lets them mix with the respectable front-yard society of ornamentals. Ecological landscapes also share traits

arrangement that works well—and repeat it, with variations.

8. Optimize edge. The edge—the intersection of two environments—is the most diverse place in a system and is where energy and materials accumulate or are translated. Increase or decrease edge as appropriate.

9. Collaborate with succession. Living systems usually advance from immaturity to maturity, and if we accept this trend and align our designs with it instead of fighting it, we save work and energy. Mature ecosystems are more diverse and productive than young ones.

10. Use biological and renewable resources. Renewable resources (usually living beings and their products) reproduce and build up over time, store energy, assist yield, and interact with other elements. Favor these over nonrenewable resources.

B. Principles Based on Attitudes

11. Turn problems into solutions. Constraints can inspire creative design, and most problems usually carry not just the seeds of their own solution within them but also the inspiration for simultaneously solving other problems. "We are confronted by insurmountable opportunities."—Attributed to Pogo (Walt Kelly).

12. Get a yield. Design for both immediate and long-term returns from your efforts: "You can't work on an empty stomach." Set up positive feedback loops to build the system and repay your investment.

13. The biggest limit to abundance is creativity. The designer's imagination and skill usually limit productivity and diversity before any physical limits are reached.

14. Mistakes are tools for learning. Evaluate your trials. Making mistakes is a sign you're trying to do things better. There is usually little penalty for mistakes if you learn from them.

How do we use the principles? As you read this book, you'll see dozens of examples of how they are put into practice. Permaculture designer and teacher Larry Santoyo calls the principles "indicators of sustainability."

Any design, whether it is of a garden, a house, or a nonprofit corporation, that uses these principles will be more efficient, effective, and ecologically balanced than one that violates them. Use them to guide your decisions and, as you create your garden, try to apply them in as many places as you can. Pay particular attention to situations where the principles aren't being followed, as those will be the spots that drain the most labor and do the most environmental damage.

The principles have deep and surprising interconnections as well. A piece of a design that strives to, say, be multifunctional will often turn out to also follow the principles "use biological resources" and "make the least change for the greatest effect." When synergies like these occur, they show we are on the right track.

Permaculture, then, is about far more than gardening. But since permaculture is grounded in the wisdom of the natural world, many people come to permaculture first through their love of plants and gardening. I will struggle in this book to limit my coverage of permaculture to the home landscape.

with wildlife gardens, they provide habitat for the more-than-human world. And since local florae gets prominent billing in these gardens, it has much in common with native-plant gardens.

But these landscapes aren't just a simple lumping together of other garden styles. They take their cues from the way nature works. Some gardens look like natural landscapes, but that's as far as the resemblance goes. I've seen native-plant gardens that require mountains of fertilizer because they're in unsuitable soil and herbicides to quell the vigorous grasses and weeds that happily rampage among the slow-growing natives. That's hardly natural. An ecological garden both looks and *works* the way nature does. It does this by building strong connections among the plants, soil life, beneficial insects and other animals, *and* the gardener, to weave a resilient, natural webwork. Each organism is tied to many others. It's this interconnectedness that gives nature strength. Think of a net or web: snip one thread, and the net still functions because all the other connections are holding it together.

Nothing in nature does just one thing. This multifunctionalism—wherein each interconnected piece plays many roles—is another quality separating an ecologically designed garden from others. In the typical garden, most elements serve only a single purpose. A tree is chosen for shade, a shrub for its berries, a trellis to restrain that unruly grapevine. But by designing a garden so that each piece can play all the roles it's capable of, not only can the gardener let nature do much of the work, the garden will be prone to fewer problems and will become a lusher, richer place. That shade tree, for example—can't it also offer nuts or other food for both people and wildlife and maybe attract pollinators that will later help fruit trees bear more heavily? Plus, the tree's leaves will build the soil when they fall, and it's harvesting rainwater and pulling dust out of the air. That tree is already doing about fifteen different jobs. We just need to connect these "yields" to other parts of the garden that need them. That will mean less work for us and better health for the landscape.

The grape arbor could be shading a too-sunny deck on the hot south side of the house; that means it will cool both deck and building and offer fruit to the lucky souls lounging beneath it. The pieces are all there, ready and waiting. We just need to link them together, using nature's marvelous interconnectedness as a model.

Also, this connectedness goes two ways. In nature not only does each piece play many roles, but each role is supported by many players. For example, each insect pest in a natural landscape is pursued by a hungry army of natural predators. If one predator bug, or even a whole species, falls down on its bug-eating job, others are there to pick up the slack. This redundancy shrinks the risk of failure. So, looking back at that lone shade tree from this perspective, don't plant just one—plant a cluster of several varieties. If one grows slowly or doesn't leaf out densely, the others are there to fill in. The combination will cast shade over a longer season, too. See the synergy? Continuing in this vein, to the grape arbor we could add a clematis to contribute color, a jasmine for scent, or some early climbing peas to lengthen the harvest season and boost the yield.

Here's another example of how connectedness can make gardens more natural and also save work. When we lived in our rural place in southern Oregon, deer were a big problem, chomping down almost any unprotected plant. They trampled a well-worn path into my yard from the southwest. So on that side I placed a curving hedge to deflect them from other tasty plantings. The hedge was built around a few native shrubs already there—oceanspray, wild roses, a lone manzanita. But I chose the other hedge species to do several jobs. I planted bush cherries, Manchurian apricots, currants, and other wildlife plants for wildlife food and thorny wild plums, Osage orange, and gooseberries to hold back the deer. But on the inside of the hedge—my side—to some of these hedgerow plants I grafted domestic fruit varieties. The wild cherries grew sweet cultivars on the hedge's house-facing side, and the shrubby apricots and wild plums soon sprouted an assortment of luscious Asian plums. This food-bearing hedge (sometimes called a *fedge*) fed both the deer and me.

I connected this hedge to other natural cycles. It was a good distance from our house, and I quickly tired of lugging fertilizer and the hose to it. So in the hedge I planted some clovers and two shrubs, Siberian pea shrub and buffalo berry, to add nitrogen to the soil. And I seeded-in several deep-rooted species, including chicory, yarrow, and daikon

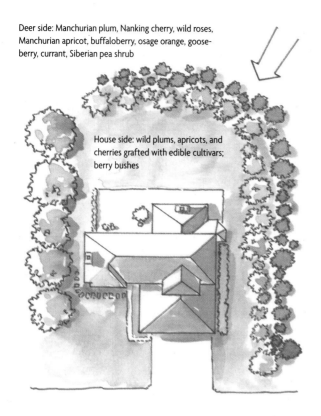

Deer side: Manchurian plum, Nanking cherry, wild roses, Manchurian apricot, buffaloberry, osage orange, gooseberry, currant, Siberian pea shrub

House side: wild plums, apricots, and cherries grafted with edible cultivars; berry bushes

A deer-deflecting food hedge, with wildlife plants on the outside, but human-used varieties on the side toward the house.

radish, which pull nutrients from the subsoil and deposit them on the surface at leaf-fall. These will build up the soil naturally. I wanted to conserve water, so I added mulch-producing species like comfrey and cardoon, a thick-leaved artichoke relative. I slashed their leaves periodically and left them on the ground to create a mulch layer that holds moisture in the soil. The hedge still needed some irrigation in southern Oregon's ninety-day dry season, but the mulch plants saved lots of water.

As the hedge matured, deer became less of a problem for us. By the time the animals had munched along the hedge to its end, they were almost to the edge of the yard and showed little interest in turning back toward the house. But everything changes, and this did too, when a new neighbor moved in

just up our gravel road. Coming from the city, he thought deer were cute and began leaving out boxes of rotting apples for them. This radically altered the approach pattern for the deer, and ever-growing herds of them began mobbing his fruit boxes via the road above our house rather than through the woods where the hedge lay. Ambling along the road to and from the bonanza at our neighbor's house, many of the deer wandered into the unhedged side of our yard. Their browsing there was too ferocious for me to establish a new hedge. Reluctantly I put up fencing on the upper side of the garden. But the food hedge still protected the downhill slope and provided us with fruit.

Nature has a broad back, and with a little ingenuity and a change in viewpoint, a gardener can shift plenty of labor to this willing partner. Nature can be the gardener's ally. We still hold vestiges of an earlier time's regard for nature as an enemy or as something to be conquered and restrained. Say the word *insect* to a gardener, and he will nearly always think of some chomping, sucking pest that tatters leaves and ruins fruit. Yet the vast majority—90 percent or more—of all insects are beneficial or harmless. A diverse and balanced ensemble of insects in the landscape means good pollination and fruit set, and quick, nontoxic control of pest outbreaks, held in check by predaceous bugs. We *need* insects in the garden. Without them our workload would be crippling—hand-pollinating every bloom, grinding fallen leaves into compost by hand.

The same applies for all the other denizens of life's kingdoms. Not only are bugs, birds, mammals, and microbes essential partners in every kind of garden, but with clever design, they can work with us to minimize our labor and maximize the beauty, health, and productivity of our landscapes. Even domestic animals can help with gardening, as I'll explain in a later chapter.

Why Is Gardening So Much Work?

One object of an ecological garden is to restore the natural cycles that have been broken by conventional landscape design and agriculture. Have you ever wondered why a forest or meadow looks perfect and stays nearly disease free with no care at all, while a garden demands arduous hours of labor? In a garden, weeds still pop up like, well, weeds, and every plant seems to be covered in its own set of weird spots and chomping bugs. This happens because most gardens ignore nature's rules.

Look how gardens differ from natural landscapes. Not only does nature never do just one thing, nature abhors bare soil, large blocks of a single plant type, and vegetation that's all the same height and root depth. Nature doesn't till, either—about the only time soil is disturbed in the wild is when a tree topples and its upturned roots churn the earth. Yet our gardens are virtual showcases of all these unnatural methods. Not to mention our broadscale use of pesticides and chemical fertilizers.

Each of these unnatural gardening techniques was developed for a specific purpose. Tilling, for example, destroys weeds and pumps air to microbes that, metabolically supercharged, release a flood of nutrients for fast crop growth. These are great short-term boons to plant growers. But we now know that, in the long term, tilling depletes fertility (those revved-up microbes will burn up all the nutrients, then die), causes more disease, and ruins the soil structure, with compaction to hardpan and massive erosion the result.

The bare soil in a typical garden, whether in a freshly tilled plot or between neatly spaced plants, is a perfect habitat for weed seeds. Weeds are simply pioneer plants, molded by billions of years of evolution to quickly cover disturbed, open ground. They'll do that relentlessly in the bare ground of a garden. Naked earth also washes away with rain, which means more tilling to fluff the scoured, pounded earth that's left and more fertilizer to replace lost nutrients.

Solid blocks of the same plant variety, though easy to seed and harvest, act as an "all you can eat" sign to insect pests and diseases. Harmful bugs will stuff themselves on this unbroken field of abundant food as they make unimpeded hops from plant to plant and breed to plague proportions.

Each of the conventional techniques cited above arose to solve a specific problem; but, like any single-minded approach, they don't often combine well with other one-purpose methods, and they miss the big picture. The big picture here, in the typical garden, is not a happy one. Lots of tedious work, no habitat for native or rare species, struggling plants on intensive care, reliance on resource-gobbling poisonous chemicals, and, in general, a decline in the garden's health, yield, and beauty unless we constantly and laboriously intervene. Yet we've come to accept all this as part of gardening.

There is another way to garden. Conventional landscapes have torn the web of nature. Important threads are missing. We can restore many of these broken links and work with nature to lessen our own load, not to mention the cost to the environment. For example, why till and add trainloads of fertilizer, when worms and other soil life, combined with fertility-building plants, will tailor the finest soil possible, with very little work? That's how nature does it. Then all we need to do is make up for the small amount of nutrients lost to harvest. (Plants are mostly water, plus some carbon from the air. The tiny amounts of minerals they take from the soil can easily be replaced if we use the proper techniques.)

"Let nature do it" also applies to dealing with pests. In a balanced landscape, diseases and insect problems rarely get out of control. That's because in the diverse, many-specied garden that this book tells how to create each insect, fungus, bacterium, or potentially invasive plant is surrounded by a natural web of checks and balances. If one species becomes too abundant, its sheer availability makes it a tasty, irresistible food source for something else, which will knock it back to manageable levels. That's how nature works, and that's a useful trick for the ecological garden.

Creating a well-balanced garden means knowing something about how nature behaves. Toward that end, this book offers a chapter on ecology for gardeners, and many examples of nature's principles at work are woven throughout the other chapters. By using nature's methods, whether for growing vegetables, flowers, or wildlife plants, the garden becomes less work, less prone to problems, and vastly more like the dynamic, vibrant landscapes found in nature. These backyard ecosystems are deeply welcoming for both the wild world and people, offering food and other products for self-reliance, as well as beauty and inspiration.

Beyond—Way Beyond—Natural Gardening

Some of what you have read so far may sound familiar. The past twenty years have seen the arrival of native plant gardens and landscapes that mimic natural groupings of vegetation, a style usually called natural gardening. Many of these gardens attempt to re-create native plant communities by assembling plants into backyard prairies, woodlands, wetlands, and other wild habitats. So gardening with nature will not be a new idea to many readers.

Ecological gardens also use principles derived from observing and living in wild land but toward a different end. Natural gardens consist almost exclusively of native plants and are intended to create and restore habitat. Some small percentage of the species planted may be endangered, although usually they are common natives. These gardens are often described, as Ken Druse writes

in *The Natural Habitat Garden*, as "essential to the planet's future." I support using native plants in the home landscape. But natural gardens, offering little for people, will never have more than a tiny effect on environmental damage. Here's why.

In the United States, all the developed, inhabited land—cities, suburbs, and rural towns, including roads, buildings, yards, and so on—covers only about 6 percent of the nation's area. You could fill every yard and city park with native plants and not even begin to stanch the loss of native species and habitat.

However, even if developed land in cities and suburbs were packed with native-only gardens, it would never be wild. Divided into tiny fragments by streets, plastered over with houses and highways, the streams culverted and run underground, filled with predatory cats and dogs, this is land that has been taken over by humans and our allies and removed from larger ecosystems, and it's going to stay that way. I don't deny that if we planted suburbia with uncommon, endangered natives we might rescue some tiny number of species. But many native species, particularly animals, are incompatible with land occupied by modern people and require large tracts of unspoiled terrain to survive. Planting suburban yards with natives won't save them.

Also, the real damage to the environment is done not by the cities and suburbs themselves but by meeting their needs. We, who live in the developed 6 percent of the land, have an insatiable appetite and use between 40 and 70 percent of America's land area (estimates vary depending how "use" is defined) to support us. Monocultured farms and industrial forests, grazing land and feedlots, reservoirs, strip and open pit mines, military reservations, and all the other accoutrements of modern civilization consume a huge amount of space, and almost none of it functions as native or healthy habitat. Each nonhomegrown meal, each trip to the lumber yard, pharmacy, clothing store, or other shop, commissions the conversion of once-native habitat into an ecological desert. The lumber for a typical American house of 2,500 square feet scalps roughly three acres of forest into barren clearcut—thus, living in a modest house will aid native species vastly more than will installing a few mountain laurels on a small suburban lot.

Certainly, natives should be included in our yards, but native plant gardens won't reduce our depredations of wild land very much unless we also lessen our resource use. A native plant garden, while much easier on the environment than a lawn, does not change the fact that the owner is causing immense habitat loss elsewhere, out of sight. But an ecological garden can change that.

Every bit of food, every scrap of lumber, each medicinal herb or other human product that comes from someone's yard means that one less chunk of land outside our hometown needs to be denuded of natives and developed for human use. Factory farms and industrial forests—pesticide-laced, monocropped, sterilized of everything but a single species—are far more biologically impoverished than any suburban backyard. But farms and tree plantations are the lands that could truly become wilderness again. Cities and suburbs are already out of the natural loop, so we should strive to make them as useful to people and as multifunctional as possible, not simply office parks and bedrooms. And urban land can be incredibly productive. In Switzerland, for example, 70 percent of all lumber comes from community woodlots. Our cities could provide the materials for many human needs and allow some cropland and tree farms to return to nature.

I'm not talking about converting every backyard to row crops. By gardening ecologically, designing multifunctional landscapes that provide food and other goods for ourselves while creating habitat for other species, we can make our cities truly bloom. But a yard full only of native plants, lacking any for human use, simply means that somewhere else, out of sight, there is a nonnative-containing farm and a factory forest, with the environmental destruction they bring, providing for that native-loving suburbanite's needs. Even organic farms are usually monocultures. In contrast, a yard planted with carefully chosen exotics (and some natives too) will reduce the ecological damage done by the human occupants far more than a native-plant garden. Taking care of ourselves in our own yards means that factory farms and forests can shrink. Somewhere a farmer won't have to plow quite so close to a creek, saving riparian species that could never thrive in a suburban lot.

The Natives versus Exotics Debate

First, a word on terminology. The term *invasive* is emotionally loaded with negative connotations. The term implies that a species by itself can invade, yet the ability to invade is not held by any one species. Whether an organism can invade a new landscape depends on the interaction between it and its environment, both living and inanimate. Dropped into one new home, a species may thrive; in another it may fail utterly. Calling a species "invasive" is not good science. Following David Jacke in his book, *Edible Forest Gardens*, I will use the word *opportunistic*, which more accurately gives the sense that a species needs particular conditions to behave as it does. Many unruly exotic species are insipidly tame in their home habitat. Even the words *native* and *exotic* have their difficulties, although I continue to use them. Does exotic mean a species wasn't here before you got here, or before the first botanist did, before Columbus, the first human, or what? Species are constantly in motion. We need to rethink these words and why we use them.

Gardening with native plants has become not merely popular in recent years, it's become a *cause célèbre*. Supporters of natural gardening can become quite exercised when someone recommends nonnative plants. Governments, agribusinesses, and conservation groups have spent millions of dollars trying to eradicate "exotic" species. Parks departments across the nation have enacted native-only policies for trails, playgrounds, and other public places. The arguments for natives have merit: of course we want to preserve our native species and their habitat. But much of the energy spent on yanking exotics and planting natives is misdirected and futile, evidenced by the failure of so many restoration projects in which the nonnatives quietly reestablish after the funding or labor pool runs out. Without major changes in our land-use practices, the campaign to eradicate exotic plants approaches futility. A little ecological knowledge shows why. Look at most opportunistic plants. European bittersweet and Japanese honeysuckle swarm over New England's forest margins. Kudzu chokes the roadsides and forest edges in the South. Purple loosestrife sweeps across the waterways of both coasts and the Midwest, and Russian olive springs up as small forests in the West. In nearly every case, these plants are invading disturbed land and disrupted ecosystems, fragmented and degraded by grazing, logging, dams, road building, pollution, and other human activity. Less-disturbed ecosystems are much more resistant to opportunistic species, though opportunists can move into them if they establish at entry points such as road cuts and logging sites.

One pro-native garden writer describes what he calls "the kudzu phenomenon, where an exotic displaces natives unless we constantly intervene." But our intervention is the problem. We assume nature is making a mistake when it creates hybrid, fast-healing thickets, so rather than allowing disturbed habitat to stabilize, we keep disturbing it. We can spray and uproot bittersweet and honeysuckle all we want, but they'll come right back.

These are species that love sunlit edges, and we've carved forests into countless tiny pieces that have more edge than interior, creating perfect habitat for these exotics. The same goes for kudzu, loosestrife, and nearly all the rest. In the East, purple loosestrife followed the nineteenth-century canals into wetlands; and in the West it has barreled down irrigation ditches into marshland and ponds. Humans create perfect conditions for exotics to thrive. I've often heard blame put on one or another opportunistic species when a native species goes locally extinct. That's understandable. When we lose something we love, we search for a scapegoat, and a newly arrived species makes a ready target. But virtually every time I've examined that charge, it turns out that the place had first been severely disturbed by development, logging, or other human use. The opportunist moved in after the primary damage was done and often in direct response to it.

Opportunistic plants crave disturbance, and they love edges. Those are two things development spawns in huge quantity. Unless we stop creating edge and disturbance, our eradication efforts will be in vain, except in tiny patches. The best long-term hope for eliminating most opportunistic species lies in avoiding soil disturbance, restoring intact forest, and shading the newcomers out with other species. In other words, we need to create landscapes that are more ecologically mature. Opportunistic plants are, with a few exceptions such as English ivy, almost exclusively pioneer species that need sunlight, churned-up ground, and, often, poor soil. For example, kudzu, Scot's broom, and Russian olive are nitrogen fixers whose role is to build soil fertility. So they prosper in farmed-out fields and overgrazed rangeland and are nature's way of rebuilding fertility with what is available.

Here's why opportunistic plants are so successful. When we clear land or carve a forest into fragments, we're creating lots of open niches. All that sunny space and bare soil is just crying out to be colonized by light- and fertility-absorbing green matter. Nature will quickly conjure up as much biomass as possible to capture the bounty, by seeding low-growing "weeds" into a clearing or, better yet, sprouting a tall thicket stretching into all three dimensions to more effectively absorb light and develop deep roots. That's why forest margins are often an impenetrable tangle of shrubs, vines, and small trees: there's plenty of light to harvest. Just inside the edge, though, where there is less light and little disturbance, forests are usually open and spacious.

When humans make a clearing, nature leaps in, working furiously to rebuild an intact humus and fungal layer, harvest energy, and reconstruct all the cycles and connections that have been severed. A thicket of fast-growing pioneer plants, packing a lot of biomass into a small space, is a very effective way to do this. Permaculture's cooriginator, David Holmgren, calls these rampantly growing blends of natives and exotics "recombinant ecologies" and believes that they are nature's effective strategy of assembling available plants to heal damaged land. Current research is showing the value and healing power of these new ecologies. If we clear out the thicket in the misguided belief that meadows should forever remain meadows even under heavy irrigation, or that all forest edges should have tidy, open understories, we are just setting the recovery process back. Nature will then relentlessly return to work, filling in with pioneer plants again. And she doesn't care if a nitrogen fixer or a soil-stabilizing plant arrived via continental drift or a bulldozer's treads, as long as it can quickly stitch a functioning ecosystem together.

The sharply logged edge of a woodland abutted by a lawn or field—so common in suburbs—is a perfect home for sun-loving exotics. If we plant low trees and shrubs to soften these margins, thus swallowing up the sunlight that pierces the forest edges,

the niche for the opportunist will disappear. Simply removing the exotic won't do much good except in a highly managed yard. The plant will come right back into the perfect habitat that waits for it. That's one reason that herbicide manufacturers are helping fund the campaign for native plants. They know a repeat customer when they see one. Nature abhors a vacuum—create one, and she'll rush in with whatever's handy. To eradicate opportunists, the habitat for it must be changed into a more mature, less hospitable landscape. The conditions that support the opportunist must be eliminated.

This approach is far from "live and let live" and more effective than an eternity of weed pulling. Pioneer weedscapes may be nature's way, but most people don't want their yard edges to be a tangled thicket. Yards can be kept free from opportunists, particularly in small spaces and if we're willing to be persistent for several seasons. But it's hard to succeed when we're stuck on the old "clear, spray, and curse" treadmill. An easier and more productive strategy is to learn from the more mature forest edges near us. Again, observing nature can teach us what species naturally nestle into the sunny margins of old woods. Look at these places, and you may find dogwood, cherry, crabapple, alder, or small varieties of maple. The species vary around the country, but edge-loving trees and shrubs are good candidates for jump-starting a yard or woodlot margin toward a more mature ecological phase. Plant them at those overgrown woody edges to fill in the gaps before something you don't want takes hold. You can't fight nature—nature always bats last—but you can sometimes be first to get where it's going.

The nineteenth-century scientist Thomas Henry Huxley likened nature to a brilliant opponent in chess: "We know that his play is always fair, just, and patient. But also we know, to our cost, that he never overlooks a mistake, or makes the smallest allowance for ignorance." Nature has a patience that humans lack. We may uproot some bittersweet or kudzu for a few seasons, but nature will keep reseeding it, year in, year out, waiting until we tire of the battle. Nature takes the long view.

It is only our limited time frame that creates the whole "natives versus exotics" controversy. Wind, animals, sea currents, and continental drift have always dispersed species into new environments. Remember that for millions of years there have been billions of birds, traveling hundreds or thousands of miles, each with a few seeds in its gut or stuck to the mud on its feet. And each of these many billions of seeds, from thousands of species, is ready to sprout wherever the bird stops. The planet has been awash in surging, swarming species movements since life began. The fact that it is not one great homogeneous tangled weed lot is persuasive testimony to the fact that intact ecosystems are very difficult to invade.

Our jet-age mobility has arguably accelerated the movement of species in unnerving and often economically damaging ways. But eventually an opportunistic species, after a boom-and-bust period, comes into equilibrium with its surroundings. It may take a decade or a century, time spans that seem like an eternity to a home owner contending with bittersweet or star thistle. But one day the new species becomes "implicated" into the local ecosystem, developing natural enemies and encountering unwelcome environments that keep it in check.

"Native" is merely a question of perspective: is a species native to this hillside, or this county, the bioregion, continent, or perhaps just to this planet? I see a certain irony in immigrant-descended Americans cursing "invasive exotics" for displacing native species. And often an opportunistic species is playing an important role, where nature is working on a problem that we may not recognize and using the best tools available. For example, purple loosestrife, perhaps the poster child of exotic-species eradication enthusiasts, turns out to be superb at both tolerating and cleaning up polluted water. It, like many other opportunistic species, is screaming out to us that there is a problem—contaminated water—and is one of nature's best agents for solving the problem by scouring out the pollutants. Also, research is showing that once pollution levels recede to relative cleanliness, the loosestrife dies back. Other researchers have found that, contrary to assumptions, loosestrife patches support just as many native pollinators and birds as surrounding areas of native plants. This shows that we need to look deeper into our reasons for demonizing certain species.

Of course, it is foolish to deliberately introduce a species known to be locally opportunistic. Permaculturists use a hierarchy of safety for choosing plants. First, use a native to fill the desired role if at all possible. If no natives for that niche exist, then use a tested exotic. Only after a great deal of research would a person then consider a small-scale introduction of a new exotic; and, to be honest, I have never done that, don't personally know anyone who has, and don't recommend it. There are thousands of species that have been tried in many habitats, and if one from that huge assortment won't work, perhaps what you have in mind doesn't need to be done.

I love native plants and grow them whenever appropriate. But nearly the whole issue—from branding certain fast-spreading, soil-building pioneer plants as evil, to creating the conditions that favor their spread—stems from not understanding nature's ways. When we think ecologically, the problem either evaporates as a misunderstanding or reveals solutions inherent in the life cycle of the opportunist. A plant will thrive only if conditions are right for it. Modify those conditions—eliminate edge, stop disturbing soil, cast shade with trees, clean up pollution—and that opportunist will almost surely cease to be a problem.

I'm also uneasy with the adversarial, polarized

relationship with plants that an overzealous enthusiasm for natives can foster. It can result in a "natives good, everything else bad" frame of mind that heats the gardener's blood pressure to boiling at the sight of any exotic plant. Rage is not the best emotion to be carrying into the garden. And we're all utterly reliant on nonnatives for so many of our needs. Look at our diet. Where did this morning's breakfast come from? I'd be surprised if many Americans regularly consume a single plant native to their state. About the only common food crops native to North America are sunflowers, hops, squash, and some nuts and berries. Nearly everything we eat originated on other continents. Get rid of exotics, and most of us would be pretty hungry until we learned to prepare local roots, berries, nuts, and greens.

This is why I advocate a sensible balance of native and exotic plants in our landscapes. We may not be able to restore our cities to native wilderness, but our gardens can play an important role in restoring the functions and services provided by our planet's environment. A major premise of this book is that our own yards can allow us to reduce our incessant pressure on the planet's health. The techniques of permaculture and ecological design allow us to easily, intelligently, and beautifully provide for some of our own needs. We can create landscapes that behave much like those in nature but tinker with them just a bit to increase their yield for people while preserving native habitat. And in so doing we can allow some of those factory farms and industrial forests to revert to wild land.

We have assembled enough knowledge from cultures that live in relative harmony with their environment, and from scientific studies of ecology and agriculture, to create gardens that offer both habitat to wildlife and support for people. They don't look like farms. Instead they have the same feel as the native vegetation but can be tweaked to provide for the needs and interests of the human residents. Picture your favorite natural landscape and then imagine plucking fruit from the trees, making a crisp salad from the leaves, clipping a bouquet from the abundant flowers, laying in a supply of garden stakes from a bamboo patch. These gardens tailor a large place for people yet still behave like ecosystems, recycling nutrients, purifying water and air, offering a home for native and naturalized flora and fauna.

Both natural gardens and ecological gardens emphasize the role of *plant communities*, that is, groupings of trees, shrubs, and nonwoody plants that naturally occur together and seem to be connected into a whole. The difference is that natural gardens attempt to mimic native plant communities, while the gardens in this book combine natives, food plants, medicinal and culinary herbs, insect- and bird-attracting species, plants that build soil, and others into synergistic, mutually beneficial groupings. These "synthetic" plant communities, which permaculture calls *guilds*, form healthy, interacting networks that reduce the gardener's labor, yield abundant gifts for people and wildlife, and help the environment by restoring nature's cycles.

Indigenous people, especially those living in the tropics, have been using guilds for millennia to create sustainable landscapes. Only recently have we understood what they were doing and how they do it. Anthropologists mistook the lush and productive home gardens that enfolded tropical houses for wild jungle, so perfectly had the inhabitants mimicked the surrounding forest. From these gardeners we've learned something about creating landscapes that work just like nature but offer a role for people.

In temperate climates, the art and science of fashioning communities of useful, attractive plants is a new and vigorous field. Many of the gardeners I spoke to while researching this book are pioneering these techniques. The last few chapters of this book explain how to design and use guilds to create vibrant "food forests" and beautiful habitats for people and wildlife. I hope that some who read this book will add to this burgeoning field.

Making the Desert Bloom, Sustainably

To help readers get a feel for an ecological garden, let me describe one of the finest examples I've seen. North of Santa Fe, New Mexico, sculptor Roxanne Swentzell has created an oasis in the high desert she calls Flowering Tree Permaculture Institute.

When I arrived at Flowering Tree, I stepped out of my car and was blasted by the mid-90s heat and the searing glare reflected from the bare, eroded hillsides nearby. But before me was a wall of greenery, a lush landscape that I'd spotted from at least a mile away, in soothing contrast to the yellow sand and gravel of the desert.

I entered the yard through a gap between arching trees, and the temperature plummeted. The air here was fresh, cool, and moist, unlike the dusty, sinus-withering stuff I'd been breathing outside. A canopy of walnut trees, piñon pine, and New Mexico black locust sheltered a lush understory of pomegranates, nectarines, jujube trees, and almonds. An edible passionflower swarmed up a rock wall. Grapevines arched over an entry trellis. Two small ponds sparkled with rainwater caught by the adobe house's roof. Winking brightly from under shrubs and along pathways were endless varieties of flowers, both native and exotic.

Roxanne, an athletic-looking woman with high, solid cheekbones bequeathed by her Santa Clara forebears, greeted me, smiling at my somewhat dazed appearance. She'd seen this before, as visitors gawked at the luxuriant growth so dissimilar to the barrenness outside. "We've got about 500 species here, on one-eighth acre or so," she told me. "We've tried to make it a self-sufficient place that will take care of us while we take care of it. So we grow whatever we can that will survive in this climate."

In 1986 she moved onto a parcel of bare land on the Santa Clara homelands. She describes the place as "no trees, no plants, no animals, just pounded-down dirt and lots of ants." She and her two young children built a passive-solar adobe house and began planting. But the climate was too harsh. Dry winds swept down from the scoured, overgrazed hills and burned up the seedlings, killing those that hadn't frozen out in winter.

Local permaculture designer Joel Glanzberg entered Roxanne's life at about this time and helped her ferret out techniques for gardening in the desert. They dragged in rocks and logs to shade seedlings and dug shallow ditches, called swales, to catch precious rainwater and create sheltered, moist microclimates. To cast much-needed shade and generate organic matter, Joel and Roxanne planted just about any useful drought-tolerant plant, native or exotic, that they could find. Thirstier species they located within reach of the *asequia*, or irrigation ditch, that surged with water once a week by tribal agreement. Without reliable water, the garden would have been impossible to establish in the desert heat.

They hauled in manure and mulch materials to build rich soil that would hold moisture through drought. Once the hardy young trees and shrubs had taken hold, they set more delicate plants in their shade. They blended berry bushes and small fruit trees into an edible hedge along the north border, to offer them food as well as block the winds that roared down the nearby canyon. All these techniques combined into a many-pronged strategy to build fertile soil, cast shade, damp the wild temperature swings of the desert, and conserve water. Together these practices created a mild, supportive place to grow a garden. Slowly the barren landscape transformed into a young, multistoried food forest.

Roxanne told me, "The garden was hard to get

Designer Joel Glanzberg stands in a barren desert plot in 1989 at Flowering Tree Permaculture Institute in New Mexico.

Four years later, Joel stands in the same spot. An intellligent permaculture design has created a lush oasis around him.

started, but once the little seedlings took off, then boy, they took off." At my visit, the landscape was eight years old, and trees, where none had been before, were as tall as the two-story house. Blessed, cooling shade, from dense to dappled, halted the searing rays of the sun. Instead of baking the soil, the fierce solar heat was absorbed by the thick leafy canopy and converted into lush greenery, mulch, food, and deep-questing roots that loosened the soil. In the bright gaps, flowers and food plants vied for sunlight. Even in the shade, a many-layered understory of shrubs and small trees divided the yard into a path-laced series of small rooms.

I caught glimpses of birds dancing from twig to twig before they disappeared into the shrubbery. A constant rustling and chirping enveloped us on all sides, and I knew that dozens more birds were hidden in the foliage. Metallic-sheened beneficial wasps dove into the blossoms that surrounded us, and butterflies of all sizes and colors soared and flapped from flower to leaf. Roxanne carried pruning shears with her as she walked and lopped off the occasional too-exuberant branch from the mulberries, plums, black locusts, and other vigor-ously growing trees and shrubs that lined the paths. These would feed her turkeys or become more mulch.

She pointed out a crimson trumpet-blossomed

Penstemon barbatus that looked unhappy in the deep shade. "Things change so fast here," she said. "This was in full sun two years ago. Now it's completely shaded out, and I think it might be rotting from the soil staying too wet. And look at all these peaches. I better get busy harvesting."

The techniques and design strategies (which this book will describe in detail) had transformed the landscape. Roxanne and her helpers had reju-venated a battered plot of desert, created a thick layer of rich soil, and brought immense biodiver-sity to a once-impoverished place. Here in the high desert was almost too much water and shade. Food was dropping from the trees faster than they could harvest, and birds that no one had seen for years were making a home in the yard.

Not everyone begins with as difficult a challenge, as devastated a site, as Roxanne. But there's quite a gap between the typical yard and what Roxanne and other similar gardeners have created. The average yard is both an ecological and agricultural desert. The prime offender is short-mown grass, which offers no habitat and nothing for people except a place to sit, yet sucks down far more water and chemicals than a comparable amount of farmland. The common, single-function plantings found in most landscapes also have their share of drawbacks. Highly bred flowers, lacking pollen and nectar, displace bird- and insect-nurturing varieties. Many ornamental plants are no more than pleasant eye candy and could be replaced by equally attractive species that have uses for people and wildlife.

Typical gardening techniques don't help much, either. A tidy layer of bark mulch, instead of more natural and protective ground plants, robs small animals and insects of their homes. The heavy chemical use in most lawns, needed because natural soil fertility and insect predators are absent, pollutes water, kills wildlife, and is almost certainly linked to many ailments. And as mentioned, unproductive home landscapes mask and contribute to the immense environmental damage our resource consumption does elsewhere, out of sight.

The ecological garden offers a solution. Our yards could be deeply connected to nature yet be more than just wildlife or native plant gardens—they could link *us* to nature's abundance as well. The techniques and strategies to do this have been worked out by resourceful and imaginative pioneers. These people have mapped a new terrain and brought back what they've learned. I spoke to many of them and visited their vibrant, naturally productive landscapes while researching *Gaia's Garden*. These pioneers shared their knowledge, which I have done my best to present in the following pages.

How to Use This Book

Gaia's Garden is divided into three parts. The rest of Part One continues this introduction to the idea of the garden as an ecosystem. Chapter 2 offers a simple guide to concepts from ecology that gardeners can apply to make their yards work more like nature. Fear not—this is not a textbook, it's a gardening manual, so I don't go into technical details. I give plenty of practical examples of ecological principles at work. Next, Chapter 3 describes

the design process and techniques that are used to create an ecological garden. Most of these ideas will be familiar to those versed in permaculture, but they may be new to people from a traditional gardening background.

Moving from theory toward practice, Part Two of the book looks at the pieces of the ecological garden. A chapter each delves into soil (Chapter 4), water (Chapter 5), plants (Chapter 6), and animals (Chapter 7), but from a different perspective from that of most garden books. Instead of viewing soil, water, plants, and animals as static, as objects to be manipulated into doing what we want, I treat them as dynamic and constantly evolving, as having their own qualities that need to be understood to work with them successfully, and as intricately connected to all the other parts of the garden.

Part Three shows how to assemble the garden's elements into a backyard ecosystem. Chapter 8 begins with simple interplanting techniques and expands on these to show how to create polycultures (blends of several to many plant species that work together) and human-designed plant communities, or guilds. Chapter 9 offers several methods for designing garden guilds. Building on these two chapters, Chapter 10 describes how to assemble plants and guilds into a multistoried food forest or forest garden. Chapter 11 offers strategies and techniques for the special challenges confronted by city dwellers. The final chapter reveals how these gardens take on a life of their own and mature into self-sustaining miniecosystems that are far more than the sum of their parts. I also give a few tips and techniques for accelerating this process.

The main text of the book explains the ideas behind an ecological garden and gives examples and descriptions of the ideas in action. Specific garden techniques are usually set off from the text in boxes so they are easy to find. Included also are lists of plants relevant to the ideas in the text (insect-attracting species, drought-tolerant plants, and so on), and the appendix contains a large table of useful, multifunctional plants and their characteristics.

Many of the techniques and ideas in this book can be used by themselves, simply as ways to make a conventional garden more productive or Earth friendly. There's nothing wrong with taking a mix-and-match approach to these ideas, using only the ones that are easy to fit into an existing land-scape. But these techniques are also synergistic; the more that you put in practice, the more they work together to create a richly connected and complete landscape that is more than a group of independent parts. These resilient, dynamic backyard ecosystems act like those in nature while providing for us and reducing our demands on the diminishing resources of this planet.

CHAPTER TWO

A Gardener's Ecology

Something was stealing the Bullock brothers' food.

Joe, Douglas, and Sam Bullock had moved to Washington's San Juan Islands in the early 1980s and set to work creating a food forest. They built up their property's soil and planted fruit trees, nut trees, and hundreds of other species, all calculated to boost the biological diversity and lushness of this once-scrubby, blackberry-entangled parcel. A decade later, walnut trees and bamboo groves shaded the paths. Plums, peaches, cherries, and apples hung in thick festoons from spreading branches, and beneath them flowers, berries, edible greens, and soil-building plants sprawled over every inch of earth. The Bullocks had created a self-renewing ecosystem that fed their families and visitors, furnished nursery stock for their landscaping business, and sheltered local wildlife.

One edge of their property bordered a wetland reclaimed a few years before from abandoned farmland. At the marsh's edge, cattails grew in thick stands. Young cattail shoots are a delicious wild food, and for several springs and summers the brothers had harvested the baby shoots, steamed or sautéed them, and added them to meals. But one year they couldn't find any shoots, only tough mature cattail stalks. Their natural food source had dried up, and the brothers wanted to know why.

A close look at the marsh revealed that some animal was gnawing the tender shoots off at the waterline.

The thieves were thorough. Nothing remained for the Bullock brothers and their families.

The culprit was quickly spotted. "We'd noticed that as the bog matured and became more productive, the muskrat population was really taking off," Douglas Bullock told me. The brothers had built garden beds that extended into the marsh, copying an idea from the ancient Aztecs. They had created peninsulas by piling straw and branches that reached out like fingers from the shoreline, covered them with rich bog muck, and planted these self-watering garden beds, called *chinampas*, with food and wildlife plants. The local animals, already enjoying the new wetland, responded to the enhanced habitat of the *chinampas* with explosive breeding. Ducks, kingfishers, herons, and other water birds now abounded, and so did muskrats. "Suddenly the bog looked like a busy harbor, criss-crossed with muskrat wakes," Douglas said. Whole flotillas of muskrats were tunneling into the rich soil along the marsh edge and nibbling down the cattail shoots. The less agile humans couldn't compete with the industrious rodents.

The brothers lamented the loss of their wild food, yet refused to begin exterminating the culprits. "For one thing, we weren't going to kill off the wildlife that we ourselves had attracted," Douglas explained. "For another, we could have shot muskrats for weeks, and they'd just breed right back again. The habitat was too good."

A cattail-less season or two went by. Then, suddenly the tasty shoots were back, and the once-busy "harbor" was more tranquil. The muskrat population had dwindled. What had happened?

"Otters moved in," Douglas said. "The muskrats were a great new food source. We'd never seen otters here before. More than otters showed up, too. We got other predators: bald eagles, hawks, owls. They cleaned up." Instead of futilely trying to trap the fast-breeding muskrats, the Bullocks sat back and let nature do the job. The brothers merely provided a rich, diverse habitat where a vigorous food web—one that included predators—could emerge and right imbalances, such as a horde of ravenous muskrats.

Three Ecological Principles

The Bullocks have built a superb example of ecological gardening, where humans and wildlife can reap the abundance and live in harmony. What happened on the brothers' land illustrates several principles of ecology that gardeners can use. The cattail/muskrat/otter progression is a good jumping-off point to look at three important and related concepts: the niche, succession, and biodiversity. I'll begin with those and then, throughout this chapter, give examples of other ecological ideas that can help create sustainable gardens. The ideas presented on the next few pages lay the foundation for the ecological garden. The examples and techniques given in the rest of this book are grounded in these principles of nature.

Finding a Niche

Decades before the Bullocks arrived, the lowest part of their property had been wetland. An industrious farmer had diked, drained, and dried up the "useless" bog and raised crops there for many years. The ecologically oriented Bullocks understood that wetlands, besides being essential for clean water and wildlife habitat, were some of the most productive ecosystems on the planet, teeming with more plants and animals than any farm. They decided to restore the wetland and tore out the dikes and drains. Water collected in the low ground, and soon the wetland was back.

While the marsh returned, the Bullocks ferried countless loads of mulch and manure onto their land in their straining pickup truck. The brothers also forked rich muck from the bog onto the shore, building soil with organic matter and nutrients. In a few years, this tremendous increase in fertility paid off many times over. Not only could the Bullocks grow more plant varieties than before, but opportunistic wild species could find homes in the enhanced habitat as well. The combination of water and fertile soil was irresistible.

Some of the earliest new tenants were the cattails. Their seeds may have been brought to the renewed bog by waterfowl, or perhaps they had lain dormant in the soil for years, hoping for the return of the wetland. In either case, the cattails capitalized on the ripe habitat, busily converting sunlight, water, and bog muck into fast-growing shoots.

Wherever there is tender greenery, there is someone to consume it—a lesson that gardeners quickly learn when rabbits, field mice, porcupines, raccoons, and all the rest descend on their vegetables. You can think of this as some horrible corollary of the "Field of Dreams" effect: if you build it, they will come and eat it; but, in ecologist's terms, this exemplifies the niche, or role played by each organism. The Bullocks, by creating habitat, opened up an opportunity for life to exploit. As if being asked to audition for a new role in a play, organisms suited to the job showed up to occupy this new niche. Think of a niche as a profession and habitat as the work space for performing that job.

As habitat becomes more varied, more niches appear. Often, providing habitat triggers a cascade of niches, which is precisely what we're trying to do in the ecological garden. The Bullocks' place is a good example of a niche cascade. The fertile habitat provided a niche for the cattails, which then furnished a new food supply that was quickly exploited by muskrats—animals that are custom-made for eating tender shoreline plants. The opportunism of the muskrats led to both their rise and fall: they fattened happily on the cattails, but that busy harbor of paddling rodents was a beacon for predators. In the still-wild San Juan Islands, otters sheltered somewhere nearby. Nature's "grapevine" is fast and effective, and it was only a season or two before the otters caught wind of the potential harvest and moved in. Just as the cattails had started small, ramped up to thriving numbers, and were chewed down to a vestige, so too did the muskrats appear, burgeon, and crash in a cycle now interlocked with those of the cattails and otters.

Eventually a form of stability descended on the

At the Bullock brothers' farm on Orcas Island in Washington State, an apple tree is surrounded by food- and habitat-creating plants that work together to benefit both nature and people.

Bullocks' land, but it fluctuates now and then as one species or other briefly gains the upper hand and is then hauled back in line. But, in a place where neither cattails, nor muskrats, nor predators could survive before, all three now thrive, because the Bullocks provided habitat and soil nutrients. The brothers supplied the beginnings, and nature did the rest. Instead of depleted farmland, the Bullocks and their friends can admire a verdant, multispecies wetland, rustling with cattails, sedges, willows, and wildflowers, ripe with blueberries and other fruit, filled with the music of waterfowl and frogs, and offering a glimpse of otters and eagles.

Gardening in Succession

In less than a decade, the Bullock brothers' property leapt from a brambled, overgrown field to a verdant young food forest. Above the bog, where blackberries once sprawled in impenetrable tangles, branches laden with plums and cherries now cast dappled shade on glowing nasturtium blossoms. Nut trees shelter a bamboo grove, and vegetable beds wind into the woods. The brothers created this rich landscape quickly by working with nature rather than against her. Some of the many techniques they used will gradually unfold throughout this book, but first we'll examine one of the overarching strategies that guided their work: accelerated succession.

When plants first colonize bare earth—for example, an abandoned farm—a progression begins. Certain types of annual grasses, herbs, and flowers are the first flora to arrive, and because of their penchant for speedy colonization, they are called *pioneer plants*. They're well adapted to invading naked or disturbed soil and mantling the floral emptiness with green. Pioneer plants fill the vegetal vacuum and restart the cycles of life. We know most of this fast-colonizing horde as weeds: crabgrass, dandelion, sheep sorrel, pigweed, plantain, chicory, wild lettuce, and many more. Abandoned fields and fresh earth are their milieu, where they have a job to do: sheltering the bare soil from erosive rains and ferrying nutrients from deep in the soil to the surface where they can be used. These fast-growing, short-lived pioneers preserve and restore the fertility of disturbed ground.

If these weeds are left alone, in a few seasons the short, early annuals are crowded and shaded out by a taller, mostly perennial crew. In the northern half of the United States, these plants include asters, fireweed, goldenrod, spurge, perennial grasses, and many others. The dense foliage, branching stems, and many textures of the tall weeds offer more niches for insects and birds to shelter, breed, and feed. The amount of living matter, called *biomass*, increases as nutrients and sunlight are gathered and transformed into tough stalks, thick greenery, and hardy seeds, which in turn become food for insects and other animals. In this way, life quickly gets a firm toehold on the bare ground. Where before the elements needed for life were confined to a thin band of topsoil, now these nutrients surge in a much thicker layer of vegetation filled with mobile animals. Life is scaffolding its way into new territory.

The progression from bare earth to short annual weeds to tall perennials is called *succession*. If allowed to continue, in five to fifteen years the weedy field will be clothed instead with perennial shrubs. With enough rain and fertility, in two or more decades the shrubs will give way to a young forest. Wherever there is sufficient rain, succession will drive a landscape inexorably toward forest.

Though succession is a nearly irresistible process, it isn't smoothly linear. At any stage, fire, wind, lightning, the plow, or another disturbance can set it back to an earlier phase. Most landscapes are a mosaic of many successionary stages, at many scales. Even in mature, late-successionary communities, species from all stages of succession lurk in the margins. Disturbances, ranging from a catastrophic forest fire to a single blown-down tree, let pioneer herbs or midsuccession shrubs slide back in, resulting in a patchy landscape of varying ages and stages.

How does this relate to gardening? Conventional gardens mimic immature ecosystems. They are usually dominated by early-succession plants. Most grasses, flowers, and especially annual vegetables are pioneers. This means that in our love of lawns and orderly gardens, we're attempting to keep our yards at an early stage of ecological development. The bare earth and disturbed soil in a vegetable garden or under clean-cultivated shrubs sing a siren song to weeds, which eagerly cover naked ground, pull nutrients out of underlying mineral soil and rock, and prepare the locale for a more mature ecosystem such as shrubland or forest. A pure expanse of well-watered grass is aching, in nature's scheme, for a blitzkrieg from seedlings and shrubs or, at the very least, a spike in diversity via fast-growing annual weeds.

We can use our grasp of succession to help solve garden problems. Most weeds are pioneer species, thriving on disturbance, sunlight, and poorly developed soils. Abandoning tilling as a garden technique alone shrank my weed problems enormously, as disturbance- and light-dependent seeds rotted underground instead of being triggered into growth by light and cultivation. A layer of mulch will often, for similar reasons, block weed seeds from sprouting.

Building soil organic matter is another weed-busting strategy. A load of so-called straw turned out, to my dismay, to contain snippets of live morning glories that I didn't notice until two garden beds mulched with this noxious blend had sprouted the familiar and unwanted green tendrils. Two of three seasons of tedious excavation of seemingly endless root networks didn't faze the morning glories. Deep mulch, even heavy wood chips, merely delayed their exuberant eruption into daylight and rapid smothering of anything else I planted. It was the closest I've come to considering herbicide. Then, one year, the morning glories were pale and patchy, and in two more years they were gone, even though I hardly weeded them. In the meantime, the soil in these beds had gone from red clay to luscious black loam after years of constant deep mulches. I've since learned from several sources that morning glories and several other challenging weeds languish in well-developed soils, much preferring youthful clays and compost-poor sands. Succession applies to soils just as much as it does to plants. Often, the stage of soil development influences which species can root in it.

A yard is a dynamic system, not an unchanging still life. By viewing our landscapes as dynamic ecosystems, rather than as static collections of inert objects, we can create gardens that inherently grow in healthy patterns and directions. This perspective lets us transfer much of the labor of maintaining our yards to nature.

With this viewpoint in mind, we can ask, What kinds of ecosystems do most yards contain? The answers tell us why yard work is so tedious and never ending. A lawn of grass edged with flowers is an ecological cousin to prairie. The other major plant arrangement found in suburbia, the archetypal turf dotted with occasional trees and shrubs, mimics a savanna. (I wonder at the ancient dreams we're acting out when we create these landscapes, which mimic those of our species' infancy on the plains of Africa.)

Prairie and savanna flourish only under certain environmental circumstances. These include low rainfall, heavy animal grazing, and frequent fire. Since few suburbanites encourage parched earth, herds of bison, and wildfire in their yards, conditions in most lawns don't favor savanna and prairie. So, what happens to these unhappy ecosystem fragments? A prairie or savanna kept unburnt, well fertilized, and bathed under the stuttering hiss of sprinklers is being urged to ripen into shrubland and forest. This is ecological succession, omnipresent and relentless.

Weeds in our lawn and maple seedlings in the flower beds are testimony to succession's power. Viewed ecologically, the standard suburban yard just wants to grow up. Understanding this lets us ally ourselves with nature's considerable might, instead of battling.

An immature ecosystem like a lawn demands that we expend time, energy, and materials to wrench back the hands of the ecological clock, holding the land at prairie phase with mowing and weeding. Yet nature—and our irrigation and fertilizers—will inexorably advance the clock another tick, sprouting seedlings and saplings, inundating us with her fecundity. With sprinkler and fertilizer we're tromping on the accelerator, yet with tiller and pruning saw we're slamming on the brake. No system runs well under that kind of schizophrenic regime.

Typical lawns, and vegetable and flower gardens, too, to a great extent, suffer from another ecological fault: they are monocultures. As we saw in the previous chapter, nature relies on multifunctionality and redundancy, neither of which can be found in a trophy lawn of Kentucky bluegrass.

Backyard Biodiversity

Even when we encourage succession to occur, not every backyard will attract muskrats and otters like the Bullocks' place. But all gardeners can profit from the same natural cycles at work there. Diverse habitat will shrink pest problems. For example, a garden bed planted all to broccoli or roses is a magnet for pests, which will happily chow down on the abundant food so kindly provided, just as the muskrats did with the cattails. When that happens in the typical garden, out come the sprays and insecticidal soaps, adding unpleasantly to the gardener's labor. But by providing habitat for these

pests' natural predators, gardeners can let nature do the bug control. Just as the otters, still abundant in the wild San Juans, came to the rescue, so too will beneficial insects, who will shelter in hedges and other naturescapes, ready to pounce on aphids and Japanese beetles. The key is providing biodiversity in the landscape. Biodiversity is the variety of organisms present, considered from many levels: cultivar, species, genus, family, and on up to include all five kingdoms, as well as the diversity of habitats and ecosystems. For our purposes, biodiversity means having a semiwild but well-designed palette of useful plants that will attract and sustain the helpful insects, birds, and other animals we need.

Garden biodiversity comes in two intersecting forms. One is the diversity that the gardener fashions by planting a broad assortment of flowers, shrubs, and trees, which creates a many-layered habitat. The second is the diversity of life that lingers nearby in still-intact wild places—the birds, bugs, and plants both imported and native that are poised to spread into this welcoming habitat. The two depend on each other.

Most towns have enough vacant lots, neglected corners, parks, and flowery landscaping to nurture a lively community of small wildlife. In any but the most impoverished landscape, these wild plants and animals have no trouble zeroing in on good habitat. If I lived inside a biological desert—for example, the pesticide-saturated megafarms that supply conventional supermarkets—I couldn't rely on the ready supply of wildlife, including insects, to find my floral offerings. That's why habitat is important. Every blossom-decked corner is a reservoir for helpful wildlife.

The idea of attracting beneficial insects is not new, but the ecological garden carries the concept a few steps further. Almost everything in such a garden has more than one function. I'll go into this idea in detail in a few pages, but here are some quick examples. To attract helpful insects, we could plant bee balm, which also makes a delicious tea, fills the air with minty fragrance, and offers a colorful pink-to-red flower. Or if we're installing a hedge, we can add a shrub such as wild apricot or Nanking cherry, ornamentals whose fruits are good for both wildlife and jam. Then we could mix in goumi (*Elaeagnus multiflora*) with flowers and berries for insects and birds, but whose roots bear soil-building, nitrogen-fixing microbes. I could continue, but the point should be clear. By filling our garden with multifunctional plants and other elements, we create a dense web full of many niches for wildlife and a rich place for humans as well: a wealth of food, flowers, medicinal herbs, and other products, and a place of beauty. Diversity offers a cascade of benefits.

Our love of tidy but not very diverse yards is imprinted on us by our culture. The immaculate lawn, under siege from ecological writers everywhere, developed in the mild and evenly moist climate of Great Britain. Its implications are deeply woven into our psyche. A lawn in preindustrial times trumpeted to all that the owner possessed enough wealth to use some land for sheer ornament, instead of planting all of it to food crops. And close-mowed grass proclaimed affluence, too: a herd of sheep large enough to crop the lawn uniformly short. These indicators of status whisper to us down the centuries. By consciously recognizing the influence of this history, we can free ourselves of it and let go of the reflexive impulse to roll sod over the entire landscape.

Our addiction to impeccable lawns and soldier rows of vegetables and flowers is counter to the tendency of nature and guarantees us constant work. But we don't need to wield trowel and herbicide with resentment in an eternal war against the exuberant appetite of chicory and wild lettuce for fresh-bared soil. Instead we can create conditions that encourage the plants we want and let nature do the work, as I'll show next.

A Mature Garden

Because landscapes have an irresistible tendency to mature, why not hop on board the successionary freight train and take advantage of nature's momentum? This is what the Bullock brothers have done, and so can we. With a nudge here and a tweak there, we can actually accelerate succession, using nature to help a garden mature much faster than it otherwise would. In the ecological garden, we're creating well-developed, productive, and lush landscapes very quickly by riding the tracks already laid down by nature.

Table 2-1 lists the differences between immature and mature landscapes. We can use this understanding to create mature ecosystems in our yards. Mature in this case does not mean a gloomy ancient forest, with closed canopy and few plants beneath—I'm not asking that you wait a century or more—but a landscape that has passed the pioneer and young shrub stages and is a young to middle-aged woods. Think of a woodland with sunny openings, rather than a thick forest. This mature landscape is a blend of trees, shrubs, and smaller plants, in contrast to the immature groupings of grasses, annuals, and occasional shrubs that is typical of most yards.

Table 2-1 reveals some important trends. As a landscape matures, organic matter builds up, in the form of plants, animals, and rich soil. This pulls carbon dioxide from the atmosphere, potentially shrinking the greenhouse effect. Fewer imports of nutrients are needed from or lost to the outside, and the cycles and patterns become more complex. To help visualize this evolution, let's compare a young ecosystem—a typical annual vegetable or flower garden that starts from seed every year—to a mature woodland.

In the annual garden, the soil is bare many months of the year. The climate is harsh and varies wildly, as the sun bakes the ground in summer, and freeze-thaw cycles heave the exposed soil in winter.

Table 2-1. Differences between Immature and Mature Ecosystems		
Attribute	**Immature Ecosystem**	**Mature Ecosystem**
Total biomass productivity	Low	High
Amount of organic matter	Low	High
Source of mineral nutrients	Non-living (rocks, rainfall)	Biological (plants, animals, humus)
Mineral cycles	Open (many imports)	Closed (recycling)
Loss of nutrients	High	Low
Role of decomposers, detritus	Unimportant	Important
Microclimates	Few, harsh, shaped by non-living forces	Many, mild, shaped by plants
Dominant plants	Annuals	Perennials
Percent of biomass that stays from year to year	Low	High
Number of different species	Usually low	High
Diversity of patterns (different layers of plants, nutrient cycles, etc.)	Low	High
Food chains	Short, simple, linear	Complex, weblike
Specialization into niches	Few, wide	Many, narrow
Symbiotic relationships	Few	Many
Average size of organisms	Small	Large
Life cycles	Short, simple	Long, complex
Breeding strategy	Many seeds or young, given little support	Few seeds or young, well supported
Stability (resistance to disturbance, opportunistic plants)	Low	High
Overall complexity and organization	Low	High
Source: Adapted from W. H. Drury and I. C.T. Nisbet, "Succession." *Journal of the Arnold Arboretum* 54 (1973):336.		

Because the short plants offer poor protection, wind blasts the ground and rain pounds the soil, washing away nutrients. Even more fertility is carried off each year as the vegetables are harvested and the bare stalks are yanked up during fall cleanup. Thus the nutrient cycles are open, in straight lines—into the garden and then out—rather than closed loops with lots of recycling. This means that fertility must be imported to replace all that is lost from leaching, erosion, and the near-total removal of plants. And unless the gardener avidly composts and mulches, there's little soil life that can survive the harsh, erratic conditions and low levels of organic matter.

Here, plant diversity is tightly controlled. In fact, true diversity is unwelcome since it's defined as weeds, pests, and raiding birds or rodents. In this environment, nature's knack for spontaneity often means trouble, rather than enjoyment and improvement.

This garden is a simple place. Plants occur in only one layer, about one to three feet high. The flora is in orderly rows or clumps, in very basic patterns. The food chain? Only two links: plants to people or, dismayingly, plants to bugs or birds. There are no symbiotic relationships or partnerships, unless the gardener is clever enough to create them through companion planting or with insect-attracting flowers. With its plants being uprooted every fall, low diversity, and high susceptibility to weeds, pests, and disease, an annual garden is unstable and easily harmed.

Painting this rather dismal portrait of a place

where gardeners derive so much pleasure, I've gotten depressed. Before I cheer myself up by examining a mature woodland, I'll mention that the reason these gardens work at all and engender so much enjoyment is the labor that humans put into them. Annual gardens need our efforts because we must replace and reconnect all the missing cycles and effort usually provided free by nature. And we often enjoy the creative effort and the therapeutic work that goes into our gardens. But if we share the work with nature and bring into our gardens the wisdom gained in three billion years of evolution, we can have all that the annual garden offers and vastly more.

Let's look at a well-developed forest and see what lessons we can extract from it for our own yards. First, the soil is covered with a layer of duff and shaded by many layers of plants that remain year-round. The vegetation softens the force of rain, sun, and wind and creates mellow microclimates where seeds quickly germinate and life nestles in comfort. The permanent presence of roots and constantly building carpet of leaf litter offer a perfect home to worms and other creatures of the soil. The abundant soil life captures nutrients and recycles them to plants before they can be washed away. These nutrients are stored, long- and short-term, in ever-present tree trunks, perennial shrubs and herbs, lichens, fungi, mulch, humus, and soil organisms. The forest builds a tremendous reserve of organic matter and minerals. All this biomass acts as a savings account, holding and recycling the forest's valuables as insurance against drought, infestation, or other stressful times.

Most of the forest spans the seasons and the decades. Each year, only a small proportion of the biomass is replaced, that is, only a few plants and animals die. Think of how most of a massive tree persists from year to year, while just its leaves and a few roots die back. Continuity is the rule, unlike the annual garden. Most of nature remains standing through the changing years.

What does die each year is recycled within the ecosystem, with almost no loss. Nearly all of life's products, from tree trunks and deer bones down to insect wings and bacteria cells, are recyclable. Nature assembles and breaks down, dissolves and renews, using the same material over and over, leaving no landfills and toxic dumps in her wake. In nature, there is no such thing as waste. Everything is food for something else, connected in life and death to many other species.

The forest contains hundreds of species of plants and thousands of varieties of animals and microbes. Biodiversity in the woodland is immense, which allows countless relationships to form. Tied together in interdependent webs, these creatures use nearly all the available food and habitat in the forest, leaving few, if any, niches open for invaders. This hyperefficient use of resources also means that no single species is likely to get out of balance. What could a new pest eat that wasn't already being eaten by some better-established creature? And since these forest species have evolved together, each has defense mechanisms—tough waxy coatings, bad-tasting chemicals—to ward off its enemies. Invaders can only take advantage of new openings, such as when a tree falls and opens fresh bare ground. But then the forest quickly closes in and will smother the invader unless the new species finds an unused, narrow niche and makes its peace within the web of life.

The forest is diverse in patterns and cycles as well. From open sky to earth, the vegetation ranges in many layers: high canopy, low trees, shrubs, tall herbs, ground-hugging rosettes and creepers, and vines that span the whole range. Amid all this varied habitat are hundreds of niches for insects, birds, and other creatures. Food webs are complex, with plants, grazers, predators, top carnivores, and decomposers entwined in a varied and many-partnered dance. Relationships among species are equally enmeshed. Trees have

The Flagstaff, Arizona, backyard of Josh Robinson of Eden on Earth Landscaping. The yard blends annuals and perennials to provide an enormous food harvest with only a few hours' work per month. It also harvests much of its own water, allowing the gardeners to rely almost not at all on municipal water. PHOTO BY JOSH ROBINSON.

symbiotic partnerships with specific fungi and bacteria that bring nutrients from soil to root. Plants extract minerals from deep in the soil for others to use. Birds and mammals ferry seeds to new locales, redistributing fertility in the form of manure along the way. If one thread of this web is broken, thousands of others stand near to hold the forest's fabric intact.

A forest is not a static, unchanging place but has a dynamic and resilient stability. Compared to a conventional garden, there is little role for pests, disease, invasive plants, and upheaval. Nature has sewn the forest together into a unified tapestry, rather than a collection of disconnected plants and animals.

With the contrasts between the annual garden and the mature forest in mind, we can think about arranging our gardens so they will mimic mature ecosystems rather than young ones. We don't need to do all the work, either. Just as in the Bullock brothers' landscape, if we lay the groundwork, nature will create many of the connections and fill in the gaps.

Here are the features of natural landscapes that are most important to include in the ecological garden:

- Deep soil that is rich in nutrients and organic matter
- Plants that draw fertility from deep in the earth, from the air, and from rainwater
- Many layers of vegetation to create varied niches for other creatures
- An emphasis on perennial plants
- Mutually helpful relationships among plants, insects, birds, microbes, mammals, and all other inhabitants, including people
- Increasingly closed cycles; that is, over time the garden should require fewer supplies from outside, producing most of its own fertilizer, mulch, seeds, new plants, and so on. Except for the harvest, little from the garden is lost by leaching and erosion—it's all recycled.

In the rest of this chapter, I'll briefly describe how to apply these insights from ecology in the garden. But the rest of the book will go into a great deal more detail.

A Few of Nature's Tricks for Gardeners

Along with differing levels of biodiversity, one of the biggest contrasts between most gardens and natural landscapes is that, if left untended, a garden falls apart, while nature doesn't. We've all returned from vacation to find our favorite plants eaten, weeds rampant, and the whole garden drooping from that unexpected hot spell. The natural condition of a garden, without the gardener, is dead—or returned to wilderness. The natural condition of a forest is healthy and vigorous. However, with a few lessons from nature, we can design gardens that will inherently become more fertile, healthy, and well-watered and will

have the dynamic stability, resilience, and exuberance of natural ecosystems. This section gives a brief overview of how to do this; the rest of the book will go into detail.

Soil Building

How can we apply nature's wisdom to the garden? First, as in any garden, start with the soil. Nature builds soil from the top down and from the bottom up. By "top down" I mean the constant rain of leaf litter from above that decomposes into fluffy earth. Nature doesn't rotary till, and we don't need to either. To create a mature soil quickly, just pile on the organic matter with deep layers of mulch. The mulch quickly composts in place to create mature soil that is bursting with organic matter, teeming with soil life, ready to nurture healthy plants. Chapter 4 gives detailed techniques for building soil with mulches.

The complement, bottom-up soil building, is done with plants. In nature, fertility comes from the vegetation and soil life, not from a bag of fertilizer. Many plants excel at pulling nutrients from deep in the earth and siphoning them to the surface where other plants can use them. These varieties are discussed in Chapter 6 and cited in the appendix. In a vegetable garden, harvesting will constantly remove nutrients, so this withdrawn fertility will have to be replaced with small additions of mulch, compost, or fertilizer. But with nutrient-accumulating plants in the garden, the task of spreading fertilizer will dwindle to almost nothing.

Together, the top-down and bottom-up techniques will quickly generate the finest soil you've ever seen.

Perennials versus Annuals

Next, the ecological garden imitates a mature ecosystem by emphasizing perennials rather than annuals. For ornamental and wildlife gardens, this is easy, as thousands of perennial flowers, shrubs, and trees are available. At first glance, though, perennials seem a tough limitation for vegetable gardens. However, I'm not saying that tomatoes and peppers are taboo. I still grow plenty. But many annuals can be replaced with perennials. Perennial greens abound: Good King Henry, perennial kale and collards, French sorrel, and many others, all described in Chapter 6. There are perennial onions, root crops, herbs, and, of course, vegetables such as asparagus, artichokes, and rhubarb. And don't forget the obvious perennial food plants, such as berries, fruits, and nuts.

The advantages of perennials are legion. They eliminate seed starting, tilling, and the opportunity for weeds that tilling brings. That slashes three chores off the list at one stroke. Perennials need less water and fertilizer than annuals. Their deep root systems tap into pockets of moisture and nutrients that annuals just can't reach. Also, because they are year-round plants, perennials offer dependable habitat to wildlife and beneficial insects.

Multiple Stories

An ecological garden has many layers, from a low herb layer through shrubs and small trees to the large overstory. Each layer can contain ornamental species, varieties for food and other human uses, wildlife plants, and flora for building soil and maintaining a healthy ecosystem. Together the layers provide diverse habitat, many products, and plenty of visual interest. In sunny climes, large trees can be closely spaced to provide shade, while in cooler or grayer zones the trees can be spread out to allow ample light and warmth. Chapter 10 tells how to create these forestlike gardens.

Plant Communities

The plants in an ecological garden, just as in nature, aren't isolated individuals but form communities. Long ago, ecologists (as well as native peoples) recognized that many plants and animals occur in distinct groups. Certain species seem always to show up with the same companions. In the arid West, piñon pine and juniper appear together, and with them frequently are Gambel's oak and mountain mahogany. In the East, a common community is the oak/hickory forest, with maple leaf viburnum and dogwoods often filling the understory. There are hundreds of plant communities, and each contains a recognizable array of trees, shrubs, and flowers whose composition varies from one community to the next. These communities can include specific animals, too. Oak/hickory forests are home specifically to blue jays, tanagers, and grosbeaks. Piñon/juniper groves harbor piñon jays and bushtits. Different environments favor different communities.

In the ecological garden, we steal a page from nature's book and often group plants in communities. Some gardeners have recreated the natural plant communities that occur in their region, while others have tinkered with plant groupings, swapping some plants with human uses or other functions in place of natives. The design of multifunctional plant communities is a new field that's in its infancy and at the cutting edge of horticulture. Clever garden designers have put together some beautiful, productive, and labor-saving plant combinations. A single garden plant community, besides providing the gardener with eye-catching blossoms and foliage, food, and herbs, might also contain plants to repel pests, generate mulch, accumulate nutrients, attract beneficial insects, and shelter wildlife. Much of this book, in particular Chapters 8, 9, and 10, tells how to create harmonious groupings of plants that nurture each other and provide for both the gardener and wildlife.

Stacking Functions

Our discussion of niches, succession, and biodiversity leads to another important principle of the ecological garden: every part of the garden does more than just one thing. Permaculture designers have a bit of jargon to describe this. They call it "stacking functions." Nothing in nature has only one function; it is furiously efficient in this way. A shrub, for example, doesn't just cast shade. It feeds winter-starved birds with its berries, offers shelter, mulches the soil with its leaves, provides browse for hungry deer and porcupines, blocks the wind, holds the soil with its roots, collects and channels rainwater, and on and on.

Nature always stacks functions, because that shrub, or any living thing, represents a big investment in matter and energy, two things that nature husbands with immense stinginess. Nature is supremely skilled at getting the most bang for the buck, squeezing every erg of energy out of that shrub, tying it into lots of other cycles to maximize the return. The shrub's berries took energy to grow, so when a bird eats them, the plant trades its effort for seed dispersal, making hard seeds that will pass unharmed through the bird's gut to germinate on new ground. The leaves gather solar energy but with no extra effort are arranged to channel rainwater to the stems and down to the roots, increasing the shrub's collection area. By making plants perform multiple functions, nature uses her energy investment very efficiently.

Do Plant Communities Really Exist?

Ecologists have been arguing for decades about whether plant communities are real or just a construct that we use for our convenience. Some say they are merely random assemblies of species that happen to like the same climate, soil, and other environmental conditions. Other ecologists believe communities form in part because of interactions and mutual benefits among the members and act somewhat like whole organisms. The jury is still out. In support of the random-grouping argument, a little botanizing shows that any two examples of a given community always contain different species and numbers of plants. No two communities are alike. Also, if you follow a community across its range—into a colder climate, for example—its makeup may vary. As the environment changes, the species that make up the community shift gradually, with one or two species dropping out here and a couple of new ones moving in there. If communities were tightly bound systems, like organisms, they should have distinct boundaries. Thus, you'd expect their makeup to switch abruptly, as if you'd traveled from one country into another, rather than gradually.

On the other hand, a community of species has a definite structure. If it lacks certain members, the community as a whole suffers. For example, Douglas fir forests that don't contain a particular fungus—a type of truffle—aren't as healthy as those that do. The truffle, which lives among the roots of the tree, provides nutrients and perhaps disease protection to the fir. If the truffle is missing, which is the case in many tree plantations, the fir forest is not just sicklier but also won't support as many other species. One of these is the red-backed vole, a rodent that feeds on the fungus. Lacking their preferred diet of voles to eat, the spotted owl population dwindles. This poverty ripples through many species, and the whole community is diminished. Thus, communities are linked together in an intricate webwork. Also, ecologists have shown that even when there are no environmental gradients—when temperature and nutrient levels remain the same over a large area—organisms still sort themselves into different, highly structured groupings that vary from place to place.

I believe that communities are held together by their interactions as well as by their environment. The ecological gardens I've seen seem to bear this out: communities—groups of plants linked in relationships— make for very healthy gardens, as we shall see.

Most human designs, in contrast, are prodigiously wasteful. We seem to hurry our goods from source to landfill in an arrow-straight stream, while nature would bend and rebend that stream into a zigzag course, extracting benefit at every turn and recycling what's left. By designing our gardens with the same principles in mind, they become far less wasteful and troublesome, far more productive and bountiful. Stacking functions is a key rule and one of the most important to follow.

Here's an example of stacking functions in a landscape design. Adjoining our Oakland house was a 5,000-gallon water tank for storing rainwater. It was mostly buried, but the ten-by-twelve-foot lid projected above the ground, an ugly gray slab of concrete next to the kitchen. To hide the concrete, I nailed a cedar deck over it, but in the blazing summer sun the deck was too hot to enjoy. Then I built an arbor over the deck and trained two seedless grapes on the arbor. A trellis on the tank's side was entwined by jasmine, wafting perfume over the deck. The cistern became a cool, shady spot beneath the fast-growing grapes, where my wife and I lingered while lunching at a small table beneath the green canopy. Our houseplants spent their summer vacation there on one light-dappled corner. In late summer, after we ate lunch, we simply reached overhead for a dessert of sweet grapes.

The grape leaves shaded our house as well, keeping the kitchen cool in summer, but in autumn the leaves dropped, allowing the much-needed sun to stream onto the deck and the kitchen window. The leaves went to the compost pile or straight to a garden bed as mulch. When I pruned the vine in winter, I took plenty of cuttings to propagate for friends. Overflow from the cistern irrigated the grapes and other plantings nearby.

By combining the water tank, grapevine, and deck in the right arrangement, I increased the usefulness of each and got benefits that none alone would provide. Nearly every element performed several roles.

Gardeners are already good at stacking functions. A simple compost pile is multifunctional: it recycles waste, creates fertile humus, boosts soil life, and even offers the gardener a little exercise through turning and spreading. Even a one-species hedge of privet can serve as a windbreak, privacy screen, and bird habitat. By recognizing the advantages of stacking functions and designing our gardens with this in mind, we can gain wonderful synergies from our own backyards.

The concept of stacking functions has two halves, two rules that reinforce each other. The first is that each element of a design—each plant or structure—should do more than one job. Our grape arbor illustrates that rule: the grapevine shaded the deck while letting in light in winter; cooled the house; provided food, mulch, and propagation stock; and beautified an otherwise ugly water tank.

The second principle is the complement of the first. Each job to be done in a design—each system or process—should be performed or supported by more than one element. In other words, always have backups in place. Once again, gardeners already follow this rule more or less unconsciously. We plant several varieties of vegetables in case one fails, or different fruits or flowers to yield over a long season. And every gardener has an array of sprinklers, drip irrigation gadgets, soaker hoses, special hose nozzles, and watering cans, all for the single purpose of delivering water to our plants. Multiple, layered systems such as these are more effective at doing the total job than any one device would be.

There are many advantages to this sort of redundancy. A quick glance at how nature does it shows some of the benefits. One is disaster protection. Most important functions in organisms and ecosystems have backups, often several layers deep. Look at our sense of balance. We use three independent methods to keep our equilibrium. First, our eyes tell us what position we're in. Second, our ears contain a fluid-filled chamber lined with hairs that are sensitive to orientation. The hairs' position tells our brain which way is up. And third, our muscles and tendons have receptors that telegraph data on our limb movements and positions. By devoting energy and organs to this "tell me three times" strategy, our bodies make a big investment in not falling over. It's worth it, because if we relied only on, say, our eyes, a flash of blinding sunlight on a steep mountain path could drop us off a cliff. Any organism or system with backups survives longer. For example, if the soil is well mulched, then when the irrigation fails during a vacation, the plants may survive the waterless glitch.

Redundancy also boosts yield. Using another example from the human body, think of how the lower digestive tract filters all the nutrition it can from food by making multiple passes on a meal. The small intestine extracts a portion of the nutrient load, then the large intestine absorbs more, and the bacteria in the gut convert yet more to a useful form. This multilayered approach ekes out nearly all available sustenance from food. In the same way, a garden with several layers of water-conserving techniques, frost protection, disease proofing, wind deflection, or soil-building strategies will gain a cumulative benefit from the multiple techniques.

These benefits of redundancy aren't lost on ecological gardeners and permaculturists, who sum up this principle with this guideline: each function should be served by multiple elements.

The two aspects of function stacking—each element performs multiple functions, and each function is served by multiple elements—can be used throughout the garden, on many levels, to align the landscape with nature's might. The succeeding chapters give plenty of examples.

Since this chapter is about ecology for gardeners, I won't attempt to cover every ecological concept. The ideas covered—the niche, succession, biodiversity, stacking functions, and others—are those that seem to me most important for gardeners to understand so they can create natural landscapes that provide for people's needs. Ecology studies the relationships among living creatures. It is those relationships that transform a collection of disparate objects into a living, dynamic landscape. With this in mind, we can now look at some design tools for building just such a landscape.

CHAPTER THREE

Designing the Ecological Garden

ardening books and magazines are packed with design ideas. They describe how to group plants according to color or how to juxtapose shapes and foliage patterns to please the eye. They can teach methods of massing plants to carry the gaze toward a stunning landscape feature. Some will reveal tricks that make a small yard look large or help a sprawling lot feel cozy and intimate. These types of garden design techniques aid in selecting plants that are quite attractive and will make your yard look very pretty.

That's not what this chapter is about.

I'm not knocking the aesthetics of garden design. An ugly landscape cramps the soul, while a beautiful one invites, relaxes, and heals the viewer. Yet a garden that is designed only to look pretty barely skims the surface of what landscapes can offer. A place designed according to principles deeper than those of surface appearance can still be beautiful but will also shelter wildlife, feed people and animals, purify the air and water, store carbon, and be an asset to Earth.

No human designed an alpine meadow, a tropical forest, or a creekside grotto, yet these wild landscapes are never ugly. They follow a larger natural order that seems to ensure beauty. In the previous chapter we began to glimpse a few aspects of nature's order. Now we can use these principles and patterns of nature to design our gardens.

A natural landscape is patterned in ways that harvest the energy (sun, wind, heat) and matter (water and nutrients) that flow through it, casting a living net that collects these resources and shuttles them into myriad cycles that transform them into more life. Nearly everything that enters a natural landscape is captured and used, absorbed and reincarnated into vibrant biodiversity. Anything produced in that landscape, from by-products such as sugary root secretions to "wastes" such as manure and molted insect casings, is recycled, swallowed up again, and reincorporated into new living tissue. And the landscape "learns" as it goes, selecting and improving the patterns that work best. Each captured bit helps build and refine a network that gets better than before at catching what comes its way.

Billions of years of evolution have left few loose ends in nature. One creature's waste is another's food. Nearly every niche is tightly held, every habitat is packed full of interconnected species. Anything faintly resembling a resource will be used: if one species can't use it, another will.

It is this interconnectedness—this linking of one species' "outputs" to another's "inputs"— that we seek to re-create in the ecological garden. Unfortunately, we don't have billions of years to wait while our gardens evolve to the immense "webiness" of the natural landscape. But we have another tool: our creative minds. We can consciously evaluate the pieces of our landscape and use permaculture principles to design the connections. Observation is the key to good design.

By observing the patterns and cycles that nature uses to solve design problems, we can replicate these forms in our gardens, not as mere static shapes but as dynamic solutions that save labor, resources, and energy. Then our gardens can be almost as interlinked as nature is, producing no waste or pollutants, needing little excess labor, ripe with habitat, yielding abundantly.

This chapter offers an introduction to design using some of the same tools that nature does. We begin with a look at how nature solves some design challenges using pattern and form and how understanding and using those patterns can make our home landscapes more functional, ecological, and beautiful. With this taste of what permaculturists call *patterning* under our belts, we will then walk through a set of steps for designing a garden that re-creates the feel and dynamics of nature.

Natural Patterns in the Garden

Anyone who has spent time looking at nature has noticed that certain patterns—spirals, waves, branches, circles—seem omnipresent and repeat at many scales. A branching pattern shows up in the convergence of streams and rivers visible out a jet window, in the graceful arch of a tree overhead and in its roots beneath us, and in tendrils of a tiny moss. Spirals appear in galaxies spanning thousands of light years and in the head of a daisy. We can see wave patterns in colliding weather fronts and at the beach, both in massive sea swells and in delicate sand ripples. In all of these cases, matter and energy are being directed into an efficient form for supporting what is needed to happen. Branching patterns are ideal for collecting and distributing energy and materials; hence trees use them to gather sunlight and disperse water and nutrients. Waves and

ripples allow two flowing bodies to move past each other with minimal turbulence. Each time we see a pattern such as these, it is nature's way of solving a design challenge—of moving, collecting, harvesting, or dispersing matter and energy in a marvelously simple and effective way. This is exactly what we are trying to do in an ecological landscape. So it's appropriate for us to study a few of these patterns, to see what they can teach us.

Humans, too, use patterns, but if the voluptuous curves and complex fractals of nature appear in our work, they are there for aesthetics, not function. Ruler-straight rows, checkerboard streets, glass-and-concrete gridwork, and the parallelograms permitted by milled lumber are our familiar patterns. Sometimes these patterns are the right ones for the job, but in landscapes such patterns are rare. Nature's shapes are rarely rectilinear, and there is good reason for that.

Choosing and applying the right shapes and patterns in a landscape, besides creating beauty, can save space, reduce labor, enhance wildlife habitat, and help bring the plants, insects, and other animals, including the gardener, into better balance.

I'll begin with a simple example of how shape and pattern can save us work and space and then move to a few richer and more elaborate ideas learned from nature's patterns.

Keyhole Garden Beds

The shape of a garden determines how much of its area can actually be used to contain plants, as opposed to paths to let us reach those plants. I regard garden paths as a necessary evil. After working hard to build up the soil, it irritates me to pound a high percentage of fluffy loam into hardpan under my feet. Every bit of path is unusable real estate that could be devoted to a rich polyculture of greens, veggies, and sweet-scented blossoms. Fortunately, changing the pattern used for garden beds can minimize the land sacrificed to paths.

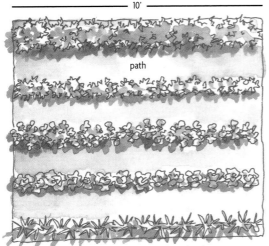

Single rows need 40 square feet of path.

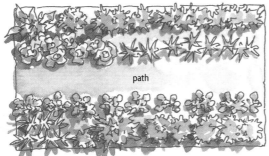

Raised beds need 10 square feet of path

A keyhole bed needs only 6 square feet of path.

Changing the shape of a garden bed—working with patterns—can reduce the area lost to paths, as seen in these beds, each containing 50 square feet of planting.

The most basic garden bed contains single rows of plants with paths between each row. In this layout, paths consume about half of the soil area. A raised-bed garden, in which paths fall between every three or four rows of plants, is an improvement, sacrificing only about 30 percent of its ground to walkways while leaving the beds narrow enough for the gardener to reach the center. Here, a simple change in geometry has eliminated almost half the path space. But we can do better and create an eye-pleasing design while we're at it.

If we bend that rectangular raised bed into a circle—or, more accurately, a horseshoe shape—even more path will disappear. By a simple trick of topology, the path shrinks to a tiny keyhole shape, which gives this space-saving garden layout its name: *keyhole bed.*

Here's what happens. If we wrap a typical 4-by-15-foot raised bed into a U shape with a small central opening for a path, we cut the path down from about 22 square feet (figuring an 18-inch-wide path down one side of the raised bed) to 6 square feet. Less than a quarter of the ground is surrendered to paths. I won't torture you with the math that would prove this to the skeptical—as any publisher knows, each successive equation in a text puts half the remaining readers to flight.

Keyhole beds have aesthetics as well as mathematics going for them. Bringing curves into a garden eliminates that "soybean field" quality that emanates from ruler-straight beds and rows. With the exception of falling apples and other gravity-driven phenomena, nature never takes the shortest distance between two points. Instead, nature meanders, drifting in graceful but efficient undulations from here to there. It's humans who have become enamored of the unswerving, direct route. But in our gardens, we meet nature more or less on her own terms. Just as a straight stretch of interstate highway invites narcolepsy, linear gardens are monotonous, too. Curves and circles lend surprise

A keyhole bed planted with cabbages, tomatoes, and pathside greens and herbs in a space 8 to 10 feet in diameter.

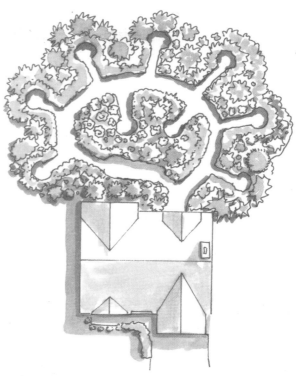

Several keyhole beds can extend from a central path to create a garden with pleasing curves and plenty of accessible bed space.

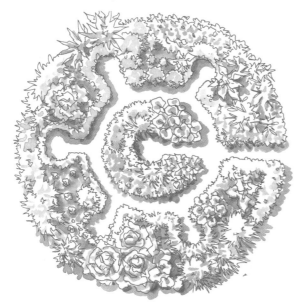

A mandala garden. A circular pattern of nested keyhole beds is both beautiful and space-conserving.

and whimsy to a garden. What a bonus it is that they happen to be more efficient, too.

More benefits of keyhole beds: if we point the central path toward the south and locate tall plants such as tomatoes or sunflowers at the back, or northern edge, the bed creates a U-shaped sun bowl that traps warmth. The toasty microclimate inside is a good place for tender or heat-loving varieties. They are easy to irrigate, too. A single minisprinkler in the center will cast a circular spray pattern to drench the whole bed.

The Herb Spiral

We can go a little deeper into the use of shape and pattern in the garden. Permaculture principles tell us to begin at our doorstep, so let's put an herb garden along the path that starts at our back door. OK, in goes the oregano, next to it a couple of types of thyme, then chives—we like chives, so let's plant five of them—and past those, a few parsley plants and a little mint. We add a dozen more favorite herbs and spices, and finish off with three

Building and Planting a Keyhole Bed

To create a keyhole bed, begin with a circle of soil about 8 to 10 feet in diameter pierced on one side by a path to the center. Keyhole beds can be created by shoveling fertile topsoil into a horseshoe shape, but I prefer to build them by layering up, lasagna-style, leaves or other compostable organic matter, newspapers, and soil, using a technique called *sheet mulching* (see Chapter 4 for details). In a keyhole bed, the plantable zone is about as wide as in a standard raised bed: 3 to 5 feet across. The access path into the bed can be narrow, a foot or so wide, but the central circle of path needs to be big enough to turn around in, about 18 to 24 inches in diameter.

You can plant a keyhole bed using the zone system (look ahead to see Table 3-3 and accompanying figures for an explanation of zones). Put the most frequently picked plants closest to the center. That means that herbs, greens, and other veggies harvested and eaten daily should border the central path. Behind these, place plants that get picked only every few days, such as peppers, bush peas and beans, eggplants, and others. These are still easy to reach without a stretch. At the back of the bed, install long-term crops and those that are harvested only once. These include potatoes, carrots, and other root crops, plus what I call the Red Queen veggies—cauliflower, iceberg lettuce, and cabbage—because it's "off with their heads" at harvest. These back-row plants might be a bit out of reach if the bed is more than 3 feet deep; thus what I am about to suggest will shock those gardeners who are zealous adherents of the double-dig method. To harvest these plants, step onto the bed (gasp!) and pluck. One footprint per season isn't going to annihilate soil porosity and structure. If the idea of stepping on light, fluffy soil is simply too appalling, lay down a board to stand on, which will limit compaction.

Keyhole beds abound with creative possibilities. A whole circle could be dedicated to tomatoes, varieties of sage. Soon, about twenty-five plants are dotted along the path, stretching well into the backyard. Those sage plants are pretty far away. On a raw wet day, we'll need to don boots and a jacket before we'll want to gather herbs. It's more likely that, with a little pang of guilt, we'll reach into the cupboard for dried sage and skip the chives. Plus, that little herb garden needs about 30 feet of path to give easy access, and every inch of path is one less inch of growing space.

What if we design the herb garden using a different pattern? Instead of a straight—or even meandering—line, let's fold up the path somehow so that the whole affair takes less space. We could just plunk the herbs into a standard raised bed, leaving a rather dull rectangular patch outside our door. That would save space, though some of the herbs might need quite a stretch to reach. But let's be more creative. Here's where a little knowledge of shapes and patterns comes into play.

This is a perfect spot for an herb spiral. An herb spiral coils up 20 or 30 linear feet of pathside plants into a helical pattern about 5 feet across. It's not just a flat spiral, either. Here's how it works.

An herb spiral begins as a mound of good soil about 3 feet high and 5 feet across. To turn this mound into a spiral, place football- to fist-sized rocks in a spiral pattern that winds from the bottom inward to the top, with the bigger rocks at the bottom. Leave about a foot of soil between the tiers of the rock spiral.

Now it's time to install the herbs, winding them up the spiral. This coils about 30 linear feet of row into a much smaller space. All the herbs can grow right outside the door, using only the path space necessary to walk around the spiral. Plus, mound-

with a few companion culinary herbs such as basil or chives at the inner margin. Or use the circular geometry to balance sun and shadow: Place crops that wilt in midsummer's full blaze to the east of taller sun-lovers, shading the tender ones on scorching afternoons. To trellis vining plants, curve a length of fencing around the bed. If salty coastal gales or the desiccating winds of the plains buffet the garden, plant tall sturdy crops such as Jerusalem artichokes or a stocky breed of sunflowers on the outside of the beds as a windbreak. Of course, keyhole beds work for flowers, too, letting us stand, shears in hand, in a circle of brilliant color as we contemplate filling a vase or three.

Keyhole beds are round, whereas most yards are square. So what about the margins, those little triangles of unused ground at the corners of these beds—isn't that wasted space? Not at all. Every garden needs insect-attracting flowers, or perennial nitrogen fixers such as Dutch clover, or a good wind-and-weed barrier at the edges to stop weed seeds blowing in from your neighbor's less-than-immaculate land. We could fill the margin with robust mulch-providers such as fava beans or comfrey. It could be a perfect spot for a small fruit tree. Or we can just expand the bed to fill the corners. There's no rule that says a keyhole bed can't be square rather than round; it's the central path that defines it.

Planting more than one keyhole bed expands the possibilities. Keyholes can extend to the left and right of a central walkway.

An undulating path flanked by keyhole beds can wrap around a house to make an attractive Zone 1 garden.

A further modification of the keyhole scheme is the mandala garden, a set of four to eight keyhole beds arranged in a circle with one more bed in the center, and a path entering the mandala from one side. A mandala garden combines beauty and efficiency to create a magical effect. Few designs can fit more growing space into less area, and the more mystically inclined would say a mandala garden brings a spiritual aspect to a piece of ground.

ing up the soil means we can reach the central herbs without bending over very far.

Combining the spiral and mound patterns into a three-dimensional helix does more than save space and effort. Its mound shape means the herb spiral has slopes that face all directions. The sunny, south-facing slope will be hotter than the north. The east-facing side, which gets morning sun, will dry out earlier in the day than the west one. The soil at the bottom will stay wetter than that at the top. We've created an herb garden with different microclimates. So we plant accordingly, locating each herb in a suitable environment. Varieties that thrive in hot, dry climates, such as oregano, rosemary, and thyme, go on the sunny south side near the top. Parsley and chives, which prefer cooler, moister climes, find a home on the north side. Coriander, which seems to bolt in too much hot sun, can be

stationed on the east side, protected from afternoon scorchings. Other herbs can snuggle into their best sites as well.

A few tips on building an herb spiral:

- The plants listed in the figure are merely examples. Choose herbs you use—not everyone needs echinacea. And they don't have to all be herbs, so feel free to include lettuce and other salad greens, strawberries, flowers, or any other small plant that you use often.
- To save on topsoil, place a few rocks, concrete rubble, or a heap of subsoil at the base of the mound, then build over that.
- To water the spiral easily, run plastic

irrigation tubing (¼ or ½ inch) inside the mound, emerging from the top, and attach a minisprinkler.

- The loose soil of the new spiral is likely to settle, so water it thoroughly (without washing it away) after piling up the soil and settle the soil without compacting it. You may need to add more soil after doing this.
- Consider sinking a small basin or tiny pond (1 to 3 feet across) at the bottom of the spiral. Watercress, water chestnuts, and other edible pond plants can grow here.

Built with attractive stone, an herb spiral can be an eye-catching central feature of any garden.

Other Natural Patterns in the Garden

Let's examine why the herb spiral offers so many rewards. This design winds a straight line into a spiral and then drapes this two-dimensional pattern over a three-dimensional one—the mound of soil. The combination spawns a wealth of what are called *synergistic effects*—the unexpected benefits of a new collaboration that neither partner alone can offer. These two patterns also interact with the environment—sun, shade, time of day, and so on—as well as with people—saving labor and space, encouraging use, looking attractive—in many more ways than a static row ever could. Clever use of natural patterns in garden design can often generate delightful bonuses.

Nature itself is full of these patterns. The spiral and the related helix (a spiral stretched into three dimensions, like a corkscrew or herb spiral) are particularly abundant. Snail shells, the pattern of seeds in a sunflower head, ram's horns, hurricanes, galaxies—all form spirals. The pattern of leaves or branches extending from a stem often unwinds in a helix, which minimizes the amount of shade cast

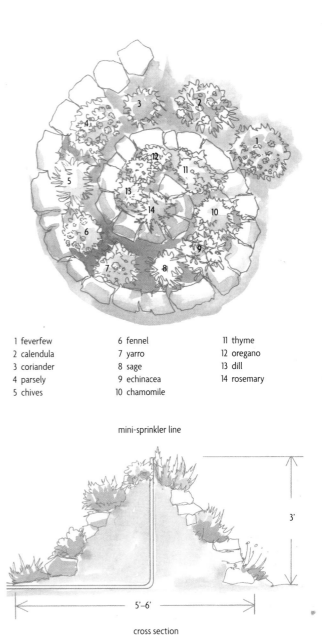

1 feverfew	6 fennel	11 thyme
2 calendula	7 yarro	12 oregano
3 coriander	8 sage	13 dill
4 parsely	9 echinacea	14 rosemary
5 chives	10 chamomile	

mini-sprinkler line

cross section

An herb spiral combines a two-dimensional pattern (a spiral) with a three-dimensional one (a mound) to form a beautiful and space-saving living sculpture that has several microclimates.

by each leaf on the one below. Spirals are often the result of growth or expansion.

Here are a few more of nature's patterns that are useful for gardeners to recognize.

A few of the many spiral patterns found in nature.

Branches. Branching patterns are used in nature to collect or disperse nutrients, energy, and water. Tree branches spread leaves over a wide area to better absorb sunlight. Forking roots gather nutrients and moisture.

We can apply our observation of branches in the garden. California designer and educator Larry Santoyo of Earthflow Design Works constantly uses patterns in his landscape designs. Inspired observation of a leaf taught him a novel design for garden paths. In one of his classes that I visited, he passed leaves to his students. "Look at the branching veins," he told us. "They use the least possible space to get sap from the green cells, the photosynthetic cells, to the rest of the plant," he pointed out. The leaf's central vein was thickest, the main branches from it were half the size, and from those extended tiny veinlets for ferrying nutrients to, and sap from, each cluster of cells. The veins themselves don't gather much light, so it behooves a plant to minimize them. "Why don't we design garden paths like that? Why didn't anyone see this?" Larry asked. "You make a big central path for a cart or wheelbarrow, and smaller ones branching off of it for foot traffic to the beds. You save a lot of space and have a natural flow pattern." I was struck by how original and useful Larry's observation was. He's designed many successful gardens using this pattern, and others have copied him.

Branching patterns are an efficient way to reach all the points in a large area, while moving the shortest distance possible. A single branch is also easy to repair if damaged, and its loss has only a small effect on the whole system or organism. Anywhere collection or dispersal needs to be done in nature, you can find branching patterns: the tributaries of a river system, the seedheads of Queen Anne's lace and other umbel flowers, blood vessels, the forking zigzag of lightning bolts, or the ever-finer divisions of tubing in a drip-irrigation system. Branches are a common pattern in nature and in our gardens.

Nets. The net or mesh pattern is found in nature in spiderwebs, birds' nests, honeycombs, and the cracking of dried mud. Nets are patterns of expansion, contraction, and even distribution. Gardeners often create a net pattern when placing seeds in a

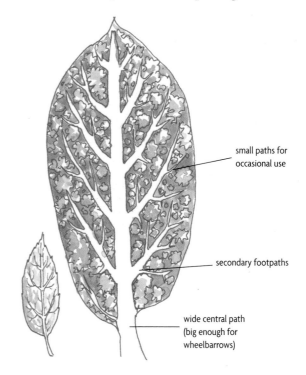

small paths for occasional use

secondary footpaths

wide central path (big enough for wheelbarrows)

Branching garden paths, modeled after a leaf. The pattern of a leaf's veins is a space-conserving way to deliver nutrients to the leaf cells without sacrificing precious light-gathering surface. We can use the same pattern for a garden's paths, which minimizes the growing area lost to our pounding feet.

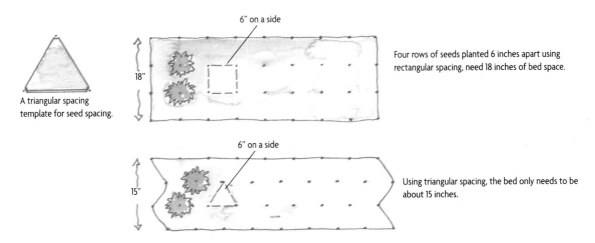

6" on a side

18"

A triangular spacing
template for seed spacing.

Four rows of seeds planted 6 inches apart using
rectangular spacing, need 18 inches of bed space.

6" on a side

15"

Using triangular spacing, the bed only needs to be
about 15 inches.

A triangular net pattern allows more seeds to be planted in the same space than the more commonly used rectangular pattern.

raised bed, setting the seeds in a pattern of triangles to create equal distances between each seed. This pattern fits the most seeds into the space available.

In drylands, orchardists plant their trees in a net pattern to collect rain and runoff. Fruit trees are planted in small depressions, and the basins are connected by a network of shallow trenches. By this clever system, rain and runoff water falling over a large area are collected by the trench network and delivered to the base of the trees.

Nature uses net patterns to build soil and ameliorate harsh conditions, and we can take a leaf from her book for our gardens. I've seen shifting sand dunes stabilized via a net pattern of plants. The blustery winds on the dunes scatter grass or other seeds randomly over a large area; as each plant grows, it creates a small shaded, windless patch around it. Bolstered by this self-created, benign microclimate, the plant sends out runners and colonizes new ground. Soon a netlike pattern of plants has captured and subdued a large patch of landscape, even though bare earth lies between the individual plants. Over time, the dispersed plants enlarge and tie together. The whole region has then been "tamed" and moderated, turned into mild and welcoming habitat.

We can use this net pattern in our yards. If our soil is poor and plants are few, the classic answer is too often a labor- and money-intensive blitz to add topsoil and blanket the place with plants all at once—a strategy that usually results in overwhelming work followed by a lot of dead plants. Vowing not to make this mistake, New Hampshire permaculturist Doug Clayton applied the net pattern to his yard. He began with a grid of small fruit trees spaced over his future orchard. Around each sapling, he added manure and wood chip mulch and planted cover crops and perennials, creating a network of mulched circles. Each tree became a small zone of healthy soil and mild microclimate. Between the circles initially was grass, which Doug more or less ignored, knowing there'd be less of it each year. "I would just mow it and rake the clippings around the base of the trees to concentrate fertility there," Doug told me. He believes this process also keeps fungal diseases in check. "The mowing, raking up leaves, putting a ring of manure on top of it in the fall, and periodically burying everything in woodchips I think interrupts the sporing cycle of apple scab. I'm not doing anything in terms of sprays for scab, but I don't have a bad scab situation. The fungus just decays."

Trees in drylands can be planted in small depressions, called net-and-pan. The basins are then connected by a network of shallow trenches. The trench network collects rain and runoff water falling over a large area and delivers it to the base of the trees. Mulch also collects in the basins, building soil.

Over the next few years, Doug expanded these circles with mulch and more plantings. Eventually, some of the circles of fertility and life began to touch each other, tying the orchard together with rich soil and lush vegetation. This is one way to use a net pattern in a garden or orchard to gradually build fertility and a diverse array of plants over a large area. Because a net pattern inherently connects, automatically building wholeness, it takes only a very manageable amount of labor and expense to nudge our yards to where this pattern is already going.

Along with spirals, branches, and nets, many other patterns occur in nature that can be applied to the garden. There are circles, waves, lobes, and fractals, as well as the complex swirling patterns of liquids and gases with exotic names such as von Karman vortex streets, Ekman spirals, and Overbeck jets. If you would like to learn more about patterns and how they occur in nature and design, see the bibliography for further reading.

Living on the Edge

Patterning by coiling a row of herbs into a spiral or scrunching a rectangular garden plot into a keyhole bed shrinks the amount of path needed. These patterns do this by reducing the amount of the bed's edge in relation to its surface area. "Edge" is a key concept in ecology, so much so that ecologists speak of "the edge effect." Edges are fascinating and dynamic places, and I'd like to delve briefly into the ways that the edges and their effects can be used in the garden.

Edges are where things happen. Where a forest meets the prairie, where a river flows into the sea, or at nearly any other boundary between two ecosystems is a cauldron of biodiversity. All the species that thrive in each of the two environments are present, plus new species that live in the transition zone between the two. The edge is richer than what lies on either side. Any fisherman knows this. He doesn't cast his lure into the center of the lake, but toward the shoreline, where fish gather to feed on the flourishing life in the shallows.

We can see edges at work in our own yards. Where do the most birds gather? Not in the middle of the lawn but along the edge of a clump of trees or shrubs; not deep in a thick mass of bushes but on the twigs at the margin. So if we want to boost the biodiversity in our yards, we should increase the amount of edge. For a start, this means encouraging plantings of varying heights. A transition between, say, lawn and trees should be gradual, softened with increasingly large perennials and shrubs to increase habitat and variety. But there are many other ways to tinker with "edge" to gain the effects we want.

Note that the permaculture principle regarding edge (see Chapter 1) says to *optimize* edge, not just maximize it. Sometimes, in fact, it pays to minimize edge, as with the herb spiral and keyhole bed. Here, edge translates into waste space and more work. The decision to increase or decrease edge depends on what lies on either side of the edge and what we want from it. Edges allow us to define spaces, see their boundaries as well as what flows across them, and work with these flows. They are places of transition and translation, where matter and energy change speed or stop or, often, change into something else. Let's examine some of the edges found in a typical yard and how we can use them:

- *House/yard edge.* The outside walls of a house create varied microclimates. The south wall will be hottest and sunniest, so heat-loving and cold-tender plants can go here, often making it possible to grow plants found one or two USDA hardiness zones to the south. The west wall will be cool in the mornings but baking hot on sunny afternoons, and the north wall the coldest and darkest. We can fit our plants and work or play spaces into them accordingly. We can also keep the house warmer or cooler by planting on these edges.
- *Pavement/soil edge.* Paved surfaces collect water, so thirstier plants can be placed alongside sidewalks and driveways to catch runoff. Pavement also stores up heat on sunny days, so the adjacent soil will be warmer.
- *Fence/yard edge.* Fences and walls act as filters, stopping some flows (such as people and views) and allowing or creating others (airflow, perching birds). Debris and snow will pile up against fences, collecting mulch and moisture. Fences can also be used as trellises, so running fencing in a zigzag will increase the edge available for trellis and fence-side plantings, as well as making the fence more resistant to wind and creating a sheltered pocket in each concave "zig."
- *Plant/soil edge.* To increase the number of plants that can fit into a given space, place them in a wavy pattern rather than a straight line. Plants at the edge of beds often yield more than the ones in the center, so patterns that increase edge in beds will boost production. Rows of tall plants can be alternated with short ones to achieve the same effect.
- *Plant/air edge.* I mentioned how a keyhole bed can be pointed south to create a sun-trap. Edges of garden beds and, on a larger scale, rows of shrubs and trees can be sculpted into undulating shapes that contain cooler, windier lobes and protected, warm bays.
- *Water/soil edge.* The shape of a garden pond affects how many plants will fit at the edge. A perfectly round pond has the least edge, whereas a pond with lobes and bays, or in a starburst pattern can hold an enormous number of bog plants and other moisture lovers. Also, the fingers of land extending into the pond will be drier in their raised

centers. Land plants can thrive in the centers, while boggy species can grow at the squishy margins. Varying the depth of the pond (another way to increase edge) will make room for more types of fish and water plants. Frogs and tadpoles can bask in the warm shallows while golden koi flash in the depths.

In general, straight lines and smooth shapes reduce the amount of edge, while shapes with lobes, notches, mounds, pits, crinkles, and crenellations will increase edge. Don't forget about extending the edge effect into the third dimension by varying the height and depth of plantings, soil, structures, and ponds. The importance of edges is simply one more manifestation of the role of connections in the ecological garden. Edges are not static places; they are the result of a relationship between two or more dynamic pieces of the living landscape.

Australian designer Geoff Lawton, who has worked closely with Bill Mollison, says that if we get a yard's edges under control, the rest of the design more easily falls into place. A careful assessment of what and where the edges in the landscape are, what flows across them or is stopped by them, and what important edges might be missing, allows us to see the patterns in our landscape and in our use

of it. Let's look deeper into the process of designing a landscape with nature as our guide.

The Ecological Design Process

An ecological design recognizes that nothing in nature stands alone and disconnected. Any garden

The benefits of increasing the edge in a pond. Though both ponds have roughly the same volume and surface area, the wavy pond has far more edge. Thus it can be surrounded by far more plants, and the extensive shallows offer more habitat for fish and aquatic plants.

One way to use the edge effect. A wavy edge can hold more plants, and expose more of their area to sun and beneficial insects, than a straight edge.

will reflect this connectedness, whether we want it to or not. Plant a swath of broccoli or roses, for example, and aphids will quickly find it, feasting on the new food source. Presto, our new plant is connected to the rest of nature, even if we'd rather it weren't. Anything we plant will instantly tie to natural cycles, taking in nutrients and water, releasing oxygen and other molecules to the air and soil, converting sunlight to greenery, and being seen as food and habitat by insects, birds, microbes, and the rest of life.

The environmentalists' adage that everything is connected to everything else is true. Any element of a design—a plant, a path, or a greenhouse or other structure—is in relationship with many other elements. How the design's pieces are connected to each other is at least as important as what the pieces are. An ecologically designed garden will do more than just accept this dynamic interconnectedness—it will revel in it and turn it to advantage. For example, if a beloved plant is also a magnet for aphids, then a good designer will discover and create conditions that discourage aphid infestations. Instead of installing a solid block of roses or broccoli, we can use a different planting pattern, scattering the plants among other species so aphids must work harder to find them. Trimming the amount of nitrogen in the soil will help, too, since aphids seek out succulent, nitrogen-fattened plants. And we can foster habitat for aphid predators such as ladybugs and parasitic wasps, a remedy that will reduce insect pests in general. The best solutions will have benefits that reach far beyond the original problem.

A rosebush, for example, is connected to many other species, including the aphids it so readily attracts. The aphids in turn lure ladybugs, the ladybugs are hungrily devoured by birds, and the birds leave their droppings to feed microbes and fertilize the rose. Everything in a landscape is busy interacting with other elements and being acted on in turn.

Thus, to have a landscape that doesn't just look natural but acts like a natural ecosystem, we need a way of thinking about the pieces of our design that goes beyond mere appearances. If we fully grasp how each design element ties to the other pieces, we can connect the parts in a way that is elegant, efficient, productive, and beautiful.

Remember how self-reliant a natural landscape is. An ecosystem provides for itself. No one brings in truckloads of fertilizer to a forest; no one carries its waste to the dump. The forest takes care of all that internally, producing fertility and recycling litter and debris. In other words, the forest's inputs and outputs are balanced, leaving little waste, and the work is powered by sunlight. This is the model we strive to emulate.

Briefly, the steps in creating an ecological garden design are:

- *Observation.* Here we ask, What do we have to work with? What are the conditions and constraints of the site and the client?
- *Visioning.* What should the design do? What do we want? What does the site need? How should it feel?
- *Planning.* What do we need to make our ideas happen? How should the pieces be assembled?
- *Development.* What will the final design look like? How will we make it happen?
- *Implementation, the final step.* How do we install the garden?

We usually think of design as the process of figuring out what goes where: "We'll put the blueberries here and the path there." But note that planning, which is the "what goes where" step, is only one of the five phases of the design process. The other steps are just as critical in a successful design. It's similar to painting a room: Wielding a wet brush is the part we think of as "painting," but it's less than half the work of getting a room of a different color. It's easy to forget, as we pick those color chips, about emptying the room, washing the walls, filling and sanding nail holes, taping trim, and reassembling the room afterward. But if you omit any of those steps, you'll wind up with something between a lackluster paint job and Jackson Pollock gone mad. Design is like that, although most of the steps are more enjoyable than washing walls. So be forewarned: Only a small portion of good design is figuring out where the pieces go. Don't be impatient or give the other steps short shrift.

One more note before we examine the design process. Every landscape design has two "clients" with their own needs: the people who live there and the land itself. When we try to force a design on a place that won't support it—expansive green lawns in the desert, for example—we're fighting an uphill battle. Only vast amounts of work, energy, resources, and money will keep an unsuitable design functioning. Those kinds of high inputs are contrary to an ecological design. Nature doesn't work that way. And if the gardener relaxes for a moment, nature will prove how unsuitable the design is. With record dry spells, freeze-thaw cycles, moisture-loving fungi, or any of a host of common but incompatible natural phenomenon, nature will outlast an ecologically unsavvy gardener and defeat an impractical design.

We're trying to design places that piggyback onto nature and work with its boundless energy, not fight against it. We can do this by recognizing that the land has its own set of requirements and tendencies just as we do.

Let's go through the design steps in detail.

Observation

The observation stage involves gathering two kinds of information, what is at the site and what resources are available for the project.

A great way to begin the process of getting to know the site is by making a map of it. The map doesn't have to be pretty, but it should include buildings, roads, and paths; existing trees and other principal plants; slope and major land features; drainage and watercourses; soil types and conditions (clay or sandy, boggy or dry, and so on); and scales and distances. Almost any good book on conventional landscape design will give details for making a simple map of a property. Several are listed in the bibliography. Landscape design and mapping software can be used, too, and they come in a range of prices and learning curves.

Making a map creates more than just a piece of paper. Each time I prepare a map, I become aware of details I would never notice otherwise. Mapmaking puts me in intimate contact with a place. Slope, view, distance, pockets of coolness and warmth, flickers of sun and shadow, all come into sharp relief as I walk the land and sketch or otherwise note what I see and feel. The knowledge deposits itself in my mind and waits for use. The place takes on a wholeness, a fullness that my senses encompass, all symbolized on a simple piece of paper that connects to an image inside me.

Observation goes far beyond simply noting the objects on the site. Observation at its best means being immersed in the place. What creatures live there? When do various birds and other animals come and go? What do they eat or otherwise use at the site? What interactions take place among the plant, animal, and human inhabitants? The first step is just to list these observations. Don't feel you have to be a professional field naturalist or geographer. Just list what you see, using this section as a guide. Later, you can research your observations in books or flesh them out with further fieldwork.

It's not easy to separate the process of observation from analysis. We almost automatically combine a raw observation, such as "this plant's leaves are turning yellow" with an analysis: "because it needs more nitrogen." But in the early phase of observation, it's important to retain a childlike quality of wonder without moving instantly to analysis. Analysis channels our thinking and reduces our options. When we leap from simply observing down the path to "nitrogen deficiency," we narrow our options to one class of solutions: This plant needs fertilizer. But by patiently remaining with the simple observation that "this plant's leaves are turning yellow," we open ourselves up to many other options. Later, with other observations to help inform us we can ask: Should we keep this sickly plant? Should we add companion plants to aid it? Is this an appropriate species to have here? What plants will be happier in these conditions? How much soil improvement do we want to engage in? Remember, we're not looking for solutions at this point but simply an understanding of what we have.

Keep track of these observations. The most common way to do this is with a written list, but not everyone's brain is wired the same way. Some people will find it more useful to make a video or tape recording with commentary or annotated sketches. Choose a method that works for you. Table 3-1 offers suggestions about the kinds of observations to make.

After making the initial observations, do research via books, local experts, or the Internet to learn more about characteristics that can't be observed directly.

The other phase of the observation step is to assess the resources on hand for the project. What supplies, plants, and tools exist at the site? How much time, money, and energy do you have to devote to the design, implementation, and maintenance of the landscape? What relevant skills and knowledge do you have? Which of these resources can come from family, friends, neighbors, or your community? A design cannot succeed without a realistic picture of the resources and limitations

that constrain it. This resource assessment will also suggest what is missing and will need to be bought, borrowed, or otherwise gotten from elsewhere.

One warning about the observation phase: Humans love to make plans and can barely keep themselves from doing it. It's excruciatingly difficult to walk around your yard observing without also thinking, "There's a great place for a path . . . and we could make a flower bed along it," and so forth. Don't do that! Try to enter a Zen mind set or whatever it takes to simply observe without planning. Instead of "We can put a path here," make an observation statement such as "There is poor access to this area." Each placement decision made too early will collapse the range of possibilities that remain. I cannot emphasize this strongly enough. Planning what goes where must wait until later.

Visioning

Now that we know what we have at the site, we can dream about what we want, what the place can look and feel like, and what could be happening there. During this phase it helps to have a notebook or tape recorder to preserve our ideas. Multiple and lengthy lists are fine. We're just brainstorming without judgments or practical considerations here. Later we'll winnow the lists.

Some designers begin with visioning, and that's fine. In truth, the observation and visioning steps inform each other. The available resources, particularly time and money, will inform your vision; and, as your vision matures, your observations may take on new focus. Some people do observation and visioning simultaneously, bouncing between one and the other, while other people work on one, then the other, and then return to the first and reevaluate. As each step is finished, it's wise to revisit the earlier steps briefly and evaluate them to see if anything needs modification in light of your new knowledge.

Table 3-1. What to Observe—a Designer's Checklist

❏ History of the land: neighbors' knowledge, library and public records, historical society, maps, photos, backyard archaeology (dig test pits)

❏ Homeowners association and government activities: covenants, easements, yard waste pickup, recycling, herbicide spraying, water rationing, zoning and construction restrictions

❏ Nearby plantings that may affect your site (now or when fully grown)

❏ Activities of neighbors that may affect design: noise, children, pets, visits, schools, industry, etc.

❏ Resources in the neighborhood: sources of organic matter, soil, and building materials such as sawmills, factories, food processors, stores, landfills, recyclers, nurseries, neighbors

❏ Utilities: power, phone, sewer, and gas lines

❏ Areas of shade and sun, and how they change over the year

❏ Wind direction, intensity, and change over the seasons

❏ Average and record temperature highs and lows, dates of first and last frosts

❏ Rainfall amounts and seasons, snow, hail

❏ Points of sunrise and sunset and their change over the seasons

❏ Topography, slope, and aspect

❏ Rock outcrops, boulders, gravel

❏ Microclimates: cool, hot, wet, dry, sheltered, and exposed spots

❏ Soil: drainage, heavy or light, sand or clay, rich or depleted, stable or slumping, compaction

❏ Water: flooding zones, drainage patterns, creeks, gullies, water movement during rain

❏ Views: good, bad, and potential

❏ Location of structures on-site and nearby, such as houses, garages, fences, and walls, and their effects on the surroundings: shade, runoff, windbreak, etc.

❏ Vegetation: species present, opportunistic or noxious plants, rare species, and their state of health

❏ Animals: pets, native and introduced, pests, "scary" animals (snakes, spiders)

❏ Traffic and its frequency, heavy or light vehicles, pedestrian traffic, bicycles

❏ Access: ease of bringing in materials, location of faucets, stairs, doors, garage, storage, etc.

The visioning phase begins with a no-holds-barred brainstorm, limited to some degree by finances (but, after all, we're dreaming here) and really only by ecological and ethical constraints. That simply means that the new landscape should be leaving Earth and its inhabitants better off, not worse, for the changes to this space. Unfortunately, many conventional landscape designs leave the planet a poorer place. Unlike natural landscapes, they are dependent on massive inputs of fertilizer, pesticides, water, and fossil fuel-driven machinery. They're devoid of habitat and offer little more to the owners than a place to park a lawn chair. It's not difficult to do better.

For a garden to be considered ecological, the new landscape should:

- Require few outside inputs, especially once it's mature
- Increase biodiversity
- Create rather than destroy wildlife and plant habitat
- Enhance air, water, and soil quality
- Eventually result in less work instead of more for the human occupants.

Further chapters of this book will detail techniques that easily meet these requirements, but we should hold these principles firmly in mind during the garden design.

With these few constraints in mind, we can create our vision. Here are the kinds of questions to ask during the visioning process:

- What do you and the other human inhabitants want and need from the landscape? What can it offer? Possibilities include food, herbs, wildlife habitat, cut flowers, privacy, inspiration, tranquility, income, play space, or all of these. Research what's available and go into a little detail, remembering that this is just the dreaming phase.

- What does the landscape and region need? Has previous abuse caused a problem that can be corrected by good design? Does the soil need rejuvenating? Are trees dying, plants struggling? Would the land benefit from more water, from wildlife habitat? Are rare native plants growing here that can be nurtured? Could the design regenerate and replenish a damaged landscape and offer a chance of survival to endangered species?

- How should the new landscape feel? Like a forest, a Garden of Eden, a meadow, a sanctuary?

- What will you do there?

- What kind of food, herbs, medicinal plants, firewood, timber, or other products would you like to have? Which of these can the land provide sustainably, for the long haul?

- Will the place have an overall theme or function such as education, sanctuary, demonstration site, self-reliant living, or market gardening?

Let your imagination run free and keep a list of the possibilities. When noting the items your want in the landscape, describe them in terms of what they do instead of giving them a static name. Rather than writing down "fence," call it a "barrier," which invites far more possibilities: It could be a hedge, rock wall, berm, or even a moat. Instead of "compost pile" think "organic matter recycling." See the difference? Listing the pieces of the design by function rather than with an inert noun description will keep far more options open.

The next step is to organize what now may be pages of notes. This begins by ranking your priorities. What are the most urgent problems or desires to address? Is it getting rid of the energy-gobbling lawn, redirecting runoff from the front walk, growing some food? Priorities can be personal, as in, "First I need a place to sit quietly; then I'll have the energy to build the rock walls I want." Examine the least important aspects of the vision, too; perhaps these contradict the more important ones or can just be dispensed with. If it helps, break priorities into several categories: personal, aesthetic, problems to be solved, environmental/ecological, and the like. See which categories and items leap out as the most important.

The final step in the visioning process is to reevaluate the goals and themes in light of the priorities to see if any goals need to be readjusted. Perhaps you've realized that a play space for children and dogs is a more pressing need than you first thought and will let that inform the overall design.

You have now collected an enormous amount of information about your site and your own desires for it. Although the observation and visioning steps don't seem like the juiciest part of the design process, doing them thoroughly greases the skids for the subsequent steps and makes them much easier to do.

Planning

This aspect of ecological garden design is demanding, but an abundance of useful tools exists to help us. With the paperwork of observation and visioning behind us, the planning phase for most people is the most fun. It's the part of the ecological design process we think of as "design," in which we figure out what goes where. I've broken this phase into two segments, conceptual design and layout.

Conceptual design. This is the "big picture" segment of design. We know our goals and the resources available that we currently have available. Now we need to find the patterns, ideas, and framework that will bring our vision to life and will support and organize all the pieces into a coherent whole. David Holmgren, the cooriginator of the permaculture concept, suggests that we design from patterns to details. This excellent advice works on several levels. The top level is: See if there is one (or sometimes more, but not often) overarching physical pattern that will support most of the goals of your design. Is there a branching, network, spiral, or other pattern that is trying to emerge from the landscape and that will best support what you want to have happen there? This pattern can become the unifying idea that ties the landscape together, appearing perhaps at different scales, each time enhancing a particular flow, aesthetic, or activity. Remember, though, not to impose a pattern on the land simply because you like, say, spirals. The pattern should emerge from your dialogue with the land and from the goals of the design. It should naturally solve design problems rather than create a series of work-arounds to be dealt with.

To help this pattern emerge, look over your lists and assessments and walk around the site to sense the flows and patterns already existing there. It may help to condense a long list of goals and dreams into two or three concise sentences that capture the essence of your goals.

At the next level, a pattern can refer to a system or strategy needed for a particular task or function of the design. Does your design need water collection, organic matter recycling, foot-traffic management? Now is the time to choose how the major goals and functions of the design will be achieved. Make a list of these goals and functions. They may include irrigation; foot and garden-cart traffic; different types of food, flower, habitat, and nutrient production; composting; storage; shade; social and family activities; pet areas; lighting; privacy; meditation; work spaces; and seating. The method chosen to do each of these tasks will, in part, dictate what elements are needed for that part of the design and how they will be organized. Water from a faucet coursing through a complex drip irrigation system will need different components and be arrayed in a different pattern than rainfall collected in a pond that overflows down a swale into an orchard. For now, just list the tasks, functions, and systems that your design needs. Figuring out what components each function comprises can wait for the next phase.

Having listed the functions, tasks, products, and strategies of our design points us smoothly toward the next step. Now we can identify the design elements—individual parts, materials, species, and other items—that make up the bigger systems and that will continue to satisfy our vision. How do we choose and assemble them? The guiding principle here, once again, is that we're not creating a static collection of objects but a dynamic, living landscape full of interactions between its inhabitants. What kinds of fruits go in the Garden of Eden? What species will attract the wildlife we want? Make detailed lists of species and structures. Later chapters and the appendix will offer many suggestions for this step.

These lists generate a lot of individual pieces. Next, and most important, is to see how the pieces of our design can be connected to create a living landscape.

Layout. Finally, at this step, we can begin determining what goes where. To do this, we need to think about how each piece of the design behaves and what its relationships are with the other pieces of the landscape and with us, the human inhabitants.

To learn about the behavior and relationships of a tree, for example, we can ask: What does this plant need to thrive? What harms it and thus should be kept away? What does it offer the other elements in the landscape? What can it take from them? What does it create? What does it destroy? Then we can search for other items in our visioning and planning lists that satisfy these needs or add new elements if they're needed. If plant A needs lots of nitrogen, find a nitrogen-producing species to install alongside it. Each clever linkage between design elements means one less job for the gardener, one less wheelbarrow load to schlep into or out of the garden. Each need not satisfied by another component of the design becomes work for the gardener; each product not used becomes pollution. The idea is to minimize both by designing wise connections.

Table 3-2 shows an example of this linking process, often called "needs and yields analysis," using a pear tree. I've listed the pear tree's products, activities (such as casting shade), its intrinsic qualities (height, color, and so forth), and its needs, including some that aren't obvious. Using this list, we can try to connect the pear tree to the other plants and structures in our design in a way that will provide or use as many items on the list as possible.

With enough time, we could make a list like this for each element in our design. Given the constraints of the real world, where we never have enough time, we could just make lists for significant and representative elements (such as important plant species; "hardscape" features, including greenhouses, paths, and fences; and other items such as ponds and hedgerows). For the items for which we don't make lists, we can just try to think about them from this "linking" viewpoint, seeing the pieces of the design as dynamic, interacting entities that connect to each other.

With our lists in hand, we can now link the products, needs, and activities to other potential elements of a design. The box on page 55 looks at a few items on the pear-tree list that might pose problems or might inspire creative uses.

Using this linking technique, people have contrived ingenious interconnections in their garden designs. In Colorado, Jerome Osentowski attached a chicken coop to his greenhouse. This setup uses the birds' body heat to warm the plants, the carbon dioxide from their breath to stimulate plant growth, and the manure for fertilizer. He also

Table 3-2. A Pear Tree's Connections	
Products and Activities:	**Needs:**
Leaves	Water
Wood	Nutrients
Seeds	Carbon dioxide
Oxygen	Oxygen
Water	Sunlight
Shade	Soil
Fruit	Pollen
Pollen	Pollinators
Bark	Protection from predators and disease
Sap	
Carbon dioxide	Pruning
Soil stabilization	
Dust collection	**Intrinsic Qualities:**
Soil loosening via roots	Color
Nutrient transport	Shape
Wildlife habitat	Size
Wind reduction	Soil requirements
Water purification	Climate requirements
Mulch and soil building	Flavor
Water transport	Scent

employs the birds' natural scratching behavior to weed and till garden beds. The chickens eat bugs, too.

A trick used by other gardeners is to dig a pond on the sunny side of a greenhouse or group of fruit trees, where the reflected light aids in ripening and

Some Pear Tree Connections

Products

- *Fruit*. We'll eat or preserve it all. If not, we should consider an animal to clean up fallen fruit or neighbors or a charity to take the surplus.
- *Pollen*. Our tree can pollinate other pears, or, combined with other pollen sources, provide food for bees. Do we want to raise honeybees?
- *Shade*. We can grow shade-tolerant plants beneath the pear or place the tree where the shade will be useful. Remember that it casts *seasonal* shade, so the tree could cool a building in summer but let needed light through in winter. We'll need to consider the final height of the tree (an intrinsic quality) when placing other sun-loving plants nearby.
- *Privacy*. When in leaf, the tree will screen an area.
- *Windbreak*. In leaf, and to a lesser extent when bare, the tree blocks wind.
- *Mulch and soil building*. Leaves and roots will help build and loosen soil,

but rotting leaves could cause fungal diseases (scab and the like) if there isn't healthy soil life to break them down quickly. If we want to rake the leaves, we should plan where to locate paths and the compost pile.

Needs

Now let's consider the tree's needs, which may be trickier to deal with than the products:

- *Water*. Is there adequate rainfall? Can we use water-conservation techniques, like mulches and dense plantings under the tree to shade and hold water in the soil? Can these plantings provide for other needs too, such as . . .
- *Nutrients*. Many plants pull nutrients from deep in the subsoil into their leaves, adding them to the topsoil at leaf-fall. We can under-plant the pear tree with some of these accumulator plants (described in Chapter 6 and the appendix). These plants can be mulched in place to build soil and offer

nutrients. Meanwhile, is there a nearby source of fertilizer that can suffice until the garden is producing its own?
- *Pollen*. Is the tree self-fertile, or does it require another variety for pollination? Do we want two fruit-bearing pear trees or an ornamental pear variety, or are there neighboring pears?
- *Pollinators*. Pollinator-attracting plants and beneficial-insect habitat should be near the pear tree. Can some of these plants also provide food, mulch, or plant nutrients?
- *Protection from predators and disease*. Do we need a deer fence? Can we use hedges or thorny plants to do this? How do we attract insects that will fight off pests?
- *Pruning*. Should we choose a dwarf tree so we won't need an orchard ladder for pruning and harvesting? Can we use the cuttings to make a woody compost pile (see the discussion of *Hugelkultur* in Chapter 4)? Or shall we just let the tree take on a natural shape?

heating. Clever connections abound; we just have to imagine and design them.

In summary, in needs-and-yields analysis, each plant, structure, or other element in a design ideally should have its needs provided by other design elements, and offer yields that nurture other elements. One benefit of needs-and-yields is that some inherent connections that use products or provide needs will be obvious, saving you the need to design them in. For example, knowing that your neighbor has a pear tree means you can probably plant only one yourself, since the nearby pear will in many cases pollinate yours. (And if your neighbor shares her fruit, you may not need to plant a pear tree at all. Social connections count too!) Once needs-and-yields analysis is done, the important linkages that are missing are the ones you must design for. If you have a pond but no water source, maybe you need to catch rainwater. The technique tells you where the holes are in your design.

Dreaming up these connections often involves a cascading thought process: We choose a design element that we want, see what it needs and can offer, then find a second element that meets some of those requirements (ideally, one that's already on one of the designer's lists), then see what connects to the second element, and so on. This process is intended to build a dense web of connections, but if done haphazardly it can create a tangled mass of confused feedback loops and dead ends.

Fortunately, permaculture offers another system to help organize the process of designing connections, one that breaks it down into small chunks that can be easily grasped and managed. It is called the zone-and-sector method. This method helps us decide where to place all the pieces of the garden so that they work with each other—and for us—most effectively (see Table 3-3).

The zone-and-sector method begins at the doorstep and extends from zone 0 to zone 5. Consider the house to be zone 0. The plants and other landscape elements that you use most often, or that require the most care, should go closest to the house. Perhaps you like fresh herbs in nearly every meal. Where should you plant your herbs? The cofounder of permaculture, Bill Mollison, offers some guidance. "When you get up in the morning and the dew is on the ground," he says, "put on your woolly bathrobe and your fuzzy slippers. Then walk outside to cut some chives and other herbs for your omelet. When you get back inside, if your slippers are wet, your herbs are too far away."

In this system, the herbs should be placed in what is called zone 1. Encompassing the area enclosed by a line about 20 to 40 feet from the house, zone 1 contains what is used most often. A typical zone 1 might hold intensively weeded and mulched salad and herb beds, a patio or tiny lawn, a shady arbor, a cherry tomato plant or two, a dwarf fruit tree, and the loveliest and most delicate plants. Any elements of the design that need continual observation, frequent visits, or rigorous techniques—such as an espaliered tree or a trellised wisteria—belong in zone 1.

This only makes sense. How often have you seen a weed-choked vegetable garden languishing fifty or a hundred feet from a house? It's not on the way to anywhere, and it's not under the kitchen window where sprouting weeds and past-due vegetables would alarm someone washing dishes. The little energetic hump created by the distance to the garden can be just enough to inspire neglect.

Zones are not neat concentric circles originating at the house. Their boundaries are permeable and bleed into one another. Zones are shaped and squeezed by topography, soil, available sunlight, access from the house, native vegetation, and the homeowner's needs.

Zones help us organize the elements and the energy flows of our property in the right relationships, allowing us to weave order according to how often we use or need to care for something.

Table 3-3. The Zone System: Functions and Contents						
	Functions	Structures	Crops	Garden Techniques	Water Sources	Animals
Zone 1: Most intensive use and care. Zone of self-reliance	Modify house microclimate, provide daily food and flowers, social space, plant propagation	Greenhouse, trellis, arbor, deck, patio, bird bath, storage, potting shed, workshop, worm bin	Salad greens, herbs, flowers, dwarf trees, low shrubs, lawn, trees for microclimate	Intensive weeding and mulching, dense stacking, square-foot and biointensive beds, espalier, propagation	Rain barrels, small ponds, graywater, household tap	Rabbits, guinea pigs, small poultry, worms
Zone 2: Semi-intensely cultivated. Domestic production zone	Home food production, some market crops, plant propagation, bird and insect habitat	Greenhouse, barns, tool shed, shop, wood storage	Staple and canning crops, multifunctional plants, small fruits and nuts, fire-retardant plants, natives	Weekly weeding and care, Spot mulch, cover crops, seasonal pruning	Well, pond, large tanks, greywater, irrigation, swales	Rabbits, fish, poultry
Zone 3: Low intensity, extensive methods. Farm zone	Cash crops, firewood and lumber, pasture	Feed storage, field shelters	Cash crops, large fruit and nut trees, animal forage, shelterbelts, seedlings for grafting, natives	Cover crops, coppicing, light pruning, moveable fences	Large ponds, swales, storage in soil	Goats, pigs, cows, horses, sheep, other large animals, free-range poultry
Zone 4: Minimal care. Forage zone	Hunting, gathering, grazing	Animal feeders	Firewood, timber, pasture plants, native plants	Pasturing and selective forestry	Ponds, swales, creeks	Grazing animals
Zone 5: Unmanaged. Wilderness zone	Inspiration, foraging, meditation	None	Native plants, mushrooms	Unmanaged, occasional wildcrafting	Lakes, creeks	Native animals

Zones are based on dynamic relationships. Rather than thinking in terms of static categories—flower, vegetable, tree—we think of how we interact with the parts of our design. Items used every day, whether salad greens, cut flowers, or a patio, go right outside the door. If we like cucumbers in our lunch, we plant accordingly. In this new order, a vining cucumber that was previously relegated to a far-off vegetable garden becomes a wonderful choice for the arbor over an attached deck, where harvest is simple. A scented rose could crouch under a frequently opened window, wafting its fragrance indoors.

Look what's happening here. The edges of the house are beginning to blur a bit. Where does the building end and the garden begin? Ordering our landscape by use and not by shape or size fuzzes some of the old categories. Those espaliered dwarf pears against the fence—is that the orchard, the hedge, or, after the wood posts rot, perhaps the fence itself?

Good design suggests that we tailor our zones to our own lives. The gourmand will want a mesclun bed and herbs by the door and baby carrots not much farther away. The "Come over to my place after work" type of person will give the patio and a cozy arbor pride of place.

Bring your garden close to home, particularly the plants you nibble every day. Vegetable gardens are ugly, you say? Then abandon straight-row garden-

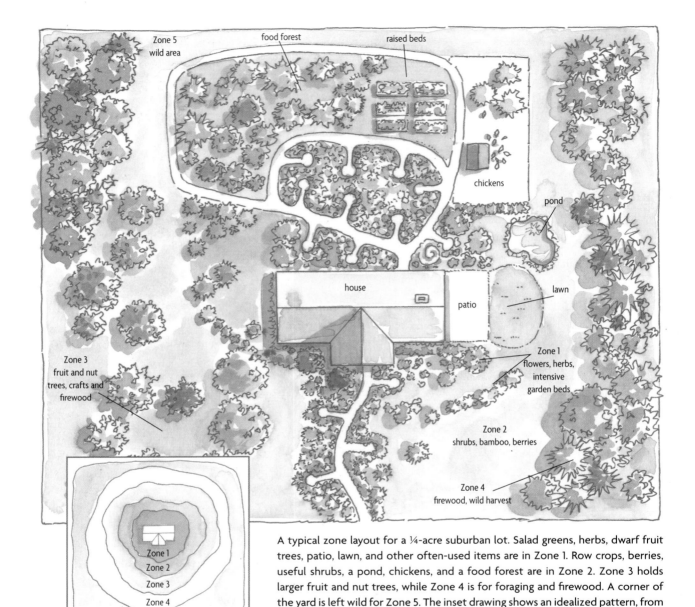

A typical zone layout for a ¼-acre suburban lot. Salad greens, herbs, dwarf fruit trees, patio, lawn, and other often-used items are in Zone 1. Row crops, berries, useful shrubs, a pond, chickens, and a food forest are in Zone 2. Zone 3 holds larger fruit and nut trees, while Zone 4 is for foraging and firewood. A corner of the yard is left wild for Zone 5. The inset drawing shows an idealized pattern, from most-often used to least, of concentric zones around a house.

ing. Curve the garden beds, follow the contours of your yard—or create some. Think of the yard as a multifunctional landscape that provides food, beauty, habitat for beneficial insects, even its own fertilizer. In zone 1, we can create attractive blends of perennials, annuals, salad herbs, shrubs, insect- and bird-attracting flowers, and nutrient-accumulating plants that build fertility.

I can attest to how well the zone method works. For years, our main garden in Oakland was 150 feet from the house, its location and eight-foot deer fence a legacy from the previous owner. With marauding deer making outside-the-fence gardening a constant source of disappointment, we placed whatever deer-proof plants we could find near the house. Two small flower beds lay at the edge of the lawn, each surrounded by "temporary" deer fencing that was looking very permanent. Maintaining these gardens became a constant battle, in part because each was surrounded on all sides by grass that was forever encroaching on the fertile, well-watered soil.

We refused to surround our home with a tall fence—the "concentration camp" aura of that arrangement was contrary to our hearts and to the openness of our landscape. But we also became less eager to visit the garden. So in the late afternoons, I would put on my boots, bid good-bye to Kiel as if I were headed to the office, and trudge out to the garden, incommunicado until my work was done. And it felt like work—the garden was where I sweated, weeded, pruned, and dug.

Finally we changed strategies and built an unobtrusive fence to enclose a semicircle around half the house. It's not eight feet tall; a determined deer could leap it, but we tried to offer them enough browse elsewhere to keep them busy. Inside the new fence, we sheet-mulched heavily and planted a dense blend of useful and ornamental plants.

What a difference it made! When we were chatting in the yard over a cup of coffee, it was nothing to stoop and yank a couple of tiny weeds. They never got much beyond tiny because we were there daily to spot them. Grass could no longer encroach from all sides. Sandwich greens came from a mesclun bed outside my study door, as did strawberries for breakfast, without a weary trudge. I distracted myself from writing—far too often—by watching bees and butterflies work the yarrow, salvia, and valerian out my window. It was nothing to toss on a handful of mulch to shield a patch of bare soil or squirt the hose on a drooping seedling. And best of all, we lived in this garden, instead of just working there. Having had it both ways, using zones is the only way I'll garden.

Beyond zone 1 is zone 2. This is home to fruit trees, terraced beds, large shrubs, berry bushes, ponds, and diversely planted hedges. It's also where the big production vegetable beds can go: potatoes, rows of canning tomatoes, trellises of pole beans. In one yard I've seen, zone 2 holds a well-interplanted mix of shrubs, less frequently picked perennial and annual vegetables, flowers, plus some orchard trees and a plastic greenhouse full of tomatoes. These are elements we don't visit every day, so management in zone 2 isn't quite so intensive: spot-mulching instead of deep continuous mulching, automatic or large-scale irrigation instead of loving visits to each plant with a watering can. In a small yard, zone 2 may begin only fifteen feet from the door and end near the neighbor's fence. On a larger property, this zone may extend fifty to one hundred feet from the house.

Small animals such as rabbits, bees, or chickens will find their best homesite at the zone 1/zone 2 boundary. Compost should molder out there, too. Ecological design is about placing the elements in the right relationship to each other, and careful thought can yield some time-saving placements. If the coop for a few urban chickens is on the way to a vegetable bed, you can toss kitchen scraps to the birds as you head out to weed and on the return trip give the weeds to the eager birds at the coop in exchange for eggs. Why make three trips?

Zone 3 contains large, rarely pruned orchard and nut trees, field crops such as grains, and commercial gardens. Some of the trees may yield firewood, wood products, or animal forage. I've seen one suburban zone 3 that holds walnuts, chestnuts, and bamboo—plants that need little attention and are harvested only once or twice a year.

Zone 4 usually applies to larger properties. It's home for grazing animals and firewood and timber trees. It is where we gather native foods, herbs, or woodcraft supplies. This is a semiwild, little-managed region, used for foraging.

Every property needs a zone 5. It's the wild land. Whether it's a corner of an urban lot dedicated to a wildlife thicket and a few rustling birch trees or a nature preserve on the back forty, it is where we are visitors, not managers. We design the other four zones, but we enter zone 5 to learn from it. There we observe, we play, we meditate, and we let the land be. Zone 5 is the instruction manual for the ecological garden and for keeping our lives in tune with nature.

Choosing the zone in which to place a design element depends on two things: the number of times we need to visit the plant, animal, or structure and the number of times it needs us to visit it. The overall strategy with garden zones is to begin at the doorstep, design and develop the places closest to the house first, and gradually work outward. That way, we can keep a continuous area under control that gets as much attention as it needs, rather than having a hodgepodge of scattered patches that are easy to forget.

Zones help us place the pieces of our design in a useful relationship with each other and with ourselves. They tell us how to work with what is on the site. But the design elements also need to be arranged in the right relationship with a second set of factors: forces coming from outside the site, such as wind, sun, and water. Again, permaculture gives us a handy tool for working with these forces by locating each one in its own specific sector. For example, the winds across a property usually come from a particular direction (the direction often depends on the time of year). Where I live in Oregon, rain-laden winter winds rage from the southwest. Thus the southwest is my winter wind sector. In summer, cool breezes waft down from Canada, so the summer wind sector is in the north. To use these observations, we move various elements of the design around with respect to the wind sector until they work best. For example, we could buffer the effects of the winter wind with windbreaks or buildings or harvest it with a wind generator. But we might welcome the summer breeze by letting it flow unobstructed toward the house. By locating and mapping out the various sectors, the pieces of a design can be placed in proper relationship to the energies entering the site and use them effectively.

Here are several other sectors:

Sun. The sun sector varies with the seasons. In North America, the summer sun rises far to the northeast and sets in the northwest, so the summer sun sector is very large. Drawn on a property map, it spans nearly 270 degrees. The winter sun sector is far smaller, since in winter the sun rises and sets in the southern sky (see below).

View. The unpleasant sight of a neighbor's dilapidated garage would fall in what we might call the "ugly view sector," a vista to be masked by a screen of plants or a structure. But a gorgeous prospect of the ocean would be preserved or emphasized.

Fire. My fire sector in Oakland pointed at me from the south. Not only did we live at the top of a dry, south-facing hill that fire could race up quickly, but my neighbors, with their power mowers, chain-saws, pyromaniac children, and other incendiary devices, lived to the south, too. Fire sectors should always be considered in a design, even in the city, and be left open, planted with fire-resistant species, or armed with sprinklers.

Wildlife. Every yard is penetrated by a wildlife sector, whether it brings marauding deer, a skulking raccoon, or a flock of cedar waxwings that flutter from a neighbor's cherry tree to yours. Wildlife can be deflected or welcomed by plantings and structures.

Other sectors include flooding and surface water; fog; pollution (noise, smells, power lines); foot traffic, such as groups of schoolchildren; and crime (a dark alley adjoining the yard).

The pieces of a design can interact with sectors in

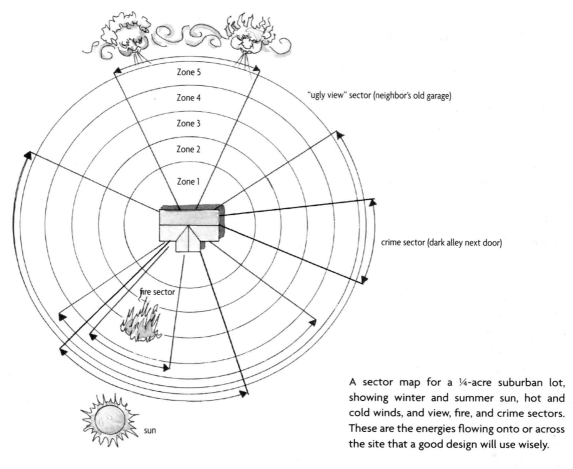

Zone 5
Zone 4
Zone 3
Zone 2
Zone 1

"ugly view" sector (neighbor's old garage)

crime sector (dark alley next door)

fire sector

sun

A sector map for a ¼-acre suburban lot, showing winter and summer sun, hot and cold winds, and view, fire, and crime sectors. These are the energies flowing onto or across the site that a good design will use wisely.

three ways. They can (1) block or screen the forces entering through the sector, as with a windbreak or shade tree; (2) channel or collect energy for use, as does a wind generator or greenhouse; or (3) open up the sector to use as much of the energy or view as possible by removing whatever blocks the sector, such as vegetation, fencing, or other deterrents. Sector energies such as sun and wind are free energy. Think of this energy as another nutrient source, like free fertilizer or water. Just placing a plant, building, path, or trellis here instead of there can nourish or otherwise improve it using the sector's energy. Just sitting there, that greenhouse, windbreak, or pond is working, benefiting the whole design while you sway in your hammock.

To sum up, zones organize the pieces of a design by how often they are used or need attention, and sectors help locate the pieces so they manage the forces that come from outside the site. Using zones and sectors together, we can make the best use of the connections within a design. If we're building a greenhouse, for example, we'd want it close enough to the house to visit regularly (in zone 1 or 2), near a faucet and tools, perhaps north of a pond to catch reflected light, in the sun sector, out of the winter wind sector to reduce chilling, probably away from the fire sector (though a metal and glass greenhouse with a sprinkler system might add to a firebreak), and maybe in the "ugly view sector" to screen that neighbor's nasty garage. Clever placements abound: A fragrant, evergreen oleander could go near a path in zone 1 or 2 to enchant passersby with its scent, in the sun sector, in the winter wind sector, and even in the fire sector since it has fire-retardant properties.

Once we know what plants and structures we want in our design, we can use the zone-and-sector method to organize them. Using a base map and sketching our ideas on overlays of tracing paper or clear plastic sheets, we can arrange the pieces of our design to connect sensibly with each other in their zones and sectors.

Sometimes when I'm stuck in the design process I use another technique, called random assembly, to break creative blocks. This consists of listing the design elements in a column:

> fruit tree
> hedgerow
> trellis
> greenhouse
> pond
> compost pile

I continue until all the major elements are listed. Then I make three copies of the list (cutting and pasting on a computer makes short work of this) and prepare a second columnar list containing connecting words. Here are all the connecting words that I could think of:

> around
> in
> facing
> between
> beside
> into
> before
> evolving into
> away from
> after
> and
> over

> hanging from
> attached to
> on
> crossing
> under
> instead of
> near
> dispersed throughout
> north (or south, east, west) of

Make two copies of this list, with the words in each list arranged in a single column. Then cut out all five columns (three lists of elements, two of connecting words) and lay them beside each other, alternating elements with connecting words. Then slide the lists around and read horizontally to see if a useful or inspirational placement results:

> vine *over* greenhouse *above* pond
> compost pile *near* toolshed *behind*
> hedgerow

This strategy gets us thinking in terms of connections among the design elements. Sometimes, of course, the placements are complete nonsense:

> pond *hanging from* chickens *between* sauna

But often a combination occurs that will jog creativity, pushing us to think in new directions. Sometimes by contemplating even a ridiculous combination, thinking about what would happen if it actually existed, we can arrive at new solutions for design problems. This system helps suspend our judgmental selves and frees us to innovate.

To sum up these methods: Needs-and-yields analysis arranges design elements in the right relationship to each other. Using zones also does this, but zones really help place elements in their best relation to the human users. Sector analysis locates the design's pieces to best use or block energies coming from off the site. And random assembly helps bust through creative blocks and hands us combinations and connections we probably would never have thought of.

Development

In the previous steps, we determined what systems and elements will be in the design and approximately where they will go. Now it's time to polish these rough ideas, working with the locations arrived at by the methods in the last section. Sketch in the various planting beds, trees, walls and fences, patios and decks, and other design elements. At first, don't go into any detail, just draw rough circles and outlines of the major components, showing their relative placement (this is often called a *bubble diagram*). Refine the connections among the components. Then sketch access routes (paths or roads) to the elements that need them. Try to minimize the number of paths. This may mean rearranging the components—trying to preserve their relationships—until the paths are most effective and occupy minimal space. This step is a bit tricky, but attention here will pay off in the long run in saved labor and a more harmonious layout. It's useful to refer back to the ideas in the "vision" step to keep the big picture in mind. Always reevaluate with respect to the observations and goals from earlier steps.

Once the layout has been refined on rough sketches, people with the skills or time may want to make more formal drawings and plans. Whether the documentation is of professional quality or not is up to the designer/gardener. Often just simple sketches will do, as long as they include distances, scale, and enough other details to implement the design. Detailed documentation of the design is very important. Don't expect to rely on memory. It's frustrating to be about to install an expensive plant and not remember where it was supposed to go. Without maps and notes, that's exactly what will happen.

This is a good time to work on color schemes and other aesthetic points. Though the design process described here gives priority to ecological considerations, once the plants, structures, and other design elements are placed in the right relationships, we can select plant varieties whose foliage and colors go well together. Any good library will offer plenty of gardening books that cover design aesthetics. A few of my favorite authors in this category are Gertrude Jekyll, Penelope Hobhouse, Rosemary Verey, Ken Druse, and John Brookes.

Now it's time to schedule the installation. What needs to be done first? A combination of factors interacts to shape this decision. These include:

- *Personal.* Is our most urgent desire food production, a patio, shade, a flower garden, or some other consideration? How much time do we have for doing the work ourselves?
- *Environmental.* Does the land most need soil building, erosion control, habitat, or something else?
- *Technical.* Will the design require earthmoving, concrete or stone work, or other hardscaping? These often must be done first to avoid disturbing the rest of the design and to reduce the expense and potential for damage done by multiple bulldozer visits. Trees and shrubs should also be planted early in the work, conforming to the old adage, "The best time to plant a tree was ten years ago."
- *Seasonal.* What can be done during the season appropriate to the work? Earth moving in the wet season will ruin soil structure; planting in summer heat may bake the transplants.
- *Financial.* Is enough money available for the whole design? If not, what aspects make sense to phase in first?

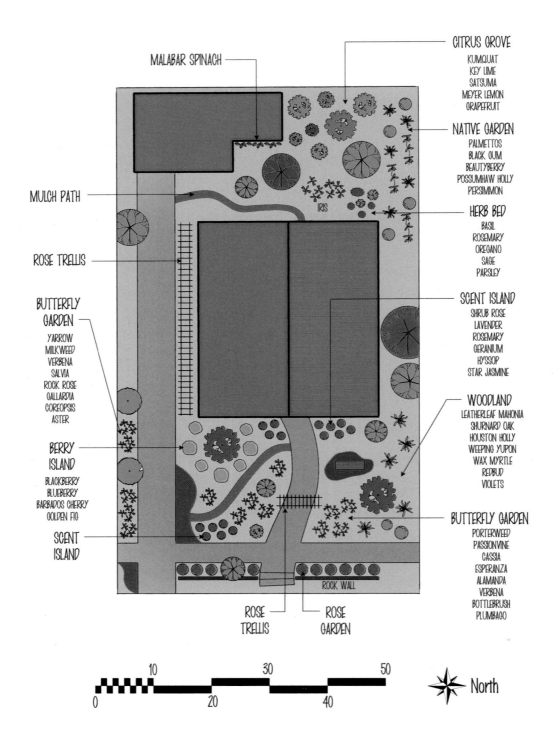

MALABAR SPINACH

CITRUS GROVE
KUMQUAT
KEY LIME
SATSUMA
MEYER LEMON
GRAPEFRUIT

NATIVE GARDEN
PALMETTOS
BLACK GUM
BEAUTYBERRY
POSSUMHAW HOLLY
PERSIMMON

MULCH PATH

IRIS

HERB BED
BASIL
ROSEMARY
OREGANO
SAGE
PARSLEY

ROSE TRELLIS

SCENT ISLAND
SHRUB ROSE
LAVENDER
ROSEMARY
GERANIUM
HYSSOP
STAR JASMINE

BUTTERFLY GARDEN
YARROW
MILKWEED
VERBENA
SALVIA
ROCK ROSE
GALLARDIA
COREOPSIS
ASTER

WOODLAND
LEATHERLEAF MAHONIA
SHURNARD OAK
HOUSTON HOLLY
WEEPING YUPON
WAX MYRTLE
REDBUD
VIOLETS

BERRY ISLAND
BLACKBERRY
BLUEBERRY
BARBADOS CHERRY
GOLDEN FIG

BUTTERFLY GARDEN
PORTERWEED
PASSIONVINE
CASSIA
ESPERANZA
ALAMANDA
VERBENA
BOTTLEBRUSH
PLUMBAGO

SCENT ISLAND

ROCK WALL

ROSE TRELLIS

ROSE GARDEN

10   30   50
0   20   40

North

A plan for an inner-city Houston lot by Kevin Topek of Permaculture Design, LLC. The aim of this design was to quiet the neighborhood association's claim that too many flowering plants were visible from the street, while preserving the biodiversity, habitat, and beauty provided by those plants. REDRAWN BY KRISTA LIPE.

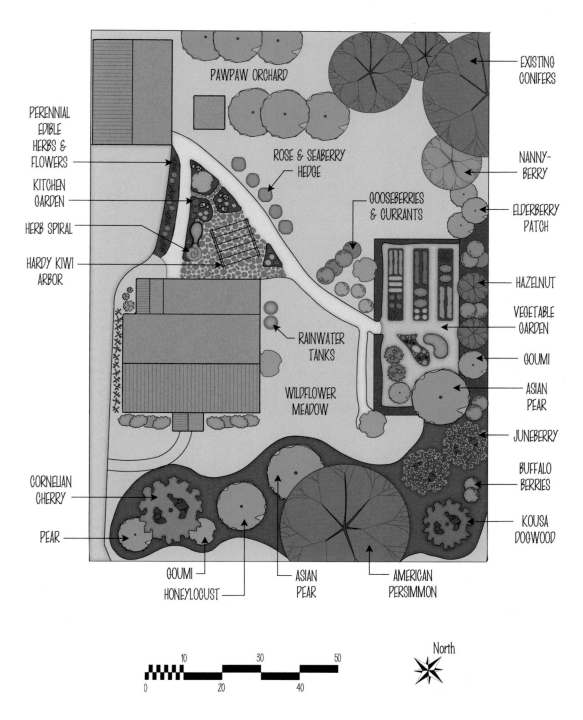

PAWPAW ORCHARD

EXISTING CONIFERS

PERENNIAL EDIBLE HERBS & FLOWERS

ROSE & SEABERRY HEDGE

NANNY-BERRY

KITCHEN GARDEN

GOOSEBERRIES & CURRANTS

ELDERBERRY PATCH

HERB SPIRAL

HARDY KIWI ARBOR

HAZELNUT

VEGETABLE GARDEN

RAINWATER TANKS

GOUMI

ASIAN PEAR

WILDFLOWER MEADOW

JUNEBERRY

CORNELIAN CHERRY

BUFFALO BERRIES

PEAR

KOUSA DOGWOOD

GOUMI

HONEYLOCUST

ASIAN PEAR

AMERICAN PERSIMMON

10 30 50
0   20 40

North

A food forest, designed by Ethan Roland of AppleSeed Permaculture, envelops this western Massachusetts home. Social spaces, salad gardens, and annual vegetables fill zones 1 and 2, while larger forest-garden shrubs and trees occupy the yard's outer zones. REDRAWN BY KRISTA LIPE.

A Summary: Designing the Ecological Garden

To provide an "at a glance" guide to the design process, I'll sum up the steps once again, this time from the new viewpoints of ecological design and permaculture offered in this chapter.

1. **OBSERVATION** Walk the site and make maps. Note what is there and how it interacts with its surroundings. Just observe, don't analyze. Make lists. Follow up with research into what was observed, the habits of species, soil types, and the like.
2. **VISIONING** Keep ecological guidelines in mind. What can the place offer us? What does the site need from us? What are our limitations and resources? What should the design do? What is most important for us and for the site?
3. **PLANNING**
   a. **Conceptual Design**. Design from patterns to details. What

is the organizing idea and goal of the design? What systems, strategies, and functions do we need to achieve the goals? Consider personal, aesthetic, environmental/ecological, and other issues, as well as trouble spots and defects to correct.
   b. **Schematic Design**. List the design elements that will satisfy the vision (plants, structures, functions, and the like). For each element (or for as many as is practical), list its products, activities, needs, and intrinsic qualities. Connect as many items as possible so that the needs of one design element are met by other elements and so that it meets the needs of other elements. Use zones to organize the pieces of a design by how often they are used or need attention and

sectors to locate the pieces so they manage wind, sun, and other forces that come from outside the site. The zone-and-sector method optimizes the connections between the design elements. Use the random-assembly method for brainstorming and to break creative blocks.
4. **DEVELOPMENT** Sketch the locations of the design elements. Research species and varieties. Optimize paths and relationships in the design. Work with color and form. Then make working drawings and enough documentation to implement the design. Determine the steps of implementation.
5. **IMPLEMENTATION** Install the design and be flexible enough to deal with the surprises that appear when a paper design meets the real world.

Remember also to apply the wisdom of zones, even to the implementation phase: Whenever possible, begin the installation at your doorstep and work outward.

Implementation

This phase of ecological landscape design is similar to installing any new landscape. Details can be found in any good home-landscaping book, such as Rita Buchanan's *Taylor's Master Guide to Landscaping* or Roger Holmes's *Home Landscaping* series. Follow this order of implementation:

- First, do any major earthmoving. Grade the site to a rough contour, if needed. Dig any swales, ponds, and drainage ditches. Install utility lines and underground irrigation pipes and wires. Then backfill the trenches.
- Add any broadscale soil amendments and compost. Mulching and shaping of intensive zone 1 beds can wait until later.
- Complete any *hardscaping*, the term designers use for wood, stone, concrete,

and other constructed elements: walls, sheds, paths, fences, and the like.

- Make any final adjustments to the grade contours with rake and shovel.
- Lay down sheet mulches (see Chapter 4 for instructions).
- Install large plants, such as trees and major shrubs.
- Plant ground covers, nonwoody plants, lawn, and cover crops.
- Adjust mulches and fine-tune the irrigation system, if any.
- Keep plants watered and help them get established by observing and caring for those that need a little extra attention.

In Chapter 12, the section "Where to Begin" covers some aspects of implementation in detail. But remember that the people, plants, animals, and landscape involved are constantly changing and full of surprises. The design and its implementation may take unexpected turns when the shovel actually strikes the soil. Don't be too rigid and be ready to revisit the early steps of the process to rework some aspects of the design so they will fit changing circumstances.

For people who want to dive far more deeply into the process of ecological landscape design, Chapters 3 and 4 in Volume 2 of Jacke and Toensmeier's *Edible Forest Gardens* is superb. Dave and Eric spend over 150 pages covering every aspect the design process for creating a food- and habitat-producing home landscape, covering much of the same ground as I have here but in vastly more detail.

In the garden, we're working with live beings, not just shapes and colors. These creatures grow, set seed, and multiply, and in time they die. Plants, insects, birds, and all the rest connect in a tight weave and enter each others' lives, creating and sharing among them food, shade, pollen, seeds, humus, perches, burrows, nests—a host of varied and valuable gifts. With a gentle, careful gaze we can peer into this wonderfully interlaced world and tease out some of the connections, transferring them to our own landscapes. Nature carries the instruction book for a sustainable world—it is up to us to read it and to preserve it.

In this chapter, I've tried to give an ecological view of garden design. Entire books—whole shelves of them—have been written about design, so a single chapter can only scratch the surface of this broad subject (though the rest of this book digs a little deeper). Design allows us to blend what we observe with what we desire. It is the way our dreams take form, sculpted by the limits of our skills, budgets, and materials. Ecological design offers a way to harmonize people with the living landscape, a harmony that is often absent from many of the places we dwell. By connecting our gardens to the rest of nature, we can bring great beauty and abundance to ourselves, share this richness with other species, and regenerate the wholeness and diversity of life that is on the verge of being lost.

Now that we have an overview of garden ecology and ecological design, it's time to look at the individual parts of the garden.

PART TWO

The Pieces of
the Ecological Garden

CHAPTER FOUR

Bringing the Soil to Life

A Latin American farmer once told my friend Ianto Evans, "Of course you have terrible soil problems in your country. What do you expect when you call it dirt?" In our culture, soil gets little respect. Most of the words for this fundamental substance are derogatory. When we want to know the worst about someone, we say, "Give me the dirt on this guy." Dirty movies. Earthy language. We hold at arm's length anything soiled, dirty, or muddy.

Yet soil is miraculous. It is where the dead are brought back to life. Here, in the thin earthy boundary between inanimate rock and the planet's green carpet, lifeless minerals are weathered from stones or decomposed from organic debris. Plants and microscopic animals eat these dead particles and recast them as living matter. In soil, matter crosses and recrosses the boundary between living and dead; and, as we have seen, boundaries—edges—are where the most interesting and important events occur.

Most discussions about soil focus on what soil is: what it's made of, where it comes from, what its physical qualities are. Of course it's important to know these things if we want to understand soil, but the physics and chemistry of soil are only part of the story. We also need to know what soil does. For years, scientists viewed soil mainly as an inert sandlike substance for holding plant roots, into which we poured fertilizer. But soil is alive. One key to having a garden that's bursting with healthy plants, well-balanced insects, and thriving wildlife is to stuff the soil with as much life as possible.

Think of soil life as the base of a pyramid. Stacked upon this base are plants, then insects, and finally animals, each dependent on the creatures below it. The greater the number and diversity of soil organisms—that is, the broader the pyramid's base—the larger and more diverse will be the flows of nutrients among them as they release the fertility stored in the soil. Bigger nutrient flows mean that more plants, both in numbers and varieties, can thrive on that abundant fertility. In turn, an extensive array of plants will attract a copious assortment of insects, and those plants and insects will provide food and shelter for a more diverse collection of birds and other animals at the top of the pyramid. Diversity builds diversity. The goal of this chapter is to give gardeners the knowledge and techniques for maximizing biodiversity in garden soil—for broadening the base of that pyramid on which the rest of the ecological garden is built.

How much life is in the soil? At least as much as above ground. When we look at a landscape, the plants and animals on the surface are obvious, but it's not easy to visualize how much life lies underground. With a few numbers, we can begin to glimpse the abundance. A teaspoon of good pasture soil may contain a billion bacteria, a million fungi, and ten thousand amoebae. It's hard to believe that

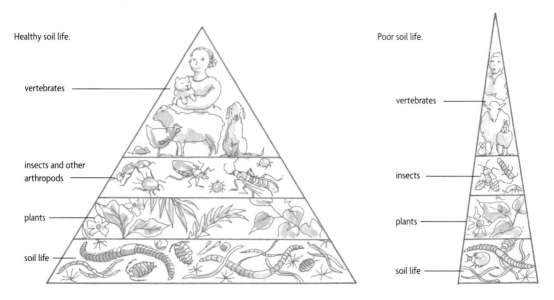

Healthy and diverse soil life supports a wide array of plants, insects, and vertebrates. Poor soil life can't support the same diversity or numbers.

anything else can fit into that teaspoon, but soil critters are small. There is still plenty of room for the clay, silt, sand, water, air, humus, and assorted small molecules that make up the rest of soil.

Above ground, an acre of good pasture may support a horse or two, say about a half-ton of animals. But living in the soil of that acre may be two tons of worms and another two tons of bacteria, fungi, and soil animals such as millipedes and mites. That one-horse-per-acre soil may contain eight or ten horses' worth of animals below ground. Vegetarians may be appalled, but much of gardening actually involves raising animals: the tiny ones under Earth's surface. Elaine Ingham, cofounder of Soil Foodweb Incorporated, a firm specializing in analyzing soil life, calls these swarms of subsurface livestock "microherds," to emphasize that we need to be wise stewards of this helpful multitude.

What are all those soil organisms doing, and how does that relate to gardening? Like most living creatures—except for a nearly hairless two-legged variety that spends much of its time thinking about things—soil organisms pass the hours searching for

food, eating, and excreting. In all of these activities, they are shuttling nutrients around: food for themselves, food for other soil life (their wastes and their bodies, living or dead), and, most relevant to gardeners, food for plants. From a plant's perspective, the main role of soil organisms is to break down matter that plants can't digest themselves and transform it into nutrients that they can readily absorb. And soil is rich in these nutrients. In all but the most abused or leached-out soils, the earth contains plenty of material for soil life to turn into plant food: rock particles and living and dead organic matter.

The soil organisms in a properly tended garden will furnish almost all the fertilizer that plants need. As the life in the soil eats, excretes, reproduces, and dies, it works an almost alchemical change on organic matter and minerals in the ground. Through soil organisms, nutrients are broken down, consumed, transformed, rebuilt into body parts and energy-containing molecules, and broken down once more. And during these many-vectored flows of matter, a small surplus of nutrients constantly trickles to the

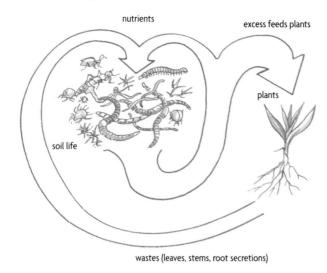

nutrients

excess feeds plants

plants

soil life

wastes (leaves, stems, root secretions)

Soil life recycles organic matter, generating plenty of excess that becomes food for plants. The more soil life, the greater the flow of excess nutrients to plants.

plants. Just as bankers and merger specialists make their fortunes by skimming money from the colossal flows of commerce, so too do plants derive their sustenance by absorbing the surplus nutrients that whirl out of soil organisms' life cycles. Fertility comes from flow. A more vigorous soil life heaves more nutrients into the flux for plants to divert, releasing a surplus of fertility during the cycle from raw material to living body to waste and back again. Here, as in so much of the ecological garden, the process, the activity, the relationship, is paramount. Healthy soil and plants are created not by the simple presence of nutrients and soil life, but by the briskness and depth of their flows and interconnections. Savvy gardeners know this and will do all they can to feed the life of the soil.

Soil Life: The First Recyclers

In nature, most fertility comes originally from the rocks. Rocks contain potassium, calcium, phosphorus, and most of the other elements that plants need

to build tissue and fuel their metabolic machinery. To convert rocks into food, plant roots and soil organisms secrete mild acids and enzymes that etch atoms of nutrients loose from rock particles. In a sense, plants and soil microbes are miners, sluicing down rocks with caustic substances that carve away precious life-supporting ores. If we create healthy soil in our gardens, the rampant soil life will coax enough minerals from the rocks for most of our plants' needs.

Once these nutrients have been chiseled out of the stone, in a natural ecosystem they are husbanded with great care. Life is the great recycler, scrupulous in not letting go of any useful substance. An example from a typical northern forest illustrates this. Researchers found that the plants and soil of 1 hectare (2.5 acres) of forest contained about 365 kilograms of calcium. Of this, only about 8 kilograms (2 percent) was lost each year in runoff. Most of the forest's calcium—98 percent—was being recycled over and over, raining down in falling leaves or dying plants, then being decomposed and held by soil life and transferred back to plant roots for another round. The washed-away 8 kilograms of calcium could easily be acquired by the forest each year: More than half that much splashed down as dissolved calcium in rainfall. The remainder of the lost calcium could be weathered from the rocks by roots and soil life. This 98 percent efficiency is a good bit better than the 30 percent or so that our cities strive for in recycling programs. And, by way of contrast, on heavily fertilized agricultural land calcium losses range from 25 percent to 60 percent annually. To have a truly sustainable society, we will need to recycle as well as nature does.

How does life do such an incredible job of recycling, and how can we duplicate this economy in our gardens? To work toward an answer, let's look at the fate of a falling leaf as it composts into nutrients and is readied for a return to life.

It's early autumn, and the oak tree in an untended corner of your neighbor's yard is shedding its leaves. One dry leaf flutters down between tall blades of unmown grass and settles on a patch of bare soil. At first, not much happens, because the leaf is too dry to be appetizing to any of the soil's many denizens (we'll assume your neighbor doesn't spray pesticides or herbicides on this corner of her yard, as these chemicals greatly diminish soil life). Also, this leaf, like most, contains nasty-tasting compounds to protect it from munching insects. The next morning, though, dew has wetted the leaf, and the protective chemicals have begun to leach out. A light drizzle accelerates the washing process. The leaf droops moistly against the soil. When the leaf is rinsed free of polyphenols and the other bitter-tasting compounds and tenderized by moisture, the feast begins. Among the first at the table are bacteria that have lain dormant on the leaf surface. They revel in the moisture and begin to bloom, secreting enzymes that tear apart the long chains of sugar molecules composing the leaf cell walls. In just hours, the leaf is speckled with the dark blotches of bacterial colonies. Wind-borne spores of fungi land and burst into life, and soon the white threads of fungal cells, called *hyphae*, knit a lacework across the leaf. Fungi possess a broad spectrum of enzymes able to digest lignin (the tough molecules that make wood so strong) and other hard-to-eat components of plants. This gives them a critical niche in the web of decomposers; without them, Earth might be neck-deep in fallen, undecomposable tree trunks.

Moistened by rain and softened by microbial feeding, the leaf quickly succumbs to attack by larger creatures. Millipedes, pill bugs (isopods), fly larvae, springtails, oribatid mites, enchytraeid worms, and earthworms begin to feed on the tasty tissue, shredding the leaf into small scraps. All of these invertebrates, together with bacteria, algae, fungi, and threadlike fungal relatives called actinomycetes, are the first to dine on rotting organic matter. They are called the primary decomposers. Earthworms are the most visible and among the most important primary decomposers, so let's watch one as it feeds on our leaf.

The earthworm grabs a leaf chunk and slithers into its burrow. With its rasping mouthparts, the worm pulverizes the leaf fragment, sucking in soil at the same time. The mixture churns its way to the worm's gizzard, where surging muscles grind the leaf and soil mixture into a fine paste. The paste moves deeper into the earthworm's gut. Here bacteria help with digestion, much as our own gut flora helps us process otherwise unavailable nutrients from our food. When the worm has wrung all the nutrients from the paste, it excretes what remains of the leaf and soil, along with gut bacteria caught in the paste. These worm castings coat the burrow with fertile, organically enriched earth. Before long, hungry bacteria, fungi, and microscopic soil animals will find this cache of organic matter and flourish in walls of the burrow, adding their own excretions and dead bodies to the supply.

Fueled by the leaf's nutrients, the worm tunnels deeper into the ground, loosening, aerating, and fertilizing the soil. Rain will trickle down the burrow, threading moisture deeper into the earth than previously. The soil will stay damp a little longer between rains. In spring, a growing root from the oak tree will find this burrow, and, coaxed by the easy passage and the tunnel's lining of organic food, will extend deep enough to tap that stored moisture. The worm, with its fertile castings and a burrow that lets air, water, and roots penetrate the earth, will have aided the oak tree and much of the other life in the soil. Worms are among the most beneficial of soil animals: They turn over as much as twenty-five tons of soil per acre per year, or the equivalent of one inch of topsoil over Earth's land surface every ten years.

Meanwhile, on the surface, the feasting invertebrates continue to shred the leaf into tiny bits—or *comminute* it, in soil-specialist parlance. Comminution exposes more leaf surface—tender inner edges at that—to attack by bacteria and fungi, further hastening decomposition. Also, the small army of mites, larvae, and other invertebrates feeding on the leaf deposit a fair load of droppings, or *frass*, which also becomes food for other decomposers (a microscope reveals that many decomposing leaves are thickly covered with frass, which adds up to an enormous amount of fertile manure). Any leaf bits that aren't fully digested on their first passage through a decomposer's gut are eaten again and again by one tiny being after another until the organic matter is mashed into microscopic particles. Soil invertebrates such as worms and mites don't really alter the chemical composition of the leaf—their job is principally to pulverize litter. Their scurrying and tunneling also mixes the leaf particles with soil, where the fragments stay moist and palatable for others. In some cases, the animals' gut microbes can break down tenacious large molecules such as chitin, keratin, and cellulose into their simpler sugarlike components. The real alchemy—the chemical transformation of the leaf into humus and plant food—is done by microorganisms.

As the soil animals reduce the leaf to droppings and microscopic particles, a second wave of

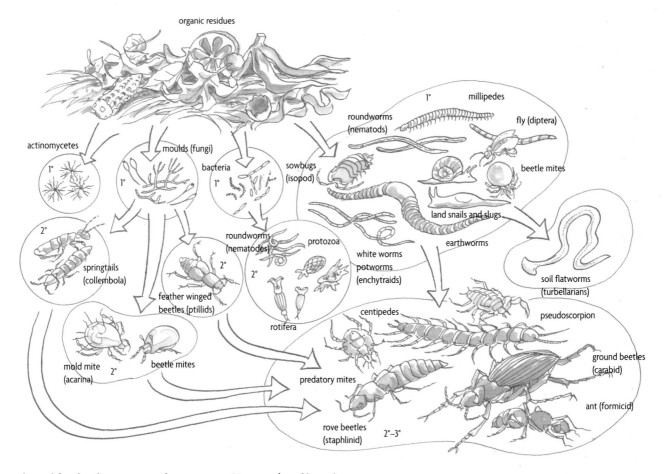

The soil food web. 1°=primary decomposers; 2°=secondary; 3°=tertiary.

bacteria, fungi, and other microbes descends on the remains. Using enzymes and the rest of their metabolic chemistry sets, these microbes snap large molecules into small, edible fragments. Cellulose and lignin, the tough components of plant cell walls, are cleaved into tasty sugars and aromatic carbon rings. Other microbes hack long chains of leaf protein into short amino acid pieces. Some of these microbes are highly specialized, able to break down only a few types of molecules, but soil diversity is immense—a teaspoon of soil may hold 5,000 species of bacteria, each with a different set of chemical tools. Thus, working together, this veritable orchestra of thousands of species of bacteria, fungi, algae, and others fully decompose not only our sample leaf but almost anything else it encounters.

Besides breaking down organic matter, these microbes also build up soil structure. As they feed, certain soil bacteria secrete gums, waxes, and gels that hold tiny particles of earth together. Dividing fungal cells lengthen into long fingers of hyphae that surround crumbs of soil and bind them to each other. These miniclumps give microbially rich soil its good "tilth": the loose, crumbly structure that gardeners and farmers strive for. Also, these gooey microbial by-products protect soil from drying and allow it to hold huge volumes of water. Without soil life, earth just dries up and blows away or clumps together after a rain and forms clay-bound, root-thwarting clods.

Microbes don't live long—just hours or days. As they die, larger microbes and soil animals consume their bodies. Also, predators abound in the soil ecosystem. Voracious amoebae lurk in films of soil moisture, ready to engulf a hapless bacterium. Mold mites, springtails, certain beetles, and a host of others feed on the primary decomposers and are called, in turn, secondary decomposers. Larger predators feed on the secondary (and some primary) decomposers that have come to our leaf: These are centipedes, ground beetles, pseudoscorpions, predatory mites, ants, and spiders, also known as the tertiary decomposers.

Although this order—primary, secondary, and tertiary decomposers—seems to suggest a linear hierarchy, the boundaries are not hard-and-fast. The frass and dead body of even the largest spider become food for bacteria and other primary decomposers, so it's hard to say who's on top. Soil ecology is a set of nested cycles, and a detailed drawing of it would be laced with arrows, almost blackened with the interconnections that tie the life and death of each species to many of the others.

How Humus Is Made

Now our leaf is almost fully decomposed. How, then, does it become plant food—how does it return to life and reconnect to plants and to our garden? The leaf's contents (those that don't forever recycle in life or dissipate as gases) end up as one of two substances, humus or minerals. Both are critical to healthy plants. We'll look at humus first.

As our leaf is shredded, chewed, and chemically dissolved by soil organisms, some parts of the leaf decompose more quickly than others. The first tissues to go are those made of sugars and starches, which soil life quickly converts into energy, carbon dioxide, or more organisms. A little harder to digest are celluloses and some types of proteins, which are chains and sheets of tightly linked small molecules. Not all soil organisms have the special enzymes needed to break the crisscrossed bonds that hold these polymers together, so these compounds decompose more slowly. Even tougher to break down are polymers known as *lignins*, which give wood its strength; *chitins*, which make up the armored coats of insects; and certain types of waxes. Only specialized soil organisms, particularly fungi, can break down these tenacious molecules. Organisms that can't crack these hardy compounds nevertheless give it their best shot. Microbes work them over, nibbling and modifying the portions they can digest. In a process that is still poorly understood, microbes and other forces of decomposition convert lignins and the other hard-core leaf compounds into *humus*, a fairly stable, complex collection of many substances that only slowly undergoes further decomposition. Humus is made up mostly of carbon, oxygen, nitrogen, and hydrogen, bonded together in ways that make it difficult for soil organisms to break them down into the constituent elements.

In a sense, humus is the end of the road for organic matter: By the time our leaf's remains have reached the humus stage, decomposition has slowed to a snail's pace. Since organisms can't easily break down humus, it accumulates in the soil. It will eventually decompose, but in healthy soil, freshly composting debris arrives at least as fast as the old humus is broken down, resulting in a slow turnover and constant buildup of humus.

When pushed, soil organisms can decompose humus, but only grudgingly and usually if there is nothing else to eat. If humus levels are dropping, it's a sign that the soil is in very bad shape. It means that all of the easily digestable organic matter is gone, and the inhabitants are, in effect, burning down the house to keep warm. Humus is critical to soil health; thus, wise gardeners keep their soil rich in humus. For now we'll see why; later we'll learn how.

Of all the ingredients of soil, humus is by far the best at holding moisture and will absorb four to six times its weight in water. Have you ever tried to pick up a wet bale of peat moss? It's monstrously heavy, and it will take months to dry out. Peat moss isn't exactly humus—it's organic matter that's been arrested on its way to becoming humus because peat bogs lack the oxygen for decomposers to finish the job—but hoisting a wet bale of peat moss gives some idea of how well humus holds moisture.

Humus also swells when it's wet, so humus-rich soil will gently heave upward after a rain. As this soil dries, the humus shrinks, leaving air spaces between soil crumbs. This expanding and shrinking process lightens the soil, acting a little like tilling but with far less disruption and damage to the soil life. In humusy, fluffed-up earth, roots and soil organisms can easily tunnel in search of nutrients, and these travelers further aerate the soil. Water penetrates the loosened soil more deeply and is stored longer by the humus. Here is another life-enhancing positive feedback loop: Humus allows moisture and soil organisms to move deeper into the soil, where they create more humus, allowing yet deeper penetration, building humus again, and so on.

Where humus really excels is in holding nutrients. The humus molecule illustrated below shows that, from an atom's-eye viewpoint, the face that humus presents to the world is a bristling array of oxygen atoms. Oxygen has a strong negative charge, and in chemistry, as in much of life, opposites attract. Thus, humus's many negative oxygen atoms serve as "bait" for luring lots of positively charged elements. These include some of the most important nutrients for both plants and soil animals: potassium, calcium, magnesium,

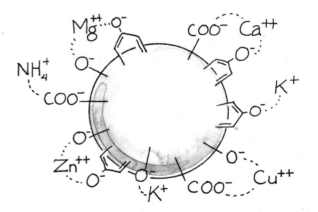

A chemical view of humus, studded with negatively charged oxygen atoms. Positively charged nutrients such as ammonium, potassium, copper, magnesium, calcium, and zinc are adsorbed to the humus. These nutrients can be pulled off the humus and used by plants and microbes.

ammonium (a nitrogen compound), copper, zinc, manganese, and many others. Under the right conditions (in soil with a pH near 7, that is, neither too acid nor too alkaline), humus can pick up and store enormous quantities of positively charged nutrients.

How do these nutrients move from the humus to plants? Plant roots, as noted, secrete very mild acids which break the bonds that hold the nutrients onto the humus. The nutrients from humus are washed into the soil moisture, creating a rich soup. Bathed in this nutritious broth, the plants can absorb as much calcium, ammonium, or other nutrient as they need. There's evidence to suggest that when plants have supped long enough, they stop the flow of acid to avoid depleting the humus.

That's the direct method plants use to pull nutrients from humus. Just as common in healthy soil is an indirect route, in which microbes are the middlemen. This type of plant feeding involves an exchange. Roots secrete sugars and vitamins that are ideal food for beneficial bacteria and fungi. These microbes thrive in huge numbers close to roots and even attach to them, lapping up the plant-made food and bathing in the film of moisture that surrounds the roots. In return, the microbes produce acids and enzymes that release the humus-bound nutrients and share this food with the plants.

Microbes also excrete food for plants in their waste. One more big plus for plants is that many of the fungi and other microbes secrete antibiotics that protect the plants from disease. All of these mutual exchanges create a truly symbiotic relationship. Many plants have become dependent on particular species of microbial partners and grow poorly without them. Even when the plant–microbe partnership isn't this specific, plants often grow much faster when microbes are present than they do in a sterile or microbe-depleted environment.

The Soil's Mineral Wealth

Having covered humus, let's look at the parts of our leaf that meet a mineral fate. Like most living things, leaves are made primarily of carbon-containing compounds: sugars, proteins, starches, and many other organic molecules. When soil creatures eat these compounds, some of the carbon becomes part of the consumer, as cell membrane, wing case, eyeball, or the like. And some of the carbon is released as a gas: carbon dioxide, or CO_2 (our breath contains carbon dioxide for the same reason). Soil organisms consume the other elements that make up the leaf, too, such as nitrogen, calcium, phosphorus, and all the rest, but most of those are reincorporated into solid matter—organism or bug manure—and remain earthbound. A substantial portion of the carbon, however, puffs into the atmosphere as carbon dioxide. This means that, in decomposing matter, the ratio of carbon to the other elements is decreasing; carbon drifts into the air, but most nitrogen, for example, stays behind. The carbon-to-nitrogen ratio decreases. (Compost enthusiasts will recognize this C:N ratio as a critical element of a good compost pile.) In decomposition, carbon levels drop quickly, while the amounts of the other elements in our decomposing leaf stay roughly the same.

By the time the final rank of soil organisms, the microbes, is finished swarming over the leaf and digesting it, most of the consumable carbon—that which is not tied up as humus—is gone. Little remains but inorganic (non–carbon-containing) compounds, such as phosphate, nitrate, sulfate, and other chemicals that most gardeners will recognize from the printing on bags of fertilizer. That's right: Microbes make plant fertilizer right in the soil. This process of stripping the inorganic plant food from organic, carbon-containing compounds and returning it to the soil is called *mineralization*. Minerals—the nitrates and phosphates and others—are tiny, usually highly mobile molecules that dissolve easily in water. This means that, once the minerals in organic debris are released or fertilizer is poured onto the soil, these mineral nutrients don't hang around long but are easily leached out of soil by rain.

Conventional wisdom has it that plant roots are the main imbibers of soil minerals and that plants can only absorb these minerals (fertilizers) if they are in a water-soluble form, but neither premise is true. Roots occupy only a tiny fraction of the soil, so most soil minerals—and most chemical fertilizers—never make direct contact with roots. Unless these isolated, lonely minerals are snapped up by humus or soil organisms, they leach away. It's the humus and the life in the soil that keep the earth fertile by holding on to nutrients that would otherwise wash out of the soil into streams, lakes, and eventually the ocean.

Agricultural chemists have missed the boat with their soluble fertilizers; they're doing things the hard way by using an engineering approach rather than an ecological one. Yes, plants are quite capable of absorbing the water-soluble minerals in chemical fertilizer. But plants often use only 10 percent of the fertilizer that's applied and rarely more than 50 percent. The rest washes into the groundwater, which is why so many wells in our farmlands are polluted with toxic levels of nitrates.

Applying fertilizer the way nature does—tied to organic matter—uses far less fertilizer and also saves the energy consumed in producing, shipping, and applying it. It also supports a broad assortment of soil life, which widens the base of our living pyramid and enhances rather than reduces biodiversity. In addition, plants get a balanced diet instead of being force-fed and are healthier. It's well documented that plants grown on soil rich in organic matter are more disease- and insect-resistant than plants in carbon-poor soil.

In short, a properly tuned ecological garden rarely needs soluble fertilizers because plants and soil animals can knock nutrients loose from humus and organic debris (or clay, another nutrient storage source) using secretions of mild acid and enzymes. Most of the nutrients in healthy soil are "insoluble yet available," in the words of soil scientist William Albrecht. These nutrients, bound to organic matter or cycling among fast-living microbes, won't wash out of the soil yet can be gently coaxed loose— or traded for sugar secretions—by roots. And the plants take up only what they need. This turns out to be very little, since plants are 85 percent water, and much of the rest is carbon from the air. A fat half-pound tomato, for example, only draws about 50 milligrams of phosphorus and 500 milligrams of potassium from the soil. That's easy to replace in a humus-rich garden that uses mulches, composts, and nutrient-accumulating plants.

A Question of Balance

Sometimes gardening books single out soil organisms as bad guys—they supposedly "lock up" nutrients, making them unavailable for plants. In an imbalanced soil, this is true. Soil life is much more mobile than plants and has a speedier metabolism. When hungry, microbes can grab nutrients faster than roots. As William Albrecht says, "Microbes dine at the first table." If the soil life is starved by poor soil, microbes certainly won't pass on any food to plants.

For example, a common soil problem is too little nitrogen. Nitrogen is used in proteins and cell membranes, and plants lacking this nutrient are pale and anemic. Gardeners are often admonished not to use wood shavings or straw as a soil amendment because they lead to nitrogen deficiency. This is because shavings and straw, though good sources of carbon, are very low in nitrogen (see Table 4-1). These nitrogen-poor amendments are fine for use as mulch, on top of the soil, but when they are mixed into the soil with a spade or tiller, decomposer organisms, which need a balanced diet

Table 4-1. Carbon to Nitrogen (C:N) Ratios in Common Mulch and Compost Materials	
Apple pomace	21/1
Bone meal	3.5/1
Clover, flowering phase	23/1
Clover, vegetative phase	16/1
Compost, finished	16/1
Corn stover	60/1
Cottonseed meal	5/1
Fish scraps	4/1
Grain hulls and chaff	80/1
Grass clippings, dry	19/1
Grass clippings, fresh	15/1
Hay, legume/grass mix	25/1
Hay, mature alfalfa	25/1
Hay, young alfalfa	13/1
Leaves, dry	50/1
Leaves, fresh	30/1
Manure, chicken	7/1
Manure, cow	18/1
Manure, horse	25/1
Manure, human	8:1
Manure, rotted	20/1
Newspaper	800/1
Ryegrass, flowering phase	37/1
Ryegrass, vegetative phase	26/1
Sawdust, hardwood	400/1
Sawdust, rotted	200:1
Sawdust, softwood	600/1
Seaweed	19/1
Straw, oat	74/1
Straw, wheat	80/1
Urine, human	0.8:1
Vegetable wastes	12/1
Vetch, fresh hairy	11/1

Data taken from *Designing and Maintaining Your Edible Landscape—Naturally,* by Robert Kourik (Metamorphic, 1986); *The Integral Urban House* by the Farallones Institute (Sierra Club, 1979); and *The Nature and Properties of Soils* by Nyle C. Brady (Prentice Hall, 1996).

of about twenty to thirty parts carbon for each part nitrogen, go on a carbon-fueled rampage. It's analogous to the whopping metabolic rush that a big dose of sugar can give you: a great short-term blast, but one that depletes other nutrients and leaves you drained.

To balance this straw-powered carbon feast, soil life grabs every bit of available nitrogen, eating, breeding, and growing as fast as the low levels of this nutrient will allow. The ample but imbalanced food triggers a population explosion among the microbes. Soon the secondary and tertiary decomposers (beetles, spiders, ants), spurred by a surge in their prey, are also breeding like fury. Whenever any valuable nitrogen is released in the form of dead bodies or waste, some tiny, hungry critter instantly consumes it before plants can. The plant roots lose out because the microbes dine at the first table. This madly racing but lopsided feeding frenzy won't diminish until the overabundant carbon is either consumed or balanced by imports of nitrogen—from the air via bacteria that pull nitrogen from the air, from animal manure, or from an observant gardener with a bag of blood meal.

The same lockups occur when other nutrients are lacking in the soil. Until the soil life is properly fed, the plants can't eat. Conventional farming gets around this problem by flooding the soil with inorganic fertilizer, ten times what the plants can consume. But this, the engineer's approach rather than the biologist's, creates water pollution and problem-prone plants. The soil life, and the soil itself, suffers from the imbalance.

Here's what happens to soil life after overzealous application of chemical fertilizer. Mixing inorganic fertilizer with soil creates a surplus of mineral nutrients (an excess is always needed, since so much washes away). Now the food in short supply is carbon. Once again, the soil life roars into a feeding frenzy, spurred by the more-than-ample nitrogen, phosphorus, and potassium in typical NPK fertilizers. Since organisms need about twenty parts carbon for every one of nitrogen, it isn't long before any available carbon is pulled from the soil's organic matter to match all that nitrogen and tied up in living bodies. These organisms exhale carbon dioxide, so a proportion of carbon is lost with each generation. First the easily digestible organic matter is eaten, then, more slowly, the humus. Eventually nearly all the soil's carbon is gone (chemically fed soils are notoriously poor in organic matter), and the soil life, starved of this essential food, begins to die. Species of soil organisms that can't survive the shortages go extinct locally. Some of these creatures may play critical roles, perhaps secreting antibiotics to protect plants, or transferring an essential nutrient, or breaking down an otherwise inedible compound. With important links missing, the soil life falls far out of balance. Natural predators begin to die off, so some of their prey organisms, no longer kept in check in this torn food web, surge in numbers and become pests.

Sadly, many of the creatures that remain after this mineral overdose are those that have learned to survive on the one remaining source of carbon: your plants. Burning carbon out of the soil with chemical fertilizers can actually select for disease organisms. All manner of chomping, sucking, mildewing, blackening, spotting horrors descend on the vegetation. With the natural controls gone and disease ravishing every green thing, humans must step in with sprays. But the now-destructive organisms have what they need to thrive—the food and shelter of garden plants—and they will breed whenever the now-essential human intervention diminishes. The gardener is locked on a chemical treadmill. It's a losing battle, reflected in the fact that we use twenty times the pesticides we did fifty years ago, yet crop losses to insects and disease have doubled, according to USDA statistics.

The other harm done by injudicious use of chemical fertilizers is to the soil itself. As organic matter is burned up by wildly feeding soil life, the soil loses its ability to hold water and air. Its tilth is destroyed. The desperate soil life feeds on the humus itself, the food of last resort. With humus and all other organic matter gone, the soil loses its fluffy, friable structure and collapses. Clayey soil compacts to concrete; silty soil desiccates to dust and blows away.

In contrast, ample soil life boosts both the soil structure and the health of your plants. When the soil food web is chock-full of diversity, diseases are held in check. If a bacterial blight begins to bloom, a balanced supply of predators grazes this food surplus back into line. When a fungal disease threatens, microbial and insect denizens are there to capitalize on this new supply of their favorite food. Living soil is the foundation of a healthy garden.

To Till or Not to Till

We've seen that organic matter keeps soil light and fluffy and easy for roots to penetrate. What then about the mechanical methods used for breaking up soil?

The invention of the plow ranks as one of the great steps forward for humanity. Farmers know that plowing releases locked-up soil fertility. Plowing also keeps down weeds and thoroughly mingles surface litter with the soil. We do all this, too, when we drag our power-tiller out of the garage and push the snorting beast through the garden beds in a cloud of blue smoke.

What's really happening during tilling? By churning the soil, we're flushing it with fresh air. All that oxygen invigorates the soil life, which zooms into action, breaking down organic matter and plucking minerals from humus and rock particles. Tilling also breaks up the soil, greatly increasing its surface area by creating many small clumps out of big ones. Soil microbes then colonize these fresh surfaces, extracting more nutrients and exploding in population.

This is great for the first season. The blast of nutrients fuels stunning plant growth, and the harvest is bountiful. But the life in tilled soil releases far more nutrients than the plants can use. Unused fertility leaches away in rains. The next year's tilling burns up more organic matter, again releasing a surfeit of fertility that is washed away. After a few seasons, the soil is depleted. The humus is gone, the mineral ores are played out, and the artificially stimulated soil life is impoverished. Now the gardener must renew the soil with bales of organic matter, fertilizer, and plenty of work.

Thus, tilling releases far more nutrients than plants can use. Also, the constant mechanical battering destroys the soil structure, especially when perpetrated on too-wet soil (and we're all impatient to get those seeds in, so this happens often). Frequent tilling smashes loamy soil crumbs to powder and compacts clayey clods into hardpan. And one tilling session consumes far more calories of energy than are in a year's worth of garden-grown food. That's not a sustainable arrangement.

Better to let humus fluff your soil naturally and to use mulches to smother weeds and renew nutrients. Instead of unleashing fertility at a breakneck, mechanical pace, we can allow plant roots to do the job. Questing roots will split nuggets of earth in their own time, opening the soil to microbial colonization, loosening nutrients at just the right rate. Once again, nature makes a better partner than a slave.

Building Soil Life

OK, enough theory: Let's get our hands dirty. What are some techniques for creating the kind of soil that gardeners dream of? To answer, I could end this chapter now with three little words: Add organic matter.

But I won't stop there. Techniques abound for building soil organic matter, and different situations call for different methods. The techniques break down into three broad categories: composts, mulches, and cover crops.

Compost: The Quick and Dirty Method of Building Soil

Most gardeners know the value of compost, and many excellent books and articles have been written about this "black gold," so I won't spend too much time recapitulating what's already out there. In brief, compost, the rich, humus-y end product of decomposition, is made by piling surplus organic matter into a mound or bin and letting it rot.

All homeowners generate excess organic matter: kitchen scraps, grass clippings, leaf piles, and debris from pruning and cleaning up a yardful of plants. Most of this can be recycled right on site and turned into a valuable source of soil life and nutrients for your plants. If you're not fussy, simply piling this stuff in a corner in your yard and waiting a few months is enough to generate compost. But the job can be done much more efficiently. The critical elements of a good compost pile are the right ratio of carbon to nitrogen, optimum moisture and air, and proper size.

Let's take size first. Chomping, multiplying microbes give off heat, which accelerates their growth and thus the breakdown of the pile's contents. But, just as important, a hot compost pile will sterilize the seeds in yard waste. Piles smaller than about three feet on a side won't insulate the burgeoning microbe population enough to raise the temperature to the critical 130 to 150 degrees Fahrenheit necessary to kill seeds. Spreading cold-processed compost on the garden imports a host of weeds and other unwanted plants. I've seen tomato seedlings pop up by the hundreds in a flower bed after the addition of poorly prepared compost. Thus, composters should save up their materials until they have enough for a three-foot heap.

What to put in the pile? Different ingredients contain varying ratios of carbon to nitrogen, and although eventually almost anything organic will decompose, an overall C:N ratio of 30:1 is ideal. Table 4-1 gives the C:N ratios of many compostable materials. If you are the meticulous type, you can calculate a proper balance of high-carbon and high-nitrogen ingredients to yield 30:1. But for the less assiduous, here's a good rule of thumb: Green materials, such as grass clippings and fresh plant trimmings (and we'll also include kitchen waste here), are high in nitrogen. Brown items, such as dried leaves, hay, straw, and wood shavings, are high in carbon. The exception here is manure, which, although brown, is high in nitrogen—consider it green. Mixing roughly half green with half brown approximates the ideal 30:1 C:N ratio. If high-nitrogen materials are scarce, sprinkle in some cottonseed, fish, or blood meal for balance.

When building the pile, add the materials in layers no more than six inches thick. For a small pile, just jumble everything together by turning. Some gardeners suggest adding soil to the pile, which I sometimes do if the soil isn't sticky clay. I also add handfuls of finished compost as I build the heap, which inoculates the pile with soil life and gives it a boost. When I'm feeling especially fanatical, I do two things. One is to inoculate the new pile with compost from another young pile if I have one, figuring that the species of soil organisms I'm transferring will be suited to the fresh pile's undigested debris. I'll also trek into the woods, into a field, to a pond margin—a variety of ecosystems—where I'll grab a quart or two of soil from each and add the blend. That way I'm maximizing the biodiversity of my soil life, importing helpful predators and decomposers.

The life of the compost heap needs water to survive. A good compost pile should be about as moist as a wrung-out sponge. If the ingredients are dry when the pile is assembled, it can take an astonishing amount of water to achieve the right moisture level. When I'm building a pile in August, I usually have a hose spraying on the pile the entire time I'm forking the dry debris in place (this is an excellent use for graywater, whose nutrient load gives the soil life an extra boost, and it assuages my guilt about using so much water). I usually cover the finished pile with a tarp or permanent lid to retain moisture on sunny days and keep rain from leaching out the hard-won nutrients.

One age-old compost question is, To turn or not to turn? Turning a pile supplies oxygen and speeds up decomposition. If you're in a hurry for compost, turn the pile as soon as the pile's initial blast of internal heat—which begins within days of a pile's creation—begins to subside. This will restoke the metabolic fires of the pile's occupants with oxygen, and the compost will quickly heat up again. Each time the pile cools, turn it again. A properly made pile can be reduced to black gold in three weeks by well-timed turning.

However, I suggest that you plan ahead so that you'll have an ample supply of compost when you need it without turning a pile more than once or twice. That's enough to incorporate and rot down the outer layers of the pile.

Here's why. A less-turned pile won't rot down as quickly as a more ambitiously forked one, but each turning amps up microbial metabolism enormously. This drives the pile's contents further down the two-forked road of fully digested humus and totally mineralized nutrients. Mineralized nutrients can leach out of soil very quickly. Completely processed humus, while great for soil texture and drought resistance, won't feed as much soil life as less-digested organic matter. A slowly rotted compost, from my experience, still gets hot enough during that first heating-up to kill weed seeds, but it seems to supply my plants with nutrients longer than the product of rapid turnings. My rule is: Turn for texture—when you need to quickly build

Woody Ways to Build Soil

Most of the techniques offered in this chapter involve the decomposition of readily broken-down organic matter such as grass and kitchen scraps. But most of us generate woody debris, too: tree prunings, logs, even rotten firewood or lumber scraps. Wood is decomposed mainly by fungi, which we welcome into the ecological garden for their superb ability to keep soil moist, break down otherwise stubborn substances, and produce disease-fighting compounds. We can't add much wood waste to a compost pile, but rather than burn or landfill surplus wood, we can use it to build soil, too. Here's how.

Hugelkultur

In the carefully tended forests of central Europe, no scrap of wood is ever wasted. Branches and brushy prunings are used in a gardening technique called by its German name *Hugelkultur* (pronounced *HOO-gul cool-Toor*), or mound culture. To create a hugelkultur, pile up branches or brush a foot or two deep in a mound four to eight feet around. Stomp on the pile to compact it a bit. Then toss compostable materials—grass clippings, sod, straw—into the pile. Moisten the pile to that wrung-out sponge stage. Sprinkle some compost on the mound and top with an inch or so of soil. Then plant the hugelkultur with seeds or starts. Potatoes really love hugelkultur—I can start potatoes in these mounds a month earlier than in garden beds. Squashes, melons, and other vines do well here, too.

The decomposing organic matter in hugelkultur beds raises the temperature just enough to boost plant growth. Another advantage: As the woody brush rots, it releases nutrients slowly, while it holds quite a bit of water. You don't need to fertilize or irrigate hugelkultur very often.

soil structure—but rest the pile for long-term nutrition.

The best role for compost, as I see it, is to give a quick fertility boost to a limited area of soil—no more than a few hundred square feet. If you've just moved to a new garden and want productivity quickly, then compost will get soil fertility on the upswing rapidly. An inch or two of compost lightly spaded into poor soil, or, if you've got enough, several inches in depleted or compacted earth, will support very dense plantings. With plant production jump-started this way, a gardener can begin more long-term soil building.

I'm going to venture once more into the heretical here: Composting isn't my favorite way to build soil, and I try to do as little of it as possible. For one thing, it's a lot of work. All that sequestering of supplies, layering, watering, turning, and then carting the whole damn pile, load by load, onto the garden bed, shoveling it out, spading it in, and, finally, raking the bed smooth. That's a bunch of materials handling, something that every efficient designer seeks to minimize.

But I also believe compost piles aren't the optimal way to raise your microherds or use their gifts. Whenever I turn or move my compost pile, I know I'm murdering billions of these wonderful helpers: smashing their homes, bludgeoning them and their children with my spading fork, desiccating all those who end up on the outer layer of the pile. I'm willing to break eggs to make an omelet but only if I can't think of another way. I'd like my gardening to be a gentle art.

And, morality aside, each disruption of the pile is a setback to the soil life. They're going through a complex ecological succession, a sweep through time from simple sugar-digesting species to protein munchers to highly specialized lignin- and chitin-eating fungi. Each stab of my fork disrupts this process. By the time I wheel my compost to the

The Dead Wood Swale

Perhaps you've observed that rotting wood can hold a large amount of moisture. Late in a rainless Northwest summer, I've plunged my arm up to the elbow into a rotten log and brought out a fistful of damp pulp. By acting like sponges, downed logs may serve as critical moisture reservoirs for water-dependent species such as fungi and soil animals. Some naturalists theorize that roots and fungal mycelia may siphon water from these woody moisture caches to plants and fungi many feet away.

Rotting wood's talent for holding water is another of nature's tricks that can be applied in the garden. We can invert the hugelkultur idea and bury wood beneath our plants. Permaculturist Tom Ward digs trenches about eighteen inches deep, tosses in woody trunks or rotten firewood, and then backfills the trenches with soil. On top of this, he plants blueberries. Tom told me, "I'm imitating how, in ponds and bogs, blueberries often root on floating logs. In my garden, all that wood is like a huge sponge sunk into the ground." Roots infiltrate this font of wetness and drink from it during drought.

Nearly any plant—not just blueberries—will grow well on a buried wood swale. Some people worry that the wood will lock up nitrogen, and thus they toss a nitrogen source into the swale (green compost materials or slow-release organic fertilizer), but I suspect that the wood decomposes so slowly that very little nitrogen is bound up by the microbes gnawing at the logs.

garden and shovel it on, does the product still retain the maximum, optimum biodiversity? I don't think so.

Also, composting can waste nutrients. A hot pile wafts volatile nitrogen into the air, now lost to the garden. And complex, life-giving metabolic liquors are dribbling out of the pile and being wasted. I know this because each time I dig up my compost heap, underneath I find a beautiful, foot-thick layer of black soil that's been transformed out of nasty clay during the pile's dance from death to life. The drip of nutritious by-products into the soil beneath triggers a growth spurt in the life there. These newly thriving creatures then chomp nutrients off clay particles, and their multiplying bodies and wastes build organic matter, turning red clay into fertile loam. I usually trundle this rich earth to the garden, too, since I am loathe to see my microherds' labors wasted. I see all those worms thriving under my compost pile, all the mites and millipedes, and

I want them in my garden, shuttling nutrients to plants, not churning uselessly a foot below a plantless pile. A technique that can harvest this otherwise lost bounty and reap countless other benefits is sheet mulching.

The Power of Sheet Mulch

Though my conversion took a number of years, I've been completely sold on composting in place, commonly known as *sheet composting* or *sheet mulching*. Sheet mulching is one of the basics in the ecological gardener's tool kit. It's a method of eradicating weeds and building soil that needs no herbicides or tilling, both of which rupture soil ecology. Sheet mulching is a variation on nature's way of building soil by accumulating and breaking down organic debris from the top down.

In its simplest form, sheet mulching is a two-step process: First, apply a layer of weed-suppressing newspaper or cardboard (or even an old discarded cloth or wool carpet) and top it with about a foot of organic mulch. Many gardeners do this in fall, so that the mulch rots to become humus-y earth over the winter. Also, the weed-stopping layer breaks down enough to allow spring-planted seeds and transplants to thrust their roots deep into the earth. But sheet mulching can be done in any season. For a more detailed description of sheet mulching, see the sidebar on pages 88–89.

Gathering the materials for sheet mulch is the most laborious and time-consuming part of the job; the rest is pretty painless. It's remarkable how much material it takes to really do it right. Fortunately, most of these items are free and easily available with a little research. If you choose materials appropriate to your bioregion, they will be easy to find. Timber country offers ample bark and sawdust, the coasts yield seaweed and salt hay, and the midcontinent and agricultural valleys always have a surfeit of straw, grain hulls, and other food-industry by-products. In big cities, canneries, food processors, and produce distribution warehouses often generate plenty of organic waste. Utility companies or landscapers will often deliver chipped tree trimmings, and almost every neighborhood offers leaves in the fall. Put the word out that you're looking for organic matter, and someone else's disposal problem will become your windfall.

Most gardeners know the benefits of mulch. A sprinkling of an inch or two of straw or shavings around plants helps conserve water, keeps soil cool on scorching summer days, suppresses weeds, and, mission accomplished, agreeably rots down into rich compost over the winter. Some gardeners have taken this idea and run with it, as in *The Ruth Stout No-Work Garden Book*. In this classic, Ruth describes how eight inches of spoiled hay applied to her garden beds built phenomenal, weed-free soil. I can vouch for the benefits.

At first I was a timid mulcher. Even after reading Stout's book, I didn't have the courage to whole-

heartedly follow her instructions. Call it fear of mulching, but I would merely sprinkle down a stingy inch or two of straw to keep the soil moist when summer warmed up. I was afraid, I think, of somehow choking out the plants, or attracting slugs, or maybe growing some malignant fungus in the straw.

These drawbacks never materialized, and eventually I noticed the real benefits of mulching, beyond water retention: fewer weeds and bigger plants.

One observation mystified me for a time. Within a day or two of laying down mulch, I would find it strewn into the garden paths as if by some evil randomizing force. I would meticulously stuff it back in place, but soon, even with no evident wind, the mulch would be back in the paths. Then I saw the culprits: Robins and towhees, hunting for worms that now were migrating into the straw since the soil was moist right up to the surface. It was observing this new interaction and understanding its implications that eliminated my mulching timidity. The mulch was clearly building a large worm population that in turn was boosting soil fertility. And the birds were helping too, pooping nitrates and phosphates into the straw.

Thus emboldened, I mulched half the garden under a foot of stable bedding, spoiled alfalfa hay, and straw. Years before, I learned the hard way not to use fresh hay for top-mulching. A light mulch of fresh hay, laden with seeds, imported throngs of weeds and grasses that took years to get under control. Straw, if harvested with a well-tuned combine, contains no seed; it's just the stems of grain plants. Hay is the whole stalk, seed-head and all.

One fall I was extending our garden into a struggling lawn. I decided to employ sheet mulch for the new beds. By spring, my lifeless red clay soil had darkened to chocolate brown, was seething with worms, and had begun to fluff to a marvelous crumbly tilth. I was sold. I still keep a compost

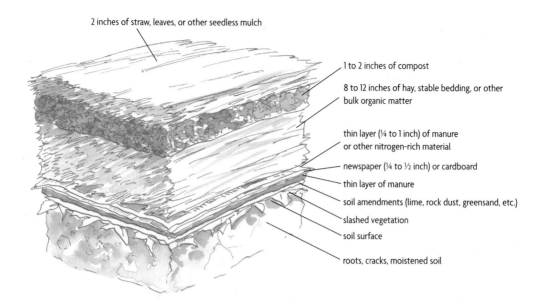

2 inches of straw, leaves, or other seedless mulch

1 to 2 inches of compost

8 to 12 inches of hay, stable bedding, or other bulk organic matter

thin layer (¼ to 1 inch) of manure or other nitrogen-rich material

newspaper (¼ to ½ inch) or cardboard

thin layer of manure

soil amendments (lime, rock dust, greensand, etc.)

slashed vegetation

soil surface

roots, cracks, moistened soil

The ultimate sheet mulch. Sheet mulch can be as simple as cardboard topped with a foot of straw, or it can be a more elaborate stack of soil-building layers, as shown here.

pile for seedling trays, a small intensive bed of greens, and soil emergencies, but sheet mulch and composting-in-place are my staple soil-building tools. Sometimes, instead of emptying the kitchen compost bucket in the compost pile, when Kiel isn't looking I tuck its contents under some mulch, where it rots very quickly.

By composting in place, the soil organisms, so essential for ferrying nutrients to plant roots, aren't disturbed. An intact subterranean ecology develops, woven by silken fibers of mycelium, riddled with the channels of traveling microfauna, bound into perfect tilth by the gummy exudates and carbon-rich liquors of metabolism. Oxygen-gulping microbes colonize the upper layers of soil, and the shy anaerobes work their complex alchemy further below. Exploding populations of wriggling worms loosen the earth deep down, churning their nutrient-rich castings into the mulch. A thousand-specied hive of interlinked subterranean activity erects its many pathways of decomposition and resurrection as sowbugs, worms, mites, amoebae, and fungi swarm in fertility-building concert. Plants tap into this seething stew and thrive. And all this is cocreated by simply piling on a fat mattress of mulch.

Sometimes I'm less than meticulous in my sheet mulching, spreading a layer of newspapers, moistening them, and then simply dumping a foot of used stable bedding on them. Here I'm thinking long-term. I know that the wood shavings in the bedding will take a couple of years to break down, so plant growth won't be maximal until then. I'll use this technique in the more distant zones 2 or 3, perhaps in circles around trees that I want to underplant or for garden beds I won't rely on heavily for a while. For heavy food production or near-the-house insectary and ornamental plant beds, I strive more precisely to achieve the proper C:N ratio in the mulch. But sheet mulch is forgiving. As long as you put down a weed barrier of paper or cardboard and top it with a foot of moist, decomposable organic matter, you'll have great soil in short order. And it can be done anywhere: I've seen sheet mulch on pavement and on rooftops.

The Ultimate, Bombproof Sheet Mulch

Sheet mulch can be as simple as a layer of newspapers topped by eight to twelve inches of nearly any mulch material. But if you want to build the perfect sheet mulch, here's how.

If this is your first sheet mulch, start small. Sheet mulch gobbles up a tremendous amount of organic matter—the roughly two cubic yards held by a full-sized pickup truck will cover about fifty square feet. But don't scrimp. It's much better to blanket a small area thoroughly than to spread the mulch too thin to smother weeds or feed the soil properly. Choose a site that's not more than 200 square feet, in the proper location for the intended plants, and preferably near the house. Remember your zones: Deeply mulched beds will soon be covered with a riot of plant life, and you want these awesomely productive areas right outside your door, to easily tend or to admire the many avian and insect visitors.

Here's a materials list for the perfect sheet mulch:

1. A two- to three-foot stack of newspaper, minus any glossy sections, whose inks may contain metal pigments (the black and colored inks on standard newsprint are soy-based and nontoxic), or about 300 square feet of corrugated box cardboard without staples or plastic tape. You can also use cloth, old clothing, or wool carpet, provided they contain no synthetic fabric, but these take far longer to decay than paper.

2. Soil amendments, depending on your soil's needs: lime, rock phosphate, bonemeal, rock dust, kelp meal, blood meal, and so on.

3. Bulk organic matter: straw, spoiled hay, yard waste, leaves, seaweed, finely ground bark, stable sweepings, wood shavings, or any mixture of these, ideally resulting in an overall C:N ratio between 100:1 and 30:1. Grass clippings are also good, but only when mixed with other "brown" mulches—otherwise their high nitrogen content causes anaerobic—and hence smelly, slimy—decomposition. You will need about four to eight cubic yards of loosely piled mulch for 100 to 200 square feet, or six to ten two-string bales of hay or straw.

4. Compost, about a quarter to half a cubic yard (six to twelve cubic feet).

5. Manure: a quarter to one cubic yard, depending on the concentration and amount of bedding mixed in. About six cubic feet of composted steer manure or other bagged product will be plenty.

6. A top layer of seed-free material, such as straw, leaves, wood shavings, bark, sawdust, pine needles, grain hulls, nut husks, or seagrass. You will need roughly one cubic yard or two to four two-string bales.

If you can't find every item, don't worry. Sheet mulching is very forgiving. As long as you have enough newspaper or cardboard, plus organic matter of almost any kind,

you'll end up with great soil. Store your supplies near the chosen site so you won't have to move them too far on sheet-mulch day. Keep them dry, too.

The day before you mulch, water the site well unless the ground is already moist from rain. The organisms that will be turning your mulch into rich earth can't work without water, and, once the mulch is in place, it takes a lot of water to moisten the bottom layers. Conversely, it takes a long time for the layers to dry out—you've got lots of water storage.

After the water has soaked in overnight, slash down any vegetation. Don't pull up weeds—leave all the native organic matter right there, including the roots. Just clip, mow, scythe, or weed-whack everything down in place. It's great worm food, and the nitrogen-rich greens and roots will be a tasty starter for the decomposers. Remove any stumps or big woody pieces.

Next, add any soil amendments. If your soil is acid, sprinkle on some lime. For alkaline soil, a little gypsum or sulfur will help. A dusting of rock phosphate or bonemeal will supply phosphorus. Greensand, kelp meal, or rock dust will add trace minerals. Use a soil test or your own understanding of your soil's fertility to guide the type and quantity of soil amendments.

If your native earth is clayey or compacted, now is a good time to open it up a bit. Just push a spading fork into the ground, rock it a little, and pull it out. Do this across the entire mulch site. Don't turn the earth, just poke some holes into it and crack it open to allow better moisture and root penetration and soil-critter movement.

Then add a thin layer of high-nitrogen material. This can be manure, blood or cottonseed meal, fresh grass clippings or other lush greens, or cast-off produce from restaurants or markets. For concentrated matter such as rabbit manure or blood meal, sprinkle down enough material to just cover the soil. Grass clippings or bedding-rich manure should go down about an inch thick. While this layer isn't essential, it attracts worms and burrowing beetles, which will aerate and loosen the soil.

Now the fun begins: putting the sheet in sheet mulch. Lay down newspapers and/or cardboard to create a continuous light-blocking layer that will smother existing plants. Cardboard is very satisfying to use since those big sheets, especially boxes from appliances and bicycles, cover the ground fast. Overlap the sheets by six inches or so to keep weeds from sneaking between them. Newspaper should be laid down one-eighth to one-half inch thick.

As you spread out the sheets, wet them thoroughly. Do this frequently if a breeze comes up—watching your sheet mulch flap away is pretty demoralizing. Soak the sheets several times to make sure the water seeps through. If you're sheet mulching with a group, this is when hose-fights usually erupt, tugging any well-orchestrated work-party toward mayhem.

Try not to walk on the paper, especially after it's wet, as this pulls the sheets apart and creates gaps. Pretend you're painting a floor: Start at the far side and work toward the access or materials pile so you won't walk on your work.

Next, toss down another thin layer of nitrogen-rich manure, meal, or fresh green clippings. This will entice the worms up through the soon-to-be rotting sheets and coax plant roots downward.

On top of this, pour on the bulk mulch, about eight to twelve inches of loose straw, hay, or other substances listed above. Weed seeds in this layer aren't a big concern, as a thick, seed-free stratum will lie atop this one. Weed seeds seem to rot rather than germinate in the slowly composting mass.

Bales of hay or straw don't have to be fluffed up to their original grassy bulk. Just break the bales into thin "flakes" about one to two inches thick and lay down about three thicknesses of these. Broken into several layers and moistened, the dense flakes will expand and compost perfectly well.

To create an easily compostable sheet mulch, pay attention to the carbon:nitrogen ratio in the bulk mulch layer. If you're using high-carbon materials such as straw or, especially, wood shavings, sprinkle on nitrogen in the form of blood meal or other nitrogen-rich source, or "dilute" the carbonaceous mulch with perhaps one part clover hay, seaweed, grass clippings, or other high-nitrogen mulch for every four of high-carbon matter (see Table 4-1

for a list of mulch materials and their C:N ratios). A mulch that is extremely low in nitrogen, such as wood shavings, will be slow to rot down and may cause anemic plant growth. You don't need a perfect C:N balance—just make sure there's *some* nitrogen in the mix to feed the compost critters.

As you build this layer, spray on water every few inches. This layer should be damp but not wet; you're looking for that wrung-out sponge state. This can require a surprisingly large volume of water. It may take a couple of minutes of soaking every few inches to achieve the damp-but-not-wet state.

Atop the bulk mulch, add an inch or two of compost. If this is in short supply, add compost plus whatever soil is on hand to reach the final thickness. Or, if the pile will have a few months to compost before planting, you can substitute manure or several inches of easily compostable material for this layer. But if you plan to plant the sheet mulch within a few weeks, a layer of compost will be necessary to act as a seedbed.

The final layer is two inches of weed- and seed-free organic matter, such as straw, fine bark, wood shavings, or any of the others listed above. Besides smothering weeds, this layer gives the project, in landscaper jargon, "that finished look," which will endear you to your more fastidious neighbors. For planting seeds and starts, push this layer aside to reach the compost/soil layer right below, just as you would with any mulch.

Some of you may be wondering: Because sheet mulching doesn't have the volume necessary to hold in heat the way a compost pile does, how can weed seeds be sterilized? The answer is: They aren't. But most weed seeds need light or disturbance to germinate. This is why it's best to cover any seed-containing mulches with a couple of inches of straw, soil, bark, or other weed-free material. One of the beauties of deep mulch is that it never needs to be—never should be—tilled. What few weeds appear are easily pulled from the loose soil. To stop future weeds, just pile on more mulch. Thus weed seeds never really get a chance to sprout. They just rot. Sheet mulch does have its weedy headaches, though. Bindweed, brought in via hay or other mulch, is the bane of sheet-mulchers and can travel for yards beneath the paper layer. The same applies to Bermuda grass, whose rhizomes can tunnel forever through the tubes in corrugated cardboard and gleefully emerge in a break for daylight at the edge of the mulch.

Another drawback to sheet mulch is slugs. In the early phase of decomposition, slug populations can explode. I compensate by extra-heavy plantings of succulent greens such as lettuce (the slugs do the thinning). For less easily seeded plants, make slug collars from cans (tin or steel, not aluminum): Remove the top and bottom, cut down one side with tin snips, unroll the can, and cut 2-inch-high rings from it. Encircle tender plant stems with these. Slugs stay out since they are irritated by the galvanic shock they receive from the metal coating.

Sheet mulch, and deep mulching in general, is a fast and easy way to boost organic matter and soil life to prodigious levels. With the bottom of the biological pyramid—soil life—built on a broad, thick foundation of mulch, your garden will support a stunning diversity of plants, beneficial insects, and wildlife.

Starting Plants in Sheet Mulch

A fresh sheet mulch won't be as productive as one that's six months old; hence it's best to prepare it in the fall. These beds seem to reach their prime the second season after construction, a productivity that doesn't fall off for several years and can be renewed by simply adding more mulch. But even a freshly built sheet-mulch bed is probably going to give plants a boost, as soil life blossoms within days, and there's plenty of fertility to be released in a foot of properly blended mulch. Starting plants in a new sheet mulch takes care, though. You can't simply sprinkle tiny seeds into the coarse, undigested mulch; they'll get lost.

If your sheet mulch hasn't broken down to soil by the time you want to plant, start seeds by making tiny pockets or trenches about three inches deep, filling them with soil or compost, and seeding these (this is why I keep that emergency compost pile). Seedlings and vegetable starts should also go into small soil pockets about three times the size of the plant's root mass. If the plant is deep-rooted, pull the mulch aside, slit the paper or cardboard in an X-pattern, and replace the mulch. Then plant above the slit, and roots will find the opening with no trouble. For shrubs or trees, either install them before sheet mulching and carefully work around them, or, after mulching, remove the mulch, slit the paper layer, peel the paper back, and dig a hole. Then place the plant in the hole with the root crown about an inch above the old soil level and carefully replace the paper to minimize the chance of weed emergence. Either push soil up to cover the root crown and tamp it in place or cover the crown with two or three inches of mulch, which in time will rot down to crown level. Don't bury the whole trunk in mulch or rodents will tunnel in and feast on the bark.

Cover Cropping for Fertility

To quickly but laboriously add fertility to soil or in zone 1 beds that are constantly being replanted, such as salad beds, use compost. For main garden beds, I prefer sheet mulch. But for large areas, for long-term fertility, and for shifting the labor to nature's ample muscles, use cover crops.

Cover crops are planted specifically to build and hold soil and to smother weeds. They range from long-growing perennials such as red fescue and Dutch white clover for undisturbed cover, to short-term green manures meant to be slashed in place or lightly tilled in after a season, such as annual ryegrass and common vetch. The aim is the same: a solid cover of plants. Their leaves shield the soil from hammering rains and carpet the earth in fall with nutritious, humus-building litter. The dense planting crowds and shades out weeds. And their roots drive deep into the soil, loosening the earth, drawing up nutrients, playing host to soil life, and placing organic matter farther down than even the deepest plowing. This last is an oft-neglected benefit of cover crops.

Roots are nature's subterranean humus builders. Above ground, leaf litter does the job; but, in the underworld, roots add organic matter in vast quantities during their constant cycles of growth and decay.

The most actively growing parts of roots are the root hairs, the almost microscopic threads growing from the very tips of roots. Root hairs lead an ephemeral existence, often living for only a few hours as they stretch toward zones of water and fertility. While alive, root hairs actively absorb nutrients and channel them to the main roots.

Plants and their roots don't grow smoothly and continuously but in spurts. These growth periods are controlled by many overlapping cycles: day/night, wet/dry, cold/warm, and even by the comings and goings of soil organisms. Roots in particular are strongly influenced by wet/dry cycles. After a heavy rain or deep irrigation, the ground becomes saturated with water, and legions of root hairs die from lack of oxygen. This explains why some plants, such as cucumbers and squash, sometimes wilt after a rain, just when we expect them to perk up again.

As the ground begins to dry after a rain, air flows into the emptying soil pores. Fueled by fresh oxygen and moisture, root hairs and tips grow eagerly toward pockets of nutrients. Growth accelerates as oxygen levels rise and the soil, no longer water saturated, approaches the perfect moisture range. But the cycle flows and ebbs: Water percolates downward, evaporates upward, and is sucked up by the plants themselves. Within hours, the soil becomes too dry for the tender root hairs. They start to wither and die. If the soil dries further, whole root sections begin to die en masse, sloughing off and decomposing. Plant growth slows. With the next rain or irrigation, new roots begin the same odyssey, surging into caches of fertility, but some of these also die in the cycle between too wet and too dry.

Interlocked loops such as these reveal nature's complexity and intelligence. The wet/dry cycle drives the root-dieback cycle, which in turn tempers the rhythm of plant and soil-organism growth. The thirsty plants themselves, as they consume soil water, alter the wet/dry cycle. Wheels within wheels spin as humus, soil life, and plants all grow.

During this cycle, plants shed huge masses of roots, hourly, daily, constantly—not just in fall when the plants die. This decaying organic matter builds humus deep in the soil and is one benefit of cover crops that can't be achieved any other way. Many cover crops send roots ten or fifteen feet deep. No plow will ever sink organic matter to a fraction of that depth.

Dozens of cover crops exist. How do you choose the best ones? As in so much of ecological gardening, diversity provides the key. While soil and climate conditions may suggest certain cover crops

Table 4-2. Cover Crops Annual Cool Weather Cover Crops
These crops are planted in the late summer or fall, and are mowed or tilled in in the spring, while they are flowering and before they set seed (the time of maximum root growth, nitrogen content, and biomass). Most are hardy to 0 to 20° F.

Common Name	Botanical Name	N-fixer	Soil preference	Tolerates poor soil	Height	Insectary	Comments
Austrian winter pea	Pisum arvense	•	Heavy		2 ft	•	hardy to 0°
Barley	Hordeum vulgare		Loam		2-4 ft		mild winters only
Bell bean	Vicia faba	•	Loam	•	3-6 ft	•	opens heavy soil
Blando brome grass	Bromus mollis		Many	•	2-4 ft		drought tolerant
Clover, alsike	Trifolium hybridum	•	Heavy		2 ft	•	can take acid soils
Clover, berseem	Trifolium alexandrinum	•	Many		2 ft	•	hardy to 18°
Clover, crimson	Trifolium incarnatum	•	Loam	•	18 in	•	hardy to 10°
Clover, red Kenland	Trifolium pratense	•	Loam		2 ft	•	short-lived perennial
Clover, sweet white	Melilotus alba	•	Heavy		3-6 ft	•	
Clover, sweet yellow	Melilotus officinalis	•	Loam		3-6 ft	•	drought tolerant
Cover, nitro Persian	Trifolium resupinatum	•	Many	•	2 ft	•	hardy to 15°
Fava bean	Vicia fava	•	Many		4-8 ft	•	hardy to 15°
Fescue, zorro	Vulpia myuros		Many		2 ft		mix with legumes
Foenugreek	Trigonella foenum-graecum	•	Many		2 ft	•	opens heavy soil
Garbanzo bean	Cicer arientinum	•	Many		3-5 ft	•	slow in cold soils
Mustard	Brassica spp.		Heavy	•	2-4 ft	•	opens heavy soil
Oats	Avena sativa		Many		2-4 ft		mild winters only
Oil seed radish	Raphanus sativus		Many		2-4 ft	•	hardy to 20°
Phacelia	Phacelia tanacetiflolia		Many	•	2-3 ft	•	hardy to 20°
Rapeseed	Brassica napus		Loam	•	2-3 ft		opens heavy soil
Rye	Secale cereale		Many		2-4 ft		
Ryegrass, annual	Lolium multiforum		Many		2-4 ft		mix with legumes
Vetch, common	Vicia sativa	•	Many		3-6 ft	•	hardy to 0°
Vetch, hairy	Vicia villosa		Many	•	3-6 ft	•	hardy to -10°
Vetch, purple	Vicia atropurpurea	•	Many		3-6 ft	*	hardy to 10°

to try, your local microclimate or variations in soil can toss in a wild card. It's best to seed a number of varieties and record which ones thrive. Another benefit of diversity: Each species secretes its own array of sugars and other compounds from its roots. Each plant's particular chemical smorgasbord attracts a different community of soil organisms to it. This means that the more species of cover

crop we plant, the more varied will be the soil life's diversity. As we've noted, this will subdue disease and boost plant growth.

The first decision to make in choosing cover crops is between annual and perennial plants (see Table 4–2 for a list). If the goal is to build fertility in a temporarily dormant garden bed—say, over winter—annuals are the answer. But perennials

Annual Warm Weather Cover Crops
These crops are planted in spring or summer, and are tilled or mowed before they set seed. With ample water and warmth, they can create enormous quantities of biomass.

Common Name	Botanical Name	N-fixer	Soil preference	Tolerates poor soil	Height	Insectary	Comments
Black-eyed peas	*Vigna unguiculata*	•	Many		3-4 ft	•	chokes weeds
Buckwheat	*Fagopyrum esculentum*		Loam		1-3 ft	•	chokes weeds
Cowpeas, red	*Vigna sinensis*	•	Loam	•	1-2 ft	•	drought resistant
Lablab	*Lablab purpureus*	•	Many		5-10 ft	•	drought resistant
Pinto beans	*Phaseolus vulgaris*	•	Loam		2-4 ft	•	drought resistant
Sesbania	*Sesbania macrocarpa*	•	Many	•	6-8 ft	•	drought resistant
Soybeans	*Glycine max*	•	Many		2-4 ft	•	mix with non-legumes
Sudan grass	*Sorghum bicolor*		Many	•	6-8 ft	•	mix with legumes
Sunn Hemp	*Crotolaria juncea*	•	Loam	•	3-6 ft	•	tolerates acid soil

Perennial Cover Crops
These are excellent for no-till gardens, and can be mowed to generate mulch and compost. Some of the shorter varieties, such as white Dutch clover, can be used as a living mulch, interplanted with other crops.

Common Name	Botanical Name	N-fixer	Soil preference	Tolerates poor soil	Height	Insectary	Comments
Alfalfa	*Medicago sativa*	•	Loam		2-3 ft	•	well-limed soil
Birdsfoot trefoil	*Lotus corniculatus*	•	Many	•	3-5 ft	•	drought resistant
Chicory	*Cichorium intybus*		Heavy	•	2-3-ft	•	opens heavy soil
Clover, strawberry	*Trifolium fragiferum*	•	Many		1 ft	•	needs moisture
Clover, white Dutch	*Trifolium repens*	•	Many		6-10 in	•	needs moisture
Clover, white Ladino	*Trifolium repens*	•	Many		1 ft	•	needs moisture
Clover, white New Zealand	*Trifolium repens*	•	Many		1 ft	•	needs moisture
Fescue, creeping red	*Festuca rubra*		Many		2-3 ft		
Orchardgrass	*Dactylis glomerata*		Many		1-2 ft		
Ryegrass, perennial	*Lolium perenne*		Heavy		2-3 ft		
Timothygrass	*Phleum pratense*		Heavy		2-3 ft		needs moisture

are in order if you're preparing a future orchard's soil, or have a "back forty" section of yard or bed to make more fertile. Perennial clovers can also be used to cover garden paths or other areas. Masanobu Fukuoka, the brilliant author of *The One Straw Revolution*, used perennial white clover as a permanent, living mulch in his garden beds. To plant crops, he simply opened up small areas in the clover and placed seeds or transplants in the resulting gaps. This is a great example of stacking functions: The greenery suppresses weeds, the shade holds moisture in the soil, the blossoms attract beneficial insects, and nitrogen fixed by the clover boosts the growth of the other crops.

This leads us to a second set of choices: between nitrogen-fixing cover crops and non–nitrogen fixers. As many gardeners know, most members of the legume (pea and bean) family, plus certain other species (such as alder, Russian and autumn olive, and ceanothus) host symbiotic microorganisms that live in nodules among their roots. These bacteria and fungi "fix" nitrogen gas from the air by combining it with carbon to make amino acids and related molecules.

The microbes pass on any surplus to their host's roots, which absorb the nitrogenous compounds. The plant converts this gift into stems, leaves, and, especially, protein-rich seeds. In return, the host plants reward their microbial partners with sugary root secretions.

Ancient farmers knew the value of legumes and other nitrogen-fixing plants. The Roman farming texts of Virgil and Cato advised farmers to sow legumes into fallow fields. Legumes need to be plowed in or mulched before the seeds set because at maturity the plant drains nitrogen from stems and leaves and concentrates it in the seeds.

Some argue that nitrogen fixers do little good until they die, when they release the nitrogen locked in the plant and microbial nodules. I disagree, and both my own observations and those of researchers support me. I've seen corn planted with and without beans in the same garden, and the corn entwined by beans is decidedly larger. On Washington's Orcas Island, the Bullock brothers routinely plant a nitrogen-fixing shrub such as autumn olive or Siberian pea shrub in the same hole as a fruit tree. Douglas Bullock categorically states, "I've seen it, and I know that trees planted with a nitrogen fixer grow faster."

Don't believe the anecdotes? Let's go to the research. William King reports in the *Journal of Agronomy* that when he interplanted ryegrass and clover, he found, using radioactive tracers, that 80 percent of the nitrogen in the ryegrass had come from the living clover. The clover was pulling nitrogen from the air and feeding it to the ryegrass.

How does this work? A few paragraphs ago I described the constant growth and dieback of roots. That's the explanation. During the wet/dry soil cycle, the clover's roots slough off, as do the nitrogen-fixing nodules. Surrounding plants and microbes then absorb these nutrients as the roots and nodules decay.

Legumes offer many benefits. The Salina, Kansas–based Land Institute found during their prairie-building work that adding more legumes to a prairie seed mix increases the total number of species—legumes, grasses, and flowers—that survive. Nitrogen-fixing species abound in early successional ecosystems such as young fields, pioneer dune communities, and freshly burned forests. Ecological gardeners can take a lesson from this observation: When building soil or feeding hungry plants, go heavy on the nitrogen fixers.

But remember that balance is important. All that nitrogen must be balanced with carbon. Soil organisms consume ten to fifty times more carbon than nitrogen, so farmers always blend a grass or other nonlegume into their cover crops. A cover crop rich in nitrogen will rekindle the soil life's metabolic fires, burning prodigious amounts of carbon to balance the nitrogenous bounty. A too-rich nitrogen fuel can actually deplete more organic matter than the cover crop adds. For this reason, commercial cover crop mixes contain 10 to 40 percent oats, annual ryegrass, or other nonlegumes.

Blending grasses with legumes provides one kind of balance in cover crops. Now that we've opened the door to biodiversity in cover crops, let's explore further. Grasses add carbon and build structure. Legumes increase soil nitrogen. What other roles can different cover crops perform?

Some cover crops are great at opening up heavy or compacted soils. Rapeseed and mustard have extensive root systems that punch through hard subsoil, aerating the earth and adding humus as the roots die. Alfalfa does the same, though it requires fertile soil to grow well. I've grown daikon radishes in heavy soil, let them flower, and then snapped them off at ground level. Each forearm-sized daikon will break up the clay and then rot, leaving a mass of organic matter in the soil.

Other cover crops can mine the soil for nutrients, ferrying minerals from the depths into their leaves and thus, at leaf fall, to the soil surface. Chicory, a warm-season perennial, is renowned for its lengthy taproot, which seeks out pockets of potassium, sulfur, calcium, magnesium, and other minerals. Buckwheat converts insoluble phosphorus to a more plant-available form. Plants that actively seek and store particular nutrients are called *dynamic nutrient accumulators.* Planting these in poor soils, or in areas that are frequently harvested and thus need replenishing, is one way to cut down on fertilizer use and let nature do that work. The plants can be left to drop their mineral-rich leaves in place, slashed for mulch, or composted. Nutrient accumulators are covered more fully in Chapter 6.

Another use for cover crops is to attract beneficial insects. The blossoms of buckwheat, phacelia, fava beans, many of the clovers, bell beans, mustard, and vetch are all abuzz with nectar hunters soon after opening.

Thus, a cover crop mix can serve multiple functions. A blend of five to ten varieties sown into the soil can build humus, add nitrogen, mine minerals, bust up heavy soil, and beckon a wide array of helpful insects. Peaceful Valley Farm Supply carries a "Soil Builder Mix" that contains bell beans, winter peas, two vetch varieties, and oats (see the resources section). And that's just the beginning. I've seen old farm texts that list fifteen varieties in their cover crop mixtures, including four grass species, five clovers, plus yarrow, fennel, plantain, dandelion, and more. That kind of biodiversity will bring many forms of nature's energy—soil life, humus, minerals, beneficial insects, and more—to work in your garden.

Sharing the Wealth of the Soil

An exuberantly healthy soil is the cornerstone of a sustainable garden. The virtues bestowed by a living, fertile soil are legion. When we pack the growing earth with organic matter, via thick mulch, self-renewing roots, and buried debris, we're beckoning the industrious workers of the soil. Worms, tiny beetles and mites, bacteria, fungi, and a host of other helpers arrive to feast on the offerings and on each other. They churn and tunnel and munch and spawn, chiseling minerals from rock and humus, all the while loosing a veritable avalanche of fertility to be shared with plants. The plants themselves shelter, feed, and are nourished and protected by whole communities of soil life in a mutually beneficent partnership. A vast commerce of shuttling minerals, sugars, acids, antibiotics, hormones, and all the molecules of life connect this thousand-specied hive together. For the price of a little mulch and a bit of care, rich and extravagant empires can be built beneath the earth, empires that will funnel their wealth upward to plants and in turn to insects, to birds, to all wildlife, and to people as well. In the ecological garden, we do all we can to broaden this river of flowing fertility, and we start with the soil.

Feeding the soil engages us in a partnership that benefits all. By applying the techniques and the point of view offered in this chapter, the base of life's pyramid—the abundance of the soil—becomes broad and sturdy. Life builds on life. Whatever we plant in this rich earth will have a far greater chance of thriving; whatever we hope to feed, whether wildlife, ourselves, or perhaps just our senses, will be deeply nourished. And serendipities we never hoped for—a surprising new wildflower, a rare butterfly, or sturdier plants that bloom longer, fruit heavier, and grow in tough conditions—will grace our lives almost daily.

CHAPTER FIVE

Catching, Conserving, and Using Water

In truth, our planet should be called Water, not Earth. About 70 percent of the globe is blanketed by this life-giving liquid, roughly 331 million cubic miles of it. But most of that is not available to us. All but 3 percent of Earth's water is salty; and, of the remaining dab of fresh water, three-quarters is locked in ice. It gets worse. About half of what's left, Earth's unfrozen fresh water, is 2,500 feet or more below ground, embedded in rock. That's too deep to recover economically. Are you following these shrinking numbers? The accessible fresh water in lakes, rivers, groundwater, and the atmosphere makes up only half of one-quarter of 3 percent—for non-Einsteins, that works out to 0.375 percent—of Earth's total water. It's precious stuff.

Yards are notorious for guzzling water. Over most of this continent, much of a home owner's summer water bill goes to irrigation. That's because conventional garden design does not create the conditions for evenly moist soil. Instead it relies on electric pumps, power plants, wells and reservoirs, a resource-intensive irrigation system, and an alert gardener to open faucets and lug hoses about. It makes you wonder how forests and grasslands survive without all that. But once again—you must be expecting this by now—nature holds the answers.

In an ecologically based design, water isn't an externally caused event—it is designed in, automatically present, naturally abundant. In the ecological garden, ample water, not drought, is the default condition. A well-designed garden doesn't have to be nudged and babied into health. It spontaneously cycles toward lush and vibrant growth, even when the gardener is absent and the skies are cloudless. Ecological design, as this chapter will show, lets us create gardens that survive the vagaries of weather without our constant care. A water-wise design saves more than just labor and frustration. It conserves resources. Turning on a sprinkler consumes energy and water that could be spared by good planning. Also, tap water's source is often a dammed reservoir that blocks fish migration and floods once-wild land. Or the water may be pumped from a well whose source is unknown and thus unreliable. The well may tap an ancient aquifer—fossil water that someday soon will be depleted. An ecologically responsible gardener is sensitive to the limits of our water supply and the energy required to use it.

This chapter will describe ways to be less reliant on distant, erratic, and expensive water sources. The methods for doing this, not so coincidentally, enhance the web of connections that link the pieces of the garden together. The result is not just less watering but also a resilient, healthy backyard ecosystem.

This information isn't just for dryland dwellers. Even though much of the country receives ample annual rainfall, it rarely arrives in perfectly timed doses. The strategies that follow will help the garden survive not only drought, but the too-wet periods as well, through better drainage, storing rain for future use, and putting water where it is needed most.

To learn how to design a garden that is naturally water-wise, we first must ask, "How does nature store water?" Besides the obvious sources—lakes and ponds—nature holds water in plants, in the air, and in the soil. Water is cleansed and recycled in wetlands, breathed into the air by trees, collected and channeled by landforms. We can use all of these relationships as the basis for a garden that has a naturally healthy water cycle.

The Fivefold Path to Water Wisdom

Recall the permaculture principle we introduced in Chapter 1: "Each function is supported by several elements." A garden that captures, holds, and recycles its water will embody that principle. If a landscape relies on only one element or device for watering—perhaps an automatic sprinkler—then one small failure spells disaster. Given Murphy's Law, sooner or later that sprinkler will clog, break, or once too often miss the tender monkey-flower in the corner. But if we support the garden's water needs by multiple tricks—say, by providing a layer of moisture-retaining mulch, plenty of rich soil that holds water, and a reliable irrigation system—the chance of all three systems failing at once dwindles to near zero.

One of the finest examples I know of this principle at work is in the garden of Charles and Mary Zemach in Los Alamos, New Mexico. This oasis in the high desert, designed by Santa Fe permaculturist Ben Haggard, can last months between waterings. Yet this is no gravelly xeriscape garden. In the glare of desert summer, fruit trees bow under the weight of juicy plums and peaches, while wispy maidenhair ferns shelter in cool shadows. Pale blossoms of mock orange and spirea peer from beneath an old apricot tree. Herbs such as burnet and French sorrel are posted near the front door, ready to enliven a salad. Here is tranquil beauty, more food than the Zemachs can eat, and abundant wildlife habitat. But in a city where water bills in summer can reach $300 per month, the Zemachs rely on almost no municipal water.

The Zemachs' garden combines five complementary techniques to support the goal of ample water: building organically rich soil, contouring the landscape to catch water and direct it to where it is needed, including drought-tolerant plants when possible, planting densely to shade the soil, and mulching deeply. (See Table 5-1.) As proof of the deeply layered strategy's effectiveness, the plantings, only three years old at my visit, had survived a five-month drought the previous year.

A little contemplation of the Zemachs' strategy reveals a synergistic bonus. Because they are skillfully combined, these techniques do more than just save water. They protect the plants from drought by keeping water in the soil, where plants can use it. Also, mulch and rich soil ensure a high level of organic matter, which boosts plant growth. Closely spaced plants, stacked in layers, boost the garden's yields. And mulch, dense planting, and contoured land all protect the soil from erosion in the infrequent but fierce downpours of the Southwest. In a good design, well-chosen techniques interlock and complement each other to create synergies and yield serendipitous benefits.

Let's look at each element of this fivefold strategy separately to understand why the parts combine to offer more than just a simple sum.

Holding Water in the Soil

In the early phases of her garden's design, Mary Zemach had envisioned an ornate drip irrigation system, a plastic webwork of emitters, spitters, and sprayers administered by an impressive

Table 5-1. Five Water-Conserving Methods and Their Benefits
Together these five techniques conserve moisture far more effectively and more certainly than any single technique, plus the benefits extend far beyond water conservation.

Method	Benefits
High organic matter content	Holds moisture
	Adds fertility
	Stores nutrients
	Boosts soil life
	Fluffs soil
	Sequesters carbon
Deep mulching	Slows evaporation
	Cools soil
	Adds fertility
	Boosts soil life
	Smothers weeds
	Arthropod and microbe habitat
Locate plants according to water needs	Conserves water
	Less labor for watering
	Survive drought
	Encourages native plants
Dense plantings	Shades soil
	Smothers weeds
	Increases biodiversity
	Increases yields
Soil contouring	Catches water
	Directs water where needed
	Helps plants and soil life survive both wet and dry periods
	Builds humus
	Adds visual interest

control panel. Designer Ben Haggard waved this off, saying it would be an unnecessary expense. He then repeated one of permaculture's mantras: *The cheapest place to store water is in the soil.*

As I mentioned in the previous chapter, humus and other organic matter act as a sponge, swelling to greedily hold several times their weight in water. I've seen just how thirsty good soil can be when I've sterilized humus-rich potting soil in the oven. The baked soil comes out of the oven bone-dry, so I add water to it before sowing seeds. A lot of water: Three quarts of dry soil will easily hold one quart of water. This means that one foot of rich, moist soil blanketing a backyard holds as much water as a three-inch-deep lake the size of the yard. To build a pond or tank that holds that much water or to buy the same number of gallons from the city would be frightfully expensive. Yet the soil will store the water for free. And soil is stingy with water. A rainstorm must first saturate the soil with water before a single drop trickles away as runoff. Plus, unlike pond water, moisture held in soil doesn't evaporate easily.

The key to the soil's capacity to hold water is organic matter. Research shows that soil with as little as 2 percent organic matter can reduce the irrigation needed by 75 percent when compared to poor soils having less than 1 percent organic matter. Most urban and suburban soils are low in organic matter because developers often strip the topsoil from new housing, sell it, and then replace the many inches of rich earth with a thin sprinkling of trucked-in topsoil. Before homeowners can achieve the lake-in-the-ground effect, they must build up that organic matter again to at least its predeveloper state.

The Zemachs built rich soil in their yard before the new plants went in. A landscaping crew stripped off the old grass, composted it, and added it back to the yard. The crew also tilled in several truckloads of compost from Los Alamos's yard-waste program

A swale, laid out on contour so that water doesn't flow along it but instead percolates into the soil, forming an underground storage reservoir. Swales can be 1 to 3 feet deep and 1 to 4 feet or more across, with a berm downslope roughly the same size, made from the soil from the swale.

and many bales of peat moss. This created a foundation of plentiful organic matter and living soil.

Rich soil holds the water that keeps our rivers flowing and our lakes full, as a friend in northern California showed me vividly. I had stopped to see seed-grower George Stevens's farm on the banks of the Klamath River, and I asked him how often he irrigates. "Not much, not until late in the summer when the rains are long gone," George answered. He directed my eyes to the Klamath Mountain foothills that ringed the valley. "Those hills are why," he said. "Water drains out of that hillside soil very slowly. The hills take most of the summer to drain. The water travels underground and goes through my farm on its way to the river. It's right under our feet. These plants bring the water up." George had seen that the soil, square miles of it lying on the rocky substrata of the hillsides and lapping down into the valley, was a giant sponge. It could hold massive quantities of water and hold it for months. Over the dry summer, this sponge would dribble its water downhill, slowly draining into the Klamath. This explains why our rivers stay full instead of just draining dry after each rain. Sure, the rivers are fed by creeks, but what feeds the creeks? There's no endlessly gushing faucet at the top. Water slowly seeps out of humic earth, drop by drop, the drops coalescing into a trickle, the trickles broadening into creeks. Each creek bank is a natural drainage ditch, collecting water that oozes from the moist earth over weeks and months. Rivers come from the soil, guardian of our water. By building our garden's soil, we can store whole rivers and lakes in our yards.

Contouring to Catch Water

The second water-holding technique that Mary used in her garden was sculpting the land to hold water. For example, in her yard is a circular patch of drought-tolerant buffalo grass that has been contoured like a dish: The center of the circle is a few inches lower than the edges. It's a gentle

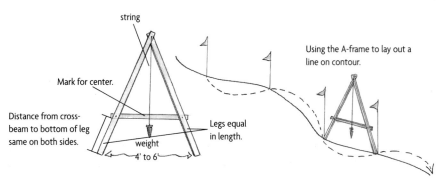

An A-frame level for laying out contour lines, made from 1x2 or 2x2 wood or metal. To calibrate, stand it upright and mark on the crossbeam where the string passes it. Then reverse the A-frame, setting each leg where the opposite one was. Mark the crossbeam again. The center is halfway between the two marks; mark it (traditionally, the object used for the weight is a beer bottle, but a rock or plumb bob will do). Or attach a bubble level to the crosspiece. To use the A-frame, place one leg at the beginning of the line to be laid out. Swing the other leg along the ground until the string aligns with the center mark. Mark this on-contour spot, and continue pivoting and marking until the line is laid out.

concavity that you can hardly see, but the rain knows it's there. Rainwater collects in the depression and soaks in, reducing the need for irrigation. This is one of many self-watering spots in the design. Others have been created by making swales.

A *swale*, in this use of the term, is a shallow trench laid out dead level along the land's contours. It's sometimes called a *bioswale*. A swale can be anywhere from one to several feet across, a foot or so deep, and whatever length necessary. A swale is shaped like a long, skinny pond. The earth dug from the swale is piled on the downhill side to make a raised mound or *berm*, so a cross-section of a swale looks like the letter S laid on its side. Surface water and rainwater run downhill into a swale, spread out along its length, and slowly percolate into the soil.

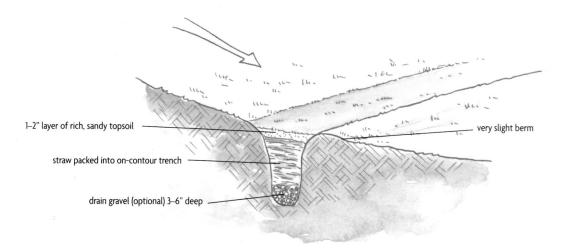

Straw-filled swale. These can be used in more formal or well-traveled parts of the yard, where a standard swale would be too deep. An on-contour trench 1 to 3 feet deep is packed with staw or hay and topped with a thin layer of sandy topsoil. Most of the excess soil is removed, leaving only a slight berm downslope to stop runoff water. The swale can be planted and will function about as well as a standard swale.

How to Make a Swale

First, if you're digging several swales, you need to determine how far apart to make them. They need to be sized and spaced so that all the runoff pouring off the area above a swale can be held by that swale without overflow. A rule of thumb is that the more rainfall, the closer swales should be spaced to catch the heavier runoff. Where rainfall is forty to fifty inches per year, swales should be about eighteen feet apart, increasing to fifty feet apart for areas receiving only fifteen inches of rain. For those in other rainfall regimes, use these numbers as guidelines to judge the appropriate distance between swales. This isn't rocket science, so exactitude isn't essential. On steep slopes, and for compacted, nonabsorbent or clayey soils, runoff will be heavier, so bring the swales closer together.

Then lay out the swale lines on the level. You're creating a contour line, just like the ones on a topographic map. For this you will need a leveling device. If you don't want to rent a surveyor's transit or buy an inexpensive peep-sight level, you can use a water level, a line level, or build your own A-frame level (see illustration). The critical point here is for the swale to be truly level so that water will infiltrate evenly and steadily.

Drive in pegs to mark the course of your swale. On hilly ground you may need to space your pegs about six feet apart to avoid height errors, but on flat ground (though no ground is truly flat!), every ten or fifteen feet will do. You'll be surprised to see that even on "flat" ground, a swale will undulate dramatically with changes in level.

Once the course is marked, begin digging. Where aesthetics aren't a concern, you can dig a rough trench one foot deep and about eighteen inches wide and mound the excavated soil along the downhill edge of the trench. For a gentler, less-visible swale, go only about six inches deep but wider (to two or three feet) and make the downhill berm wider, too. Periodically check the bottom of the swale to make sure that it's level along its length. If you want, you can dig pits or other deep spots in the swale above water-loving plants to coax additional water to their roots.

The general principle is: The more water, the bigger and more numerous the swales. If gullywasher storms that dump two inches of rain regularly inundate your region, you'll want swales that can handle a lot of runoff.

After the swale is dug, you can partially fill it with mulch, which will help hold and absorb water and make the swale less noticeable. Planting along the berm will make the swale more stable and multifunctional. Most any plant will help, but trees and shrubs are ideal, because their deep roots will hold the berm in place, and the leaves will add humus to the soil. The shade will also slow evaporation.

This underground water then seeps downslope, forming a lens of moisture that is held together by hydrostatic tension. The stored water creates an underground reservoir that aids plant growth for tens of feet below the swale. Swales also prevent gullies from forming by intercepting rainwater, slowing it, spreading it, and storing it in the soil.

In the Zemachs' yard, aesthetics dictated that the swales be small and delicate, almost ripples in the ground. After all, this was a public space where the feet and gaze of friends and passers-by would fall; farm-scale ditches wouldn't do. So the swales have been laid out to curve in eye-pleasing lines, softened yet further by the leafy silhouettes of plantings. Gentle swales lead from downspouts and along paths to the roots of shrubs, toward fruit trees, into perennial beds, all in soft arcs and windings. When the rain comes, each swale stops runoff and directs the water into the ground.

Mary says that in heavy rains some of the swales fill with water, but they rarely overflow. If they should spill over, another swale always lies just downhill to

Fishscale swales. If existing trees or other obstacles make long swales impossible, shorter, overlapping swales can be dug to harvest runoff water.

catch the excess water and coax it into the soil. And all these soft contours are almost invisible.

Swales aren't just for deserts. I was once skeptical that swales could be useful in my Northwest climate. Why would I want to catch water in winter when it's constantly raining? And when summer comes, we often go ninety days with no rain, so how could swales help during the dry season? But at the urging of more experienced permaculturists, I dug a swale anyway, an eighty-foot-long, three-foot-wide affair on the slope below our Oakland house. It made a tremendous difference, holding moisture long after the winter rains were gone. Come summer, above the swale the grass shriveled and browned within days after the rains stopped. Below it, not only did the greenery remain verdant for weeks longer, but the wild grasses below it began to fill with many wildflower species, favored by the now-welcoming microclimate. Humus began to build, diversity expanded. Letting water concentrate and soak in via swales will store it in the soil deeper and longer than if the water simply spreads across level ground. Suffice it to say, I'm now sold on swales.

Swales can take many forms. In places where even the gentle undulation of a standard swale would be inappropriate, a level trench can be dug and stuffed full of straw or other absorbent organic matter. When the ground is planted and mulched, you'll never know this swale is there, but it will be thirstily intercepting water and storing it in the earth. If a long, yard-spanning swale is impossible because of trees and other obstacles, a series of short, overlapping swales above and below the obstacles will work. These are called fish-scale swales.

Plants That Are Parsimonious with Water

Water-conservation strategy number three is to use plants that are suited to the available water. Note that I'm not recommending only drought-tolerant plants. There are several ways to match plants to the water on hand, including using a mix of natives that are adapted to local climate, drought-tolerant varieties, and plants whose water use changes seasonally. Thirsty plants can be located where they can get water with minimal human effort, near hoses, swales, sidewalk runoff, and downspouts. Plants should be in the right relationship with the overall climate, microclimate, landforms, soil, and surroundings. Here's how to do this.

Begin by using native plants where you can.

Table 5-2. Useful Plants from Mediterranean Climates			
Common Name	**Botanical Name**	**Common Name**	**Botanical Name**
Abelia, glossy	*Abelia grandiflora*	Lilac, California	*Ceanothus spp.*
Almond	*Prunus dulcis*	Lupine	*Lupinus spp.*
Aloe vera	*Aloe vera*	Madrone	*Arbutus menziesii*
Bamboo, golden	*Phyllostachys aurea*	Olive	*Olea europaea*
Alstroemeria	*Alstroemeria ligtu*	Oregano	*Origanum vulgare*
Barberry	*Berberis vulgaris*	Oregon grape	*Mahonia aquifolium*
Bead tree	*Melia azedarach*	Pistacio	*Pistacia vera*
Blackberry	*Rubus fruticosus*	Quince	*Cydonia oblonga*
Bladder senna	*Colutea arborescens*	Quinoa	*Chenopodium quinoa*
Borage	*Borago officinalis*	Rock rose	*Cistus albidus*
Cardoon	*Cynara cardunculus*	Rocket	*Eruca vesicaria sativa*
Catmint	*Nepeta faassenii, N. mussinii*	Rosemary	*Rosmarinus officinalis*
Fennel	*Foeniculum vulgare*	Rue	*Ruta graveolens*
Fig	*Ficus carica*	Russian olive	*Elaeagnus angustifolia*
Flax, New Zealand	*Phormium tenax*	Sage	*Salvia spp.*
Garlic, golden	*Allium moly*	Salal	*Gaultheria shallon*
Garlic, society	*Tulbaghia violacea*	Sage, Jerusalem	*Phlomis fruticosa*
Grape	*Vitis vinifera*	Scorzonera	*Scorzonerica hispanica*
Hackberry	*Celtis spp.*	Sea buckthorn	*Hippophae rhamnoides*
Hawthorn	*Crataegus spp.*	Sea holly	*Eryngium maritimum*
Hazelnut	*Corylus avellana*	Snowberry	*Symphoricarus albus*
Hind's black walnut	*Juglans hindsii*	Summer savory	*Satureja hortensis*
Honey locust	*Gleditsia triacanthos*	Strawberry tree	*Arbutus unedo*
Italian stone pine	*Pinus pinea*	Thyme	*Thymus vulgris*
Jujube	*Ziziphus jujuba*	Tree mallow	*Lavatera spp.*
Lavender	*Lavandula angustifolia*	Wormwood	*Artemisia absinthum*
Lemonadeberry	*Rhus integrifolia*	Yarrow	*Achillea millefolium*
Licorice	*Glycrrhiza glabra*		
These plants are from parts of the world with moist winters and dry summers. Though drought tolerant, they can survive wet periods far better than many so-called "drought tolerant" plants that originate in deserts. Most of these plants serve several functions, such as offering both food and habitat.			

Whatever the water regime in your locale, native plants are adapted to it. And your region's wildlife will appreciate the familiar food and habitat. Books abound on native plants for every region. A little research will uncover a wide array of natives for wildlife habitat and a somewhat lesser but still broad palette for culinary and medicinal herbs, food, show, and a host of other uses.

Unless you're committed to a natives-only garden, you'll probably want to broaden the horticultural palette to include other plants. Now we can move on to drought-tolerant plants. First, some ecological background: Plants adapted to drought have evolved principally in two climate types, desert, where there's little water, period; and Mediterranean climates, where summers are dust-dry but winters are amply watered. "Mediterranean climate" in this sense means any region with a climate similar to that of coastal Mediterranean lands: much of North America's west coast, portions of coastal Chile, parts of South Africa, southern and western Australia, and of course, the Mediterranean coast itself.

Mediterranean-climate and desert plants differ in their approaches to water. Some desert plants can't survive for long with wet roots. If planted in, say, the American Midwest, desert plants may weather the corn-killing droughts but be felled by a lengthy rainy spell. A Mediterranean-climate plant, however, is adapted to shifts between dry and wet and may work better in nondesert climates. If rains in your region are irregular enough to droop common vegetables and flowers, Mediterranean plants will reduce both your water bill and drought headaches.

Keep in mind that Mediterranean climates are mild, rarely getting colder than USDA Zone 6. If Mediterranean plants are cold-hardy enough to survive your winter, they are a good choice for outlasting the unpredictable dry spells we're experiencing in this era of wild weather. Including these plants expands the selection of water-conserving species beyond native and desert plants. Table 5-2 lists some useful Mediterranean plants. You can enlarge this introductory list on your own by finding other varieties that hail from the world's Mediterranean zones.

What about all those luscious plants that we love but that need regular water? Here, proper location is the answer. For starters, remember your zones. Stationing water-hungry plants where you'll see them, in zone 1, will not only remind you to water

them but will make it easier to drag out the hose or watering can to quench their thirst.

Also, find and use the wet spots in your yard. Where does runoff accumulate? Often, driveways and sidewalks are sloped or crowned and act as water catchments that direct rain to the adjacent soil. That's a good location for water-dependent plants. Check near downspouts, under unguttered eaves, at low spots in the yard, beneath faucets, and near foundation drain outlets. Every property has its own microclimates, with specific sites that are a bit moister than others. Do you have a spot in your lawn that stays green when the rest is beginning to brown? That's a likely candidate. Observe, assess, and then station your thirstiest plants in the naturally wet places. Contour the soil to catch water as suggested above. Let nature and gravity do your watering for you.

Dense Plantings to Banish Drought

The next step in this multilayered water strategy is to densely pack and stack plants together to create shade. That way, the blanket of fronds and leaflets will block desiccating beams of summer sunlight before they reach the soil. Shading soil can reduce evaporation loss by over 60 percent. Shade, like mulch, also keeps root temperatures down, slowing the moist exhalations of transpiring leaves that would otherwise pump water into the sky.

Plants can also shade each other to reduce water loss. It's a rare plant that absolutely requires all the sunlight of a fourteen-hour summer day. In particular, cool-season vegetables such as brassicas and leafy greens do best when shaded for part of a hot afternoon. Many perennial flowers, including lady's mantle, astilbe, monarda, geranium, and others, originated in forests or on shady riverbanks and will flower with a half-day of sun. We can stack our plants in layers to hold moisture beneath the canopy yet still harvest all the sunlight that each variety needs.

Watch how nature works in a forest. In spring, the first plants to leaf out are the tiny herbs and ground covers. Once these have gathered sunlight for a few weeks, building sugary sap and healthy roots, the shrubs above them begin to burst their buds. The low trees follow, and last come the spreading forest giants. By the time the heat of summer arrives, the canopy is nearly closed, and only a few dancing sunflecks shimmer on the forest floor. But by now everything is in full leaf, with branches arrayed in alternating whorls to catch the shifting rays and efficiently convert solar energy into sugars, starches, and the other molecules of plant life.

Once the forest canopy has closed, the air and soil beneath it stays far moister than in the open. Desiccating sunlight can't reach into this grotto to dry the air and earth, and the temperature stays cool, further slowing moisture loss.

The time-delay approach used by nature can work in a garden, too. We'll cover the multilayered approach to gardening in detail in Chapter 10, on forest gardens. For now, be aware that covering the soil in a blanket of plants will curtail water loss.

Mulching for Moisture

The final element in the fivefold water strategy is mulch. A two- to four-inch mulch layer (or more) will squelch moisture loss by slowing evaporation from the soil and by keeping plant roots cool, which will reduce transpiration. Organic mulches also soak up rain rather than letting it run off. And as organic mulches break down, they add humus to the soil, which compounds the soil's water-holding power. Mulches also prevent erosion, protect the soil structure, and soften temperature swings.

Mulch materials are nearly limitless: straw, alfalfa and other seedless hay, wood shavings, bark, leaves, corncobs, shredded cornstalks, seaweed, husks and hulls, even sand. For acid-loving plants, sawdust or pine needles work well. One warning: Mulched soil won't warm up in spring as fast as naked earth, so to speed the growth of heat-loving plants, strip the mulch off in spring and replace it when the soil is warm.

Rocks can also be used for mulches. A mulch of stone may sound bizarre, but in dry country a rock mulch (one- to four-inch cobbles, four to six inches deep) picks up morning dew and dribbles it into the soil. These mulches help during the day, too, when the rocks are shaded by plants and thus cooler than the air. Hot air drifts into the cool, dark spaces between stones. Moisture then condenses out of the warm air onto the chillier rock surfaces and trickles into the ground. In these ways a rock mulch can significantly boost the amount of water that plants receive. Rock mulches also hold heat from sunny days, helping the soil warm in spring and keeping plants toasty on chilly nights. A rock mulch can extend the growing season or help grow hot-weather plants in cool regions.

By combining these five water-holding techniques—rich soil, contouring and swales, the right plants, dense plantings, and mulch—Mary Zemach's land is far more drought-proof than if she'd used only one method. Not only does this redundancy protect against the failure of any one strategy, but the combination of complementary techniques fuses to create a garden that's far less susceptible to drought than any one method used alone. This synergy is one of the great benefits of gardening with ecological principles.

What if your garden's problem is *too much* water, not too little? Oddly enough, these same techniques can help, with little modification. They're not just for drought proofing. More broadly, they moderate any extreme water conditions, dry or wet. Humus-rich soil and mulch can absorb vast volumes of water without losing the ability to hold air, and it's the lack of air that drowns waterlogged plants. Plus, soil rich in organic matter drains better than nearly any but the sandiest soil. And mulches, dense plantings, and contoured ground will prevent erosion from pounding rains. In boggy yards where water really pools, swales can be dug just slightly off contour, at about a 2 percent grade, to carry water to an appropriate catchment area (ideally a pond, creek, or a dry slope, but in the city, a storm drain may have to do).

Conserving Water with Catchment

You'll notice that Mary's multipronged approach to water wisdom doesn't include an irrigation system. She's never needed that imposing array of valves and sprinklers mentioned earlier. Because water is held so thriftily in the soil, the little irrigation that's needed can come from occasional brief sessions with a hose and watering can. However, even here, the Zemachs' yard takes its cue from nature. In an effort to use as little city water as possible, Mary has plugged into natural cycles and those of her own household. Much of her irrigation water comes from stored rainwater and from recycled domestic wash water, or *graywater*. She's recently installed two 1,500-gallon water tanks that collect water from her roof, half-sunk in the ground and topped with planters and benches to make them unobtrusive. As pumping water from the ground or over long distances becomes less economical, more people are turning to free, environmentally friendly ways of irrigating their gardens. Irrigation water doesn't need to be as clean as household tapwater, hence rainwater and graywater are practical alternatives. Let's look at rainwater first.

Harvesting and Storing Rainwater

Every home has a handy rainwater collection system built right into it: the roof. Rainwater splashes on rooftops, drips into the gutters, sluices through downspouts, and then goes . . . away, usually into a storm-drain system. Even in the desert, rainwater usually is treated as a problem to be disposed of, not as the valuable resource it is. I've watched countless acre-feet of rainwater collect on summer-baked parking lots, swirl uselessly down drains, and gurgle toward the ocean, while nearby sprinklers hiss and stutter the last remaining bits of some fossil aquifer onto lawns. Those lawns could easily be watered by that parking-lot catchment system or by rooftop-collected water.

How much water can a roof catch? The box on page 108 labeled "How Much Water Will Your Roof Collect?" gives a simple method for calculating that number, and it's a lot. The average 2,000-square-foot, two-story house has over 1,000 square feet of roof (most houses plus the garage have far more). If that house is in a region receiving forty inches of rain a year (the average for much of the United States), the roof will collect 25,000 gallons of water each year. That's enough to keep a 1,000-square-foot garden watered for 250 days of drought.

A 25,000-gallon tank is a little large for the typical backyard, but it's also rarely necessary. In the eastern half of North America, summer rain usually falls every two or three weeks. To drastically reduce municipal or well water use in that part of the country, we only need to store enough to tide us over between rains, or a couple of weeks' worth of irrigation water. How much water is that? A typical garden that covers 1,000 square feet needs roughly 100 gallons per day to thrive (and that's generous water use). Two weeks' worth of water would thus be 1,400 gallons, which would fit into a circular pond two feet deep and ten feet across, or a tank five feet high and six feet on each side. A pond or tank that size will easily fit into a typical yard.

We can further shrink the amount of water storage needed, of course, by using water-conserving techniques such as mulches, lots of organic matter, and drip irrigation. I know people who get most of their irrigation water from just four fifty-five-gallon drums, one at each downspout. These drums are easy to camouflage with plantings and paint.

A 600-gallon rainwater tank made from galvanized metal culvert that gravity-irrigates a perennial front-yard garden in Prescott, Arizona, with trellising on the tank for vines. The warm microclimate created by the southwest exposure of the tank, which heats the water on sunny days and creates a warm microclimate, means that when there are late frosts the adjacent apple tree fruits only on the side facing the tank. PHOTO AND DESIGN BY ANDREW MILLISON OF MILLISON ECOLOGICAL DESIGN.

Rainless periods can last longer than two or three weeks anywhere on the continent, so for those who truly want to be water-independent, water storage needs to be larger. If you have the space and resources to build a large water tank or pond, then go for it. My point here is simply to show that it's easy to harvest rain, which greatly reduces our dependence on uncertain and energy-consuming water sources.

Compared to Easterners, those in the American West are in tougher shape because rainfall in the West is rarely sufficient for gardening. Outside help is essential. Total rainfall on the Great Plains is less than twenty-five inches, not enough for most garden plants. On much of the West Coast a summer stretch of ninety rainless days is common. Water storage in the West simply needs to be larger. The 5,000-gallon rainwater tank in my Oakland yard,

Planning a Water-Harvesting System

Because many books and articles have been written on ponds and other water storage systems, I won't duplicate those efforts here by describing basic construction. The bibliography lists several good sources. But here are some tips to help with planning.

When designing a rainfall catchment system for your yard, there are five factors to consider:

1. How much rain falls in a year? National Weather Service data will help here, although local features such as which side of a hill you're on or elevation changes can cause big variations in rainfall. A rain gauge, or a neighbor who's kept track of rain for years, is a more accurate source of information.
2. How much water is consumed? By implementing the "fivefold water-saving strategy" described in this chapter, using drip irrigation, and

How Much Water Will Your Roof Collect?

A rule of thumb is that every 1,000 square feet of roof area will catch about 625 gallons of water per inch of rain. For those wishing to be more exact, here's a formula.

First determine these numbers:

A = area of roof in square feet (area of ground covered by the roof, not total area of sloping roof)
R = rainfall in inches per year

Then calculate

$$\frac{A \times R}{12} = W \text{ cubic feet}$$

This is the number of cubic feet of rain the roof collects each year. Because there are about 7.5 gallons in a cubic foot, to convert to gallons, calculate:

W × 7.5 = rain collected in gallons per year

Here's an example: A 30-by-36-foot roof covers 1,080 square feet. If the average rainfall at that site is 35 inches, Area × Rainfall = 1,080 times 35, which equals 37,800. Dividing this by 12 inches gives 3,150 cubic feet of water. To convert to gallons, multiply 3,150 by 7.5, and this yields 23,625 gallons of rainwater per year collected by the roof.

sunk in the ground and camouflaged with a deck and grape arbor, took us through only six weeks of drought.

Tanks are utilitarian, but ponds add habitat and visual pleasure to the list of water storage's possible roles. On a hot day the sight of sparkling water edged by lush greenery seems to drop the temperature by ten degrees. Ponds are also cheaper than tanks and can hold far more water if needed.

The secret of storing water in a pond is depth since the smaller surface area needed by a deeper pond to store a given volume means less evapora-

tion. A twelve-by-twelve-foot garden pond that's four feet deep instead of the usual two can store over 4,000 gallons of water. Obviously, if you're pulling water from the pond for irrigation, you will have to develop some strategies for protecting plants and fish when the water level drops toward the bottom. One possibility is to have one pond strictly for irrigation and a second, smaller one for finny and leafy inhabitants.

A typical garden pond is lined with flexible plastic and edged with flat rocks. In nature, you'll never see a pond that looks like this—a tidy opening in

watering only when needed rather than when an automatic timer decides, you can greatly reduce water consumption.

3. What is the available area of roof or other catchment? The amount of roof area available often depends on the pattern of gutters and downspouts; some sections of roof may not be usable without elaborate plumbing schemes. Pavement and other hard surfaces can also be called into service. I know someone who tosses a sand-bag into the street gutter when it rains, diverting a huge volume of water up his driveway and into a swale to fill a pond and irrigate some trees.

4. What size storage can be built? Here, budget, space, and aesthetics are all factors. Tanks are more expensive than ponds but take up less space. Ponds are much nicer to look at than

tanks, but tanks can be hidden underground, or even, as in many houses dating from the 1800s, built in the cellar.

5. Where should the storage be placed relative to the catch-ment? If the storage can be higher than the garden, gravity, rather than a pump, can power the irrigation system. Aesthetics and ease of construction will also play a role in placement decisions.

Note that all of these factors except the amount of rainfall are controllable. This gives the gardener a lot of leverage. The four other factors can be tinkered with to design the best system for your region.

A warning: The system I am describing is for irrigation water only, not for household use or drinking. Household systems require

measures for keeping out debris, dirt, bird droppings, and other contaminants. Those methods are beyond the scope of this book but are described in the permaculture and water-harvesting books in the bibliography.

Awareness of the rainfall patterns in your area—not just how much it rains, but when—will help you design an effective water storage strategy. Rain that reliably replen-ishes a pond every fortnight or so will dictate a different approach than one forced by regular two-month droughts. But, as we will see in the next section, there are more ways of obtaining water than turn-ing on a faucet or praying for rain.

the ground rimmed with an even border of flag-stones—and that design creates problems. Birds, small mammals, and many insects can't drink from a pond with such a sheer rock edge. Earle Barnhart, a landscape designer on Cape Cod, has evolved a more natural pond edge, replacing some or all of this abrupt rock drop-off with a gently sloping beach, as shown in Figure 5-5. Small animals can sip at the water's edge in this design. One warning: Larger animals, such as dogs and children, may also be attracted to this backyard beach, with possibly messy results.

To see how a pond can be both a landscape focal point and a practical water source for the garden, let's look at what forestry consultant and permacul-turist Tom Ward did in his Ashland, Oregon, yard. Tom built a 3,000-gallon pond on the uphill side of his vegetable garden. "After we dug the hole for the pond," Tom told me, "we added three coats of a product called plastic cement, troweled onto bird netting, for reinforcement." He could have used a rubber or plastic liner but chose a less-expensive but more labor-intensive method since he's got plenty of friends to help him build. The pond is fed by down-

This pond edge, based on a design by Earle Barnhart of Great Work, Inc., allows animals and birds access to the water. At the same time, the gravel beach looks far more natural than ponds edged with rocks, a pattern rarely seen in nature.

spouts from the house next door and from a shed in the lot behind Tom's. Both neighbors responded readily to his request for their runoff water.

The pond was new when I visited, but Tom intended to stock it with edible fish and a variety of useful and attractive plants. However, the pond's benefits extend beyond its boundaries. A swale runs alongside the pond. Overflow dribbles out of the pond, down a rock waterfall, and into the swale. The water is captured by the level swale and sinks into the soil. Tom's vegetable garden is just downhill from the swale, and the expanding lens of subterranean wetness from the swale moves down the slope toward the crops like a slow underground tide. The pond and swale thus form a subsurface irrigation system for the nearby garden. Once again, placing the pieces in the right relationship lets nature do the work and substantially cuts Tom's reliance on municipal water.

At the outlet end of the swale, about twenty feet from the waterfall inlet, Tom planted blueberry bushes. Any water that flows the entire length of the swale and spills out the far end is captured by these shrubs.

This is a fine example of ecological design. The pond harvests rainfall from his neighbors' roofs, the swale collects any surplus from the pond, and the garden and blueberries benefit from moisture taken in by the swale. Tom has integrated a pond into his garden that is attractive and practical and that connects once-separate elements—even from beyond his own property—into a healthy, smoothly functioning whole.

Closing the Cycle with Graywater

The typical American family uses 100 to 200 gallons of water a day in their home (not including irrigation water). Though some of that water goes down the toilet as "blackwater," most of it leaves via sink, shower, and laundry drain, contaminated only by a few drops of soap, the odd flake of dead skin, and a smattering of the bacteria that coexist peacefully with us. This is "graywater," nearly clean, but just dirty enough to be unfit for direct human reuse.

The vision for this once-typical suburban backyard in Santa Maria, California, was to create an abundant food forest with an aquatic element for relaxation. A bare expanse of struggling lawn with a thin perimeter of young fruit trees was transformed into a diverse aquaculture pond system with mini-chinampas growing celery, taro, celeriac (*Apium graveolens* var. *rapaceum)*, Japanese parsley (*Chryptotaenia japonica)*, with watercress, mints and mini-cattails accompanying the fish in the water. Surrounding the pond, amongst the grasses, are sorrel, rhubarb, and the tall and lush achira (*Canna edulis)*, an edible-rooted canna from the Andes. A variety of birds, frogs, and other wildlife now make their home here. Designer Larry Santoyo sits by the pond. PHOTO BY JORDAN HOSEA.

However, plants and soil organisms will gratefully accept the watery part of graywater and eagerly consume the solid and dissolved contents as food.

Reusing graywater reduces pollution and the strain on sewage and septic systems. Just as we now separate our compostable garbage and recyclables from landfill-bound trash, it makes sense to split easily reusable, almost-clean graywater from toilet wastes.

Does the idea of using wastewater in the yard seem, well, a bit unsavory? Don't worry. By following a few simple guidelines, you can easily reuse graywater with no health risk, odor, or any other unpleasantness. Far from it. Health authorities in

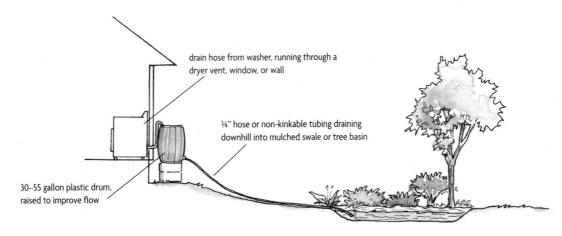

drain hose from washer, running through a
dryer vent, window, or wall

¾" hose or non-kinkable tubing draining
downhill into mulched swale or tree basin

30–55 gallon plastic drum,
raised to improve flow

A washing machine set up to pump graywater into a drum that will then drain to a planted, mulched swale or tree. REDRAWN WITH PERMISSION FROM *CREATE AN OASIS WITH GREYWATER*, BY ART LUDWIG (OASIS DESIGN 2000).

many states have deemed graywater systems safe and legal. Graywater guru Art Ludwig reports that not a single incidence of illness has been traced to a legal graywater system.

Graywater can be an important resource, helping to build yet another resilient, life-enhancing cycle into the ecological garden. Let me describe graywater's benefits, then we'll see how to add this new resource to the garden's living structure.

In earlier chapters, I described the crucial role of the decomposers that make up the detritus cycle. In a healthy ecosystem, the decomposers play as large a part, both physically and energetically, as do the producers (such as plants) and the consumers (animals). The decomposers ingest body wastes and corpses and transform them into the raw feedstocks of life, ready to be cycled once more as the breath and bodies of animate beings. Yet in most human ecosystems, including our yards, the detritus cycle is sadly lacking, destroyed by a lack of topsoil and too many pesticides. Without decomposers and their products, organic matter becomes as rare as precious gems. (I've known gardeners who, when they move, take their compost pile with them.) Ecological gardening attempts to restore the detritus cycle to its rightful, central role by using deep mulches and composting and by avoid-

ing toxic sprays. Incorporating graywater is one more method to do this recycling.

Graywater closes a loop. The usual linear flow of water through a household goes like this: We import items such as soap and food into the home ecosystem, mix them with pure water to create slightly dirty water, and send this dilute waste out of our house (and our awareness) through the drain. This graywater is piped through a massive sewer system and processed in an expensive treatment plant; the contaminants are turned to sewage sludge and the cleaned-up water dumped into a river, lake, or ocean. In this way, valuable resources are speedily converted to garbage and lost from our cycles, yielding along the way only a fraction of the energy and value they contain and costing lots of money to clean up.

In contrast, reusing graywater creates a tight, local cycle and uses far less energy and infrastructure. In such a system, water, food, and biodegradable soaps are imported into the household ecology, mixed with a little dirt and skin effluvia in shower and laundry, and sent into the soil or a backyard wetland. There, the whole mélange is processed by the microbes and plants in the yard, which consume the nutrients within. The result is not waste but clean water and fertilizer, ready

CATCHING, CONSERVING, AND USING WATER

Tips for Using Graywater

- Graywater is a legal gray area. The southwestern states are the most graywater-friendly, but even their building codes mandate systems that are more complex than necessary. Many graywater systems have been built without code approval, yet function safely. Become aware of the codes in your area before building a graywater system.

- Avoid watering food plants directly with untreated graywater. Graywater should be applied to the base of nonfood plants or fruit trees and shrubs. It can also be delivered by subsurface irrigation using perforated leach lines, like a septic system. The risk of disease or toxicity from graywater is slight, but putting graywater directly on food is asking for trouble. Processing graywater by passing it through microbes and plants in an artificial wetland or similar system removes and detoxifies its contaminants. The water can then be collected and used for food-plant irrigation.

- Be careful of what you put in a graywater system. Chlorine bleach, detergents containing boron (borax), and some household chemicals and solvents are toxic to plants and should never go in a graywater system. Hydrogen peroxide–based bleaches are safe to use. If you must use chlorine or boron, install a diverter valve so that your laundry outlet can be temporarily sent to the septic tank or sewer (that is, be treated as blackwater).

- Most common detergents will make graywater alkaline, which is hard on most plants if soil organisms don't have a chance to clean the graywater first. Many stores sell detergents that are graywater compatible and are labeled as such. But filtering graywater through a layer of mulch and fertile soil, or a home wetland, is usually enough to restore pH balance.

- In climates where the ground freezes more than a few inches deep, graywater systems may not work in the winter. Here it's a good idea to be able to divert graywater back into the sewer or septic system until spring thaws.

- Never store untreated graywater for more than a day or two. The normally low numbers of bacteria can multiply quickly in the nutrient-rich water and create unpleasant smells at best and health hazards at worst. Get raw graywater on the ground quickly.

- Graywater is too "lumpy" for drip irrigation systems unless filtered by sand or some other fine filtration system. Lint, hair, and other debris will quickly clog pumps and pipes or openings less than one-half inch across. Use large-diameter hose and pipes to deliver graywater or invest in an appropriate filter system.

for recycling and already in the right place to do it. The soaps and food bits are transformed into fertilizer, then absorbed into the home ecosystem as soil, trees, and flowers. These captured nutrients are spun into an ever-enlarging dance from leaf to litter and back again, harvestable by us or our wild friends. With every shower or laundry load, this circle's connections grow thicker and stronger, and the garden grows greener.

By using a graywater system, most of the water used in the household grows our plants and is lofted into the air by transpiration, cooling us on a hot day, and wafting skyward to return soon as rain, instead of burdening a sewage treatment plant as garbage.

Although the amount of soaps, food, and other material in graywater may seem trivial, it adds up over time, building biomass, becoming plants and wildlife and food. And obviously, the water involved, at about 100 gallons a day, is by no means trivial. I've seen graywater systems that have quickly and dramatically boosted the fertility and lushness of a yard. There's something magical in creating these simple cycles, as if nature recognizes the service and showers us with gifts in return.

If we think of a garden as a living being, then a graywater system acts as one of its organs, a sort of liver and kidneys that process waste and liquid. These "organs" are missing from most gardens. No one can function without kidneys; the only substitute is elaborate machinery of life support. Our gardens are the same. Given a full complement of organs, a garden comes to life. Then we can withdraw resource-gobbling life-support systems such as automated sprinklers and doses of fertilizer. A graywater system helps a garden be more self-sustaining.

A thorough guide to building graywater systems is beyond the scope of this chapter. Good books and articles have been written on the subject. My favorite resource is *Create an Oasis with Greywater* by Art Ludwig (see bibliography). This easy-to-read booklet describes how to choose and install a range of graywater systems. For now, the present chapter will look at a few simple graywater setups, to show how easy and sensible it is to incorporate graywater into the ecological garden.

The simplest possible graywater system—maybe too simple for most people—is a basin in the sink. When it's full, just empty the basin into a well-mulched garden bed. The mulch will absorb the graywater instead of letting it run off, and it contains ample soil life to quickly and hungrily process the graywater's contents. Avoid pouring graywater directly on vegetation, as soaps or oils could clog leaf pores or otherwise harm the plant.

For those who want to recycle their graywater but don't feel like sloshing outdoors with a full soapy basin every few hours, the next level is

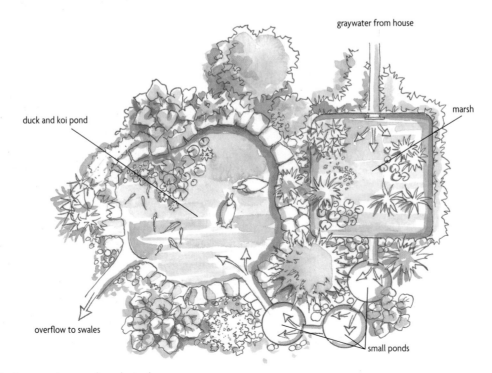

graywater from house

marsh

duck and koi pond

overflow to swales

small ponds

Penny Livingston's graywater marsh and ponds.

what Art Ludwig calls a "drain to mulch basin" system. This involves a little do-it-yourselfing or hiring a plumber to tap into the outlet of a washing machine, tub, or shower and isolating it from the drain lines that carry toilet wastes. Rigid plastic drainpipe (ABS) is then connected to the drain to carry the graywater out of the house. Outside the house, more ABS pipe or flexible, nonkinkable one-inch hose (such as Spa-flex hose) directs the graywater downhill into a mulched swale or to mulched basins around trees. The outlet hose must be unkinkable—not just a garden hose or irrigation polypipe. A kinked hose can cause a drain to back up or burn out a washing-machine pump. (See the illustration on page 112 for details of this setup.) This system can be varied to include a thirty- to fifty-five-gallon drum outside the house to temporarily hold the graywater. The drum will cool water that's too hot for plants and briefly store large volumes of water, such as a tub's contents, that flow too fast for a narrow-diameter outlet hose.

This arrangement, which provides regular doses of ten to thirty gallons from a shower or laundry load, is ideal for trees, shrubs, and large mulched beds. The flexible hose outflow can be moved from bed to bed every day or two, so that no single area will get too soggy. Ludwig's booklet also describes systems that drain to multiple beds so you won't have to move a hose around.

Some very complex graywater systems exist, full of automatic backflush pumps, multistage filters, and leachfield distribution lines. However, for me, the next step in graywater beyond the "drain to mulch basin" system is no more mechanically complicated but far more biologically rich. An ideal example is one created by Penny Livingston, in her yard north of San Francisco.

Penny's graywater system is a set of four shimmering ponds, complete with water plants, fish, and ducks. Graywater from bath and laundry first flows through a small marsh that brims with bog plants

Ducks bob happily in clean, treated graywater that has been purified by a backyard wetland.

and ornamental grasses. This artificial wetland, just a few feet across, removes most of the graywater's contaminants and converts them into vegetation. The mostly clean water then trickles over rocks through three small ponds, where it is joined by rainwater from the roof of Penny's backyard office, home of the Permaculture Institute of Northern California. The final destination is the duck pond, a deep ten-by-ten-foot affair that glimmers with golden koi and ripples with the splashes of mallards. The ducks serve as water-quality monitors. In the system's early days, before the marsh was installed, the ducks wouldn't swim in the not-clean-enough water. That was because the residual soap in the ponds washed the oil from their feathers resulting in sinking ducks. Now, the marsh-cleaned water suits them perfectly.

The pond network is strategically located just south of the office so that winter sun is reflected through the windows, brightening the building's interior. A patio and arbor lie beside the pond, where Penny and the rest of the staff sit on pleasant days or on any other excuse to enjoy this soothing spot.

Penny's backyard was my introduction to the dynamic nature of graywater. During a visit, I quickly learned that when I showered, the pond network came alive, so some mornings I would dash from the shower, half-dressed and dripping, outdoors to the ponds to watch the show my bathing had triggered. As my shower's water surged into the tiny wetland, plant-filtered water flowed out, over the rocks, past the meditating Buddha and under the dwarf peach tree, filling the first pond to overflowing. The second pond topped up, then the third, and water soon cascaded into the final pond. The gentle surge of water set the ducks bobbing, and their soft quacks sounded like laughter.

Here was living water that needed no pump to force its fluid motion. With graywater, every yard, no matter how landlocked or desert bound, can gurgle and splash with the lively rhythms of moving water, without pumps or huge utility bills. And these simple systems give a tremendous boost to the diversity of plants and wildlife that a yard will support while decreasing water consumption. Adding water to a yard creates a whole series of new edges and new flows of both energy and living beings, as any pond owner knows. Treated and cleaned in a backyard wetland, graywater not only provides this bounty guilt free, it eases the burden on overtaxed sewer systems.

Wetlands are nature's way of purifying and recycling water. As dirty water wends sluggishly through a marsh or bog, the resident plants, microbes, and animals dine leisurely on the water's contents, converting pollutants to biomass and purifying the water. Cities from Shelburne Falls, Massachusetts, to Arcata, California, have copied nature, building "artificial" wetlands to process municipal wastewater. Many of these projects are beautiful, threaded with paths for nature lovers who gather to watch the waterfowl, otters, and other creatures that thrive in

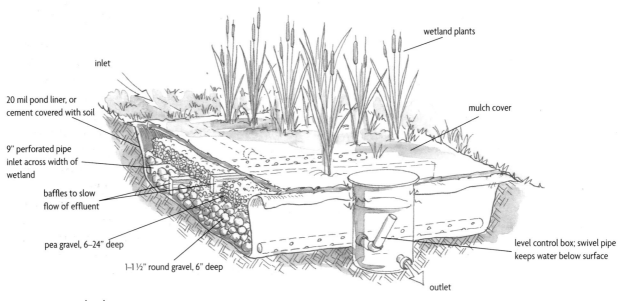

A graywater wetland.

Creating a Backyard Wetland

Building a backyard wetland is relatively straightforward. It's really just a shallow pond, filled with gravel, covered with mulch or soil, and planted with bog and water plants. The water level is kept below the top of the gravel to thwart mosquitoes. Graywater enters the wetland, passes through the gravel, is purified by the plants and attendant microbes, and exits to a pond, swale, or irrigation system (running graywater through irrigation pumps and sprinklers may require additional filtering). Table 5-3 suggests some plants for this wetland. The plants in the first section of the table—cattail, bulrush, reed canary grass, and canna lily—are essential for treating graywater, and all graywater wetlands should contain a majority of one or more of these species. They are special water-cleaning plants, able to supply oxygen to their roots and to the soil nearby. This creates an aerobic zone around each root, resulting in countless aerobic and anaerobic microsites in the wetland and plenty of edge between them. These diverse microniches support many different kinds of pollution-eating microbes. A wetland lacking these special plants might not clean water effectively.

Once a preponderance of the essential plants is in place, other plants, such as those in the second section of Table 5-3, can be added to increase diversity.

Graywater wetlands function effectively only when the plants are growing. Gardeners in very cold climates should install a diverter valve to direct water to the sewer or septic system when the plants die back in winter. This also will keep the outdoor graywater plumbing from freezing.

To build a backyard graywater wetland, select a site that is downhill from your home's graywater outlet so the wetland can be gravity fed (otherwise you'll need a sump pump or other power-using system). The wetland should be able to hold three days of graywater volume. For a family that uses 200 gallons of water per day on a busy day (several showers and laundry loads), that means a 600-gallon wetland. That translates to 80 cubic feet (600 gallons divided by 7.5 gallons per cubic foot), or a wetland two feet deep, four feet wide and ten feet long. This can be any shape: a long trench, a circle, a wavy-edged pattern that maximizes the edge effect, or even more than one wetland in series or parallel.

The wetland should be 12 to 24 inches deep and lined with a plastic pond liner. If your soils are relatively impervious clay, you may not need a liner. Local building codes may offer guidelines for size and materials, although home graywater wetlands are a little avant-garde for most codes to even consider. Some of the systems I know of are of the guerrilla variety or have required special code variances.

Once the wetland is dug and lined, install plumbing as per the diagram. Cover the inlet and outlet pipes with one- to three-inch round gravel. Then fill the liner with three-eighths to one-half inch of pea gravel. The wetland can be covered with mulch or an inch or two of topsoil to help get plants established. Then add the plants. Now graywater can begin to fill the wetland.

The water depth is controlled by a water-level box such as that shown in the diagram on page 116. This is not absolutely required, merely a nice control feature. A spillway for the water to exit will serve almost as well. In the water-level box, changing the height of the pipe, lets the water level be adjusted to the optimal height, about two inches below the top of the gravel (this will prevent mosquito growth). If you want to be extra nice to the plants, once a month or so pull the level control pipe all the way off to drain the wetland. Once it's drained, reinsert the pipe. Periodic draining aerates the bottom of the wetland, helping roots get deeply established. For a simpler system without the level box, a two-foot-wide spillway for the water to exit will do the job, as long as it keeps the water level about two inches below the surface. Rocks can be set across the spillway to keep the mulch and gravel in place.

Table 5-3. Plants for a Graywater Wetland

Essential Wetland Plants
One or more of these varieties should make up the majority of any graywater wetland, as they are particularly effective at purifying water.

Common name	Botanical name	Comments
Bulrush	*Scirpus validus*	
Canna lily	*Canna* spp.	ornamental, cold-intolerant
Cattail	*Typha* spp.	wildlife value, dwarf varieties available
Soft rush	*Juncus effusus*	fiber plant
Reed canary grass	*Phragmites communis*	on some "invasive" species lists, accumulator

Additional Wetland Plants
These species can make up 20% to 30% of a constructed wetland. If warm shower and laundry water is entering the wetland, even the less-hardy species here can survive winters to USDA Zone 6 or below.

Arrowhead	*Sagittaria* spp.	ornamental
Chokeberry	*Aronia* spp.	wildlife value
Comfrey	*Symphytum officinale*	mulch, insectary
Cranberry	*Vaccinium macrocarpon*	wildlife value, foliage
Daylily	*Hemerocallis fulva*	alkaline tolerant
Elderberry	*Sambucus* spp.	ornamental, wildlife
Hedge hyssop	*Gratiola virginiana*	aromatic, ornamental
High-bush blueberry	*Vaccinium corymbosum*	wildlife value, foliage
High-bush cranberry	*Viburnum trilobum*	wildlife value, foliage
Horsetail	*Equisetum* spp.	accumulates nutrients, opportunistic
Lotus	*Nelumbo lutea, N. nucifera*	ornamental
Ostrich fern	*Matteuccia pennsylvanica*	ornamental
Pickerel weed	*Pontederia cordata*	ornamental, opportunistic
Sedge	*Carex* spp.	
Spike rush	*Eleocharis* spp.	
Sweet flag	*Acorus calamus*	ornamental, opportunistic
Taro	*Colacasia esculenta*	cold intolerant
Umbrella palm	*Cyperus alterufolius*	cold intolerant
Water canna	*Thalia* spp.	ornamental
Yellow iris	*Iris pseudoacorus*	ornamental

the restored habitat. The know-how for building these wetlands has trickled down to home owners, coincidentally, at a time when growing bog and water plants is very popular. By creating a backyard wetland for graywater, we can meld the beauty of water gardens with ecological responsibility.

Water Brings the Garden to Life

If I were designing a landscape from scratch, I'd try to incorporate nearly every idea in this chapter; that way, the garden would be nearly self-watering, sparing the gardener most of the work and expense of irrigation. But the reasons go much deeper. Catching water from rooftops also spares our overtaxed municipal supplies and groundwater aquifers. Thinking of the soil as the best place to store water encourages deep mulching and other practices that, in addition to conserving water, create fertility and abundant soil life. This, in turn, keeps plants healthier. Using graywater allows us to harvest and use both water and fertility that would otherwise be wasted. And wetlands and ponds are beautiful and incredibly productive garden features that attract a marvelous range of wildlife.

The result is that, by using these methods, we get one step closer to creating a home ecosystem. Each rainfall is captured by rooftops and sent, not to a storm-drain's banishment, but to where it can be used, just as a tree harvests water with its leaves and directs it to its roots. In this garden, rain collects in cisterns and ponds, is slowed by gentle contours and swales, and then is stored in the soil to be slowly released and used, mimicking a natural watershed. Plants form a continuous cover, keeping the soil shaded and moist, cooling the air, offering a home to plentiful wildlife, and pleasing the eye and palate with their bounty. When the human inhabitants of this ecosystem use water in their home, bog plants thrive and grow, ponds and waterfalls gurgle, and the glint of flowing water reflects on the leaves overhead. Who would choose the mechanical chatter of sprinklers drenching a sterile lawn over this verdant paradise?

All the techniques in this chapter help us think of our gardens as living systems, humming with energy and busily shuttling nutrients to and fro. These living places are laced with a webwork of interdependent pathways and feedback loops, with plants, soil, insects, microbes, birds, and others all connected via water. Without water, there is no life.

In a conscious, ecological design, water becomes an integral part of a landscape: designed in, not added on. In a well-designed garden, perfectly watered plants—not parched, not drowned—are the natural state. Drought and flood are foreigners here. A healthy garden tunes its relationship with water toward harmony, using rich soil, ponds, a wetland, and the intelligence of the gardener to survive both drying and drenching.

CHAPTER 6

Plants for Many Uses

In most gardens, each plant is chosen for a single purpose. A silver maple tree in the front lawn, for example, has probably been selected for its stunning fall foliage, while a spreading white oak in back is for shade. Those Shasta daisies in the perennial bed? Their white blossoms accent the hues of nearby plantings, while the cylindrical juniper against the house was picked because it was slender enough to fit between two windows. This is how most conventional landscape designs work: a selection of isolated pieces placed together because they look nice. Nature never works this way. Natural plant groupings form through dynamic relationships among species and the environment—yet nature always manages to create landscapes that rival and often surpass the beauty of human designs. And natural landscapes work: They harvest water, build soil, minimize disease, reproduce themselves, have copious yields, support an enormous diversity of species, and function in dozens of other ways that we hardly recognize—all this while looking pretty.

This chapter lays the groundwork for understanding how plants actually work together. We'll explore the different functions that plants can have—the roles they play in the ecological theater—plus how they cooperate and aid each other and how they change and are changed by their environment. Then we'll see how to select plants that fill the needs of both the gardener and the landscape.

Of course, we want to live in an attractive land-scape. But if we can go beyond what plants look like and examine what they are doing, we can begin to create gardens that have the health, resilience, and beauty of natural ecosystems while yielding abundant gifts for people and for other species.

The Many Roles of a Tree

As I've said, when we look at a plant, we often see it as doing one thing. Take the hypothetical white oak I referred to above. Some home owner placed that tree in the backyard to create a shady spot. But even this single tree, isolated in a lawn, is giving a rich performance, not simply acting as a leafy umbrella. Let's watch this oak tree to see what it's doing.

It's dawn. The first rays of sunlight strike the canopy of the oak, but most of the energy in these beams is consumed in evaporating dew on the leaves. Only after the leaves are dry does the sunlight warm the air within the tree. Above the oak, however, the air has begun to heat, and a cloud of just-awakened insects swirls here. Below the canopy, it's still too chilly for the bugs to venture out. They roil in a narrow band within the thin layer of warm air above the tree. Together the sun and the oak have created insect habitat, and with it, a place for birds, who quickly swoop to feast on the swarm of bugs.

In the cool shade of this tree, snow remains late

into the spring, long after unprotected snow has melted. Soil near the tree stays moist, watering both the oak and nearby plantings and helping to keep a nearby creek flowing. (Early miners in the West frequently reported creeks disappearing once they'd cut nearby forests for mine timbers.)

Soon the sun warms the humid, night-chilled air within the tree. The entrapped air dries, its moisture escaping to the sky to help form clouds. This lost moisture is quickly replaced by the transpiring leaves, which pull water up from roots and exhale it through puffy-lipped pores in the leaves, called *stomata*. Groundwater, whether polluted or clean, is filtered by the tree and exits through the leaves as pure water. So trees are excellent water purifiers, and active ones. A full-grown tree can transpire 2,000 gallons of water on a hot, dry day. But this moisture doesn't just go away—it soon returns as rain. Up to half of the rainfall over forested land comes from the trees themselves. (The rest arrives as evaporation from bodies of water.) Cut the trees, and downwind rain disappears.

Sun striking the leaves ignites the engines of photosynthesis, and from these green factories oxygen streams into the air. But more benefits exist. To build sugars and the other carbon-based molecules that provide fuel and structure for the tree, the leaves remove carbon dioxide from the air. This is how trees help reduce the level of greenhouse gases.

As the leaves absorb sunlight and warm the air within the tree, this hot, moist air rises and mixes with the drier, cool air above. Convection currents begin to churn, and morning breezes begin. So trees help create cooling winds above them.

Closer to the ground, trees block the wind and make excellent windbreaks. Wind streaming past a warm building can carry off a lot of heat, so one or more trees on a house's windward side will substantially reduce heating bills.

The oak's upper branches toss in the morning breeze, while down below the air is still. The tree has captured the energetic movement of the air and converted it into its own motion. Where does this energy go? Some scientists think that captured wind energy is converted into the woody tissue of the tree, helping to build tough but flexible cells.

The morning breeze carries dust from the plowed fields of nearby farmland, which collects on the oak leaves. A single tree may have ten to thirty acres of leaf surface, all able to draw dust and pollutants from the air. Air passing through the tree is thus purified—and humidified as well. As air passes through the tree, it picks up moisture exhaled from the leaves, a light burden of pollen grains, a fine mist of small molecules produced by the tree, some bacteria, and fungal spores.

Some of those spores have landed below the tree, spawning several species of fungus that grow symbiotically amid the roots, secreting nutrients and antibiotics that feed and protect the tree. A vole has tunneled into the soft earth beneath the tree in search of some of this fungus. Later this vole will leave manure pellets near other oaks, inoculating them with the beneficial fungus—that is, if the owl who regularly frequents this oak doesn't snatch up the vole first.

This tree's ancestors provided Native Americans with flour made from acorns, though most contemporary people wouldn't consider this use. Now, blue jays and squirrels frolic in the oak, snatching acorns and hiding them around this and neighboring yards. Some of these acorns, forgotten, will sprout and grow into new trees. Meanwhile, the animals' diggings and droppings improve the soil. Birds probe the bark for insects, and yet other birds and insects depend on the inconspicuous flowers for food.

Later in the day, clouds (half of them created by trees, remember) begin to build. Rain droplets readily form around the bacteria, pollen, and other microscopic debris lofted from the oak. These small particles provide the nucleation sites that raindrops need to form. Thus, trees act as cloud seeders to bring rain.

As the rain falls, the droplets smack against the oak leaves and spread out into a fine film, coating the entire tree (all ten to thirty acres of leaves, plus the branches and trunk) before much rain strikes the ground. This thin film begins to evaporate even as the rain falls, further delaying any through-fall. Mosses and lichens on this old oak soak up even more of the rain. We've all seen dry patches beneath trees after a rain: A mature tree can absorb over a quarter inch of rain before any reaches the earth, even more if the air is dry and the rain is light.

The leaves and branches act as a funnel, channeling much of the rain to the trunk and toward the root zone of the tree. Soil close to the trunk can receive two to ten times as much rain as that in open ground. And the tree's shade slows evaporation, preserving this moisture.

As the rain continues, droplets leak off the leaves and splatter on the ground. Because this tree-drip has lost most of the energy it gathered during its fall from the clouds, little soil erodes beneath the tree. Leaf litter and roots also help hold the soil in place. Trees are supreme erosion-control systems.

The water falling from the leaves is very different from what fell from the sky. Its passage through the tree transmutes it into a rich soup, laden with the pollen, dust, bird and insect droppings, bacteria and fungi collected by the leaves, and many chemicals and nutrients secreted by the tree. This nutritious broth both nourishes the soil beneath the tree and inoculates the leaf litter and earth with soil-decomposing organisms. In this way, the tree collects and prepares its own fertilizer solution.

The rain eases toward sundown, and the sky clears. The upper leaves of the tree begin to chill as night falls, and cold air drains down from the canopy, cooling the trunk and soil. But this chill is countered by heat rising from the day-warmed earth, which warms the air under the tree. The leafy canopy holds this heat, preventing it from escaping to the night sky. So nighttime temperatures are warmer beneath the tree than in the open.

The leaves, however, radiate their heat to the sky and become quite cold, often much colder than the air. All these cold surfaces condense moisture from the air, and the resulting dew drips from the leaves and wets the ground, watering the tree and surrounding plants. Leaves can also gather moisture from fog: On foggy days the mist collects in such volume that droplets trickle steadily from the leaves. On arid but foggy coasts, tree-harvested precipitation can be triple the average rainfall. By harvesting dew and fog, trees can boost available moisture to far beyond what a rain gauge indicates.

As we gaze at this huge oak, remember that we're barely seeing half of it. At least 50 percent of this tree's mass is below the ground. The roots may extend tens of feet down, and horizontally can range far beyond the span of the tree's branches. We've already learned how these roots loosen and aerate soil, build humus as they grow and die, etch minerals free from rocks with mild acid secretions, and with sugary exudates provide food for hundreds or even thousands of species of soil organisms that live with them.

Roots gather nutrients from deep in the ground, and the tree uses them to fashion leaves. When these leaves drop in the fall, the carbon and minerals collected from the immense volume of air and earth around the tree are concentrated into a thin layer of mulch. Thus, the tree has harvested a diffuse dusting of useful nutrients, once sprinkled into thousands of cubic yards of soil and air, and packed them into a rich, dense agglutination of topsoil. In this way, trees mine and concentrate the sparse ores that surround them to build fertility and wealth. This wealth is shared with many other species, which root and burrow, feed and build, all nourished by the tree's gatherings.

But there is more: This tree's roots have threaded toward those of nearby oak trees and fused with them. A tree's roots, researchers have shown, can graft with those of its kind nearby, exchanging nutrients and even notifying each other of insect attack. Chemical signals released by an infested tree prompt its neighbors to secrete protective compounds that will repulse the soon-to-invade bugs. If an oak has grafted to its neighbors, does it remain an individual tree? Perhaps trees in a forest are more like branches from a single subterranean "tree" than a group of individuals. One of the largest organisms in the world is a forest of aspen trees that is in fact a single individual. Above ground, it looks like a grove of separate trees, but beneath the surface, they are all connected via their entwined roots. Each of these aspen trees is genetically identical.

The ways in which a single tree interacts with other species and its environment, then, are many. I've barely mentioned the swarms of insects that this oak supports: gall wasps and their hymenopteran relatives, beetles that tunnel into twigs and bark, and all manner of sucking and chewing bugs and their many insect predators. Then there are the birds that feed on these bugs. And we shouldn't forget the myriad nearby plants that benefit from the rain and nutrients collected by this tree.

Through this tree, we glimpse the benefits of ecological thinking. Instead of viewing a tree simply as something that looks nice or provides a single offering such as apples or shade, we can begin to see how deeply connected a tree is to its surroundings, both living and inanimate. A tree is a dynamic element embedded in and reacting to an equally dynamic landscape. It transforms wind and sunlight into a variety of daily and seasonally changing microclimates, harvests nutrients, builds soil, pumps and purifies air and water, creates and concentrates rain, and shelters and feeds wildlife and microbes. Add to all this the better-known benefits

for people: fruit or nuts, shade, climbing and other fun for kids, and the beauty of foliage, flowers, and form. We start to see how tightly enmeshed is a simple tree with all the other elements in a landscape. Now we can begin to imagine the richness of a landscape of many plant species, all interconnected by flows of energy and nutrients, nurturing and being nourished by the animals and microbes that flap and crawl and tunnel among them.

Each plant modifies its environment. These changes in turn support or inhibit what lies nearby, whether living or not. Recognizing that plants don't stand alone can radically affect the way we place the features of our gardens.

Multipurpose Plants

We've seen how one oak tree has many qualities. This oak isn't exceptional. All species are just as multitalented, albeit in different ways. What good does this knowledge do us? Granted that a plant can harvest rain, build soil, attract insects, and do umpteen other things, how do we use this in our yards?

When we understand a few of the roles that a particular plant can play, we can place that species so that it complements what is nearby. Any given plant can have a positive or negative relationship with nearby plants, animals, structures, and limitations of soil, light, wind, and water. Acknowledging and using these relationships can benefit the plant, its neighbors, the environment, and, not incidentally, the gardener.

We can choose plants according to function—and not just one function. These multiple and often overlapping uses of plants allow us to have some real fun in garden design. For example, if a yard contains a dry spot in poor soil under a shade tree, that's a perfect place for a drought- and shade-tolerant, nitrogen-fixing shrub such as indigo (*Indigofera tinctoria*), which incidentally is a good "green manure" plant and attracts insects to its lovely purple blossoms. Other nitrogen-fixing shrubs can take extreme cold, such as Siberian pea shrub (*Caragana arborescens*); there are drought-tolerant, nitrogen-fixing shrubs that revel in full sun and buzz with bees such as wild lilac (*Ceanothus* spp.) and Dyer's greenwood (*Genista tinctoria*).

Plant functions can be combined in just about every permutation you could ask for. Want an insect-attracting, deerproof, and edible flower with medicinal properties? Try bee balm (*Monarda didyma*). For a plant that yields salad greens and poultry forage and has roots that break up clay

soil and make a coffee substitute when roasted, use chicory (*Cichorium intybus*). How about a nitrogen-fixing shrub that is great for erosion control and hedges, with edible berries that are packed with vitamin C? That would be sea buckthorn (*Hippophae rhamnoides*). The combinations can even be whimsical. At a recent workshop, one student listed twenty medicinal plants that could also be used for toilet paper.

To see how multifunctional plants can be used in the landscape, let's look in some detail at a few species with many functions and some ways to take advantage of them. Then I'll describe some general roles that plants take on.

Table 6-1. Stacking (Bodily) Functions: Twenty plants having medicinal properties as well as leaves broad and soft enough to be used as toilet paper. Not to be taken as medical advice; for information only.

Common Name	Botanical Name	Medicinal Use
Alum root	*Heuchera glabra*	Antiseptic
Balsamroot	*Balsamorhiza sagittata*	Anti-rheumatic, diuretic
Baneberry	*Actea rubra*	Analgesic, emetic
Black cohosh	*Cimicifuga racemosa*	Birthing and menstrual aid
Burdock	*Arctium minus*	Detoxification
Coltsfoot	*Tussilago farfara*	Demulcent, expectorant
Comfrey	*Symphytum officinale*	Anodyne, hemostatic
Corn	*Zea mays*	Diuretic, hypoglycemic
Figwort	*Scrophularia californica*	Detoxification
Large-leaved avens	*Geum japonicum*	Astringent, poultice
Mallow	*Malva sylvestris*	Demulcent, laxative
Mullein	*Verbascum thapsus*	Demulcent, expectorant
Nasturtium	*Tropaeolum majus*	Antibiotic, expectorant
Skunk cabbage	*Lysichiton americanus*	Blood purifier, poultice
Thimbleberry	*Rubus parviflorus*	Tonic, stomachic
Trillium	*Trillium ovatum*	Birthing aid, ophthalmic
Usnea*	*Usnea* spp.	Antiviral, antibacterial
Vanilla leaf	*Achlys triphylla*	Emetic
Western coltsfoot	*Petasites palmatus*	Pectoral, salve
Yellow dock	*Rumex crispus*	Laxative, poultice

*Usnea is a lichen, not a plant, but otherwise satisfies the criteria.
List compiled by Tricia King.

Maximilian Sunflower

Just south of our Oakland house, we planted a mixed border filled with shrubs, herbs, and flowers. Below this, the ground angles downhill. On this slope, we placed a hedge of Maximilian sunflower (*Helianthus maximilianii*). Maximilians are one of the few perennial—not annual—sunflowers, which is a benefit right there because they don't need replanting every year. They grow five to seven feet tall and sport four-inch yellow blooms in the late fall, giving a fine flash of color when most everything else is spent. A big plus is that deer don't eat them—in fact, the stems are covered with a coarse fuzz that discourages deer from poking through them. The plants aren't invasive, but they grow thickly, forming a superb deer barrier that deters the hungry beasts from strolling up the hill to munch on the mixed border. In winter, I trimmed the stalks to about four feet high, and the deer really hated the stiff spikes that remain. The bare stems, a potential eyesore, were downhill and thus hidden from our view. But the trimmings, especially when I cut them to the ground in early spring, were copious and created plenty of biomass for mulch or compost.

The benefits continue. Maximilians, a relative of Jerusalem artichokes, have edible shoots that are delicious raw or cooked. The seeds are attractive to birds (they also yield a useful oil, but I confess I'm not following up on this aspect). They are very hardy, to −30 degrees Fahrenheit. The plant is very drought tolerant. It can handle many soil types, all the better because on my land it was growing in some very nasty red clay.

Below the Maxies sprawled a grassy savanna that I converted to a food forest (more about that in a later chapter). Here, the sunflowers' thick growth stanches the tide of grass that would love to spread uphill into the mixed border.

So here's a plant that I placed in this particular spot primarily to create a deer barrier but that is

Maximilian sunflower (*Helianthus maximilianii*).

also quite pretty and blooms late, has edible parts, attracts birds, generates mulch, stops grass invasion, and is very low maintenance. It's an excellent multifunctional plant.

Goumi

I'll offer a second many-purpose species. Goumi (*Elaeagnus multiflora*) is a nonopportunistic relative of Russian olive that is hardy to −20 degrees Fahrenheit. It was bred in Asia to yield tasty berries. Red, three-quarter-inch fruits thickly festoon this six-foot-tall shrub in late summer and are good eaten out-of-hand, but they are more often made into jams, sauces, and pies. The berries are very high in vitamin C, contain compounds that help break down fats in the blood, and are reputed to reduce cholesterol levels. Birds love the berries, too. Where I lived, wild turkeys gathered to feast on goumi berries and those of other *Elaeagnus* shrubs.

Once established, goumi is very drought tolerant, so it's a good wildlife shrub for the far, unwatered margins of the yard. Deer do a little nibbling of the leaves and young growth, but I've never seen

Goumi *(Elaeagnus multiflora)*.

them strip and annihilate an entire shrub as they do with so many other woody plants.

Spring finds goumi vibrant with hundreds of fragrant, cream-colored flowers that are adored by bees and other pollinators. The leaves of goumi are attractive, too. Gray-green on top and silver below, in a breeze they shimmer and sparkle as the light catches the bright undersides.

One heavyweight benefit of goumi for the ecological garden is that it fixes nitrogen. *Elaeagnus* species bear root nodules that harbor a nitrogen-producing filamentous fungi called *Frankia*, making these shrubs one of the few N-fixers outside the pea family. Goumi's gift of nitrogen boosts the growth of neighboring plants; thus, many gardeners interplant this or other N-fixers among plants that don't fix nitrogen. Nitrogen-fixing shrubs also help restore soil and, interspersed in a young landscape, can speed the repair of battered land. The fast-growing greenery can be slashed back heavily to yield mulch.

Ecological landscapers often go heavy on N-fixers such as goumi in the early phases of a design to build fertility and create a supportive environment for other plantings. Later, as the landscape matures and these pioneer qualities are less needed, differ-ent shrubs can be gradually substituted for many of the N-fixers.

Thus, in goumi we have a nitrogen-fixing perennial that attracts insects and birds, offers healthful food, needs little care, nurtures young landscapes, generates plenty of mulch or compost, and bears lovely foliage, flowers, and fruit. That's a multifaceted plant.

Maypop

Moving from shrubs to a different growth form, let me offer a vining passionflower, maypop *(Passiflora incarnata)*, as our next many-talented species. This fast-growing climber is native to the southeast United States and is hardy to 0 degrees Fahrenheit. Like all passionflowers, maypop offers an exquisite and exotic-looking blossom; this one has a lemony fragrance. The flowers attract bees, butterflies, and admiring humans and develop into an edible fruit about the size of a hen's egg that tastes a little like apricot. (You will notice that food forms a common

Maypop *(Passiflora incarnata)*.

theme through these selections; though not essential, edibility considerably raises my esteem for a plant.) The fruit can also be used for jam and juice. Even the young leafy shoots are edible and can be chopped raw into a salad or cooked as a green.

Vining deciduous plants fill an important niche. Trellised on the sunny side of a house or patio, or over a greenhouse, they leaf out in early summer just as the heat comes on. This creates much-treasured shade, keeping a house cool or allowing an unbearably hot space to become usable in summer. Then, when the warm weather ends, the leaves drop, and sunlight can stream in again. Vines such as maypop can also climb up bare tree trunks or into nonflowering shrubs to provide color with their blossoms.

Maypop won't shade out other shrubs, as it leafs out late in the spring, giving other plants a chance to get started. In climates with heavy winter freezes, maypop dies back to its roots. But it's a vigorous grower, leaping from eighteen-inch sprouts in June to as much as twenty-five feet of growth by fall. Spreading can be a problem: The roots can send up new plants fifteen feet away, though usually only a few of them each year.

Maypop, then, attracts insects and birds, has edible parts, and is ideal for trellising, creating a seasonal shady spot that's bright with exotic blooms and offering tasty fruit and greens.

Comfrey

A quintessential permaculture plant, comfrey (*Symphytum officinale*) offers a range of uses that is tough to match. Its pink and purple blossoms are certain bait for bees and other beneficial insects, which buzz deep into the tubular flowers in search of pollen and nectar. Used traditionally for wound healing, comfrey was once called knitbone, and research confirms that a root extract speeds recovery from bone injuries. The plant manufactures a substance called allantoin, which promotes wound healing and moisturizes the skin. Poultices of

Comfrey *(Symphytum officinale)*.

mashed leaves have long been used to heal cuts and scrapes.

Comfrey is also a stellar nutrient accumulator, reaching deep into the soil to pull potassium, calcium, and magnesium into its roots and leaves. The spongy aboveground parts can then be composted or mulched to draw these nutrients into the home ecosystem's cycles. Speaking of mulch, it's a vigorous biomass producer, with soft, lush leaves and stems that can be slashed down two to four times each growing season and either composted in place or shuttled to where the fertility and cover are needed. Or it can be grown as a living mulch. Ecological orchardists often plant a ring of comfrey around a fruit tree and periodically practice "chop and drop" mulching, which triggers the plant to regrow, converting yet more nutrients from the earth into biomass and then topsoil.

Comfrey's fat vigorous taproots push far into the soil and can break up hardpans and heavy clays. Chopping off the top-growth causes some root dieback, leaving the roots' organic matter deep in the soil to decompose and nourish the underground microherds.

It is the roots that have struck fear of this wonderful plant into a few hearts. Comfrey does not usually set seed—many varieties are sterile—but it can grow exuberantly from root divisions. A chunk the size of one finger joint is enough to found a new plant, so if a gardener digs or tills into the root system, the plant will spread wherever cuttings land. Power-tilling recklessly through a single large plant is enough to sow comfrey successfully and persistently across a surprising expanse of garden. Thus one caveat about comfrey: Don't dig or till close to it. Following that simple advice will spare any trouble. I had comfrey plants growing in a garden for over a decade, cultivating near them occasionally—but not too near—and they did not spread. When I wanted to eliminate a plant, sheet mulch did the job. There is, however, one other way besides tilling that can cause comfrey to migrate around a yard. In a friend's garden, comfrey would periodically emerge in new spots even though she was careful not to dig near the established plants. Curious enough to investigate, she dug up a tiny comfrey shoot that had just appeared in virgin territory. Beneath it was a gopher den, holding a stash of sprouting comfrey roots and carrots laid out in a neat row—the gopher's winter larder. But, wise to comfrey's many uses, my friend felt this rodent-propelled propagation was a modest price to pay for the plant's favors.

Mashua

Another plant with useful parts both above and below ground, mashua (*Tropaeolum tuberosum*) is an edible nasturtium. It's common knowledge that nasturtium flowers are tasty, but this species also offers edible tubers. Finger-shaped and -sized and ranging in color from white to yellow and occasionally purple, the raw tubers have a radish-like

pepperiness that disappears on cooking. Baked or roasted, the tubers become sweet and delicious. The leaves are also edible, having a watercress-like sharpness. Mashua was an Inca staple, grown high in the Andes, and thus can take some frost. But like many tubers grown in cold regions, cool winter storage indoors is best. Smaller than the most famous Inca tuber, the potato, mashua makes up for diminutive size by yielding copiously: A harvest of 30,000 pounds per acre is common, and twice as much is possible. One healthy plant can provide eight pounds of tubers, each one, incidentally, packed with vitamin C.

The tubers have a reputation for being a male antiaphrodisiac and were supposedly fed to Inca troops "that they should forget their wives," writes the Jesuit priest Bernabe Cobo. Studies on rats show that the effect is real, but it takes a steady, heavy diet of mashua—what you'd expect from Army chow—to measurably suppress testosterone

Mashua *(Tropaeolum tuberosum)*.

levels. The occasional portion isn't apt to deflate anyone's ardor.

More usefully, mashua contains compounds that repel nematodes, fungal diseases, and some harmful insects. Interplanting it with other crops such as potatoes, corn, and beans can control pests of those plants. Its cream to orange flowers are also edible, and although not the stellar insect attractor that umbel and composite flowers are, they offer nectar and pollen to bees and other beneficial insects that will regularly visit. Unlike the ground-sprawling nasturtiums more familiar to us, mashua is a vine, trellising easily up a six-foot fence; thus it makes a fast-growing screen to block unpleasant views or hot sun.

In mashua, then, we have a plant whose roots, leaves, and flowers are edible and nutritious; one that is able to protect other plants from all manner of pests, suitable for trellises and fences, and very pretty; and one that offers a unique expansion to our diet.

Bamboo

Bamboo is the queen of the useful plants—whole books have been written in loving description of its many roles. More than 1,580 human uses for bamboo have been found, including paper, flooring, poles, food, baskets, bridges, fans, fences, hats, acupuncture needles, and xylophones. Thomas Edison used bamboo for the filament of his first successful light bulb.

Yet bamboo, so important in Asia that it is often called "the brother," gets a bad rap in this culture. Many temperate varieties are "running" (or *monopodial*) bamboos, which if placed in the wrong spot will seemingly sprint across the ground via fast-growing rhizomes. The most common question asked about bamboo seems to be, "But won't it take over?"

In my mind, and in that of many bamboo-loving *bambuseros*, the benefits of the plant vastly outweigh

Black bamboo *(Phyllostyachys nigra)*, one of hundreds of useful bamboo species.

its drawbacks, which are relatively easy to overcome. Here are some of bamboo's uses in a typical yard: Birds build nests from the leaves and twigs, and bamboo stands attract bush tits, chickadees, song sparrows, and many others to warble from within the dense, rustling foliage. The canes have endless uses around the home, whether for trellis uprights and overhead lattice, an eternal supply of garden stakes, temporary or permanent fences, or a Huck Finn–style fishing pole for the kids. For those with tool savvy, bamboo poles can be transformed into furniture, flutes, wind chimes, mats, handmade paper, and—literally—a thousand other items.

Bamboo is deerproof, so suburban and rural gardeners can add it to the "outside-the-fence" plant list. The roots, like those of other grasses, don't expand in girth, thus it can be planted over septic drain fields without fear of clogging the pipes. On steep slopes it's a natural for erosion control because its rhizomatous roots interlace into a tough webwork. Bamboo has been used for restoration work, healing clearcuts and other abused lands (in Vietnam bamboo has thrown a green bandage over landscapes defoliated by Agent Orange). Bamboos vary in hardiness, from tropics-only species to those that will survive below-zero temperatures.

It's a beautiful, restful plant. Few sights and sounds are as soothing after a wearying workday as a shady, sussurating grove of bamboo, enfolding and quieting a space within a forest of soaring green canes that arch overhead. Its leaves remain throughout the year, so it forms a permanent haven and screen. A bamboo grove, however small, is a meditative place that quiets the outside world.

With dozens of species to choose from, a home owner can select varieties ranging from knee high to forty or fifty feet tall and thicknesses from pencil size to four-inch timber bamboo. The shapes and colors vary too, with straight, curved, or zigzag stems; green, golden, striped, bluish, or black canes; and solid, variegated, or striped leaves.

Bamboo is also a source of food. The young white shoots of most varieties are edible and delicious when steamed or sautéed. In fact, the best way to control bamboo's potentially rampant growth is to eat any shoots that venture outside the chosen bamboo zone. Now that's stacking functions!

Here are a few other tips for control: Remember to think like bamboo. It needs water to thrive, and the rhizomes run most furiously in loose soil. Thus, in the arid West, bamboo can be thwarted by simply not watering outside the desired growth area. In wetter climates, plant bamboo next to a pond, compacted path, or gravel driveway. A sidewalk or paved driveway might stop the plant, but the rhizomes of some energetic varieties relish the lack of competing roots and zip under the pavement, bursting joyously into daylight on the other side. For the truly bamboo-fearful, nonspreading clumping bamboos—called *sympodial*, as opposed to running, or *monopodial*, bamboos—are available.

For physical containment, a specific product

called bamboo barrier can be bought. Less expensive used or new fiberglass roofing sheets (metal won't last more than a few years) can be sunk twenty inches deep in the ground, sloping slightly outward to deflect rhizomes upward. A similar blockade of concrete can be created. Some growers dig out a bed about a foot deep, line and edge it with a pond liner, and fill it with soil.

But the very best way to contain bamboo is to use it. It is a plant that seems to cherish an active relationship with people, often languishing without human companions. So eat any errant shoots, thin out and use the poles when they are three or four years old, and perhaps with some creativity you can add to the long list of known uses for bamboo.

These are just a few examples of multifunctional plants and the attitude toward them that can inspire creative use. In the appendix, I've listed many others along with their roles, but the list is far from exhaustive. Nearly every plant is multifunctional, and only the gardener's imagination sets limits on how many ways a plant can be used. The key is to remember that plants don't merely supply products, such as fruit and flowers. More importantly, plants are busily performing processes such as soil building, water harvesting, pest suppression, and insect attraction. Viewing plants as dynamic, not static, requires a subtle shift in thinking—after all, plants just seem to sit there most of the time. But with experience, we can learn to see plants as active participants in garden ecology. In the next section we'll examine some of the roles plants play.

The Roles of Plants in the Ecological Theater

We'll never know all the roles that plants play. We can see the obvious activities, such as shedding leaves and casting shade. And with some observation we can understand that plants build soil and nurture insects. But many of the jobs that plants perform are hidden from our eyes: pulling nutrients from deep in the earth and sharing them with microbes or even with other plants via entwined and connected roots or pumping nitrogen into the soil to prepare barren ground for colonization. I'm sure there are other quiet relations among plants and the rest of the world that we don't even glimpse. Thus, any list of plant's roles must be incomplete, as we mere humans aren't equipped to detect the subtle activities of the green world. I'll attempt to describe the roles plants play that are important for the ecological garden, knowing that they surely have many less detectable vocations as well.

Mulch Makers

Plants build soil in many ways, and one is by the continual rain of leaves, flowers, twigs, and bark that patters on the earth as the seasons turn. All this debris quickly composts into rich humus. Every plant drops litter, but some are truly prodigious mulch makers, and it is these that we especially welcome when the soil is young or has been abused. Mulching is simply composting in place, but it brings other benefits, such as moisture retention, soil cooling, and habitat creation.

Soft-leafed plants make mulch the fastest. These include artichoke and its relative cardoon, rhubarb, comfrey, Jerusalem artichoke, ferns, reeds, and nasturtium. Many varieties used for "green manure" cover crops can be used for mulch, such as the clovers (especially sweet clover, which grows five feet tall), vetches, many grasses and grains (such as oats, wheat, and barley), mustard, crotolaria, and buckwheat. These plants and many others can be slashed or mowed down, often several times a season, and used as mulch wherever needed. Mulch plants should be cut before they go to seed unless you want mulch growing in your beds. Some gardeners interplant mulch makers among their crops and simply chop-and-drop the whole plant to deliver its benefits right in place. If the mulch looks too messy, it can be tucked under a layer of straw or wood shavings.

Woody plants can also make great mulch. Many shrubs, especially nitrogen fixers such as alder, *Elaeagnus*, Scotch broom, and ceanothus, break down very quickly. Trimmings from shrubs and trees that have small branches (pencil-thick or thinner) are fine for mulch. There's no need to send them through a chipper as long as they're in contact with the soil, which greatly speeds rotting. A tall pile of brush won't break down nearly as fast as some stomped-down branches that get ground contact. Again, if aesthetics are a factor, brush can be mulched out of sight or under a more attractive top layer.

Then there are living mulches. A soft undercover of greenery offers many of the same benefits as dry mulch, plus those of living plants (flowers, habitat, and so on). Living mulches include dwarf yarrow, thrift, *Ajuga*, wild strawberry, stonecrop, yerba buena, and white clover.

Nutrient Accumulators

Certain species draw specific nutrients from deep in the soil and concentrate them in their leaves. The long taproots of these plants dredge up important nutrients such as potassium, magnesium, calcium, sulfur, and others. As these plants lose their foliage in fall, the nutrients build up in the topsoil. Such plants are obvious candidates for the ecological garden because they keep nutrients cycling within the yard and reduce the need for purchased fertilizers.

Nutrient accumulators include yarrow, chamomile, fennel, lamb's quarters, chicory, dandelion, and plantain. Table 6-2 lists many others.

A warning: Many of the species that accumulate metals such as copper and zinc also pick up lead and in fact are used to clean up contaminated sites. If soil contains lead, such as along the foundation of old houses where lead-based paint may have weathered, these plants can concentrate the metal in their leaves. On one hand, metal-accumulator

Table 6-2. Dynamic Nutrient Accumulators													
Common Name	**Botanical Name**	**Nutrient Accumulated**											
		N	**P**	**K**	**Ca**	**S**	**Mg**	**Mn**	**Fe**	**Cu**	**Co**	**Zn**	**Si**
Alfalfa	*Medicago sativa*	x							x				
Apple	*Malus* spp.			x									
Beech	*Fagus* spp.			x									
Alyssum	*Alyssum murale*				x			x				x	
Bentgrass	*Agrostis* spp.					x		x		x		x	
Birch	*Betula* spp.		x										
Borage	*Borago officinalis*			x									x
Bracken, eastern	*Pteridium aquifolium*		x	x				x	x	x	x	x	
Buckwheat	*Fagopyrum esculentums*		x	x									
Burdock	*Arctium minus*							x					
Caraway	*Carum carvi*		x										
Carrot leaves	*Daucus carota*			x			x						
Cattail	*Typha latifolia*	x											
Chamomile, corn	*Anthemis arvensis*			x	x								
Chamomile, German	*Chamomilla recutita*		x	x	x								
Chickweed	*Stellaria media*		x	x				x					
Chicory	*Cichorium intybus*			x	x								
Chives	*Allium schoenoprasum*			x	x								
Cleavers	*Galium aparine*				x								
Clovers	*Trifolium* spp.	x	x										
Clover, hop	*Medicago lupulina*	x	x										
Coltsfoot	*Tussilago farfara*			x	x	x	x		x	x			
Comfrey	*Symphytum officinale*	x		x	x		x		x				x
Creosote bush	*Larrea tridentata*									x			
Dandelion	*Taraxacum vulgare*			x	x	x			x	x			x
Dock, broad leaved	*Rumex obtusifolias*			x	x	x			x				
Dogwood, flowering	*Cornus florida*			x	x	x							
Duckweed	*Lemna minor*	x								x		x	
Dulse	*Palmaria palmata*				x		x		x				
Fat hen	*Atriplex hastata*			x					x				
Fennel	*Foeniculum vulgare*	x	x										
Fescue, red	*Festuca rubra*									x		x	
Flax	*Linum usitatissimum*			x				x	x				
Garlic	*Allium sativum*					x		x					
Geranium, scented	*Pelargonium* spp.							x	x	x	x	x	
Groundsel	*Senecio vulgaris*								x				

Table 6-2. Dynamic Nutrient Accumulators (continued)													
Common Name	**Botanical Name**	**Nutrient Accumulated**											
		N	P	K	Ca	S	Mg	Mn	Fe	Cu	Co	Zn	Si
Hickory, shagbark	*Carya ovata*		x	x	x								
Horsetails	*Equisetum* spp.			x	x		x		x		x		x
Kelp	(Several genera)	x			x		x		x				
Lamb's quarters	*Chenopodium album*	x	x	x	x			x					
Lemon balm	*Melissa officinalis*		x										
Licorice	*Glycyrrhiza* spp.	x	x										
Locust, black	*Robinia pseudoacacia*	x		x	x								
Lupine	*Lupinus* spp.	x	x										
Maples	*Acer* spp.												
Marigold	*Tagetes* spp.		x										
Meadow sweet	*Astilbe* spp.		x		x	x	x		x				
Mosquitofern, Pacific	*Azolla filiculoides*							x		x			
Mullein, common	*Verbascum* spp.			x		x	x		x				
Mustards	*Brassica* spp.		x		x	x		x		x		x	
Nettles, stinging	*Urtica urens*	x		x	x	x			x	x			
Oak, bark	*Quercus* spp.			x									
Parsley	*Petroselinum crispum*			x	x		x		x				
Pennycress, alpine	*Thlaspi caerulescens*									x		x	
Peppermint	*Mentha piperita*			x			x						
Pigweed, red root	*Amaranthus retroflexus.*		x	x	x				x				
Plantains	*Plantago* spp.			x	x	x	x	x					x
Primrose	*Oenothera biennis*	x											
Purslane	*Portulaca oleracea*			x			x	x					
Rapeseed	*Brassica napus*		x		x	x		x		x		x	
Salad burnet	*Poterium sanguisorba*				x	x	x		x				
Savory	*Satureja* spp.			x									
Scarlet Pimpernel	*Anagallis arvensis*						x						
Shepherd's purse	*Capsella bursa-pastoris*			x	x								
Silverweed	*Potentilla anserina*			x	x					x			
Skunk cabbage	*Navarretia squanosa*						x						
Sorrel, sheep	*Rumex acetosella*		x		x								
Sow thistle	*Sonchus arvensis*			x			x			x			
Sunflower	*Helianthus annuus*			x				x		x		x	
Spurges	*Euphorbia* spp.												
Strawberry	*Fragaria* spp.									x			
Tansy	*Tanacetum vulgare*			x									

(continues)

Table 6-2. Dynamic Nutrient Accumulators (continued)														
Common Name	Botanical Name	Nutrient Accumulated												
		N	P	K	Ca	S	Mg	Mn	Fe	Cu	Co	Zn	Si
Thistle, Canada	*Cirsium arvense*								x				
Thistle, creeping	*Sonchus arvensis*		x	x					x				
Thistle, nodding	*Carduus nutans*								x				
Thistle, Russian	*Salsola pestifer*								x				
Toadflax	*Linaria vulgaris*				x		x		x				
Tobacco, stems/stalk	*Nicotiana* spp.	x											
Valerian	*Valeriana officinalis*												x
Vetches	*Vicia* spp.	x	x	x						x	x		
Walnut	*Juglans* spp.		x	x	x								
Watercress	*Nasturtium officinale*		x	x	x	x	x		x				
Willow	*Salix* spp.						x					x	
Yarrow	*Achillea millefolium*	x	x	x						x			

Sources: Cocannouer, Joseph. *Weeds: Guardians of the Soil*. Devin-Adair, 1976. Famulari, Stevie. University of New Mexico. Unpublished. Jacke, David and Eric Toensmeir. *Edible Forest Gardens*. Chelsea Green, 2005. Kourik, Robert. *Designing and Maintaining Your Edible Landscape—Naturally*. Metamorphic, 1984. Pfeiffer, Ehrenfried. *Weeds and What They Tell*, Biodynamic Farming and Gardening, 1970.

plants might remove lead from your soil. But you don't want to eat lead-laden leaves or put them into a compost pile. If your soil contains toxic metal, pay attention to where leaves and stems from these plants end up.

You'll note that many of these plants are considered weeds. In nature's more tolerant scheme, most weeds make their living as pioneer species: tough, sun dependent, fast growing, and short lived. These early colonists invade bare or depleted soils, where one of their roles is to accumulate nutrients in their roots and leaves. Each fall, these plants die and rot, pumping a fat load of minerals into the soil. The enriched earth is then ready for the next successionary phase of less ephemeral, more fastidious plants, such as perennial herbs, shrubs, and trees.

Ecological gardeners turn the features of pioneer plants to their advantage, letting them draw nutrients from deep in the earth to create fertile, balanced soil. As the soil improves, nutrients will begin to recycle from leaf to soil and back again.

No longer will deep roots be required to tug scarce nutrients from the depths. The accumulator plants will then be redundant and will begin a natural decline that the gardener can accelerate by pulling them up and replacing them with other varieties.

Not incidentally, many of these species are also considered medicinal. A plant coursing with minerals stands a good chance of being healthy food, too.

Nitrogen Fixers

We have met this third group of soil-building plants before. These plants harbor bacteria or fungi among their roots that extract nitrogen from the air and convert it to plant-available form. Though arguments still rage about how and when these plants deliver their nitrogenous bounty to the soil, there is no doubt of their benefit. Some people believe that nitrogen fixers must die to release their nutrients, but both research and my own experience show that live N-fixers are at least as growth boosting as dead ones.

Table 6-3. Nitrogen Fixers					
Common Name	Botanical Name	Comments	Common Name	Botanical Name	Comments
Acacia	*Acacia* spp.		Genista	*Genista* spp.	
Alder	*Alnus* spp.		Golden-chain tree	*Laburnum anagyroides*	Flowers toxic
Alfalfa	*Medicago sativa*		Goumi	*Elaeagnus multiflora*	Tolerates air pollution
Amur Maackia	*Maackia amurensis*		Groundnut	*Apios* spp.	
Autumn olive	*Elaeagnus umbellata*		Hog peanut	*Amphicarpa bracteata*	
Barrel medic	*Medicago truncatula*		Kentucky coffee tree	*Gymnocladus dioica*	
Bayberry	*Myrica pensylvanica*		Licorice	*Glycyrrhiza*	
Bean	*Phaseolus* spp.		Lupine	*Lupinus* spp.	
Bird's foot trefoil	*Lotus corniculatus*		Mesquite	*Prosopis glandulosa*	
Black Locust	*Robinia pseudoacacia*		Milkvetch	*Astragalus* spp.	
Bladder senna	*Colutea arborescens*		Mountain avens	*Dryas octapetala*	
Blue false indigo	*Baptisia australis*		Mountain mahogany	*Cercocarpus montanus*	
Broom	*Cytisus* spp.		Pencil flower	*Stylosanthes biflora*	
Buffaloberry	*Shepherdia argentea*	Drought resistant	Prairie turnip	*Psoralea esculenta*	
Bush clover	*Lespedeza thunbergii*		Russian olive	*Elaeagnus angustifolia*	
Butterfly pea	*Clitoria mariana*		Sea buckthorn	*Hippophae rhamnoides*	
Carolina bush pea	*Thermopsis villosa*		Sesbania	*Sesbania exaltata*	
Cattail	*Typha latifolia*		Siberian pea shrub	*Caragana arborescens*	
Chamomile	*Chamaemelum nobile*		Silk tree or mimosa	*Albizzia julibrisin*	
Chicory	*Cichorium intybus*		Silverberry	*Elaeagnus commutata*	
Chinese artichoke	*Stachys affinis*		Spanish broom	*Spartium junceum*	
Chives	*Allium schoenoprasum*		Sunn hemp	*Crotolaria juncea*	
Clover	*Trifolium* spp.		Sweet gale	*Myrica gale*	
Collards	*Brassica oleracea viridis*		Sweet pea	*Lathyrus* spp.	
Columbine	*Aquilegia vulgaris*		Sweet vetch	*Hedysarum boreale*	
Comfrey	*Symphytum officinale*		Sweetfern	*Comptonia peregrina*	
Common milkweed	*Asclepias cornuti*		Trefoil	*Desmodium* spp.	
Cowpea	*Vigna unguiculata*		Vetch	*Vicia* spp.	
Elaeagnus	*Elaeagnus × ebbingei*		Wax Myrtle	*Myrica cerifrea*	
False indigo	*Amorpha fruticosa*		Wild Bean	*Strophistyles umbellata*	
Fava Bean	*Vicia faba*		Wild lilac	*Ceanothus* spp.	
			Wisteria	*Wisteria* spp.	

Most plants in the pea or bean family (the *Fabaceae*, more commonly referred to as legumes) fix nitrogen, as do ceanothus, mountain mahogany, buffaloberry, and *Elaeagnus* species such as goumi and autumn and Russian olive. Nitrogen fixers come in all sizes, from ground covers such as clover, to shrubs, to trees such as black locust, alder, and acacia. These fast-growing plants can be slashed down or trimmed to provide a rich stock for mulch or compost. Table 6-3 lists many that are suitable for the home landscape.

Soil Fumigants and Pest Repellents

Some plants secrete compounds that repel a few specific pests that live either in the soil or just above it. Examples include nasturtium, false indigo, elderberry, and certain marigolds. Nasturtiums seem to deter whitefly, though the data are a bit ambiguous. The wild marigold, *Tagetes minuta*, repels soil nematodes, although cultivated varieties, such as *T. patula* and *T. erecta*, are less effective. The rule seems to be: The more highly bred and less odoriferous the marigold, the less effective it is as a pest deterrent. Some hybrid marigolds, in fact, stunt the growth of nearby plants and attract pests. Pest-repellent plants are not well researched, and I'd advise planting them in limited quantities.

Insectary Plants

Plants that attract beneficial insects are legion: Almost any pollen- or nectar-producing flower will lure our six-legged friends. Beneficial insects fall into two main groups: pollinators, needed for fruit and seed set; and predators, which gobble up the bugs that munch our plants. These insects will be covered in more detail in Chapter 7. A few choice insectary plants are yarrow, buckwheat, lavender, golden marguerite, bee balm, and many clovers. Nearly all of the celery or carrot family (the *Apiaceae*), which includes fennel, Queen Anne's lace, dill, and coriander, are excellent insectary plants. Other plant families that are loaded with insect-attracting species include the onion or lily family (the *Lilaceae*), the sunflower or composite family (the *Asteraceae*), and especially the mint family (the *Lamaceae*). Not only will insectary plants improve your garden's health, but the flash and shimmer of multicolored buzzers and flutterers will both delight the eye and attract many varieties of birds to eat them, further increasing your yard's biodiversity. Chapter 7 contains a special section on insectary plants.

Fortress Plants

I use the term *fortress plants* for species that prevent invasive plants from swarming into more delicate areas of the garden. They work by producing a wall of thick growth above and below ground that shades out and physically restrains invaders. They'll stop the rampages of grass, weed seeds, creeping vines such as bindweed, and other unwanted marauders. Some, like the above-mentioned Maximilian sunflower, secrete mildly toxic compounds that inhibit seed germination and root growth. Other fortress plants include comfrey, Jerusalem artichoke, lemongrass, red-hot poker, and any other thickly growing perennial with a dense root system.

Spike Roots

When a soil is compacted or clayey, plants offer excellent tools to restore tilth and fluffiness. Many species have deep, soil-busting taproots that are perfect for the job. These include daikon (Japanese radish), chicory, comfrey, artichoke, and dandelion. Others, such as mustard, rapeseed, and alfalfa, don't have a single taproot but instead thrust a massive, fibrous root system deep into the earth to accomplish the same soil loosening. You can use these plants in either of two strategies: Sow them into a future orchard or garden to work a year or two before the final planting, or intercrop them among the beds or under trees to continually break up the soil. An added bonus of spike roots is that most of these species will add organic matter as their giant root systems decay. After they've done their work, these plants can be cut down, shaded out by taller plants, or sheet-mulched.

Wildlife Nurturers

In the late 1970s, gardeners began to discover the joys of attracting wildlife to their yards, not only via bird feeders and salt licks but by choosing plants that sheltered and fed the animals they loved. If you choose appropriate plants, rare birds, mammals, and butterflies—not deer and raccoons—will appear. A few of my favorite wildlife plants include dogwood, elderberry, chokeberry, blueberry, native roses, hawthorn, ceanothus, and various wild cherries. Chapter 7 contains a table listing more. With so many plants to choose from, a wildlife zone need not be a brushy tangle but can be attractive as well as functional.

Shelterbelters

Plants can create effective windbreaks and shelterbelts to modify harsh winds, keep out unwanted browsers such as deer, screen an unwanted view, or create U-shaped suntraps for warmth. Shelterbelt species are limited only by the designer's imagination, as these hedges can be delightfully multi-functional. For a large windbreak, why not mix together some junipers and hollies for year-round protection, fruiting trees and shrubs for food, nitrogen fixers such as black locust and laburnum—which incidentally are beloved by bees—and some wildlife species? As a rule of thumb, windbreaks should be constructed to allow 40 to 70 percent of the wind to pass through them (if they are denser, they create turbulence downwind). They will protect an area two to five times as long as the windbreak is high. A hedge of shorter plants can shelter garden beds, but remember that these, too, can be multifunctional. I've used Maximilian sunflowers and Jerusalem artichokes around my garden, and I know of other gardens protected by bamboo, basketry willows, wildlife shrubs, or berry bushes.

Deciduous plants can also be used for their seasonal shade. Trellised on the south or west side of a building, over a deck, or even over a roof, their shade will drop the temperature substantially, yet let in sunlight in bare-branched winter.

garden beds

A U-shaped sun-trap. Open to the sunny south side, but closed to winds by a semicircle of plants, the microclimate of this suntrap is warm and protected, and suitable for tender plants. Evergreens can be planted on the north side as a year-round windbreak.

A tangle of thorny shrubs can thwart plant-munching deer (or discourage trespassers). I've redirected deer with a hedge of Osage orange, hawthorn, native roses, Manchurian plum, gooseberries, and a few nonthorny wildlife species mixed in for filler. Once these are established, the deer can nibble on the outside to their heart's content, but they can't get through.

In this necessarily incomplete listing of plant functions, I've omitted purely human-oriented uses such as edible species, flowers for cutting, timber trees, and craft material. My focus is on the ecological role that plants can play, and I'll leave it to the clever gardener to note the many uses that these plants also have for people. A well-designed ecological landscape will benefit all of nature, humans included. When a garden supports pollinators, builds soil, discourages pests, and moderates climatic extremes, its gifts for people will also be marvelously abundant, flowing from the landscape almost as a by-product. Those spike-rooted artichokes (whose leaves make great mulch) just happen to be edible; that group of wildlife shrubs yields berries for a tangy jelly (and incidentally hides the neighbor's house); the bamboo windscreen, in addition to sheltering a chickadee family, also provides tomato stakes and edible shoots.

By recognizing that plants and the other elements of a garden can serve many purposes, we can create richly connected, productive landscapes that relieve the gardener of many tasks that nature will gladly do. Why make compost when you can have plants that build their own soil? Why weed when a living mulch will smother any unwanted invaders? It may take a little work to design and install a well-working ecological garden, and there may be some trial-and-error before all the pieces fit perfectly; but, in the long run, understanding that in nature "nothing does only one thing" will result in lively, dynamic landscapes.

Annuals and Perennials

You may have noticed that nearly every plant I've mentioned in this chapter is a perennial. That's not a coincidence. Sure, my garden has its share of tomatoes, peppers, and beans, but I'd trade them in a minute for perennial varieties if they existed (although tomatoes, peppers, and many beans are perennial in the tropics). I grow few annual flowers because there is a fine perennial substitute in nearly every case. And many of my salad greens are either perennial, such as French sorrel, perennial kale, and Good King Henry, or self-seeding, such as arugula, chard, red mustard, and lettuce. In part, the cause is simple laziness: Why slave over seed trays, grow lights, cold frames, and transplanting when I don't have to? But I prefer perennials for ecological reasons, too.

Planting annuals every year means disturbing the soil, which is rough on the soil life and brings weed seeds to the surface, where they germinate. Tilling to prepare a seedbed also flushes the soil life with oxygen, and the revved up little critters burn a lot of organic matter in response. This uses up nutrients that could otherwise be feeding plants. Plus, the bare soil erodes in the rain and wind.

Perennials, on the other hand, eliminate the drawbacks of tilling, plus they hold the soil in place year-round with their roots and prevent erosion with nearly continuous cover. Their roots often go far deeper than those of annuals, so they can tap water and nutrient reserves. This means less irrigation and fertilizing.

That burly root system is part of what ecologists mean when they say that perennials have more "standing biomass" than annuals. Standing biomass is simply the part of the plant that's permanent, such as branches, trunks, and large roots, as opposed to seasonal, such as fruit or deciduous leaves. Here's an example showing why standing biomass is important. I grow perennial bush kale (*Brassica olera-*

cea var. *ramosa)*, which resembles annual kale but reaches five feet in height and spread and has thick multiple trunks. When I pick leaves from my perennial kale for a dinner, I'm removing much less of the plant than if I were to snip a head of cabbage for the same meal. The remaining biomass on the perennial kale—the leaves, stem, and roots— helps it recover from harvest much faster than the cabbage (if indeed the cabbage survives my assault). The roots grab nutrients, the remaining foliage captures sunlight, and the plant quickly sprouts new leaves. The plant rebounds speedily from my harvest. I've removed only a tiny percentage of my garden, leaving plenty of biomass behind to keep all those important nutrients cycling and recycling. The biomass is the garden's essence: Remove it, and everything stops.

Also, by removing only a bit of the biomass, the larger cycles of the garden ecosystem remain more intact than if I hacked down a head of cabbage (to me, harvesting annuals is like small-scale clearcut logging). The perennial kale continues to offer habitat and food for bugs and birds, the roots harbor soil life, the leaves protect the soil from sun and rain, and so forth. That's a lot more than a stub of cut-off cabbage will provide.

As we saw in Chapter 2, ample standing biomass is a quality of mature ecosystems such as forests, and in ecological gardening we're trying to create mature ecosystems, rather than immature, pioneer systems such as vacant lots, conventional lawns, and farmland. Mature ecosystems need far fewer inputs since they cycle nutrients internally. Perennials, with their permanent roots and stems, are a feature of mature ecosystems, annuals of immature ones.

Perennials can replace many (though not all) annual plants. Fruit and ornamental trees; bushes for berries, blossoms, and wildlife; shrubs, vines, herbs, edible greens, and flowers—all come in perennial varieties. Hundreds of books describe perennial plants. But one niche is tough to fill

with perennials: vegetables. Most fruits are perennial, and perennial greens abound, but not many temperate-climate veggies return each year. The only ones commonly used in the United States are asparagus, rhubarb, and artichoke. Egyptian or walking onions, which set shallot-like bulbs above ground on stalks, can be added to the list. A perennial broccoli exists, called Nine-Star, that must be picked before it sets seed or it may die. Another that I've already mentioned is bamboo, with its edible shoots. Scarlet runner beans are perennial in mild climates (USDA Zone 8 and above). And, as mentioned, in the tropics tomatoes, peppers, and many others are perennial, too, but not in most of the North America.

Let's broaden the horizon with some less-familiar perennial vegetables. (I thank Eric Toensmeier, author of the very useful *Perennial Vegetables*, and Ken Fern's book *Plants for a Future* for introducing me to many of these varieties. See the Resources section for seed sources.)

Perennial Vegetables

Garlic chives (*Allium tuberosum*) have tangy shoots, leaves, and flowers, and they make an attractive ornamental as well.

Chinese mountain yam (*Dioscorea batatas*) pushes long tuberous taproots several feet into the ground and is hardy to 0 degrees Fahrenheit or colder. The cooked tubers have a mild, flourlike taste and store well.

Perennial groundcherry (*Physalis heterophylla*) is a wild relative of the tomato, hardy to at least −20 degrees Fahrenheit, with small golden berries that are tangy and sweet.

Groundplum milkvetch (*Astragalus crassicarpus*) has pods that look like plums, with a pealike flavor and purple flowers. It also fixes nitrogen.

Sea kale (*Crambe maritima*) has broccoli-like heads and shoots that can be blanched and eaten. The leaves are edible, too.

Lovage (*Levisticum officinale*) is an old European vegetable whose stalks, seeds, and leaves are edible and have a strong celery-like flavor. The huge flowers attract beneficial insects.

Mitsuba or Japanese parsley (*Crytotaenia japonica*) is a perennial parsley that prefers moist, shady spots and can tolerate temperatures of −20 degrees Fahrenheit or below.

Ramps or wild leeks (*Allium tricoccum*) have tasty, flat, and broad greens and edible bulbs, and they incidentally thrive in shade.

Udo (*Aralia cordata*) is a Japanese plant that grows to nine feet or more. The blanched shoots are eaten, either sliced very thin and soaked in ice water or boiled in several changes of water. It prefers partial shade.

Watercress (*Nasturtium officinale*) has edible stems and leaves and grows in streams and flowing water. It can, however, be invasive.

Chinese water lotus (*Nelumbo nucifera*) has edible roots, young leaves, and seeds that taste like chestnuts. An aquatic, it's hardy to Zone 6 if planted in deep soil and water.

Perennial Herbs

To expand the list of edible perennials yet further, we can include several herbs, especially those that can be used in quantity. Some examples are chives, fennel, parsley, various mints, and garden cress. Many other herbs are perennial, such as oregano, sage, marjoram, and other culinary herbs, but as they are never eaten in substantial amounts, it might be stretching things to include them.

Weeds and Other Wild Food

Another low-maintenance source of food lurks at the garden's margins. These are the weeds, a highly subjective category of maligned plants that even the United States Department of Agriculture admits are simply "plants that interfere with human activities." But one person's weed is another's treasured specimen. A surprising number of so-called weeds have edible greens, including dandelion, chicory, pigweed, lamb's quarters, chickweed, sheep sorrel, and cleavers. In Ashland, Oregon, permaculturist Tom Ward has cultivated an intimate relationship with his weeds. He has encouraged edible weeds in his lawn and prepares diverse and highly nutritious salads from his front yard. "Domesticated greens like lettuce can't compare with wild greens," Tom says. "When we bred out those tangy or slightly bitter flavors, we bred out the nutrition. There's probably more nutrition along the edges of most gardens—in the weeds—than in the crops. So mothers should be telling their children not, 'Eat your greens,' but, 'Eat your weeds.'"

Weeds are supremely multifunctional plants. They are the pioneers, covering, protecting, and fertilizing bare soil, preparing it for others. Many weeds are superb nutrient accumulators—in fact, that is often their primary role, pulling widely scattered nutrients from deep in the earth and concentrating them in the surface soil. That also explains why they are so nutritious: They accumulate health-giving minerals in their tissues. Weeds can also tell the gardener about soil conditions. Some weeds, such as curly dock and horsetail, grow in ground too moist for most fruit trees. Eastern bracken and silvery cinquefoil point to soils that are acid, while white campion and salad burnet reveal alkaline soil.

In addition to these uses, weeds furnish critical food and habitat at various times of the year for songbirds, game birds, and other wildlife. Insects that feed on abundant spring weeds afford crucial nourishment for hungry nesting birds, while weed seeds help carry many animals through lean winters.

Weeds have been our partners at least since the dawn of farming. Some weeds are semidomesticated, onetime food plants used by early

Perennial Greens

Perennial greens abound. These include French sorrel (*Rumex scutatus*), Good King Henry (*Chenopodium bonus-henricus*), dandelion greens (*Taraxacum officinale*), bush kale (*Brassica oleracea ramosa*), New Zealand spinach (*Tetragonia tetragoniodes*), Malabar spinach (*Basella rubra*), and Turkish rocket (*Bunias orientalis*).

Roots and Tubers

We can sneak a few roots and tubers into this list. I consider them almost-perennial foods because you must disturb the soil to harvest them, and if you harvest the entire root, it doesn't matter if it's a perennial—the plant is gone. But by leaving a section of the root, or allowing the plant to grow large enough to send out smaller roots, some species can be perennialized. They include Jerusalem artichoke, salsify or oyster root, Chinese artichoke, horseradish, shallots, garlic, cinnamon vine or Chinese yam, American groundnut, burdock, and chicory.

Even plain old potatoes left in the ground will grow and form new tubers, but they seem to become woody and small if left in place for more than a year or two.

A group of ancient Peruvian tubers, including mashua, is now becoming popular, so let's add them to the list. These include the following:

- Oca (*Oxalis tuberosa*) grows three-inch tubers with a lemony flavor.
- Yacon (*Polymnia edulis*) is a frost-tender plant with large, crisp, and juicy tubers.

humans, tried but found wanting as full-scale agricultural crops. Perhaps they had too much genetic variability or didn't set seed regularly. Thus, they fell by the wayside—quite literally—yet were so well adapted to our landscapes that they have followed us ever since. Other weeds coevolved with humans because they thrive in the disturbed or cultivated soil at our settlements. Wanted or not, they have lurked at the edges of our culture since culture began.

Many of the weeds in North America are imports, brought with food, animals, ship's ballast, or via less obvious avenues. Plantain was named white-man's foot by Native Americans because its tiny seeds lodged in the wooden soles of early colonials' boots. As the colonists blundered about the unfamiliar woods, plantain seeds dropped and sprouted, revealing where the Europeans had walked. Plantain is often cursed as a noxious weed, yet like so many others, it offers both food and medicine to those who understand it.

Acknowledging the usefulness of weeds can eliminate some of the warlike sentiments that we often bring into the garden. I want my garden to be a place of relaxation and sustenance for myself and others, but if I grow furious at every sprout of chickweed or sheep sorrel, the garden becomes merely one more trigger for high blood pressure. Now I see weeds as my allies, protecting soil that I've inadvertently left naked, quietly boosting fertility until I'm ready to plant. And most of them are a source of food, which further raises them in my esteem. Not incidentally, eating them becomes a way of controlling them, too.

Native plants offer another source of low-maintenance food, though without special training not many of us will make a meal from natives. Unless you're a serious survivalist, you probably won't do more than snack on the occasional huckleberry, currant, or wild strawberry. Food is one of the least compelling reasons to include native plants in the garden; their value for wildlife habitat and biodiversity preservation is far greater. Natives play an important role in the ecological garden but share the landscape with many useful nonnative plants.

Common Name	Botanical Name	Edible part
Burdock	*Arctium lappa*	Root
Chamomile, German	*Matricaria matricarioides*	Flower
Cheese mallow	*Malva parviflora*	Leaf, seed
Chickweed	*Stellaria media*	Leaf,
Chicory	*Cichorium intybus*	Leaf, root, flower
Cleavers	*Galium trifidum*	Leaf
Dandelions	*Taraxacum officinale*	Leaf, root (roasted), flower
Dock, curly	*Rumex persicarioides*	Leaf, root
Dock, yellow	*Rumex crispus*	Leaf, root
Epazote	*Chenopodium ambrosioides*	Leaf
Garlic mustard	*Allicaria officinalis*	Leaf, root, seed
Garlic, wild	*Allium ursinum*	Leaf, root, flower
Goldenrod	*Solidago* spp.	Flower (for tea or spice)
Horseweed	*Conyza canadensis*	Young leaves
Knotweed	*Polygonum cuspidatum*	Shoot
Kudzu	*Pueraria lobata*	Leaf, root (powdered as starch)
Lamb's quarters	*Chenopodium album*	Leaf
Lettuce, wild	*Lactuca scariola*	Leaf
Milk thistle	*Silybium marianum*	Young leaves, flower buds
Mint	*Mentha* spp.	Leaf
Mustard, wild	*Brassica* spp.	Leaf, flower, seed
Pigweed	*Amaranthus retroflexus*	Leaf, seed
Pineapple weed	*Matricaria matricarioides*	Leaf (for tea)
Plantain	*Plantago* spp.	Leaf, seed
Purslane	*Portulaca oleracea*	Leaf
Queen Anne's lace	*Daucus carota*	Leaf, flower, root
Shepherd's purse	*Capsella bursa-pastoris*	Leaf, seed, seedpod
Sorrel, sheep	*Rumex acetosella*	Leaf
Sow thistle	*Sonchus oleraceus*	Leaf
Stinging nettle	*Urtica dioica*	Leaf (cooked)
Wintercress	*Barbarea vulgaris*	Leaf

Table 6-4. A Sampling of Common Edible Weeds

• Mashua (*Tropaeolum tuberosum*) is a vining nasturtium with a small, peppery tuber that becomes deliciously sweet on baking.

Perennialized and Reseeding Annuals

Some annual plants can be "perennialized." For example, if leeks are allowed to set flowers, many small bulblets will form at the base. If you pull only the main stem and bulb, the bulblets can grow the following season. In mild climates (USDA Zone 6 or warmer), cutting back broccoli or cauliflower after harvest can keep it growing for several years.

We can stretch the list still further by including plants that reseed naturally. Good choices here are arugula, chard, lettuce (though eventually lettuce reverts to its more bitter wild ancestor), red mustard, corn salad, and lamb's quarters. Many common vegetables, such as tomatoes, brassicas, and squash, will self-seed, but they too easily hybridize or revert to wild types, giving flavorless or unpredictable varieties.

You can see that the perennial food garden can contain a wide variety of crops. Supplement these with the better-known perennial fruits, berries, and herbs, and you can have a very low-maintenance, ecologically sound way of producing food.

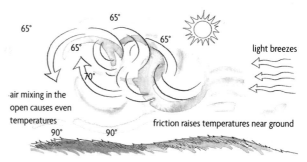

Few microclimates exist in the open.

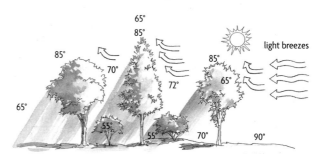

Many microclimates form when trees block air mixing, reduce radiative heat loss, and cast shade.

Microclimates for the Garden

Whether perennial or annual, a plant will thrive only under the right growth conditions. A drought-loving rosemary bush that will drown too close to a downspout will perk up in a hot, sunny corner. But a sweet woodruff that is withering in a sunny site will sigh in relief when shaded by some nurturing shrub. Each plant requires a certain range of soil type, acidity, temperature, light, moisture, and other factors. I've described how to improve soil and moisture conditions. Now let's see how to change the climate in your yard—the microclimate—to support the plants we want. The right microclimate is crucial to a plant's survival.

In turn, the plants we choose will change the environment around them. Some species—pioneers in particular—bring on their own destruction, changing soil pH and fertility until other species, better adapted to the new conditions, can easily crowd them out. Other plants wage environmental war to squelch competition by secreting mild toxins or casting such dense shade that nothing else can survive. Vegetation can also make a homesite more or less hospitable for the people who live there. My rural neighbor cut down all the trees south of his house to improve the view, only to find that indoor and yard temperatures in summer soared 10 degrees as the sun blistered the now-exposed house and soil. A scalding breeze now scorches them where cool shade once refreshed.

In contrast, Seattleite Kevin Burkhart trained a hardy kiwi vine onto wires over the southern half of his roof, and the seasonal shade has significantly lowered the summer temperature of his home. Yet after leaf fall, the bare vines don't block Seattle's scanty winter light. An added plus—stacking functions again—is the huge harvest of delicious fruit that Kevin enjoys in autumn.

We can think of the give-and-take between plants and their environment as microclimate gardening. With a little background, and, of course, some observation, we can identify the right microclimates for our greenery and understand how nearby plants will affect our environment in turn.

The big force that creates most microclimates is heat transfer. I won't get too technical here: Heat transfer is simply the movement of energy from one place to another. Heat transfer occurs when the sun sends radiant energy into the ground, when warm ground radiates heat to the sky, or when wind mixes hot air with cold.

That warm spot on the south side of your house, where snow melts soonest, exists because of heat transfer and is a good lesson in microclimate. If your house weren't there, the sun would still heat the ground, but most of the resulting warmth would simply radiate back to the open sky. The rest would be swept away by the wind.

When the south wall of your house enters the scene, the picture changes dramatically. Sun heats the ground just as in the open, but now the sunlight also warms the south-facing wall. The wall's warmth then bounces onto the ground, warming the earth further. That's heat transfer. Also, the heat radiating from the ground—which in the open would disappear skyward—is partially blocked by the wall and can't escape. A vertical wall blocks up to two-thirds of heat loss from a nearby "radiant body"—the ground in this case. (Let's not go into the math—microclimatology is called "the mathematician's paradise" because of the dense formulae that choke most books on the subject.)

The wall also alters heat transfer in a third way: It blocks air movement, preventing cool air from mixing with the warm air against the wall. A chilly wind over that hot spot would conduct heat from the ground. By stopping these gusts, the wall reduces the wind-chill factor (which is simply the rate that a breeze sucks heat away from a "radiant body," most commonly your shivering torso).

The mixing of air is a key element in creating microclimates. When wind sweeps across a bare plain, the air at head height or above mixes well. Temperatures from that height to a few hundred feet above are fairly even due to good air mixing. At the ground, however, friction slows the air and prevents good mixing. On a sunny day, the temperature an inch from the ground can be twenty degrees warmer than at eye level. A steep vertical temperature gradient forms: uneven air mixing. If we add some trees, walls, and houses to this bare plain, friction of the wind against these obstacles causes turbulence. Eddies of stillness form; pockets of hot air gather. Uneven air mixing now occurs horizontally as well as vertically. Microclimates are born.

We can use this very basic overview to find—and create—useful microclimates in the yard. Trees, shrubs, and other vegetation alter the way heat transfer and air mixing occur. A leafy canopy, even that of a good-sized herb, will block sunlight during the day, slowing the warming of the ground beneath it. At night, that canopy prevents the escape of heat from the earth to the sky, so temperatures below any plant won't fluctuate as much as in open ground. Also, the air below the greenery is more humid, and moist air uses more energy to heat than dry air. This further reduces temperature swings.

The benefits of a canopy become even more apparent in winter, when the sloping rays of the horizon-skimming sun reach under the leaves of, say, an evergreen shrub to warm the soil while at night the leaves block heat loss. Tender perennials can shelter there. Overhanging eaves of a house can have a similar effect, especially on the south and west sides, creating another spot for less hardy or warmth-loving plants. This all means that cold-sensitive plants can survive under canopies and eaves in climates where, in the open, they would be frozen out. Protection like this can often let the gardener use plants suited to one USDA zone farther south.

Just as capturing warm air is important, eliminating cold air is critical, too. Cold air drains downhill, so it's important not to block its escape routes. I know of some gardeners who planted a fine stand of bamboo just downslope of their garden, only to find that it stopped cold air drainage, turning their garden into a chilly frost pocket. They moved the bamboo, and the garden warmed considerably. Thus, slope can affect microclimate, too. Since cold air sinks, orchardists know that fruit trees on high ground can survive frosts that blacken the blossoms of trees just a few feet lower. This knowledge can be used in reverse: In regions with late frosts, gardeners often set fruit trees in the coldest part of their yard (for example, in a low spot, or on the northeast side of the house) so the trees will stay chilly. That way they won't bud out until late in spring, after the final frosts.

We can use more than just theory to find microclimates; we can observe them. A perfect time to locate warm and cool spots is just after a light frost. Watch which places lose the hoary rime of ice the soonest. These may be ideal sites for starting early flowers or cool-weather vegetables. The plants themselves can tell you, too. In Oakland we had three Lattarula fig trees, but one, in a little south-facing bowl against a hedge, held its leaves long after the other two were bare and leafed out earlier. That tells me it's in a great spot for other cold-sensitive or late-fruiting plants.

If you have pets, they'll let you know where the hot spots are. North Carolinian Jeff Ashton has written that since his dog, Dakota, has gotten a bit elderly, he's become picky about where he naps. Using the same instinct that cats employ to identify favorable microclimates on top of the fridge or water heater, Dakota has helped Jeff locate several warm sites in his yard. Jeff then uses these hot spots for specialized plantings. We hope Dakota is agreeable to being relocated.

Insects are savvy microclimate users. Bees often sleep inside daffodil blossoms because on a sunny morning the flower's interior can be 15 degrees Fahrenheit warmer than outside (due mainly to reduced air mixing). The bees heat up to flying temperature bright and early and are out pollinating much sooner than their outside-sleeping companions.

Color creates microclimates, too. A dark wall absorbs heat, while a light one reflects light. Researchers found that peaches grown against a dark wall grew faster but didn't ripen fruit any earlier than in the open. However, when peaches and grapes were grown against a light-colored wall, the fruit set was heavier and earlier. The reflected light had more of an effect on fruiting than the heat.

The color of the soil also affects microclimate. Light-colored soils heat up slower than dark ones. Maori farmers darken their soil with a sprinkling of charcoal to help it heat up in spring. Tibetans toss dark rocks on snow-covered fields to speed the thaw.

Soil density matters as well. A dense clay warms far slower than a fluffy, sandy soil. And mulch, with its many insulating air pockets, can keep soil from freezing but retards the warming of soil in spring. Pull mulch aside when spring temperatures rise to speed soil heating.

By understanding microclimates, we can find better homes for our plants, but we can also use our plantings to make our own homes more comfortable. Deciduous trees on the south side will cool a house and yard dramatically in summer, yet let in light in winter. On the windward side of a house (in this country, usually the west), evergreens can block winter winds. Here in Oregon, winter storms come from the southwest, so conifers should be located there. Summer breezes here come from the north, so I plant trees and high shrubs only sparsely in that direction.

I've mentioned the benefits of planting deciduous vines on arbors, trellises, even roofs and walls. Summer temperatures can be lowered substantially this way. Shading a yard works the same way, especially with a high canopy of trees. The sun doesn't penetrate, but breezes can still waft through the open space beneath the treetops. Now that the trees and shrubs around our house are beginning to mature and cast ample shade, not only do we stay cooler on those withering August afternoons, but I don't need to water these and the plants they shelter nearly as often.

Anywhere that slope or shape or density or color alters the way heat enters or leaves, anywhere friction or other forces change the mixing of air, this is where microclimates form. Microclimate gardening can extend the growing season by weeks, reduce heating and cooling bills substantially, and make living in any site far more pleasant.

Nurses, Scaffolds, and Chaperones

Now that I've shown how plants can be used to alter microclimates and introduced the concept of nutrient-accumulating species, I'd like to combine the two notions. Melding these two concepts yields a powerful gardening technique: using plants to modify both soil and microclimate to spur the growth of other flora. Species that do this are called nurse, chaperone, and scaffold plants.

In many ways, creating an ecological garden is a restoration project. The soil in most yards is poor, important species are missing, and healthy cycles are broken. Thus, people who restore damaged landscapes for a living—restoration biologists— have some things to teach us.

One trick the restorationists have learned from nature is the use of nurse plants. These are species that create shelter and other favorable conditions in which more delicate plants that would otherwise never survive can get a start. In Roxanne Swentzell's New Mexico garden, she and permaculture designer Joel Glanzberg, who helped create the site, planted

Siberian pea shrubs and other nitrogen fixers along a swale to provide shade and nutrients for less hardy plants. This nurse-plant strategy helped overcome some inhospitable conditions.

In Roxanne's yard, Joel showed me a black walnut tree about eight years old that towered over a tired-looking Russian olive. The Russian olive, though it had grown ten feet tall, was now clearly struggling. They had planted it to shield the young walnut from the withering sun, as well as to pump nutritious nitrogen into the soil, boost organic matter and soil life, and mulch the eroded ground with leaf litter. Now in deep shade and possibly suffering from years of the walnut's toxic juglone secretions, the Russian olive's work was done. Its walnut protégé had thrived under the Russian olive's care, then overtopped it and, a little sadly, driven it into decline.

This is often the fate of nurse plants, to be spurned by the youngsters they coddled into maturity. Sometimes it's possible to save a desirable nurse plant by pruning back its competitors, but often the best nurse plants are short-lived pioneers that rarely survive more than a decade or two, so their decline, though lamentable, is natural.

Many nitrogen fixers make great nurse plants since their symbiotic microbes force-feed them nutrients, even in poor soils, so they grow quickly (think of the astounding growth of wisteria and alder, both nitrogen fixers). Other candidates are the fast-growing species found in young shrub communities. See Table 6-5 for a list of potential nurse species.

Nurse plants can be used in several ways. In the example above, Joel and Roxanne employed nitrogen-fixing shrubs as what I call "chaperone plants." These are species that protect seedlings from harm until the juveniles are ready for life on their own. Chaperone plants are common in nature. Piñon pines under the protection of oak tree canopies survive far better than pines in the open. And mesquite, a nitrogen fixer, chaperones seedling saguaro cacti by sheltering them until the saguaros are tough enough to take the full desert sun. As with many chaperone species, mesquite's benefits are many-fold. In addition to providing fertility and shade, mesquites also aid saguaro reproduction. Mesquites are the favorite nest-trees for white-winged doves, which feed saguaro fruit to their young. The nestlings regurgitate the saguaro seeds, which then sprout in the shaded, rich litter beneath the mesquites.

Understandably, chaperone plants for shade are more needed in hot-sun climates toward the south. But many plants, especially shrubs and small trees for the understory layers of the garden, will profit from sun protection during their early years.

Woodland plants evolved in the dappled sunlight

Table 6-5. Nurse Plants

All of these plants are fast growing and can take harsh conditions, though they should be watered and fertilized while getting established. Other plants can be planted beneath and near them to benefit from their protection, leaf litter, and nutrient accumulation.

Common name	Botanical name	Comments
Acacia	*Acacia* spp.	Nonhardy N-fixing trees
Alder	*Alnus* spp.	N-fixing trees and shrubs
Autumn olive, Russian olive, goumi	*Elaeagnus* spp.	N-fixing shrub, edible berries
Black locust	*Robinia pseudoacacia*	N-fixing tree
Bladder senna	*Colutea arborescens*	N-fixing shrub
Bush clover	*Lespedeza thunbergii*	N-fixing shrub
Casuarina	*Casuarina* spp.	Nonhardy N-fixing tree
Crab apple	*Malus* spp.	Hardy small tree
Crimson-spot rock rose	*Cistus ladanifer*	Fast-growing small shrub
Elderberry	*Sambucus nigra*	Shrub with edible berries
Flowering quince	*Chaenomeles* spp.	Small deciduous ornamental tree
Golden-chain tree	*Laburnum anagyroides*	N-fixing small tree
Hackberry	*Celtis occidentalis*	Drought-tolerant shrub
Hawthorn	*Crataegus* spp.	Hardy small tree
Hebe	*Hebe salicifolia*	Fast-growing shrub
Hybrid broom	*Cytisus × spachianus*	N-fixer. Hybrids do not spread, unlike non-hybrids
Mesquite	*Prosopis* spp.	N-fixing, drought-tolerant tree
Mulberry	*Morus* spp.	Pioneer tree, but can tolerate shade
Sea buckthorn	*Hippophae rhamnoides*	N-fixing shrub, edible fruit
Siberian pea shrub	*Caragana arborescens*	N-fixing shrub
Silk tree, mimosa	*Albizia julibrissin*	N-fixing tree
Spanish broom	*Spartium junceum*	N-fixing shrub
Tree mallow	*Lavatera* spp.	Small shrub to medium tree
Tree of heaven	*Ailanthus altissima*	Tolerates pollution, opportunist
Wild lilac, buckbrush	*Ceanothus* spp.	N-fixing shrub
Willow	*Salix* spp.	Small tree or shrub for moist areas

beneath the forest canopy and can be fried by even the mild sun of a Maine summer. Plus, chaperones bestow more than just shade. Their roots loosen the soil, build humus, and secrete sugary juices for beneficial microbes; the leaf litter creates mulch and keeps soil moist; and the leafy canopy slows evaporation and forms a microclimate that damps temperature swings and holds humidity.

This is why nurse plants are used by many gardeners to restore battered landscapes and build biodiversity. On Orcas Island, the Bullock brothers swear by them. As I mentioned in Chapter 4, the brothers poke a nitrogen-fixing shrub or small tree alongside the fruit and nut trees they plant, sometimes even in the same hole. When the protected plant is mature, or if the chaperone begins to compete with it, they slash the chaperone back for mulch. They aver that this "two plants in every hole" system speeds growth immensely, and not just from sun protection.

A second use for nurse plants is as scaffolds. Here, the helpers' physical presence lets young or otherwise vulnerable plants get established. Then, like the temporary staging that workers use for erecting buildings, the scaffold plants can be removed or used for a different job. For example, ornithologist David Wingate relied on scaffold plants when he attempted to create habitat on a denuded island for an endangered Bermudan bird, the cahow. In the 1960s, Wingate tried to restore the native cedar forest, destroyed by overgrazing and a subsequent blight, that was once the cahow's home. But fierce ocean winds scoured down the seedling trees. So he turned to nonnative scaffold plants, tamarisk and the fast-growing nitrogen-fixer casuarina, to create a windbreak and replanted cedars in their shelter. The cedar forest quickly grew and was tough enough to withstand Hurricane Emily in 1987. Wingate has since guided the vegetation closer to its native composition by girdling many of the scaffold plants (removing a ring of bark

from around the trunk). This kills them but leaves them standing, reducing the ecological stress on the cedars that wholesale removal of the scaffolds might cause.

Other uses of scaffold plants are to hold soil in place on eroding hills and gullies, to stabilize and catch windblown soil, and to create thorny or dense fencing that protects young plants from deer and other animals. Thus, scaffold plants can be placed thickly in these trouble spots. Once the scaffold plants' mission is accomplished and other, more permanent vegetation is established, the scaffolds can be removed.

Nurse plants can also create wildlife habitat and attract new species. For example, the wild chile, or chiltepine, increasingly endangered by development, requires nurse plants to protect it from strong sun. Scientists noticed that the wild chiles grew mainly under hackberry bushes, even though many other shrubs provided similar shelter. In part, this was because hackberries create denser shade than most other shrubs. But the big factor was the hackberry's superior wildlife habitat. Several species of birds that are insensitive to the fiery-hot taste of chiltepine fruit prefer hackberry bushes for perching and nesting. The denser shade and tasty fruit makes hackberries a favored bird hangout. The birds thus dispersed most of the seeds of the chiltepines they'd eaten under hackberries.

Hackberries and other wildlife plants can serve many functions. They can protect tender or rare plants, attract animals, and put out the welcome mat for animal-imported species such as the chiltepine. Here we get a sense for the interconnectedness of natural communities and how they are assembled. A Johnny Appleseed–like broadcasting of chiltepine seed probably won't save this rare species. It is connected to a set of chile-insensitive birds, and both are tied to the hackberry. So creating supportive plant communities via nurse plants and other network-building techniques will furnish places for many species to thrive. This increases the odds that new species will survive, whether they're chosen by the gardener or imported via squirrel fur and bird poop.

The accompanying table lists many proven nurse, scaffold, and chaperone plants. To find additional candidates for your region, observe natural edges and abandoned fields that are transitioning from pioneer herbs to shrubs and trees. Nurses often appear as the pioneer phase is ending. Plants—often sturdy shrubs and small trees—that appear to be stopping wind, casting light shade, and otherwise sheltering the next generation of inhabitants are prime choices for nursing your landscape to maturity.

Summary: Blending the Many Functions of Plants

Ecological gardening moves beyond the "one role for each plant" philosophy. Here, plants are intimately connected to the sun, soil, water, and air; to each other; to insects and other animals; and to people. Also, they transform all that they are tied to. When we understand the multiple roles that plants can play, we can link together their many functions in intelligent ways. Then we can design gardens full of resilient, interconnected networks of life.

Through creative choice of plants, a simple hedge, for example, becomes not merely a screen but a deer-blocking, wind-reducing, wildlife- and people-feeding, mulch-producing, insect-attracting source of medicinal plants and craft materials. Curve it to enfold the north side of a garden, and it becomes a suntrap. And that's just getting started; a clever designer could probably come up with ten more roles for that hedge.

In thinking of plants not simply as passive objects but as active, dynamic performers, we can begin to see some of their many aspects. In this chapter, I've pointed out that plants can play a wide range of ecological roles, as mulch makers, nutrient accumulators, nitrogen fixers, insect attractors, pest repellents, fortress plants, spike roots, wildlife nurturers, and shelterbelters. Any functioning ecosystem—or ecological garden—almost certainly needs plants that play each of these parts. A few species that fill these functions have been described in this chapter, and more are listed in the appendix.

How do we combine all these performers? The final section of this book," Assembling the Ecological Garden," will show how. But for now, we need to look at one more important piece of the ecological garden.

CHAPTER 7

Bringing in the Bees, Birds, and Other Helpful Animals

My wife, Kiel, loves birds. To attract them, she hung a feeder from a tree in our front yard, and we both enjoyed the chickadees, goldfinches, grosbeaks, and others that flocked to this seed-stuffed larder. As the birds scrambled to eat, they flung seed to the ground in pattering cascades. The fallen seed drew first ground-feeding towhees and then a covey of California quail. These larger birds would scratch and claw in their search for seed, and I noticed that the quail tilled the ground thoroughly, leaving behind speckles of guano, a phosphorus-rich fertilizer.

Then, for various reasons, we moved the feeder. The quail-worked ground, now birdless, quickly grew lush and green with grass and wildflowers. Those quail and other ground-scratchers had acted as birdseed-powered tractors, scratching out all the vegetation, loosening the soil, and adding a little bonus of fertilizer. The same thing happened in the feeder's new spot, but instead of letting random greenery take hold after the birds worked their magic, I planted herbs and shrubs. They grew quickly.

It was comforting to know that while I sat at my desk and sipped tea, the birds were tilling and fertilizing a new garden bed for us. We didn't enslave the quail, just took advantage of their by-products. We merely put the feeder in the right place. In ecological gardening at its best, that's all the work that's necessary: putting things in the right relationship. Nature will do the rest.

Those busy birds illustrate how animals can be one of the gardener's most powerful allies. In the wrong place, an animal can wreak havoc, but when the garden's elements are in clever relationships, animals will eliminate a lot of labor for the gardener. Animals include not just the feathered and the four-legged varieties, but insects, spiders, and the zillion-legged soil critters, too. They all can help us.

My simple "quail tractor" barely scratches the surface of what animals can do for the garden. Animals don't just till and fertilize. They pollinate, disperse, and process seed; prune vegetation; eat pests; dispose of waste; circulate nutrients; and provide food for us if we wish. By attracting birds, small animals, and insects to our yards, we not only increase biodiversity but make our gardens more balanced, disease free, and productive as well.

From an ecological viewpoint, animals are a critical part of the home ecosystem: the consumers. Remember that the cycle of energy and matter in an ecosystem whirls from producers to consumers to decomposers and back to producers, over and over. Without all three roles, the cycle is broken and the ecosystem won't work. The principal producers are plants, which turn sunlight into leafy and woody tissue. The decomposers, as we have seen, live mostly in the soil, working their alchemy to transform organic matter into a new and useful state. The consumers are primarily animal: humans and other mammals, insects, birds, and all the rest. Animals are opportunists, living off the bounty produced by plants. But animals aren't mere parasites; we have our place as well. Animals, though they represent only a tiny portion of the total biomass of nature, are the "regulators" of an ecosystem. Whether they are loggers removing whole forests, browsing deer or cattle scalping shrubs and grasses, or gypsy moths defoliating an oak grove, animals channel and control huge flows of matter and energy through ecosystems.

Animals control the growth rates of many other species, by pollinating, dispersing seeds, grazing, hunting, and choosing where to nest or drop manure. Add to this their trampling, burrowing, and scratching, not to mention the large-scale effects of human endeavors, and we see that animals have altered the face of the planet.

Without animals, a garden cannot function. We need them, in the right place and numbers. In this chapter, we'll look at the ways that animals of many types can work in the garden. First we'll examine the role of insects and see how to attract and nurture beneficial ones. Then we'll do the same with birds and other wildlife. Last, we'll see how small domestic animals, such as ducks, rabbits, and chickens, can play a valuable part in the garden, even in the city.

More Good Bugs than Bad

Not long ago, I visited Occidental Arts and Ecology Center, an environmental learning institute north of San Francisco renowned for its marvelously productive organic gardens. Ecologist Brock Dolman was leading a tour, and one of the participants asked Brock how he dealt with a noxious insect that ravaged local crops. "I'm not a good one to ask about insect pests," Brock answered. "Our gardens are in such good ecological balance that no single pest ever does much harm. All the pests here have natural enemies that keep them in check. So we've never had to become experts on specific bug problems."

This perspective is a far cry from that of most conventional agriculturists. The main emphasis of most agricultural extension agents, master gardener clinics, and numerous textbooks—not to mention several multibillion-dollar industries—is on pests. A gardener who confesses ignorance about problem insects must be living in another, more benign universe.

Insects aren't high on most gardeners' lists of favorite things. It's too easy to notice the bug-ravaged leaves of broccoli and ignore the benefits of pollination and the role of pest-killing predator insects. Yet most insects are either helpful or neutral. Only a minority harm plants. Without insects, there would be very little for us to eat, no compost or topsoil, few birds, fewer mammals—they're an essential, major thread in the web of life. Biologist E. O. Wilson calls them "the little things that run the world." Yet most gardeners hate them: On a visit to a hardware store I heard a man ask, "What can I get to kill all the bugs in my yard?" I nearly began shrieking.

There's no doubt that insects damage food plants and ornamentals. Fourteen percent of all crops are lost to insects and disease, according to the USDA. However, there's more to that number than meets the eye, as fifty years ago crop loss was only 7 percent. Three factors have caused this alarming trend. The first is loss of soil fertility. Healthy, pest-resistant plants need healthy soil, and we've lost or impoverished much of ours. The other two causes fit with this chapter's theme, because they are responsible for the death of the beneficial insects that once kept pests in check. These are fencerow-to-fencerow "clean" cultivation and heavy and ill-timed pesticide use.

Up until a few decades ago, farmers divided their

fields with multispecies hedgerows and left wild vegetation along creeks and back pastures. The diversity of plants in these untamed places gave a home to a wide variety of insects, which sheltered among the leaves and supped from the nectar and pollen of the many blossoms. Spiders and birds, too, thrived in these thickets. Whenever pests swarmed into the adjacent fields, predators were waiting in the wings to gobble up this new food source. With all of nature standing ready in hedgerows and fallow fields to right any imbalance, pest problems rarely got out of hand.

Then, the advent of herbicides and high-powered tractors and the incentive to squeeze every dollar from farmland destroyed the good bugs' habitat. The broad, wildlife-filled hedgerows were replaced with wire fence or removed to make larger, trac-tor-tilled fields. Creeks were drained. Herbicides vaporized the wild places, which were disdained as unproductive and as wellsprings of weed seed, pests, and disease. The farm flowed over the last scraps of wild landscape, drowning it in a uniform sea of crops.

The second of the one-two punches that knocked out beneficial insects was widespread insecticide use. The ecology of pests and their predators tells us how this contributed. Insects that feed on plants reproduce at staggering rates, quickly surging to astronomical numbers. But the insects that prey on these pests reproduce more slowly and are far fewer in number. This is because a predators' food supply is less abundant (there are more leaves to eat than bugs), and it takes more energy to hunt than it does to mill around and graze. Less energy is available for predator breeding than for that of their prey. Just as a predator such as an owl is fairly uncommon and has only a few offspring per year, a predaceous lady beetle doesn't reproduce as quickly or prolifically as its prey. Predators always occur in much smaller numbers than their prey. This makes them vulnerable to extinction when prey declines.

Also, a time lag falls between the breeding of prey and of their predators. An outbreak of aphids can reach pestilential proportions in a week or two (frighteningly, aphids can give birth to already pregnant young). Lady beetles—you may know them as ladybugs or ladybird beetles—will reach the scene quickly and attack the aphid population before even a sharp-eyed gardener knows they are there. But without habitat for lady beetles to shelter and breed, not enough will live nearby to quell the outbreak. And fence-to-fence farming means the hedgerows and wild places where they abide are rare.

Aphids, or any rich food source, will trigger the lady beetles to breed, but they need time to lay and hatch eggs. The larvae, which look like alligators, are even more voracious predators than their parents, but they take a few days to get going. Hence there's a time lag before their numbers can build. Meanwhile, the aphids are multiplying to astounding numbers.

In this unfortunate cycle, just as the lady beetles have bred thickly enough to control the aphids, the farmer or gardener notices the aphids and sprays insecticide. This kills lots of aphids—and most lady beetles. The fast-breeding aphids recover within a few days, but the lady beetles remain at critically low numbers until the aphids can feed their young. Just as the lady beetles begin to breed again, the gardener sees that the aphids are back. Fearing another plague, he sprays again, hammering the struggling lady beetles. A few rounds of this and the lady beetles are all dead, while some aphids are bound to survive. Now the pests are predator-free and can multiply unchecked, and the farmer—or gardener—is on an expensive and toxic insecti-cide treadmill. He or she has eliminated nature's safeguards and must spray and spray or take the time—and the short-term crop loss—to restore the natural balance.

How can we create gardens that have this balance

A predatory lady beetle larva and adult.

and that provide what beneficial insects need? First, we need to get to know these helpful insects a little. We can distinguish four types of beneficial insects: predators, parasitic insects (or parasitoids), pollinators, and weed feeders. Let's look at each in turn.

Predatory Insects

Predators come from several different categories, called *orders*, of insects: beetles, true bugs, flies, wasps and their relatives, and a few smaller orders. They eat their prey either by crunching them with fierce mandibles or by piercing them with tubelike mouthparts and sucking out the body fluids. (It doesn't sound pretty, but just wait till you hear how parasitoids use their prey.) Some are specialists, preying on only one or a few species, but many eat anything that comes their way, whether helpful or harmful. In many cases, both the adult and immature insects are predators. Lady beetles are a prime example: The ravenous young have huge, powerful jaws on a crocodile-like body. These larvae look nothing like the cute spotted adults heralded in nursery rhyme.

Allow me to add spiders to our list, though they are arachnids and not insects, since they are superb pest predators. They shelter in dried grass and mulch, which provide the high humidity and refuge from temperature changes that they prefer. A cleanly cultivated garden is poor habitat for them: Researchers found thirty times more spiders and far less insect damage to plants in mulched gardens than in unmulched ones.

Parasitic Insects

Parasitic insects, also called *parasitoids*, are small wasps and flies that lay their eggs inside other insects or insect eggs. Their life cycles are quite gruesome stories, a sample of which I'll share here. One species of the group of parasitic wasps called braconids hunts down cabbageworm caterpillars. On finding one, the wasp thrusts its sharp ovipositor, or egg-laying tube, into the caterpillar and pumps twenty to sixty eggs into the hapless creature. The cabbageworm is perfectly alive when this happens. In two or three weeks, the wasp eggs hatch inside the cabbageworm and begin to feed. Death comes only slowly, as the wasp larvae avoid eating vital organs until ready to emerge. Finally, the growing larvae chew their way out through the caterpillar's flesh, killing the miserable host and leaving an empty, wrinkled husk behind.

I have heard that the makers of the film *Alien* got their inspiration from parasitic wasps. Other parasitic wasps lay their eggs on leaves, where caterpillars will eat them. Once consumed, the eggs hatch inside the caterpillar, and the whole ghoulish story begins again.

Parasitoids are often specialists, preying on only one or a few species of pest, so they rarely harm helpful insects. Most adult parasitoids are not carnivorous and feed mainly on pollen and nectar (perhaps they got meat eating out of their system at an early age). Flowers and wild vegetation near or in the garden are critical for their survival.

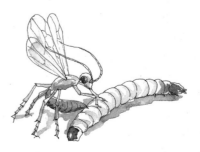

A parasitic braconid wasp injecting eggs into a cabbageworm larva.

Many parasitic wasps are barely visible to the eye, and most are stingless, so those averse to bees and wasps have nothing to fear from these helpful insects.

Pollinators

The link between plants and animals is dusted with pollen. Without insects to begin fruit and seed growth by fertilizing flowers with pollen, humans would starve. Vegetable gardens and orchards would be bare except for corn, grapes, and a handful of other wind-pollinated plants. Flowerbeds wouldn't exist.

The story of coevolution between plants and

A tawny mining bee pollinating an apple blossom.

insects is a long one, stretching back tens of millions of years to the end of the dinosaur age. Back then, insects learned that protein-rich pollen was excellent food, and flowering plants found that pollen-covered insects were more effective than

A Gallery of Beneficial Insects

Though thousands of species of bugs are beneficial to gardeners, most of them fit in a few major categories. Here are the principal insect allies of the gardener.

Predatory beetles include the familiar lady beetle, also called the ladybug or ladybird bug. They feed mainly on aphids but also eat mites, soft-bodied insects, and insect eggs. They overwinter in leaf litter, under rocks, and in other protected places. Ladybugs and their ferocious-looking alligator-like larvae consume fifty to five hundred aphids each day. When hungry, the adults can survive on nectar and pollen from shallow flower clusters such as yarrow and sunflower, but they greatly prefer insects.

Other important predaceous beetles are the iridescent green- or blue-winged beauties known as ground beetles, which feed on potato-beetle eggs and others,

and rove beetles, which consume cabbage maggots, onion maggots, and other root maggots.

Lacewings are found all over North America—green lacewings east of the Rockies and the smaller brown lacewings in the West. The larvae attack aphids, mealybugs, thrips, caterpillars and their eggs, mites, and scales. The young have hollow mandibles through which they suck the body fluids of their victims. Larvae spin yellow, pea-sized cocoons on leaves that hatch in about two weeks. Some adults eat aphids and mealybugs, but others rely on pollen and nectar for food. If adults are released where no other food exists, they will eat each other.

Predatory wasps include both social and solitary wasps. Social, colony-forming wasps such as yellow jackets and paper wasps prey on caterpillars, eating them or feeding them to their larvae. Solitary wasps,

such as digger wasps, do not form colonies but make one-critter nests and feed on weevils, crickets, and caterpillars. Some predatory wasps paralyze their prey with a surgically accurate sting to a specific nerve bundle, leaving the victim alive but helpless in the nest for the larvae to consume at leisure. Most adults need pollen and nectar for food. Composite flowers (such as daisy, chamomile, and golden marguerite) and mints (including spearmint, peppermint, and catnip) will attract and feed predatory wasps as well as hoverflies and robber flies, described below.

Parasitic wasps fall into three main groups. The braconids are tiny, often brightly colored wasps that lay their eggs on or in cabbageworms, tomato hornworms, and other caterpillars. Gardeners can sometimes spot caterpillars studded with dozens of eggs, usually the work of braconids.

the wind in delivering their male DNA to a female ovary. A partnership began. Plants developed easily reachable pollen organs, bright flowers as signals to bugs, and nectar sacs brimming with sweet sugars to further reward the industrious pollinators. In turn, insects grew pouches to hold freightloads of pollen, extendable mouth parts to delve deep into blossoms, and, in some cases, the ability to buzz loudly at just the right frequency to send pollen boiling out of the blooms.

The best-known pollinator is the European honeybee. Imported with many of America's food plants, these honeybees are generalists, pollinating almost anything they can reach. But honeybees, bred like other domestic animals for docility and high yield, aren't as tough as wild bees. Recently they've fallen prey to parasitic mites and diseases that have killed up to 80 percent of their colonies. This means that native and other pollinators are more important than ever.

Fortunately, native bees and wasps and their imported kin are abundant. The Maya and other Native Americans cultivated local bees both for pollination and for their honey, often keeping several species of them in their dooryard gardens. Remember, too, that predator and parasitic insects, like the rest of nature, play multiple roles. They can be pollinators as well. Many insects imported

A second group, chalcids, are small (1/32-inch) wasps that parasitize mealybugs, aphids, and the larvae of moths, beetles, and butterflies. They may be golden-colored or black. The third group, ichneumonid wasps, insert their characteristic long ovipositor into moth and butterfly larvae and lay eggs within. All these wasps rely on pollen and nectar as adults. Plants with tiny flowers, including fennel, angelica, coriander, dill, and Queen Anne's lace, provide their favorite food.

Syrphid flies, which include hoverflies (also called flowerflies) and robber flies, are members of the Diptera, the fly order, though many of them look like bees. They are stingless. Hoverfly larvae eat aphids, mealybugs, leafhoppers, and scale, hoisting their prey aloft like wineskins while draining their innards. Adults feed on pollen and nectar and can be lured by keeping blossoms blooming all season. Robber flies are large and attack many insects, including useful or harmless ones, so it is the grub- and egg-eating larval stage that is most helpful.

Tachinid flies also are dipterans and are dark and bristled like houseflies. They are parasitic, injecting their hosts with eggs or maggots or leaving eggs on leaves to be consumed by hosts, inside whom they will hatch. One species, *Lydella stabulans,* is often written about because the young sometimes hatch inside their mother and consume her from within. When not eating mom, tachinids destroy stinkbugs, caterpillars, cutworms, armyworms, and the larvae of gypsy moths and Japanese beetles. Adults need flowers since they feed on nectar and pollen as well as aphid honeydew.

Minute pirate bugs and their relatives, insidious pirate bugs, are true bugs (order Hemiptera), about 1/8-inch long, black with white wing patches. Both adults and young feed by sucking juices through a needle-like beak. They eat thrips, spider mites, insect eggs, aphids, and small caterpillars. Spring- and summer-flowering shrubs and weeds will entice them to stay since they eat pollen and plant juices when they can't find prey. Pirate bugs particularly like elderberry, mountain ash, hairy vetch, and wild and domestic buckwheat.

Big-eyed bugs are about 3/16-inch long and silver-gray, resembling tiny cicadas with bulging eyes. They have a distinctive waggle when they walk. Both the adults and young feed by sucking juices from their prey through a needlelike beak. They munch eggs and larvae of bollworms, tobacco budworms, and all stages of whiteflies, mites, and aphids. Big-eyed bugs also eat seeds, and planting sunflowers boosts their numbers. They also feed on nectar and like cool-season cover crops such as clover.

to battle pests have become naturalized and now pollinate both native and exotic plants.

I've mentioned that most of our food crops and many weeds are not native; neither are a large percentage of their pollinators. Imported beneficials play major roles in pollinating many exotic species that came from the same region. Scientists found that when European honeybees were kept away from the invasive weed star-thistle, also from Europe, thistle reproduction plummeted. This suggests that it will be very hard to eliminate many weeds unless we kill off their insect allies, a difficult or even undesirable task. Given a welcoming environment, exotic insects, like exotic plants, eventually become part of their new ecosystem.

Weed Feeders

Not all pest insects chomp solely on vegetables and prize flowers, though I know it seems that way. Some insects specifically eat unwanted plants. For example, purple loosestrife, loathed in the United States for being rampantly opportunistic in fertilizer-polluted waterways, is a valued wildflower in its native Europe, where it is controlled by a large web of natural enemies and competitors. A beetle and a weevil that feed only on loosestrife have been brought from Europe to control the plant and in

A weed-eating agapeta moth larva feeding on a knapweed root.

experiments have left only dead stubs where loosestrife once thrived.

Then there is the larva of the yellow agapeta moth, which eats the roots of several knapweed species. Certain flea beetles dine on leafy spurge, a rangeland weed that sickens cattle.

Of course, importing a new insect is risky, as it may misbehave in its new home by attacking valued species. This is a fairly esoteric field that most gardeners probably shouldn't pursue on their own, but if your property is being invaded by a well-known exotic such as loosestrife, you could contact your county extension agent to learn if a specific weed-feeding control insect is appropriate. But we're tinkering with a complex system here, so be cautious.

Attracting Beneficial Insects

Now that we've met our insect friends, we can put out the welcome mat for them. Like all animals, insects need food, shelter, water, and the right conditions to reproduce. Let's look at some ways to provide those.

Table 7-1 is a list of insect-attracting plants and the beneficials that frequent them. These plants may offer pollen and nectar, foliage for the larvae to feed on, or habitat for prey species; they all furnish food in some form. Many of these florae are very attractive and can (and should!) be included in even the most formal garden bed. Note that plenty of these plants are multifunctional, yielding food, herbs, medicine, or other bonuses.

Without a reliable supply of prey, predators and parasitoids won't stay around. This is another benefit of hedgerows or weedy spots, which always harbor a few aphids and other prey, encouraging beneficials to lurk about. Some gardeners fear that weeds or other "trap crops," as noncrop prey homes are called, are the breeding source for pests,

Table 7-1. Host Plants for Beneficial Insects

Common Name	Botanical Name	Bloom Time	Lady bug	Tachinid Fly	Minute Pirate Bug	Hoverfly	Parasitic Wasps	Big-eyed Bugs	Lacewing
Alfalfa	Medicago sativa	Sum-Fall			•			•	
Alpine cinquefoil	Potentilla villosa	Spr	•			•	•		
Angelica	Angelica gigas	Mid-late Sum							•
Anise hyssop	Agastache foeniculum	Sum		•			•		•
Basket of gold	Alyssum saxatilis	Early Spr	•	•		•			
Buckwheat	Fagopyrum esculentum	Early Fall	•	•	•	•			•
Bugle	Ajuga reptans	Late Spr or early Sum	•			•			
Butter and eggs	Linaria vulgaris	Sum, early Fall				•	•		
Butterfly weed	Asclepias tuberosa	Sum	•						
Caraway	Carum carvi	Sum				•	•		•
Clover	Trifolium spp.	Late Spr-Sum	•		•				•
Coriander	Coriandrum sativum	Sum-Fall	•			•	•		•
Cosmos	Cosmos bipinnatus	Sum-Fall				•	•		•
Crimson thyme	Thymus serpyllum coccineus	Sum		•		•	•		
Dandelion	Taraxacum officinale	Spr, Fall	•						•
Dill	Anethum graveolens	Sum	•			•	•		•
Dwarf alpine aster	Aster alpinus	Sum				•			
English lavender	Lavandula angustifolia	Sum				•			
False indigo	Amorpha fruticosa	Sum					•		•
Fennel	Foeniculum vulgare	Sum	•			•	•		•
Fern-leaf yarrow	Achillea filipendulina	Sum-Fall	•			•	•		•
Feverfew	Chrysanthemum parthenium	Sum-early Fall				•			
Four-wing saltbush	Atriplex canescens	Sum	•			•			•

(continues)

Table 7-1. Host Plants for Beneficial Insects (continued)

Plant			Insect Attracted						
Common Name	Botanical Name	Bloom Time	Lady bug	Tachinid Fly	Minute Pirate Bug	Hoverfly	Parasitic Wasps	Big-eyed Bugs	Lacewing
Gloriosa daisy	Rudbeckia fulgida	Late Sum-Fall				•			
Golden marguerite	Anthemis tinctoria	Spr-Fall	•	•		•	•		•
Goldenrod	Solidago virgaurea	Late Sum-Fall			•	•			
Hairy vetch	Vicia villosa	Sum-Fall	•		•				
Lavender globe lily	Allium tanguticum	Sum				•	•		
Lemon balm	Melissa officinalis	Sum		•		•	•		
Lobelia	Lobelia erinus	Sum				•			
Marigold	Tagetes tenuifolia	Sum-Fall	•			•	•		
Masterwort	Astrantia major	Sum				•			
Maximilian sunflower	Helianthus maximilianii	Late Sum	•						•
Orange stonecrop	Sedum kamtschaticum	Sum				•	•		
Parsley	Petroselinum crispum	Sum		•		•	•		
Pennyroyal	Mentha pulegium	Sum		•		•	•		
Phacelia	Phacelia tanacetifolia	Late Spr-early Sum		•					
Poached-egg plant	Limnanthes douglasii	Sum				•			
Purple poppy mallow	Callirhoe involucrata	Sum				•	•		•
Queen Anne's lace	Daucus carota	Sum-Fall	•			•	•		•
Rocky mountain penstemon	Penstemon strictus	Late Spr-Sum	•			•			
Spearmint	Mentha spicata	Sum				•			
Spike speedwell	Veronica spicata	Sum	•			•			
Statice	Limonium latifolium	Sum-Fall				•	•		
Stonecrops	Sedum spurium & album	Sum				•			
Sulfur cinquefoil	Potentilla recta 'warrenii'	Sum, early Fall	•			•	•		

| Table 7-1. Host Plants for Beneficial Insects (continued) | | | | | | | | | |
| Plant | | | Insect Attracted | | | | | | |
Common Name	Botanical Name	Bloom Time	Lady bug	Tachinid Fly	Minute Pirate Bug	Hoverfly	Parasitic Wasps	Big-eyed Bugs	Lacewing
Sweet alyssum	*Lobularia maritima*	Sum				•	•		
Tansy	*Tanacetum vulgare*	Late Sum-Fall	•	•			•		•
Toothpick ammi	*Ammi majus*	Sum-Fall		•	•	•			
Wild bergamot	*Monarda fistulosa*	Sum				•			
Wood betony	*Stachys officinalis*	Spr-Sum				•			
Yarrow	*Achillea millefolium*	Sum-early Fall	•			•	•		•
Zinnia	*Zinnia elegans*	Sum-frost				•	•		

but research shows that their value as snack bars for good bugs far outweighs any possible harm from pests. It seems counterintuitive, but having a few pests around is better than having none at all. If you temporarily eliminate all pests (and temporarily is all that's possible), good bugs will disappear, too, leaving you defenseless when the faster-breeding pests return.

Helpful bugs also require shelter, which includes dense foliage, mulch, dead brush and leaves, and rock piles and walls. Shrubs, hedges, and thick perennial beds are ideal. Research shows that many beneficial insects overwinter or lay eggs in dead vegetation, so gardeners should delay their postseason cleanup until spring. That fastidiously neat garden is poor habitat for beneficials. (Isn't it wonderful to find sound ecological reasons for procrastinating?)

Drinking water isn't usually a concern since many insects get moisture from nectar or foliage. Some species of bees and wasps drink from open water, however, and other insects have an aquatic larval stage, so it's never a bad idea to have a pond or other water feature.

Offering food, shelter, and moisture goes a long way toward creating the right conditions for beneficials to reproduce. Food also needs to be available at the right time, and here diversity is once again the key. Grow many species of flowers so that several types are always in bloom. This gives beneficials a better chance at fattening up enough to breed. Multispecies hedgerows, wild and weedy spots, mixed and perennial borders, and flowers sprinkled in vegetable beds all provide habitat. You could take a scientific approach and select specific plants for individual beneficials, or you could be like me and use the shotgun method: Plant everything under the sun and enjoy the resulting orgy of buzzing, flittering, iridescence, nectar-slurping, pollinating, and garden health.

Remember, too, that no insect is an island. All organisms evolved in concert with others, and bugs are no different. They have plant and animal partners, and if we can recreate these partnerships in our gardens, better balance and fewer problems will result. A good example of this is the sunflower plant. Sunflowers are native to North America, and over 150 species of insects, including weevils, beetles, and caterpillars, feed on their foliage, roots, flowers, and seeds. When large-scale commercial planting of sunflowers began in the 1970s, some of these pests moved from wild to domestic sunflowers. Yet only a few became significant problems. That's because an equally enormous array of predator and parasitic insects—over 100 species—had also evolved with the sunflower-eating bugs and were on hand to squelch outbreaks. Dozens of insects have evolved as sunflower pollinators, too.

This gives a glimpse of how complex plant–insect relations are. We can think of plants and their insect companions as occurring in orchestras—or as miniecologies—each playing a role, each being in balance with dozens or hundreds of species. This is one advantage to working with native plants: The partners needed for healthy growth and reproduction (including soil microorganisms, rodents, or birds) are likely to be on hand. But after several centuries of commerce and travel between continents, plenty of the partners of exotic plants have arrived here, too. Many of the beneficials buzzing in an ecologically designed American landscape came from other countries, yet they can find their way to a healthy garden's welcoming habitat with little effort.

Many garden-supply companies sell beneficial insects, and this is one surefire way to obtain them. But it would be silly to buy expensive bugs if you don't offer them habitat. They'll just leave for greener pastures or, at best, eat the nearby pests and then die without reproducing. Perhaps for farms or large gardens with rows and rows of vegetables, buying insects is a short-term solution, but I've never resorted to it, and my yard hums with helpful bugs. Besides, an ecological garden won't have rows and rows of monocultured veggies but a diverse array of many varieties blended together, including flowers. To attract beneficials, just plant flowers and provide habitat, and the beneficial insects will come—and stay.

Each year, I add more useful flowers, and I'm astounded at the almost exponential increase in insect life. Insectary plants do more than just attract insects. A garden laden with bug-attracting plants can—and will—be multifunctional. My plants are healthier, and my garden is simply prettier. Plus, the scientist in me gets to scrutinize dozens of tiny stingless wasps and weirder critters as they flit from blossom to blossom. Also, many of these flowers are edible; I can pop calendula, bee balm, mustard, borage, or many other blooms into a salad or use foliage from these and others as herbs. The medically inclined can make tinctures and salves from insectary plants. Because insects are a big part of the avian diet, I've seen a jump in bird visitors, too. The relationship among plants, insects, and birds is fascinating and one we'll explore next.

The Gardener's Feathered Friends

My story of the "quail tractor" at the beginning of this chapter hints at the roles birds can play in the ecological garden. But, as with insects, many gardeners don't welcome birds into the garden or orchard with unambiguously open arms. Birds can decimate a berry crop, peck holes in fruit, and scratch up small seedlings. Often these problems arise because good bird habitat is lacking, and the birds are reduced to making do with what's available (in other words, your plants). I'd argue that in a well-designed, balanced landscape, birds do far more good than harm. They are supreme insect predators, attacking both leaf-munching caterpillars and flying bugs. Many birds eat seeds, reducing the number of weeds. In return for this food, they leave small gifts of rich manure. Individual bird droppings may not amount to much, but when a gardener concentrates manure by hanging a feeder or by some other tactic, plenty of fertilizer can accumulate. Birds also scratch the soil, simultaneously tilling the ground, removing insects and weed seeds, and uprooting weed seedlings. Some small birds are good pollinators. And then there is the simple joy that birds bring, with their bright plumage, burbling song, nest building and family raising, and their endlessly varied behavior as they hunt, court, stake out turf, and socialize. A yard without birds seems a sterile place.

To see how to attract birds to the landscape and to benefit from them, let's once again take the ecological view. What kind of habitat gives birds all that they need? Once we've answered that, we can see how to blend bird habitat, and all the gifts birds offer, into the garden.

Imagine a backyard of bare ground. A little bare earth is useful for birds, which will take dust baths in dry soil to subdue mites and other parasites. Birds also eat grit to aid digestion. But without shelter from predators and the elements, no bird can live here. Occasional visitors might come to pluck worms or ground-dwelling insects from this empty place, but they will not stay for long.

Allow a low ground cover to carpet the soil, and the friendly microclimate and greenery will attract several types of insects. Now ground-nesting birds such as meadowlarks and certain sparrows may appear to feed on bugs and seeds. These two types of food foster diversity in bird residents, because insect-eating birds have long, slender beaks to pluck insects from foliage, while the bills of seed-eaters are short and thick to crack tough seeds. As the environment grows more complex, bird anatomy and behavior diversify as well. In other words, more species of birds can coexist in complex habitats than in simple ones.

Bring in a little more plant diversity: tall grasses. Thick, high grass offers birds protection from predators but also hampers bird flight. Birds that live in tall grass are different from ground-nesters. They have short wings and tails to nimbly maneuver through the grass, hopping rather than flying.

This is still a fairly impoverished home. Let's add some shrubs, which encourage diversity in several ways. One is by moving firmly into the third dimension, height. This provides perches for birds, where they can sit and watch for prey rather than hopping about in continuous search. Sit-and-wait hunting conserves energy, leaving more for breeding and social behavior. Perches also encourage flying, so the wings and tails of shrub-dwelling birds are bigger than the sawed-off stubs of grass residents. Also, birds that hunt bugs on the wing have broader bills to raise the odds of nailing insects with each swoop. Nests, now off the ground, are safer, cooler, and drier, so more nestlings survive.

Perching birds are superb seed dispersers and can bolster plant diversity on their own. Researchers found that when they provided perches in a field, the number and variety of seeds brought by birds skyrocketed. If in our landscapes we offer birds a few shrubs for perching, they'll introduce many new plant varieties on their own. This in turn will attract new insects, which will bring more new birds, which will ferry in more seeds, and up and up the cycle builds.

Another boost to diversity offered by shrubs is from woody tissue. Grass and herbs have soft stems and foliage; thus insects can munch them with ease. But the woody stems of shrubs will resist a soft-mouthed bug. Woody stems offer a whole new niche, drawing insects with tough jaws or piercing mouthparts. Thus, a shrub-filled landscape is home to yet more species of insects, and that means more types of birds to eat them.

Within the shrubby canopy, small birds are protected from predators. These birds can hop from twig to twig, snapping up insects. They need sharp, pointed beaks to poke into small places in search of food. So here come some more new species.

The move to the third dimension hugely boosts diversity, opening up many new opportunities for food sources and consumers of that food. As the habitat diversifies, more and more birds find niches, and this creates more variety in turn. Also, a combination of herbs and shrubs will nurture not only the birds dependent on each but also new species that colonize the edge between the two habitats. Once again, the whole is more than the sum of the parts.

Now we can add some trees to the mix. The combination of tree trunk and canopy creates a new structure, where birds can glide in the open expanse below the crowns. More flying birds will arrive, and bigger ones, too, since thick branches can support large birds. And once again, this creates new insect niches. The tree trunks, with thick bark and broad surfaces, allow new species of bugs to feed, hide, and lay their eggs. The birds that eat these bugs need specialized beaks to probe the bark and an anatomy modified to hang sideways on trunks instead of perching upright. So trees hike bird diversity still further. Life among the trees is safer, too. Birds and nests in the canopy are protected from predators lurking on the ground, which must now learn to climb for their food.

This shows how a diverse habitat, with many shapes, sizes, and varieties of plants, attracts birds (and insects) of many species and lifestyles. Birds play a critical role in any ecological garden, for the reasons given at the beginning of this section. Although some people landscape their yards specifically to attract birds, every yard can have some bird-friendly elements in it. Of course, we can design so that most of these elements will have more than one function, benefiting the human and other occupants and contributing to the health of the entire miniecosystem. Let's see specifically what needs to be included in the ecological garden to bring birds into it, and how those pieces fit in.

An ideal, diverse habitat for birds will have four key elements. They are:

1. *Food.* Bird foods fall into three main categories: fruits and berries, insects, and seeds and nuts. Some birds are specialists, eating mostly from one group, while others aren't so fussy. Hummingbirds and a few others also drink nectar, but even hummingbirds get over half their nutrition from insects. To feed a wide variety of birds, a garden needs insectary plants (many of which offer nectar, too), grasses and herbs that yield seeds, and shrubs and trees with nuts, fruit, and berries. A wide variety of species to continuously provide food over a long season is best. Many fruits and berries hang on into winter, and these species will invite birds all year. Table 7-2 is a brief list of plants that are all-around useful ones for birds and have other functions as well. A more comprehensive list of plants that feed birds would fill many pages, so I will refer the reader to the bibliography for some good books on the subject.

2. *Water.* The most natural source of water for birds is a pond or small stream with shallow edges. An alternative is a birdbath or other container less than two inches deep. A shrub or other shelter very close by will give birds an escape route and allow them to check out the water from a safe perch. Birds will also frolic in a sprinkler's spray or other moving water.

3. *Shelter and protection.* Birds know that death from predators or bad weather is always near. Thus, food and water offer little enticement for birds unless accompanied by shelter from the elements and protection from predators. Dense shrubs, tangles of vines, plants with thorns, and leafy tree

| Table 7-2. Useful Plants for Birds | | | | | | | |
| Name of Plant | | Provides | | | | | |
Common Name	Botanical Name	Seeds	Insects	Fruits	Winter Fruits	Shelter and Cover	Nest Sites
Alder	*Alnus* spp.	•					•
American cranberry	*Viburnum trilobum*			•	•		
Amur cork tree	*Phellodendron amurense*				•		
Amur honeysuckle	*Lonicera maackii*				•		
Apple and Crabapple	*Malus* spp.			•	•		•
Ash	*Fraxinus* spp.	•					•
Autumn olive	*Eleagnus umbellata*			•	•		
Bamboo	*Phyllostachys* spp.					•	•
Barberry	*Berberis* spp.					•	•
Bayberry or wax myrtle	*Myrica* spp.			•	•		
Birch	*Betula* spp.	•	•				
Blackberry and raspberry	*Rubus* spp.			•			
Blueberry	*Vaccinium* spp.			•			
Buckthorn	*Rhamnus* spp.					•	•
Cherry	*Prunus* spp.			•			
Dogwood	*Cornus* spp.			•			•
Douglas fir	*Pseudotsuga menziesii*						•
Eastern red cedar	*Juniperus virginiana*				•	•	•
Elderberry	*Sambucus* spp.					•	•
Elm	*Ulmus* spp.		•				•
Euonymus	*Euonymus* spp.	•					
European cranberry	*Viburnum opulus*			•	•		
Fir	*Abies* spp.					•	
Firethorn	*Pyracantha* spp.			•			
Greenbrier	*Smilax* spp.					•	
Hackberry	*Celtis* spp.				•		
Hawthorn	*Crataegus* spp.			•	•		•
Holly	*Ilex* spp.			•	•		•
Honeysuckle	*Lonicera* spp.			•			
Maple	*Acer* spp.	•	•				•
Mountain ash	*Sorbus* spp.			•	•		
Mulberry	*Morus* spp.			•		•	•
Persimmon	*Diospyros* spp.			•	•	•	•
Pine	*Pinus* spp.					•	•

(continues)

Table 7-2. Useful Plants for Birds (continued)							
Name of Plant		**Provides**					
Common Name	**Botanical Name**	**Seeds**	**Insects**	**Fruits**	**Winter Fruits**	**Shelter and Cover**	**Nest Sites**
Rose (wild, bramble, etc.)	*Rosa* spp.			•	•	•	•
Russian olive	*Eleagnus angustifolia*			•	•		•
Salal	*Gaultheria shallon*			•		•	•
Serviceberry	*Amelanchier* spp.			•			•
Smooth sumac	*Rhus glabra*				•		
Spicebush	*Lindera benzoin*			•			
Spruce	*Picea* spp.					•	•
Staghorn sumac	*Rhus typhina*				•		
Sycamore	*Platanus*		•				
Toyon	*Heteromeles arbutifolia*			•			
Tulip tree	*Liriodendron tulipfera*				•		
Willow	*Salix*		•				
Wolfberry	*Lycium* spp.			•		•	•

canopies all provide safe havens from predators. Thick evergreen foliage will shelter them from wintry winds, heavy snows, and extreme cold. For nesting, birds need plants with foliage that will exclude rain, hot sun, and sharp-eyed predators. Birds often nest at specific heights, so a diverse array of shrubs and trees will offer potential homesites to many species. Wide, dense plants are useful since lots of birds prefer to nest deep inside a broad hedge or bush.

4. *Food and habitat diversity.* To attract and nurture numerous birds from many species, a yard should furnish many food sources that stretch yields over the whole year, diverse places for shelter and protection, and plenty of private spots at varying heights for nest sites. To provide all this, a landscape needs plants from each of seven overlapping categories:

- *Evergreens.* Evergreen trees and shrubs with needles (pine, fir, cedar, spruce, yew, hemlock, juniper, and others) and broadleaf evergreens (holly, arbutus, large bamboo, eucalyptus, bayberry) offer winter shelter, summer nesting sites, and escape cover. Some of these provide buds, seeds, and sap for food.
- *Grasses, flowers, and herbs.* Tall grasses, annual and perennial flowers, and herbs provide cover for birds that feed or nest on the ground. Many offer seeds and nectar or are hosts for insects.
- *Nectar-producing plants.* Nectar-producing plants with red tubular flowers (such as *Penstemon barbatus,* trumpet vine, and columbine)

are irresistible to hummingbirds. Larger nectar producers (including sugar and big-leaf maple, *Elaeagnus*, honeysuckle, banksia, and black locust) are used by orioles and other small birds to supplement their diet.

- *Summer-fruiting plants.* Plants that produce fruits or berries from May through August are the mainstays of many bird-attracting gardens. Examples include blackberry, blueberry, cherry, chokecherry, honeysuckle, raspberry, serviceberry, mulberry, elderberry, and wild plum, but there are dozens more.

- *Fall-fruiting plants.* Migratory birds must build up fat reserves for their long voyage southward, and nonmigratory varieties need plenty of food to survive winter freezes. Fall-fruiting plants are essential for this; they include dogwood, mountain ash, snowberry, sea buckthorn, buffaloberry, and cotoneaster.

- *Winter-fruiting plants.* Especially valuable are plants whose fruits cling to the branches into winter. Some of these fruits need repeated freezing and thawing to be palatable. Winter fruits include black chokecherry, snowberry, sumac, highbush cranberry, many varieties of crabapple, barberry, hawthorn, strawberry tree, bittersweet, eastern and European wahoo, hardy kiwi, medlar, Virginia creeper, and chinaberry.

- *Nut and acorn plants.* These include oaks, hickories, butternuts, walnuts, buckeyes, chestnuts, piñon and stone pine, and hazels. These trees also provide good nesting habitat.

Most of these plants will complement any home landscape, and many are multifunctional, offering food as well as beautiful foliage and flowers. A few, such as buffaloberry and sea buckthorn, are nitrogen fixers. In turn, the birds these plants attract will provide entertainment and insight into animal behavior as they forage, nest, and interact. They'll help keep insect problems in check, while their gifts of fertilizer and tilling can be significant, too. The next section shows how to consciously harvest these animal benefits, using them to improve the garden.

Other Backyard Helpers

The chances are good that your grandparents or great-grandparents, whether they were farmers or not, kept small livestock. Before World War II, the sound of clucking chickens or the sight of rabbit cages was common in backyards even in the cities. On apartment rooftops, flocks of pigeons cooed and groomed in specially built lofts and dovecotes. Not a few iceboxes were stocked with meat and eggs from homegrown animals, and feathers or fur often found a use as well. Manure, of course, went to the garden (or sometimes to other uses—citizens in Elizabethan England were exhorted to raise pigeons because bird guano yielded nitrate for gunpowder).

But in the postwar era, small livestock disappeared from urban and suburban yards. It was easier to buy meat, eggs, and even composted manure at the store than to raise small livestock. Suburbanites were also eager to distance themselves from the unsophisticated aura of the farms where many of them had grown up. Towns passed laws against keeping livestock—especially roosters, whose unpredictable crowing disturbed the sleep of nine-to-five commuters.

The past decade has seen a resurgence of small animals in backyards. Antichicken ordinances are toppling (often permitting hens but not roosters), and chicken yards, duck ponds, rabbit hutches, and even pens for dwarf pot-bellied pigs are cropping up in suburb and city. Some of this renaissance is spurred by a desire for humanely raised, hormone- and antibiotic-free meat, but even vegetarians or those unwilling to butcher their own animals are finding advantages to small livestock.

Small animals suited for the backyard are legion and include chickens, turkeys, pigeons, doves, ducks, quail, and peafowl, as well as rabbits, guinea pigs, and pot-bellied minipigs. (Geese and guinea fowl, though also small animals, are a little too noisy for the city or suburbs.) Occasionally I've spotted pygmy goats in suburban yards.

If animals are intelligently raised, their advantages are multifold: They can fertilize, till, clip grass, weed, eat scraps and leftovers, hunt insects and slugs, process compost and yard waste, and warn of intruders (OK, rabbits and guinea pigs aren't great alarm-sounders).

Feeding kitchen scraps to livestock cycles more nutrients into yields for us than composting the scraps directly, while creating about the same amount of fertilizer. That's because when any creature eats those scraps, be it bird, rabbit, or soil organism, roughly the same proportion of food passes through the creature to become fertilizer, whether as compost or as animal manure. Another portion is exhaled as carbon dioxide. In a compost pile the remainder is reincarnated as soil life, which we can't eat, instead of chicken, which we can.

We can think of other benefits of raising animals. When small animals are housed in or adjoining a greenhouse, their body heat warms it in winter, and they boost plant growth with carbon dioxide from their breath. Less tangibly, they can entertain us for hours, become our companions and friends, and teach adults and children about the cycles of birth, mating, and death. Given all that, their ability to provide us with food seems almost trivial.

Does raising livestock in the city or suburb seem shocking? It's a matter of perspective. We raise dogs and cats with nary a second thought, yet they require expensive feed and intense care, their excrement is extremely noxious, they destroy property, and barking dogs and love-smitten cats are every bit as noisy as roosters. Their benefits do include companionship, and dogs make great burglar alarms, but if you're looking at tangible benefits, other small animals provide far more with less trouble. We've just gotten used to dogs and cats while we've become prejudiced against the barnyard taint of livestock. I'd like to see us expand our small-animal horizons. I love dogs and cats, but they can raise hell in the garden, while many other animals are garden assets and can provide useful labor and fertilizer as by-products of their daily activities, as well as fur and meat.

Sometimes the biggest obstacles to keeping animals in the city are the neighbors, who may need to be educated gently about animals' benefits and trouble-free nature. Many people have quieted their neighbors' worries and turned them into allies by treating them to fresh, wholesome eggs or meat.

Chicken Tractors

One secret to integrating small animals into the garden is a small mobile pen, called an animal tractor (see the illustration on page 168). By keeping livestock in a movable enclosure, animal tractors let the gardener decide where the animal will work best, rather than allowing the critters to wander and wreak havoc in freshly seeded beds. The bottomless pens concentrate the animals' weeding, tilling, and manuring in a small space, which is the key to successfully melding animals and gardens. With an animal tractor, you can have weed-free, surface-tilled, perfectly manured raised beds with only a few minutes of (your) work per day.

Chickens are ideally suited to animal tractors, although ducks, rabbits, pigs, and guinea pigs have been used in these mobile pens. Andy Lee has written an entire book on the subject, *Chicken Tractor*, which I recommend to anyone planning to use an animal tractor.

A chicken tractor is a bottomless pen on wheels that fits over a garden bed. A typical one might be four feet wide by eight feet long and about two feet high. This design, one of many, is an open wood-frame box, covered on the sides with one-inch chicken wire (poultry netting), roofed with plastic panels, having wheels or skids at one end and a door to let the birds in and out. Inside, food and water containers hang from the roof; in some models, perches project from the sides. There are other designs, including circular styles, but that's the gist. To move the pen, just lift one end and roll it on the wheels or skids. Animal tractors work best with garden beds as wide as the tractor, and ideally, in lengths that are an even multiple of the tractor length.

The number of birds per tractor varies with the breed, but as a rule of thumb, a laying hen needs four square feet of room, while a broiler need two square feet. Thus, a thirty-two-square-foot tractor can hold up to eight layers or sixteen broilers.

You can use a chicken tractor to build soil in three basic ways: rotation, sheet mulching, and deep mulching.

In the *rotation* method, first thing in the morning you wheel the pen and chickens to an unused garden bed. The birds can stay inside while you move it—they'll scurry along inside the pen. Withhold their feed until they've been on the new bed for an hour or so. That way the hungry birds will eat the vegetation inside the tractor area. Let the birds weed, till, and manure the soil all day. The

next morning, wheel the tractor down the bed to the next fresh spot and sprinkle some mulch on the first bed. Rotate through all the unused beds. This system requires that some of your garden beds go fallow part of the time so the chickens have soil to improve. Andy Lee's garden is twice as big as he needs, which lets him rotate chicken tractors through each bed every other year.

As the tractor leaves each raised bed, you can sow a cover crop of buckwheat, or winter rye and vetch, and bring the chickens back to eat and till it again when the cover crop is about four inches high. Not only does this boost fertility and soil life enormously, but it cuts down on chicken feed bills. The result is superb soil with little labor, plus eggs and meat if you wish.

To *sheet mulch* with chickens, leave the tractor in one spot for several days. Each day, add about an inch of mulch and let the chickens work over the mulch and add manure to it. When the mulch is about four inches deep, move the chickens to a new spot and repeat the process. This way, you (and the chickens) are adding both nutrients and organic matter to the soil. The mulch binds the nitrogen and other nutrients in place while the whole mixture composts. Treat this bed as you would any new sheet-mulched bed and plant it with seedlings in soil pockets or seeds in a top layer of potting soil.

You can also use a chicken tractor to make a *deep-mulch* garden bed, useful in gardens too small to move the tractor every day or where the soil is very poor. Leave the chicken tractor in one place and add about an inch of mulch each day. After about five weeks—or the time it takes broilers to grow from chicks to mature—you'll have a thick raised bed to plant. Andy Lee warns that leaving the tractor in one place this long may give predators—dogs, skunks, foxes—time to dig under the pen and attack the birds. If you're building a deep-mulch bed, he recommends laying chicken wire on the ground

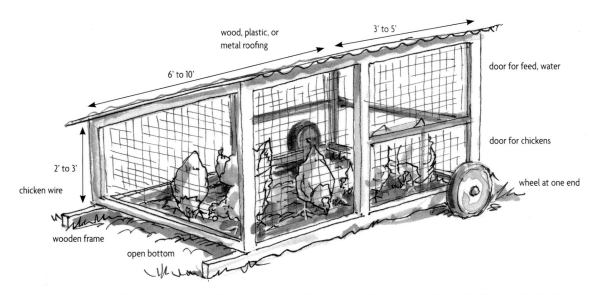

An animal tractor: a moveable pen that lets small animals such as chickens or rabbits weed, till, and fertilize garden beds.

around the pen and pinning it in place to frustrate digging predators.

Both mulch techniques work well on sloping as well as level ground. On a slope, the chickens—and gravity—will leave the mulch thicker on the downhill side of the pen, resulting in a level, terraced bed.

Chickens can also graze free-range in the garden, where they will glean insects, slugs, and weed seeds, but it's best to keep an eye on them in case they find a crop they really like, such as berries or tomatoes. Wait until garden plants are mature before letting the chickens into the garden, as poultry will happily eat tender seedlings. If you allow the birds into the garden in the late afternoon, they won't be there long enough to do any damage and will naturally return to their coop or tractor at dusk, sparing you the trouble of a lengthy chicken chase.

Growing some of the chickens' food will cut down on costs and reduce imports to your site, but it's not realistic to expect to grow all their food. A hen needs about eighty pounds of grain a year, which could be grown on about 1,000 square feet. The numbers add up fast: Feeding a small flock of eight hens would require an eighty-by-one-hundred-foot garden and countless hours of labor to grow and harvest the food. Instead, I'd suggest growing multifunctional plants around the yard to supplement the chickens' diets, which will cut costs and provide valuable vitamins and fresh foods. These plants could be nicely integrated into the garden design, supplying habitat, food, nutrients, and all the other needs of the ecological garden, rather than just the single function of chicken feed. And growing chicken forage creates yet another closed cycle for the garden. As the chickens build the soil, the resulting food plants will be healthier and more lush, and the chickens in turn grow stronger and more productive.

Table 7-3 lists some plants that can be included in a chicken yard or integrated into a landscape for chicken forage.

Ducks, Rabbits, Worms, and Other Small Animals

Animals not well suited for tractors but useful in the garden are ducks and their relatives the muscovies. Penny Livingston's ducks, those inhabitants of her graywater pond system, patrol her garden rigor-

Category	Common Name	Species	Notes
Table 7-3. Plants that Provide Poultry Forage			
Trees			
	Black locust	*Robinia pseudoacacia*	Pods can be ground
	Fruit trees	Various	Fallen or fresh fruit
	Mulberry	*Morus* spp.	Fruits eaten
	Nut trees	Various	Cracked nuts for feed
	Oak	*Quercus* spp.	Acorns high in protein
	Pistachio	*Pistacia* spp.	Nuts eaten
	Honey locust	*Gleditsia triacanthos*	Pods can be ground
Shrubs[1]			
	Autumn olive	*Elaeagnus umbellata*	
	Barberry	*Berberis* spp.	
	Boxthorn	*Lycium* spp.	
	Buffaloberry	*Shepherdia* spp.	
	Coffeeberry	*Rhamnus* spp.	
	Currant	*Ribes* spp.	
	Elderberry	*Sambucus* spp.	
	Hackberry	*Celtis* spp.	
	Hawthorn	*Crataegus* spp.	
	Manzanita	*Arctostaphylos* spp.	
	Passionfruit	*Passiflora* spp.	
	Privet	*Foriestiera* spp.	
	Russian olive	*Eleagnus angustifolia*	
	Serviceberry	*Amelianchier* spp.	
	Siberian pea shrub	*Caragana arborescens*	edible pods
Herbaceous plants[2]			
	Alfalfa	*Medicago sativa*	
	Buckwheat	*Fagopyrum esculentum*	
	Swiss chard	*Beta vulgaris*	
	Chickweed	*Stellaria medea*	
	Chicory	*Cichorium intybus*	
	Cleavers	*Galium aparine*	
	Clover	*Trifolium* spp.	
	Comfrey	*Symphytum officinale*	
	Cucumber	*Cucumis sativus*	
	Dandelion	*Taraxacum officinale*	
	Dock	*Rumex* spp.	
	Fava beans	*Vicia faba*	

(continues)

Category	Common Name	Species	Notes
	Fennel	Foeniculum vulgare	
	Lamb's quarters	Chenopodium album	
	Mustard greens	Brassica spp.	
	Nettle, stinging	Urtica dioica	
	Pigweed	Amaranthus retroflexus	
	Plantain	Plantago spp.	
	Rye (shoots)	Secale cereale	
	Shepherd's purse	Capsella bursa-pastoris	
	Vetch, hairy	Vicia villosa	
Seed crops			
	Amaranth	Amaranthus	
	Barley	Hordeum vlgare	
	Corn	Zea mays	
	Millet	Panicum miliaceum	
	Oats	Avena sativa	
	Quinoa	Chenopodim quinoa	
	Sunflower	Helianthus annuum	
	Wheat	Tritium aestivum	

Table 7-3. Plants that Provide Poultry Forage (continued)

1. All fruits and many of the greens of these shrubs can be eaten by poultry.
2. The seeds, flowers, and greens of these herbaceous plants can be eaten by poultry. Young greens may be more palatable.

ously for slugs and insects, leaving behind a little fertilizer. Many of the plants in Table 7-3 are suitable for ducks as well as chickens.

Ducks are gentler on plants than chickens and don't scratch much, thus they don't need close supervision in the garden. Khaki Campbells and Indian Runners are good egg layers, while Pekins and Improved Mallards are bred for meat. Muscovies, a South American fowl intermediate between ducks and geese, are very quiet, making them good candidates for the urban or suburban yard.

A nonfeathered animal that works well in a tractor is the rabbit. You'll need to put a chicken-wire bottom on the tractor since rabbits are burrowers and will quickly tunnel out of a bottomless pen. They don't scratch the way chickens do, so they're less effective tillers, but their manure is high in nutrients, and they're voracious vegetarians that will quickly eliminate weeds.

Rabbits can be grown as pets or for their products. Angoras provide wool (French angoras are easier to raise than the English variety, which can develop eye problems and must be brushed daily or their hair will mat). For those so inclined, a few rabbits can provide meat for a family. Five breeding rabbits, each birthing per year an average of three litters of five kits, will yield ample meat for a typical family. That's an intensive breeding rate, and those who care about their rabbits will let the mothers rest every other year, or the exhausted animals will die young. Good breeds for meat include California and New Zealand rabbits. Their fur also has commercial value.

Since rabbits don't eat insects or scratch the soil,

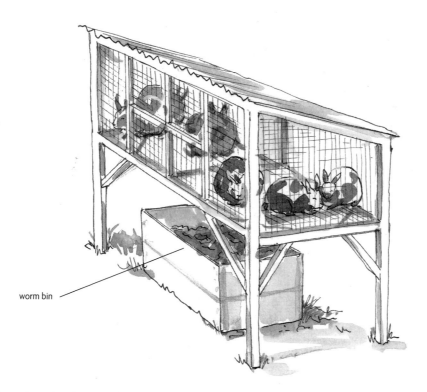

worm bin

A rabbit hutch combined with a worm bin. The rabbit manure is quickly converted into rich compost by the worms.

some gardeners think they aren't ideally suited to animal tractors. Instead they employ rabbits in the garden by combining rabbit hutches with worm bins to naturally process manure into a perfect compost (see illustration). This technique links two animals together and, like all well-connected relationships, provides benefits—great compost and fat worms—and solves problems, by conscientiously using rabbit manure and urine.

In this system, a wire-bottomed rabbit hutch is built elevated on posts. Below the hutch, set an open wooden or plastic bin eighteen to thirty inches deep and big enough to catch the droppings. Place shredded newspaper plus peat moss or shredded dry leaves into the bin to a depth of six inches. The bin will collect rabbit manure, urine, and spilled food. Once this bin is full, add 100 to 300 red worms to it, cover the box, and set it aside. Place a second box containing the newspaper/peat moss mixture

under the rabbit hutch. By the time the second bin is full, you should have beautiful worm compost in the first box and can sift out the worms and add them to the second bin.

These worm bins can also process kitchen scraps. Worm bins are a first-rate composting system that can be used indoors. The virtually odorless bins are ideal for creating indoor compost in northern winters, when the outdoor compost pile is a frozen lump. Check the bibliography for more details on constructing and using worm bins.

With animals, we extend the reach of our garden into yet another kingdom of nature. In the rich soil teem the unseen wonders that bring the dead back to life, the decomposers who work their magic on wood and leaf, on bone and chitin. Above ground are the plants, green marvels that capture the sunlight and build sugar and sap, the flowers, fruits, and seeds that feed us all. And now we bring in the animals that flit and buzz, scamper and scratch, nibble and manure. Animals are the final link in nature's cycle. They are nature's mechanics, accelerating growth here with seed dispersal and fertilizer, retarding it there with a vigorous browse and trample. They haul nutrients and seeds great distances, from a lush lunch nook to a dry bare patch used for a dust bath, inoculating the barren soil. They process seedheads through their bodies and hooves, mash seed into the soil, trim branches, thin the hordes of bugs. Without animals, our labor is doubled and redoubled, and we must pollinate, spray, dig, cart and spread fertilizer and fill the thousand other tasks easily and cheerfully done by our marvelous cousins. Without animals, nature just limps along, and in a garden lacking animals we must supply the crutches. By creating a garden that nurtures our two-, four-, and more-legged friends, we close the cycle and shift the burden more evenly, letting nature carry her share.

PART THREE

Assembling the Ecological Garden

CHAPTER 8

Creating Communities for the Garden

It's time to assemble the pieces of the ecological garden. We know that our garden needs water, which is stored best by the soil but also held within plants and in ponds and cisterns. Our garden's soil is alive, charged with fertility and bustling with microbes to shuttle that fertility to plants. Rooted in this living soil are the plants themselves, in all the many roles they play. The plants we've chosen will collect and cycle Earth's minerals, water, and air; shade the soil and renew it with leafy mulch; and yield fruits and greens for people and wildlife. In the ecological garden, animal companions abound. Birds scratch the soil, scatter seed, munch malevolent larvae, and leave an offering of nutrient-packed droppings. Here are insects to subdue pests and to pollinate the many flowers. Perhaps, too, this garden holds a few chickens, ducks, or rabbits for soil tilling, weed and bug control, and for their gift of manure. In the wilder edges, deer pass by to prune and harvest; mice and voles scuttle off with seed—some of which, far off and forgotten, will sprout to widen our garden's reach yet further.

But these are merely the pieces. Left unconnected, water, soil, plants, and animals create little more than a collection of fragments: pretty potsherds that hold nothing until glued back together. These fragments, as should be clear by now, do not come to life until they are assembled in the proper relationships. In this chapter, we'll examine those relationships.

We'll begin our work of connection simply, blending a few plants together to glimpse what synergies emerge from their juxtaposition. Then we'll create communities of plants using both wild and domesticated varieties. Each member of these communities supports, enhances, and benefits from the others. Although our communities are based on plants, their participants extend beyond the floral realm to include insects, birds, mammals, soil organisms, and people.

Interplanting and Beyond

Vegetable gardeners have some experience in creating plant communities. Food-growers have long attempted to avoid the drawbacks, both aesthetic and ecological, of large blocks of a single crop. Monocultures deplete the soil, provide a sumptuous feast for pests, and dull the senses. To avoid these faults, many gardeners practice *interplanting*, mixing different varieties together to save space and avoid solid clumps of one vegetable. Interplanting strategies, while usually limited to vegetables, illustrate some of the principles of combining varieties that work together to deter pests and aid each other in other ways. Once we've learned the basics of interplanting, we can broaden our spectrum and look beyond vegetables toward garden plant communities that benefit not just people but all of nature.

One simple interplanting scheme mixes onions, carrots, and lettuce in the same garden bed. These three plants have different leaf forms, light requirements, and rooting depths, which makes them compatible both physically and in terms of their resource needs. The cylindrical leaves of onions grow virtually straight up, casting little shade. Feathery carrot leaves bush out a bit but don't create deep shadows. Lettuce, although it forms a solid mass of greenery, is short and casts its shade below the other plants. The three leaf forms fit well together, allowing ample sunlight to bathe each plant. Also, lettuce needs less sun than onions and carrots, so the slight shade cast by the latter two won't impede lettuce's growth. In summer, lettuce tends to bolt and taste bitter unless shaded, which is a good reason to grow it beside taller plants. And, lastly, the roots of these three plants don't compete for space: Onions are shallow rooted, lettuce reaches to an intermediate depth, and the taproots of carrots go deep but straight down. Each searches for nutrients in a different place. These three vegetables, with their varying shapes, light requirements, and rooting patterns, can be interplanted very successfully.

Other combinations: Interplanting Brussels sprouts, parsley, spinach, and onions is effective because the spinach and onions are ready before the sprouts mature, and the parsley can tolerate some shade. Also, their root depths and nutrient needs are divergent. Radishes, lettuce, and peppers work well for similar reasons; the radishes grow fast, the lettuce doesn't mind the shade of the young peppers, and by the time the peppers are full-grown, the other plants have been harvested.

Though interplanting saves space, it doesn't go far enough for me. Most interplanting, as in the

An interplant of lettuce, onions, and carrots, which allows dense planting while avoiding competition for nutrients and sunlight.

above examples, simply combines plants to avoid negative interactions, such as competition for space or light. This form of interplanting doesn't blend plants into dynamic, interactive associations the way nature does. What's more, interplanting rarely capitalizes on the mutual benefits plants can provide each other, such as deterring pests or transporting and storing nutrients.

A second technique, *companion planting*, takes

advantage of some of these mutual benefits. For example, planting sage near carrots reputedly repels the carrot fly. Carrots themselves are thought to exude a substance that stimulates the growth of peas. Companion planting is a step in the right direction; but, unfortunately, many traditional combinations turn out, in careful trials, to provide no benefit at all. Surprisingly, some old recipes even produce detrimental effects. Robert Kourik, in his excellent book, *Designing and Maintaining Your Edible Landscape—Naturally*, summarizes a wealth of research that debunks many old-time companion-plant recipes. For example, gardeners have long edged their beds with marigolds to deter pests, and Kourik notes that certain marigolds, especially Mexican marigolds (*Tagetes minuta*) can repel harmful soil nematodes. However, other varieties of marigold actually attract pests, and most simply don't help at all. I've seen gardens randomly strewn with marigolds as a general panacea, but the research makes me wonder if the benefits extend beyond offering something nice to look at.

Hence, without supporting data I'm skeptical of planting basil alongside tomatoes in the hopes of getting bigger beefsteaks—to choose an old-time companion recipe at random. Companion planting in its highest form can create beautiful mixed beds of flowers and vegetables. In its simplest and most common mode, however, companion planting merely combines plants in what is not far from monoculture: nice orderly beds of two or perhaps three species—static, perfectly weeded, and ecologically dead. We can do better.

Gardening Goes Polycultural

What if we could blend the best qualities of interplanting and companion planting? Interplanting combines crops that minimize competition for sun and nutrients. Companion planting blends varieties that enhance each other. Natural plant communities, tuned by billions of years of evolution, do both. Why not emulate these plant communities in our gardens?

Plant communities are dynamic, not static. As we saw in Chapter 2, they are constantly changing their composition, swapping species in and out as ecological succession lurches on. In succession's early stages, aggressive pioneer plants—usually annuals—colonize bare earth. As they grow and die, their leaf litter scatters mulch on the soil. Their roots crack open the hard ground, and, after death, decay into fingers of humus that fan deep into the soil. This prepares the ground for later, more choosy species. Conditions are right for longer-lived perennials to move into this now-fertilized soil, followed by shrubs. Eventually, if rainfall is ample, trees appear.

The living plants themselves create conditions attractive to other species. When pioneers move in, the once-bare ground, with its uniform temperature, humidity, and sunlight, is subdivided by plant life into myriad habitats and microclimates. Beneath the pioneers' leafy protection, the soil becomes moist and cool, a perfect milieu for seeds of new species to germinate. Soon the once-naked earth is swaddled in plants of contrasting height, width, leaf size and shape, succulence, scent, flower form, reflectance and absorbance, and a host of other qualities. Diversity cascades on diversity. As microclimates multiply, favorable conditions evolve for yet more species. Niches abound, and new varieties will move into these niches, attracting more insects, more birds, more life.

The typical vegetable garden, however, has only one niche: loamy soil, at neutral pH, in full sun. (OK, we all don't have gardens like that. Your garden may have acidic clay hardpan that's shaded by a neighbor's tree, but most gardeners aspire to have the so-called ideal conditions listed above.) This ideal, however, reduces a diverse ecology to an impoverished uniformity. The many plants that

Ianto Evans's Polyculture

Prepare a garden bed, allowing about twenty square feet of bed for each person who will be fed from the polyculture.

- *Two weeks before the last frost:* Indoors, start about five cabbage plants per twenty square feet of bed. The cabbages should be ready for transplanting a month or so after the seed mixture below is sown. To extend the season, choose both early- and fall-maturing cabbages.
- *Week One (at the last frost date in your region):* In early spring, sow seeds of radish, dill, parsnip, calendula, and lettuce. For a lengthy harvest season, select several varieties of lettuce. A mix of looseleaf, romaine, butter, iceberg, and heat-tolerant varieties such as Summertime or Optima will stretch the lettuce season into summer.

  Broadcast all the seeds over the same area to create a mixed planting. Sow at a density of about one seed every couple of square inches and cover the entire bed with a light scattering of seed. Sow each seed type separately—don't mix the seeds and toss them all onto the bed, because the heavy seeds will be flung the farthest, and you'll wind up with all the radishes on one end and all the parsnips at the other. Then cover the seed with about a quarter-inch of compost and water gently.
- *Week Four:* Some of the radishes should be ready to pluck. In a few of the gaps left by the radishes, plant cabbage seedlings about eighteen inches apart.
- *Week Six:* The young lettuce will be big enough to harvest. The dense sowing of lettuce will yield a flavorful mesclun blend when the plants are young. Pick the whole plant to make space for the rest to grow. With continued thinning, the remaining lettuce will grow up full sized. If you've chosen varieties carefully, you'll be crunching lettuce for up to four months.
- *Late Spring/Early Summer:* When the soil has warmed to above 60 degrees Fahrenheit, plant bush beans in the spaces left by the lettuce. If more openings develop in early summer, sow buckwheat and begin thinning their edible greens shortly after they appear. The next crops to harvest after the lettuce will be the dill and calendula (calendula blossoms are edible and make a tasty addition to salads). The early cabbages will be coming on at about this time, too, followed in midsummer by the beans. Parsnips are slow growing and will be ready to eat in fall and winter. As gaps in the polyculture appear in early autumn, mild-winter gardeners can plant fava beans; others can poke garlic cloves into the openings, to be harvested the following spring.

grace our gardens were collected from hundreds of ecological niches that differ in soil type, available sunlight, and many other variables. Sentencing our garden plants to a single uniform habitat erodes the broad potential available to us. A garden that offers varying soil, light, and temperature enlarges the palette of species that will thrive there.

One of the biggest factors that shape the garden environment is the plants themselves. Our plants coevolved in dynamic environments, molded by neighboring plants. Species evolved under tree canopies, amid grasses and herbs, or shouldering their way between shrubs, but never alone, always competing and cooperating with the other members of their communities. Isolating these mostly gregarious plants and plunking them into beds and borders extracts them from their original niches.

To re-create or mimic the original niches of our now-domesticated plants, we can use a gardening technique called *polyculture*, a word hybridized from the Greek *poly*, meaning "many," and the Latin *cultura*, "to tend or cultivate." Polycultures are dynamic, self-organizing plant communities composed of several to many species.

Interplanting and companion planting are elementary forms of polyculture, which in its simplest form is simply growing many plants together. But in more sophisticated polycultures, the plants themselves tune their environment to the best conditions for their growth. Given the chance, heat-shunning lettuces will snuggle for protection under a leafy canopy of cauliflower. Slow-germinating wildflowers will bide their time in the moist shade of an early-leafing currant bush. We can encourage these relationships to flourish in our gardens. By blending a carefully chosen but highly diverse assortment of varieties, we can create gardens in which plants nestle together in minimally competitive patterns, bolster each other with beneficial interactions, and shift their composition in ecological succession, all combining to provide a lengthy and varied harvest of food, blossoms, and habitat.

We'll look at a simple polyculture system that introduces this ecological gardening technique, followed by a more elaborate version. Afterward, I'll present guidelines for designing your own polycultures.

Traditional societies have long used polycultures, but most of these employ plants unfamiliar to most North American gardeners. Recognizing the need for polycultures based on European and American varieties, a team headed by Ianto Evans, a transplanted Welshman living on our West Coast, pioneered several temperate-climate polycultures in the 1980s. Ianto is an inventor, teacher, and architect who spoons out his accumulated wisdom in thoughtful and sometimes curmudgeonly dollops. He has traveled at length in the less-developed world, and his creations, which include new bean varieties, fuel-efficient woodstoves, and sculpted earthen houses, temper industrial technologies with the wisdom of traditional cultures. Ianto's polycultures follow suit, infusing indigenous knowledge into Western gardens.

After observing polyculture gardens used in traditional cultures, Ianto extracted a set of basic principles that allowed him to blend common vegetable varieties into combinations that would ripen, one variety after another, over many months to give up to nine months of continuous food. His efforts, originally limited and tentative, gradually evolved into polycultures of up to thirty species, and his work has been continued by others.

Ianto devised a seven-variety polyculture that mimics natural succession and fills ecological niches—and a garden bed—densely. As the early-germinating plants in this polyculture grow, they create habitat for the other members of the assemblage, and they attract beneficial insects for pollinating as well as fighting pests. The thick planting forms a living mulch for the soil, curtailing evaporation and the need for water. This polyculture yields a steady harvest for several months from a very small space. All these benefits stem from placing the plants in the right relationship, one that takes advantage of the dynamic qualities of living beings.

Ianto's polyculture blends early-sprouting radishes, insect-attracting and edible dill and calendula, lettuce, parsnips, cabbage, and nitrogen-fixing bush beans. Detailed instructions for planting this polyculture are given in the accompanying sidebar.

How do the elements of this polyculture interact? The fast-growing radishes cast shade, which keeps the soil moist and cool. This protects slow-germinating seeds—particularly the parsnips—from the desiccating sun. Strongly scented dill and calendula will confuse insects searching for tender young radishes. Dill also hosts tiny predatory wasps that attack cabbage loopers. Cabbages, which grow through the fall and into winter, protect the soil from erosion by heavy rains. Beans add nitrogen to the soil. The variety of leaf shapes and root depths minimizes competition for sun, space, and nutrients.

The polyculture as a whole provides enough diversity to bewilder most pests. The thick planting creates a living mulch that protects the soil from sun, rain erosion, and heat, thus conserving soil texture, humus, and moisture. I've pushed my hand into a polyculture on a blazing summer afternoon and found the lower leaves and soil deliciously cool and moist. Also, because most plant niches are filled, weeds are denied access. The overall yield is greater than if the plants were grown in monocultural blocks covering the same area. And this polyculture offers a long and varied harvest from just one major sowing and a few minutes of later care.

Further Adventures with Polycultures

Others have expanded on Ianto's work, adding new species to his seven-part polyculture. A village self-development organization in Nepal, the Jajarkot Permaculture Program, has created an enlarged polyculture that, with the modifications I have made, can be planted in spring in most North American gardens.

This polyculture begins by planting a dense ground cover of edible greens interspersed with slower-growing salad plants and herbs. As these are harvested, beans and other vegetables take their place. In all but the most bitterly cold regions, this polyculture can yield food for six to eight months of the year. In northern climes, installing spun row cover or greenhouse plastic over the bed can extend the productivity of this planting well into the fall and spring.

With Jajarkot's polyculture (see the accompanying sidebar), you'll be harvesting herbs for a month or two—longer if you trim some of the dill, fennel, coriander, and basil rather than pulling up the whole plant. Salad greens will yield for three to four months. The early brassicas and peas will come on by late spring, and bush beans, favas, and alliums in summer. If you've chosen a few fall-heading brassicas, these will be ready for your table in autumn.

The interactions and benefits of Jajarkot's polyculture are much the same as in Ianto's, just on a larger scale. The several umbelliferous herbs attract beneficial insects. A variety of legumes fix nitrogen, and the fava beans also attract parasitic wasps. Once again, the dense greenery shades and protects the soil and excludes weeds. And of course, the lengthy harvest is a big benefit for the gardener.

Designing Your Own Polycultures

Temperate-climate polyculture design is still in its infancy. Plenty of research still needs to be done to develop successful combinations and to broaden the number of plant varieties that work well. I encourage gardeners to experiment with their own polyculture versions. A polyculture that succeeds in one climate, such as my native Northwest with its long, cool spring and fall, might bolt or bake in the hotter "shoulder seasons" of the South or Midwest.

One tip for a successful annual-vegetable polyculture is to use plants from each of these three groups: fast-growing greens and early vegetables such as radishes and the spring brassicas (broccoli, raab, early cauliflowers), midseason veggies such as beans and onions, and slow-growing plants including fall cauliflower and cabbage, Brussels sprouts, parsnips, and leeks.

Jajarkot's Advanced Polyculture

To create Jajarkot's polyculture, prepare a garden bed, allowing twenty to thirty square feet of space for each person to be fed.

- *One month before your last frost date:* Start, per person, four to eight seedlings each of cabbage, cauliflower, or broccoli indoors. Select a blend of varieties that will ripen over a long season.
- *Week One (at the last frost date in your region):* Create an edible ground cover by densely sowing a mix of mustard greens (Osaka Purple mustard, tatsoi, mizuna, garden cress, and the like) and other cool-season greens such as arugula, garden purslane, and shiso. In regions where spring is warm (May temperatures reaching 80 degrees Fahrenheit), also sow buckwheat. Young buckwheat greens are delicious in salads or stir-fried.

Then add some salad crops. Lightly sow the seeds of radishes, chard, lettuces, and carrots among the previously sown seeds.

Herb seeds go in next. Sow fennel, dill, and coriander somewhat more densely than the salad crops since they don't seem to germinate as well.

Now add legume seeds to the mix. Push fava beans, bush peas, or a blend of these, into the soil roughly one foot apart.

Add some of your favorite alliums, such as onions, garlic, garlic chives, or leeks. Plant either seeds or starts of these, about six to twelve inches apart.

- *Weeks Two to Four:* Begin harvesting the edible ground cover. Don't just trim the leaves; pull the whole plant to create openings. Take care not to disturb the young beans or alliums. Pull a few of the young herbs to thin them out; they'll make a tangy addition to salads and stews. In some of the resulting gaps, plant cabbage, cauliflower, or broccoli seedlings about eighteen inches apart.
- *Late Spring/Early Summer:* When soil temperatures reach 60 degrees Fahrenheit, plant basil and bush beans in the openings.

As the spring warms up, many of the greens will bolt. Speed up your harvesting of these to eliminate them before they set seed. Alternatively, if you want to naturalize these greens in your garden, let a few go to seed, then pull the whole plant and lay it on the soil to compost and reseed. Continue harvesting all plants as they mature or crowd.

To help gardeners design polycultures, Ianto Evans has developed a set of guidelines based on his long experience. His time-tested tips are:

1. Seed several varieties of each species. This lengthens the harvest season, teaches you about the best types to plant, and more fully occupies ecological niches.

2. Don't sow seed too thickly. The recommended sowing rates on seed packets are based on heavy thinning. You'll be eating nearly every plant, so you'll be "thinning" after your plants are at least adolescent size, which is later than in conventional gardens. If you sow ten species, reduce your sowing density accordingly, to about

10 percent of the suggested rate. One seed per couple of square inches is plenty. Any more than that and you'll be inundated with hundreds of tiny salad plants about one month after sowing. This not only makes harvesting/thinning tedious, but the speedier-growing greens can overwhelm the less sturdy herbs.

3. Begin your harvest early. Harvest your plants, especially greens, when they begin to crowd, not when they are mature. Overcrowding will inhibit rapid growth. Young plants are especially tasty, as the continuing infatuation with baby vegetables demonstrates.

4. Mix plant families, not just species. Closely related plants compete for the same nutrients, so a polyculture that's heavy on the brassicas (broccoli, cauliflower, cabbage, kale, Brussels sprouts) or any other single genus won't grow well. In addition to preventing fertility shortages, diversity will confuse pests in search of big blocks of their favorite food.

5. Include many seeds of fast-growing, shallow-rooted species. Radishes, mustard greens, fenugreek, and buckwheat will cover the soil quickly to thwart weeds and will get your harvest off to a fast start. You'll eat a lot of these small plants, so plant them the thickest.

6. Overlap the harvests. To extend the harvest season, plant several varieties of each species, each with a different ripening time. For example, leaf lettuce is ready for the salad bowl much sooner than head lettuce. In

addition, blend fast-growing vegetables with slow ones and early-season crops with late. Examples are radishes followed by cabbage, peas followed by bush beans followed by fall fava beans, or spring herbs such as dill succeeded by summer basil.

7. Avoid root and light competition. Sprawling plants such as tomatoes and potatoes may not be appropriate for polycultures since they'll shade out many other plants. A preponderance of root crops will compete for soil space. Think about the mature size and shape of each variety before you plant and avoid competition.

8. Harvest whole plants. With the exception of some long-lived herbs that can be prevented from bolting by regular trimming, polyculture plants should be pulled up whole. This allows room for the other many contenders for the same space. Be gentle; don't disturb the roots of adjoining plants. Harvest from the densest zones and select plants whose harvest will release their slower companions from competition.

9. Save a few plants for seed. Let a few of the healthiest individuals of each species go to seed, for natural reseeding or for seed saving. Plants saved for seed should, if possible, be left on the north side of the bed, so they won't shade the other flora.

10. Examine your polyculture every day. Things happen fast in polycultures. After about three weeks, your polyculture will be at maximum density and will need daily harvest to continue rapid growth. The payoff is

a nice salad or stir-fry every day. Your polyculture will appreciate this daily attention. As the Chinese say, the best fertilizer is the gardener's shadow.

Guilding the Garden

By now, readers who are wildlife gardeners are growing impatient with all this talk of lettuce and broccoli. The above polycultures reside firmly in the realm of vegetable gardening. They are heavily cultivated, omit native plants, and allow few roles for wildlife beyond insects. These polycultures, while more "natural" than clean-cultivated row crops, are still far from behaving like wild ecosystems. We need to remedy this. I began with vegetable-based polycultures because they illustrate some of the basics of assembling plants into interactive communities, without being overwhelmingly complex. Now it's time to consider a wider variety of species that can more closely mimic a natural plant community. In these systems, the needs of humans are balanced with those of the rest of nature.

The more complex polycultures mentioned above have some of the qualities of natural communities. Polycultures undergo succession, offer many niches, and play a large role in creating their own structure, as do plant communities and ecosystems. We can think of ecosystems as intricate polycultures, with far more complex interactions. Because ecosystems are so multifaceted, they can behave in more interesting and adaptive ways than simple systems. In ecosystems, we see qualities such as succession, predator-prey relations, adaptation to fire, climate control, and so on, that you won't see in conventional farms and gardens. The ability to develop patterns and qualities such as these make ecosystems more robust, more adaptive, and less prone to disaster than human-designed systems such as gardens. What qualities of ecosystems can we use in our gardens to nudge our yards into more ecological patterns?

Here's one useful quality: Ecosystems are fundamentally cooperative places. Yes, there is plenty of competition, but the underlying dynamic is one of mutual aid. In an ecosystem, microbes build soil, soil nourishes plants, plants feed animals, and animals disperse seed and leave their waste and corpses to be transformed by microbes into soil. Here spins a cycle of mutual interdependence, rich with many specific partnerships.

We can re-create some of these partnerships in our gardens. I'm not talking about simple companion planting, with its nebulous and difficult-to-identify fellowships. Let's begin with qualities we can easily spot. Plants display outward, measurable characteristics, such as nitrogen fixation, insect attraction, and mulch production. By identifying and combining these qualities, we can create the floristic equivalent of a mutual-aid society in our garden.

Nature, as we saw in Chapter 2, binds plants into interdependent communities and associations. Indigenous people, too, have crafted plant combinations that weave synergies among species. In the past two decades, ecological designers also have blended plants into communities that contain partnerships. Permaculturists call these imitations of natural associations *guilds*.* Formally defined, a guild is a group of plants and animals harmoniously interwoven into a pattern of mutual support, often centered around one major species, that benefits humans while creating habitat. The remainder of this chapter explores the role of guilds in bringing nature's dynamics into our own gardens.

---

* The term *guild* is used by ecologists to mean something slightly different (a set of different species that use a common resource in a similar way, as in "the guild of seed-eating birds"). This overlap is unfortunate and potentially confusing, but permaculture's use of the term *guild* is well established, and I will stick with this common usage rather than introduce another term.

Guilds are one way to bridge the broad gap between conventional vegetable gardens and wildlife gardens by creating plant communities that act and feel like natural landscapes but that include humans in their webwork. Vegetable gardens benefit only humans, while wildlife or natural gardens specifically exclude people from their ecological patterns.

Gardens for wildlife are immensely valuable, but they are only a partial answer to habitat loss. As I've said before, if we ignore the material needs of humans in our urban and suburban landscapes, we're doomed to continue our voracious consumption of wild land for factory farms and tree plantations. Ecological gardens, using guilds and the other tools described in this book, help our developed land to blossom into nourishing places for both humans and wildlife.

The Three Sisters (or Is It Four?)

Let's begin our exploration of guilds with a very simple example that illustrates some essential principles. Then we can proceed to more complex guilds—ones that go beyond vegetables.

Familiar to many gardeners is the Native American triad of corn, beans, and squash, a combination often called the Three Sisters. The trio qualifies as a guild because each of these plants supports and benefits the others. The beans draw nitrogen from the air and, via symbiotic bacte-

Growing the Three Sisters Guild

Mark out a series of planting mounds about three feet apart, a couple of inches high, and a foot or so in diameter. (To calculate how many mounds you need, figure that you'll get about four or five ears of corn per hole.) Then poke three or four kernels of corn into each mound. Your favorite sweet corn variety will do, although Native Americans developed shorter, multistalked cultivars specifically for this guild, such as Black Aztec, Hopi White, or Tarahumara sweet corn, so you might consider a similar many-stalked variety. When the corn sprouts, start mounding the soil up around the young stalks. Don't cover the sprouts; just build up earth around the base. These mounds, by exposing soil to the air and sun, will warm the sprouts, speeding their growth. The mounds also improve drainage. Don't thin the corn—you want two or three stalks per mound,

hence the greater-than-usual distance between mounds.

About two weeks after planting the corn, select some pole beans, rather than a bush variety. Common pole bean varieties such as Blue Lake work well enough, although I've been told that very vigorous hybrid pole beans clambering up skinny hybrid corn stalks can pull the spindly corn down. Again, old-style varieties used traditionally in the Three Sisters work best. These include less-vigorous climbers such as Four Corners Gold and Hopi Light Yellow. But plants are forgiving, and most varieties will do well enough.

If you can, coat the bean seeds with a legume inoculant specific for beans (available from many seed suppliers). This ensures that the all-important nitrogen-fixing bacteria will find a happy home among the bean roots. Plant two or three bean

seeds near the edges of each corn mound.

At the same time you start the beans, plant squash or pumpkins between each mound. Don't use zucchini, as their tall stems will push the corn aside. Grow a vining squash variety that will sprawl over the soil.

Aside from these trio-specific instructions, grow the Three Sisters by following the cultural guidelines on each vegetable's seed packet. After harvest, leave the stalks, vines, and other organic debris on the ground to compost in place. This returns some of the extracted fertility to the soil and protects the ground from erosion. Although much of the bacterially fixed nitrogen will be concentrated into the protein-rich bean pods, plenty will remain in the vines and roots, ready to go back to the earth.

ria, convert the nitrogen to plant-available form, boosting the growth of all three vegetables. The cornstalks form a trellis for the bean vines to climb. The rambling squash, with its broad leaves, forms a living parasol that densely covers the ground, inhibiting weeds and keeping the soil cool and moist. Further cementing this trio together comes the news from scientists that the roots of the corn ooze specific sugars that are the perfect nourishment for the nitrogen-fixing bacteria.

Together, the Three Sisters produce more food, with less water and fertilizer, than a similar area planted to any one of these three crops in isolation. Jane Mt. Pleasant, an agronomist at Cornell University who has blended her Iroquois heritage with her research, has shown that total yields of this guild, measured in calories, are about 20 percent higher than comparable yields of corn grown alone in an equal-sized plot.

Look at how many interconnections this guild bears. Beans furnish nitrogenous fertility for themselves, the corn, and the squash; squash shades soil for the benefit of all three; corn feeds the bean-hugging bacterial nodules and creates a trellis for the beans. Three plants, weaving at least eight connections. The Three Sisters guild is a perfect place to begin creating a richly connected garden.

In the Southwest, a fourth "sister" is found in this guild: Rocky Mountain bee plant *(Cleome serrulata)*. Often found growing near former Anasazi settlements—it's virtually an indicator plant for ancient ruins—this two- to five-foot-tall, pink-flowered cleome is a powerful attractant for beneficial insects that pollinate beans and squash. The young leaves, flowers, and seedpods of bee plant are edible, and native people boiled and ate them or made a paste from the plant for later use. Bee plant also accumulates iron and is the source of a deep-hued paint used to create the characteristic black designs on Anasazi pottery. Songs and blessings of New Mexico's Tewa people mention corn, beans, squash, and bee plant, indicating that this multifunctional flower is an integral member of a sacred plant pantheon.

I was pleased to learn of this fourth sister, as it connects the web of this guild's beneficial interactions with the insect realm. Part of the strength of the corn/beans/squash triad comes from its tie-in with a nonvegetable domain: that of the symbiotic nitrogen-fixing bacteria carried by the beans. And now, by adding a fourth plant to the guild, the web's pattern strengthens further, drawing insects into the network. Lured by bee plant, these nectar sippers will pollinate the squash and beans (corn is wind pollinated), ensuring good fruit set. By extending the Three Sisters, we've moved into three kingdoms: animal, plant, and bacterial. Creating this connectedness allows us to draw on three billion years of life's wisdom for aid.

The lesson here is that by hooking into the cyclical rhythms of many-kingdomed nature, a guild can capitalize on enormous sources of energy and experience. Focusing only on food plants sucks fertility from the soil while giving little in return. In contrast, offering a little something extra—a habitat for bees, a home for soil organisms—ties the small cycles of our garden into the generous and large cycles of nature. Growing a few early-blooming flowers encourages bees and other beneficial insects to stick around when the fruit trees need pollination and the aphids begin to swarm. Leaving last fall's leaves to compost on a flower bed nurtures a healthy crop of worms to till and aerate soil and to deposit nutrient-rich worm castings down among the roots. Our small offerings bring large rewards. In effect, if we buy the first round of drinks, nature picks up the tab for dinner and a show. We can leverage our assets into a not-so-small fortune by piggy-backing onto the pooled resources of the natural economy. By making nature our partner, our yields multiply, and risk of failure declines.

The Inca and other New World peoples added their own fourth member to this guild: amaranth.

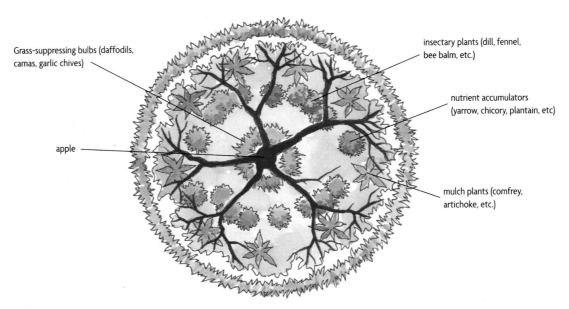

Grass-suppressing bulbs (daffodils, camas, garlic chives)

apple

insectary plants (dill, fennel, bee balm, etc.)

nutrient accumulators (yarrow, chicory, plantain, etc)

mulch plants (comfrey, artichoke, etc.)

A typical apple-centered guild. Below the apple tree, a ring of attractive and grass-suppressing bulbs encloses flowering and food-producing plants that also provide mulch and habitat for beneficial insects. The apple tree is nurtured by this community of multi-functional plants, making less work—and more food and flowers—for the gardener.

Amaranth is a high-protein grain with tasty leaves. The Hopi stewed the flowers to make a red dye. Amaranth, then, is doing a fine job of stacking more functions into this already-magnanimous guild.

The addition of bee plant or amaranth boosts the Three Sisters into a more powerful foursome. This illustrates a useful rule for guild design, which is to start with something familiar and simple and gradually add connections. This gives us a jumping-off point for creating our own guilds. Let's see how a more complex guild is constructed, and then we can develop more guidelines for building our own.

Building an Apple-Centered Guild

Courses in permaculture often proffer, as an introduction for students, a basic guild whose dominant member is an apple tree. Just as the Three (or four) Sisters bolster each other, the members of this new guild support the apple tree in numerous ways: by luring beneficial insects for pollination and pest control, boosting soil tilth and fertility, reducing root competition, conserving water, balancing

fungal populations to counter diseases such as scab, diversifying the yield of food, creating habitat, and several other functions. The result is a healthier apple tree and a varied ecology. Also, this biological support replaces human intervention, shifting the gardener's workload onto the broad back of nature.

The apple guild is a useful learning tool. It illustrates some general principles of guild building. I'll describe an apple guild briefly, and then we can examine it in more detail to see how each piece functions.

In the center of a typical apple guild, not too surprisingly, is an apple tree. Under the tree's outermost leaves, at the drip line, is a ring of thickly planted daffodil bulbs. Inside the bulbs is a broken circle of lush comfrey plants, each topped with purple blossoms that buzz with bees. Between the comfrey are two or three robust artichoke plants. Dotted around these grow flowers and herbs: yellow bursts of yarrow, trailing orange nasturtiums, and the airy umbels of dill and fennel. A closer look shows a number of plants that are normally considered weeds, such as dandelion, chicory, and plantain. Crowding between all this flora is a thick ground cover of clover, and we can spot some fava beans and other legumes growing in the dappled sun beneath the branches.

Each species in this guild performs a valuable function. Just as an automobile needs parts that perform certain functions—steering, power, braking—organized in the proper relationship, every guild has elements to do the tasks—disease control, fertilizer production, pollination—necessary for the guild to be healthy and low maintenance. Good guild design lets nature perform all these jobs by fitting different plants and animals into each role. If we leave out one of the guild's pieces, we're stuck with performing that part's task. And if we're short-sighted enough to simply plant an apple tree in isolation, we have to do it all: spraying for disease, watering, fertilizing, and importing bee hives for pollination. No wonder fruit trees are considered high maintenance. Conventional orchards have broken the gears that mesh our fruit trees into the rest of nature.

Now that we have an overview of this guild, let's dive in and examine its pieces to see how they fit together to create a harmonious community. In keeping with ecological gardening's emphasis on processes rather than pieces, I've organized the guild members by function instead of plant type. You've seen most of these plant functions before, in Chapter 6, but here I relate them more specifically to guilds. These are the elements that are common to almost every well-designed guild.

The central element. In this guild, we've chosen an apple tree as the centerpiece, though almost any fruit or small nut tree could be substituted. Usually the central element is a food-producing plant, though other types of guilds may feature wildlife-attracting or nitrogen-fixing trees or perhaps a timber-producer. Apple trees come in many sizes, from thirty-foot-tall standard trees to six-foot minidwarfs, with semistandards, semidwarfs, and dwarf trees in between. All are fine for guilds; but obviously, a small tree won't support as many associated plants as a big one. The size you choose will be based on your property size, how high you like to reach or climb to harvest, and other similar variables. The tree should be pruned to an open shape to allow light to reach the plants below.

Grass-suppressing bulbs. The shallow roots of bulbs keep grasses from moving into our guild. Grasses, though planted deliberately by many orchardists, are surface feeders and thus vie for nutrients with trees, whose principal feeding roots also lie near the surface (where most nutrients reside). Eliminating grasses near fruit trees will lessen the need for fertilizer. With less root and nutrient competition, the fruit trees may be more vigorous and grow to their maximum size.

Bulbs should be planted in a circle at the drip line of the tree based on its full-grown size. Because spring bulbs curtail their growth in early summer, they won't rob water from the tree as the heat comes on. Useful bulbs include daffodils, camas, and alliums (preferably perennial alliums such as garlic, garlic chives, ramps or wild leek, or Egyptian onions rather than annual onions).

Daffodils are particularly useful bulbs, as they contain toxins that animals abhor. Deer eschew the aboveground parts, and gophers are repelled by the bulbs. Planting one circle of daffodils around the trunk and a second thick circle of them at the drip line will temper the depredations of browsers, burrowers, and bark-chewers.

Bulbs such as camas and alliums, besides occupying ground that would otherwise be choked with grass, are edible. Camas bulbs were a principal food of western Native Americans and are having a resurgence among wild-food enthusiasts. Be very

A mature apple tree guilded with currants, fennel, mint, and comfrey.

cautious, though, about planting edible bulbs near daffodils, as eating a daff by mistake could cause serious gastric distress.

This selection of multifunctional bulbs can yield food, protect from pests, and reduce grasses. You've probably noticed that they look nice, too. In general, bulbs for this guild should be spring flowering and summer dormant and ideally have at least one function beyond shouldering aside the grass, such as edibility, pest repellence, or beneficial-bug luring.

Insect- and bird-attracting plants. The tempting blossoms of flowering plants will lure pollinators for boosting fruit set and attract predatory wasps that feast on pestiferous larvae such as borers and codling moths. Choices include edible herbs such as dill, fennel, and coriander, as well as many of the insectary plants described in Chapter 6 and listed in the appendix. If you want to be a fanatic, the commercial orchardists tell us, select flowers that will bloom just before and after—but not during—

apple blossom time, so pollinators will be abundant but not distracted by competing blooms. For home orchards, I suspect this timing is not critical.

A few flowering shrubs such as butterfly bush and fuchsia, or perennials such as red-hot poker and salvia varieties, placed not necessarily under the tree but nearby, will encourage insectivorous birds, who will probe the apple tree's bark crevices for larvae and eggs.

Mulch plants. Growing mulch under the tree eliminates trudging around with a compost-filled wheelbarrow since the guild will build its own soil. Mulch makers include soft-leafed plants such as comfrey, artichokes, cardoon, rhubarb, clovers, and nasturtiums, all of which can be slashed and left to compost in place. A ring of comfrey around the tree can be hacked down four or five times a summer. As the nutrient-rich greenery rots, it delivers a huge dose of minerals and organic matter to the soil. The resulting thick layer of compost is home to a thriving and diverse population of worms, fungi, bacteria, and other helpful denizens of the soil. This rich and living soil will suppress diseases because the churning soil life competes fiercely for food and habitat below the ground. With all the resources divvied up among the soil's many inhabitants, no one microbial species can get out of balance and become a pest. This means that buildups of harmful fungi such as apple scab are less likely—there are too much competition and too many predators for a single-species population explosion. In contrast, a clean-swept and chemically fertilized orchard floor, devoid of organic matter, ensures that the only fungi able to thrive will be pests since they are adapted to feeding on the one remaining source of food: your trees.

Nutrient accumulators. Examples of plants that accumulate nutrients are chicory, dandelion, yarrow, plantain, and others found in Table 6-2 (see page 132). The deep taproots of these plants plunge far into the mineral soil and dredge up important nutrients: potassium, magnesium, calcium, sulfur, and others. As the guild matures, nutrients will begin to recycle within the guild rather than requiring extraction from mineral soil by deep roots. The accumulator plants will then become redundant and begin a natural decline that the gardener can accelerate by pulling them up and replacing them with others.

Nitrogen fixers. I've mentioned the benefits of nitrogen-fixing plants throughout this book, so it should be no surprise that they are a critical component of guilds. Adding nitrogen fixers to guilds is one more way of keeping nutrients cycling within the plant community and reducing the need for fertilizer and other inputs. Since all-important nitrogen is so freely available from the air, it seems silly to be constantly lugging bags of it into our gardens.

The list of potential N-fixers for guilds is long and includes clovers, alfalfa, lupines, cowpeas, beans, peas, vetch, and others listed in Table 6-3 (see page 135). Which is best? I opt for the perennials, such as Dutch or New Zealand white clover, alfalfa, or lupine. However, many of the others, including vetch and some beans, reseed freely, giving them nearly perennial status. Cowpeas and fava beans are edible, which stacks yet another product into the guild. In late summer, I usually poke one or two dozen fava seeds into the soil beneath each of my fruit trees, and in the following spring I harvest the pods and mulch the stalks in place. Gardeners not similarly blessed with mild winters can start favas in early spring for summer harvest and for mulch material.

I've already mentioned another N-fixer strategy, which is to plant a young nitrogen-fixing shrub, such as goumi, bladder senna, or Siberian pea shrub, in the same hole or close to a new fruit tree.

Just keep cutting back the shrub to roughly half the size of the tree until the tree is five years old or so and then remove the shrub altogether. It can be left and the pruning continued beyond age five, but the fruit tree's extensive root network will be drawing nitrogen from a vastly greater area by then. Two or three small N-fixing shrubs can also be placed at or just outside the edges of the mature drip line of the central tree when the guild is created.

Soil fumigants and pest repellents. Certain plants exude substances that repel pests. Examples are nasturtiums and certain marigolds. Their merits and drawbacks were presented in Chapter 6. Pest-repellent plants are the least understood of the guild members; and, although nasturtiums seem to be useful in guilds, few other pest repellents have been well tested, and they should be used with caution, as they may repel beneficials as well.

Habitat nooks. Piling up stones, logs, or brush near the apple guild and creating small ponds and puddles will attract lizards, frogs, snakes, and birds. I tucked individual and piled-up rocks unobtrusively around our rural yard, and vast numbers of helpful garter snakes and lizards nested under them. Soon I couldn't move a rock without uncovering a reptilian home. That was OK—I wanted a ready crew of these beneficial animals for gobbling up slugs, leaf-eating insects, and harmful larvae.

Predators such as these are important for preserving balance. If any prey species—caterpillars, aphids, slugs, or the like—finds a home in the lush garden and begins to reproduce exuberantly, a waiting population of predators will cull their numbers with chilling efficiency.

These are the roles that should be filled in any guild. Guild design is still a young science: and, as we learn more about the connections necessary to build a thriving plant community, we may need to insert other roles into our guilds. So far, ecological gardeners around the country have had good results from a blend of grass suppressers, insect and bird attractants, nutrient accumulators, mulch plants, nitrogen fixers, soil fumigants, and pest repellents, all surrounding a central food-producer tree.

Several Pieces, Many Functions, One Guild

You'll note that many of the apple-guild members have more than one function. Clover and alfalfa are nitrogen fixers, but they also attract bees. Plantain and yarrow sequester nutrients and are medicinal as well; artichokes produce both mulch and food; and mineral-collecting dandelions and chicory are also edible. The winner in the multifunctional sweepstakes is comfrey, which yields mulch and medicine, attracts insects to its flowers, pulls potassium and other minerals from the soil into its leaves, and can be made into a tea for drinking or for fertilizing the garden. Clever guild designers will choose as many multifunctional guild members as they can. This begets a guild that swells with connections, which, as we saw in Chapter 2, makes a plant community—and our garden—flexible, responsive, and robust. Plants acting in community can survive weather extremes, soil problems, pest invasions, and other onslaughts far better than can isolated species.

All that remains to create the apple guild is to fit the plants together. The illustration on page 186 shows one arrangement that will work in most gardens, although it is more stylized and formal than most guilds turn out to be—it's a schematic drawing, after all.

To decide how many plants to use, let the mature size of the central tree be the guide. A dwarf or semi-dwarf apple tree will support fewer guild members than a large standard tree and will require smaller plant varieties. With dwarf trees, I'd avoid climbers such as vetch, which might trellis up the apple and shroud it with vines. Also, artichokes are almost too large to fit under a dwarf tree unless they are planted toward the tree's drip line or just outside it. Think about each plant's habits and mature size when you construct your array. As a rule of thumb, the larger the plant, the fewer of its kind in the guild: one apple, one or two artichokes, several comfreys, a dozen insectary plants, dozens of bulbs, a hundred or so clovers.

There's one potential drawback to our apple guild: New guild-builders often place plants too densely under the tree. Come harvest time, the apple may be surrounded by a thicket of vegetation that will ensnare the legs of an orchard ladder. Fortunately, by the time mid- to late-fruiting apple varieties are ripe, much of the undergrowth will have died down, and harvest will be easy. But harvesting summer apples will necessitate a bit of care during ladder placement. However, there's no hurry—this

isn't a commercial orchard, and the extra bounty and reduced maintenance bequeathed by the guild should balance any slight inconvenience felt while parking the ladder. But do remember to leave room for access.

This guild restores nature's role as the gardener's partner, transforming a solitary apple tree into a plant community that immensely lightens the human workload. By creating a guild such as this one, gardeners weave a strong web that builds fertile soil and mulch; attracts pollinators and pest-fighting insects; reduces fungal disease; provides a diverse array of food, flowers, and herbs; creates wildlife habitat; and reduces water and fertilizer use. These benefits stem not just from choosing the right parts—the right plants—but also from placing the guild's parts in the right relationship.

CHAPTER 9

Designing Garden Guilds

Nature has much to teach us about designing guilds. The resilience and abundance of natural plant communities are incentive enough for us to listen to nature, but there's more to learn. A healthy plant community recycles its own waste back into nutrients, resists disease, controls pests, harvests and conserves water, attracts insects and other animals to do its bidding, and hums along happily as it performs these and a hundred other tasks. To lay the groundwork for building our own guilds, we can look at natural communities—what they're made of, how they're organized, and how the pieces are connected. Although simply copying the guilds found in this book may satisfy some gardeners, more experimentally inclined readers may want to create their own guilds. The next few sections show how. Also, not all guilds are appropriate for every soil, climate, and terrain, thus it's useful to know how to customize guilds without severing their interconnections.

This chapter offers three techniques for learning about guild design from natural plant communities. The first method is based on intimate, firsthand knowledge—hanging out with a plant community long enough to see interrelationships among the various members. The second technique is more of a "paint-by-numbers" approach for those lacking the time for lingering meditations in the woods. This method uses plant identification books and library research

to assemble a guild. (A note on nomenclature: When I refer to a *community*, I mean a natural grouping of species in the wild. A *guild*, on the other hand, is a human-made assemblage that mimics a natural community.) The third method lets us assemble guilds based on function. The apple guild from the last chapter introduced this method. There the guild's function was to support an apple tree in its need for pollinators, healthy soil, and so forth. Guilds can be designed to meet a host of other functions, such as wildlife attraction, erosion control, or toxic soil cleanup.

Using this guilds-by-function method, guilds can also provide products for us. For example, an herbalist and wild-crafter might create a guild that provides medicine and first aid, another for perfume and scent, and a third offering basketry and fiber supplies. Although these guilds may have specific designed-in functions, some of the guild species need also to provide nutrients and other basics of life for the guild. Every guild will be rounded out with a few members that build soil, attract pollinators, and offer similar other forms of support.

After learning about guild design, we'll see how to combine several guilds to create landscapes that offer an incredibly diverse assortment of fruits, vegetables, and wildlife habitat while minimizing the gardener's work by letting nature do her share.

An Intimate Way of Guild-Building

Every region has its own set of plant communities, whether we're in the oak-hickory woodlands of the Northeast, the chaparral of California, the saguaro-mesquite lands of the low desert, or the Southeast's pine forests. Local field guidebooks, especially recently published ones, often list the dominant plant communities of the region. A brief walk with a field guide through the native plant communities where we live (or those remaining near our city or suburb in nature parks and preserves) will teach us which species regularly occur together. Each community has an almost palpable feel; and, as we become more experienced, we can sense the shift from, say, a dry and open oak-hickory woods to the cool dampness of a maple and beech grove. Soon we begin to see relationships. We might note that currant bushes seem to thrive beneath the maples, but they are thin and rare below the oaks; or that squirrels extend the spread of oak woods by stashing and forgetting acorns.

What about hybrid plant communities, those novel mixtures of natives and exotics that we encounter increasingly often? In and around many cities and suburbs, when we spot native plants, they are often jumbled together with garden escapees, bird-imported shrubs, and disturbance-loving newcomers. Although abhorred by plant purists, these new communities are robust and vigorous and are adapting speedily to altered environments that no longer favor many of the former inhabitants. Nature doesn't recognize the division between native and exotic but will use whatever is available as long as it suits the current conditions.

In fact, these hybrid communities may be telling us more than the native communities about what plants will work well in our surroundings. Both kinds of communities can teach us the general principles of how plants can be combined, but the hybrids might tell us more about which specific species will work best in our area. A native community in a forest preserve outside of town or groomed by a conservation group in a city park is a fine guide to the rules of guild building in nature and to which species have called a particular region home for the last few hundred years or more. But that happily thriving mélange of native and imported shrubs, flowers, and weeds in the vacant lot down the street is probably growing in conditions more like those in your yard than are the plants in the forest preserve. The hybrids may include pioneer soil-builders that can survive and replenish soils stripped and compacted by developers, insectary plants pollinated by local bees, shrubs whose abundant seedlings prove that regional birds enjoy their berries and shelter, and trees that tolerate—and perhaps help clean—exhaust-laden air. We don't want to mimic the frowzy appearance of a vacant lot, but the mingling of these scrappy species signals that a powerful synergy is taking place. In the right context, some of these plants or their more domesticated relatives could be arrayed in attractive and useful combinations.

Eventually, our observations will allow us to understand plant communities well enough to build analogous guilds of plants that will work for us in our yards. By blending a native or hybrid community's original species with similar domesticated plants we can try to re-create the community's original interconnections while tilting the community's offerings a bit into the human realm. We'll take a look at how one experienced observer designed a successful guild, and then we'll use this example to develop some general rules for guild building.

Arizona permaculture designer Tim Murphy has created a guild centered on a walnut tree, based on his intimate knowledge of a walnut-containing plant community. Let's follow Tim's observations, reasoning, and hunches to see how an experienced guild-builder uses nature to design a useful plant assembly. Since walnuts grow in much of the United

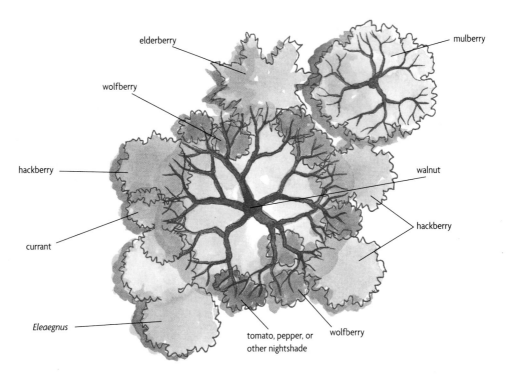

elderberry

mulberry

wolfberry

hackberry

walnut

hackberry

currant

Eleaegnus

tomato, pepper, or
other nightshade

wolfberry

A walnut/hackberry guild. Ornamental yet habitat-providing shrubs such as elderberry, hackberry, and wolfberry grow well under the stately walnut tree. Currants, tomatoes, and peppers supplement the walnut harvest. The mulberry and Elaeagnus create a transition to other plantings in the yard, protecting neighboring plants from the walnut's allelopathic effects.

States, this example of guild creation can be applied by gardeners all over the country.

The walnut tree is one of the patriarchs of the plant kingdom. Behind my parents' home in Illinois, a mighty black walnut arched over the back deck, and on many mornings I lounged in its soothing shadows with a good book and a mug of coffee. Along with shaded pleasures, walnut trees offer many other benefits. They yield delicious nuts and delight us with the scampering of squirrels among the branches in search of the tree's bounty. Even the nutshells have uses, for dye and abrasives. Walnuts also provide premium-quality timber that brings in a hefty sum and is a cabinetmaker's delight. The trees are drought-tolerant, too, and can thrive in the arid Western states as well as in less harsh locales.

Choosing companion plants for walnuts is tricky because this genus is *allelopathic*—that is, the plants

secrete a toxic substance (in this case, one called juglone) that suppresses competing plants. Very few species can thrive under the canopy of a walnut, and vegetation near the trees is often stunted. But once again, observing nature nudges us toward a solution. By observing what juglone-tolerant species naturally associate with these stately trees, Tim Murphy has evolved a guild of walnut-friendly plants.

Murphy noticed that in Arizona a vigorous pioneer shrub called hackberry (*Celtis* spp.) often sprawls in the dry shade of walnut trees. Hackberry's leaves and berries yield good wildlife forage, and the fruit, while small, is tasty, making this shrub a candidate for the ecological garden. Since hackberries seem to thrive beneath walnut trees, the shrub's growth is evidently not squelched by juglone. Like walnuts, hackberries secrete a competition-suppressing substance; an intriguing harmony vibrates between these two allelopathic birds-of-a-feather. The toxins from the two species almost seem to complement each other. Juglone, though stunting the growth of many plants, doesn't have much effect on grass, whereas hackberry's toxins inhibit grasses and other shallow-rooted plants.

Here is a subtle interweaving that leaves a highly specialized niche. What rare combination of qualities results in plants that can grow amidst walnuts and hackberries, unscathed by this broad spectrum of toxicity? We can look to nature to tell us what grows with walnuts and hackberries, but how their companions survive in toxin-laced soil is little understood. We know only superficialities about plant relations and are reduced to simple, empirical observations at this point. Some plants can tolerate walnut and hackberry toxins, while many others cannot.

To create a useful guild, we need to find more species that can survive this allelopathic bath. Tim has noted currants growing under a walnut canopy. An odd thing about these currants: Tim generally finds them under walnut trees only when hackberries are present. Why is that? Does the mingling of walnut and hackberry create some currant-enhancing condition? Tim offers up a few hypotheses for the walnut/hackberry/currant confederation. He notes that decomposing walnut leaves and husks release insect-repelling citronella fumes. Since aphids and other soft-bodied bugs are a prime currant pest, the odor of citronella wafting through currant leaves may protect this low-growing shrub. Also, currants probably benefit from the absence of competing grasses under hackberries, and the dappled shade cast by these larger chaperones provides the half-gloom that currants favor. Perhaps, too, the berry bushes profit from some subterranean molecular commerce between the microbial associates of walnut and hackberry roots. A combination of these and other less obvious qualities may explain the allure that walnuts and hackberries hold for currants.

These three plants—walnuts, hackberries, and currants—furnish the foundations of a guild. The three species provide nuts and timber, habitat for wildlife, and berries for munching or jam. That's still a meager harvest, though. Can we build on this framework?

Tim has recorded two other species found under hackberries: chiltepine (*Capsicum aviculare*) and wolfberry (*Lycium* spp.). Chiltepine, a perennial, is the feral parent of the chile pepper and bears habañero-hot half-inch fruits. Wolfberry is a thorned shrub that drops its leaves in severe drought and holds berries relished by birds. Both are members of the Solanaceae, the nightshade family, which also includes tomatoes, peppers, potatoes, and eggplants. Tim notes that the Solanaceae are narcissistic—that is, they thrive in the leaf litter of members of their own family. This raises the possibility that certain of the domesticated Solanaceae could fit into the walnut/hackberry guild. (It's well known that potatoes are stunted by juglone, but the pepper and tomato branch of the family seems less sensitive and could provide good candidates.)

Now we have a framework for a nature-based guild: walnuts, hackberries, currants, and perhaps peppers or tomatoes. Let's flesh out this skeleton still further. Nitrogen-fixing plants are obvious candidates to plug into our guild. Their ability, via symbiotic bacteria, to convert atmospheric nitrogen into fertility-giving nitrate means they simultaneously enhance soil ecology and accumulate nutrients. These multiple functions brand them as near-mandatory components of guilds. Most nitrogen fixers are legumes, the plant family that includes beans and peas. A few other plant families also bear nitrogen-fixing members. For the walnut/hackberry guild, Tim proposes a nonleguminous nitrogen fixer called Russian olive. Other members of Russian olive's genus, *Elaeagnus*, will also work, as the drought-tolerant *Elaeagnus* species seem insensitive to juglone. The berries of wild *Elaeagnus* are prime wildlife food, and domesticated varieties, such as goumi and *Elaeagnus × ebbingei*, sport fruit good enough for humans. Native plant enthusiasts may want to include indigenous nitrogen fixers such as ceanothus, or, in the Southwest, Apache plume (*Fallugia paradoxa*).

Finally, Tim suggests placing other walnut-tolerant species near the margins of the guild to buffer juglone's effect on other plants. Candidates include mulberries, elderberries, black locusts, and acacias. The last two also fix nitrogen and are beloved by bees. Beyond this buffer zone, useful plants not tolerant of juglone, such as fruiting trees and shrubs, can be woven into the assemblage.

How to assemble this guild? The illustration on page 194 gives one possible arrangement. Just as in the apple guild, the rule for determining numbers is: The bigger the plant, the fewer in the guild. Begin with a single walnut tree. Around it, within the roughly thirty-foot circle that will be the future drip line of the walnut, plant one to three each of hackberry, currant, wolfberry, and *Elaeagnus* or other N-fixer. Then scatter the solanaceous plants (peppers, tomatoes, eggplants) in the interstices. In the reduced sunlight of northern climates, sprinkle these last toward the brighter margins of the circle. In the South, however, these vegetables will appreciate the walnut's dappled shade. Radiating outside of this circle, place the mulberries and other buffer plants.

The resulting varied array will create a lively web of connections to beckon many ancillary components: birds to spread seeds and guano, insects for pollination, soil microorganisms to release and transport nutrients, and small mammals to till, prune, and fertilize.

Several gardeners have installed variations of this guild. Los Alamos resident Mary Zemach has put many of Tim's observations to work in her own walnut/hackberry guild, which also holds currants, wolfberries, elderberries, silverberries, and *Elaeagnus*. Mary acknowledges that her guild is still an experiment, but when I visited the plants were thriving.

Guilds for Bookworms

The most successful guilds are those designed after prolonged observation of a natural community. These guilds have the best chance of clicking into the dynamic relationships that wild plant communities embody. But gaining enough knowledge to design on the basis of prolonged observation takes special dedication. For ecological gardeners who haven't the time or inclination to spend hours— or years—with a natural community, I present a more academic, armchair method of guild design. Remember, though, that nothing substitutes for observation, and even a brief field trip to a plant community can yield critical insights that books can't give.

The armchair method begins with a search for lists of the major plant communities native to your area. This information resides in ecology and plant field books, forest service websites, and journal articles in university libraries or online databases. This literature is abundant and dense and may require some digging to extract the relevant nuggets. In my own neck of the woods, I would begin by searching under "Plant Communities, Oregon" in a university library catalog or database index. In your search, plug in your own state's name. When the lengthy list of references comes up, watch for titles such as "Plant Associations of (your state)," or "Vegetation of (your county)." If you know the dominant native tree in your region, you can narrow down the search by seeking research on that species. I have a handy paper called "The *Quercus garryana* Forests of the Willamette Valley," which describes the Oregon white oak forests that rule the dry hillsides of my region.

Using Natural Plant Communities to Guide Guild Design

Based on the work of Tim Murphy and other guild designers, we can develop some guidelines for creating guilds from local plant communities. Here are some questions to ask that will help select plants for useful guilds:

1. What is the dominant species of the community? Is it useful for humans, via nuts, fruit, particular beauty, animal feed, or other benefit? Is a related plant even more useful?

2. Which plants are offering food to wildlife? What wildlife uses them? Are these animals desirable in the yard?

3. Are any plants capable of providing food for humans? Do any plants in the community have domesticated relatives that can provide fruit, berries, tubers, greens, herbs, or other products for people?

4. Which species are common to more than one community, as opposed to those unique to only one? These may be possible buffer or transition plants to connect a guild to the rest of the yard.

5. Does any species show exceptional insect damage or have large numbers of harmful insects living on it? This might not be a desirable variety.

6. What species generates most of the leaf litter? Would it make a good mulch plant?

7. How well, and by what mechanisms, does the community withstand drought or flood? Some desert plants shed their leaves in extreme dryness, a useful quality but not an attractive habit for a major planting.

8. Do any plants have bare ground or stunted vegetation near them? This may simply be due to deep shade, but if sunlight reaches the soil near this plant, the species might be an allelopath and worthy of caution.

9. Are any plant families heavily represented in the community? If so, domesticated relatives might be successfully substituted.

10. Does the community contain any known nitrogen fixers or other nutrient accumulators? These may be critical members and necessary for a related guild.

The answers to these questions will generate a list of species that can form the backbone of a potential guild.

If this research process seems daunting, some legwork can be circumvented by calling the nearest college botany department or USDA Forest Service office and asking where to find descriptions of the plant communities of your area. Someone in the department will know the name of the best books or journal articles for you and may even be willing to give an impromptu telephone lecture on local plant communities.

Here's how I built an armchair guild for my bioregion when we lived in southern Oregon. On my bookshelf sits the bible of plant communities for my locale, *Vegetation of Oregon and Washington*, by Jerry Franklin and C. T. Dyrness. Though it's more than twenty-five years old, the species lists are still valid. Thumbing through this book, I see that plant communities are listed not only by region but also, bless the authors' hearts, by climate and soil preference. Our former home in Oakland hugs the brow of a south-facing hillside that bakes to withering dryness in summer; thus, for that microclimate, I needed to find a native plant community that tolerates hot, dry, clayey slopes. Franklin and Dyrness suggest that Oregon white oak, *Quercus garryana*, will thrive in those conditions. This was no surprise, as both my woods rambles and the paper cited above taught me that Oregon white oak loves it there. It was reassuring, though, that the professors and I agreed.

White oak communities, Franklin and Dyrness reveal, come in several varieties, each named for the most prevalent understory shrub. These communities are called white oak/hazelnut, white oak/serviceberry, and—gulp—white oak/poison oak, which unfortunately is all too common down there. Each community contains a dozen or more associated plants that are listed in the text or in a table.

Next, I scanned these lists for species that are useful in themselves or have relatives that yield food, habitat, or other gifts. My goal was to use the original community members or related substitutes to create a guild with a structure similar to the native community but one that provides products for humans in addition to its many natural functions. The white oak/hazelnut community has excellent potential since it includes several nuts, fruits, berries, and herbs. The members of the community are shown in Table 9-1.

With a little exploration and fine-tuning, the white oak/hazelnut community can be transformed into a very useful guild. Let's walk through the species list.

Oregon white oak has subtle virtues. It's a lovely shade tree, and mature specimens bear abundant acorns cherished by wildlife. Oaks often swarm with birds probing the bark for insects. The acorns were a major protein source for Native Americans, roasted whole or ground into flour. White oak acorns contain less bitter tannic acid than others and thus don't require the complex leaching process that renders many acorns palatable. They also make excellent animal feed. Will suburban gardeners eat acorns? I confess I've only experimented with them, and I'd wager their acceptability as modern food is limited. The tree also takes a decade or more to bear acorns, so they're not an ideal human food plant. Oak wood is valuable timber, but unless

Table 9-1. Members of the White Oak/Hazelnut Community	
Common name	Botanical name
Oregon white oak	Quercus garryana
California hazelnut	Corylus cornuta
Pacific madrone	Arbutus menziesii
Mazzard cherry	Prunus avium
Black hawthorn	Craetagus douglasii
Saskatoon serviceberry	Amelanchier alnifolia
Creambush oceanspray	Holodiscus discolor
Round-leaved snowberry	Symphoricarpos albus
Thimbleberry	Rubus parviflorus
Trailing blackberry	Rubus ursinus
Sweetbriar rose	Rosa eglanteria
Broad-petaled strawberry	Fragaria virginiana
Poison oak	Rhus diversiloba
Yerba buena	Satureja douglasii
Sweet cicely	Osmorhiza chilensis
American vetch	Vicia americana

you've got some acreage, cutting down a major yard tree is potentially disastrous, and it certainly disrupts the guild.

Thus, white oak's food value for humans is limited, and its timber value in a suburban yard is doubtful. Is Oregon white oak useful enough to hold down a guild? Here is my reasoning: If I demanded that every guild's central tree provide me with copious food, I might substitute an oak relative, the chestnut, and hope that it wove well into this guild. I might even rove far afield and experiment with a fruit tree or other species, especially if I could take advantage of a mature specimen already present. But with all of oak's gentle benefits, especially for wildlife, plus its status as one of our most charismatic trees, I'm inclined to overlook its slight food value for humans. For me, the oak is a fine focal tree for a guild. I grow other trees for fruit and nuts.

The second major component of this oak community is the California hazel. No major substitution is needed here, just a little domestication. Hazelnut is a very useful plant. The hazelnut genus has been bred into a suite of heavy nut-producers such as European and Turkish filberts, filazels, hazelberts, and the tree hazel or trazel. Not only are the shrubs attractive, but birds love hazelnuts, too, and you'll probably share your harvest with them, like it or not. With white oak and a domesticated hazelnut, we're on our way to a useful guild.

Often the Oregon white oak community harbors another tree species, Pacific madrone. Here we have several choices. The madrone is an outstanding tree, luring immense flocks of birds to munch the prolific flowers and berries. Its smooth red bark is gorgeous, flaking off each summer to bring in birds in search of insects under the cracking fragments. Should the tree come down, the firewood is denser than walnut and burns hot and long. However, I'm hesitant to place both oak and madrone—large trees with limited food value—into a guild, especially in a small yard. Unless you live on a half-acre or more, you might declare that this guild just ain't big enough for the both of them. But there is hope. The madrone's genus, *Arbutus*, also contains several smaller species, and my suggestion for using this genus is to plant madrone's close relative, the strawberry tree, *Arbutus unedo*, which bears creamy and sweet, somewhat seedy fruit. Strawberry tree in its full-sized version grows twenty feet tall, but there are bush and dwarf cultivars that will nestle under an oak easily.

The understory of the white oak community holds two small trees, mazzard cherry and black hawthorn. Coopting these species into our guild is easy because each is useful in wild or domesticated form. Mazzard cherries are relished by birds, though humans will find the fruit good only for an occasional sour mouthful or for pies. Promisingly, mazzard is also a commonly used cherry rootstock, available at nurseries grafted onto sweet or pie cherry scionwood. These grafted cherries could be introduced into our guild. The second small tree,

black hawthorn, is not only beautiful but a superb wildlife plant as well, with berries that carry many birds through the winter. It's a close relative of the pear and can be easily grafted to become a pear-bearing variety. Pruning will keep these two already small trees at manageable height. With cherry and hawthorn, we now have an understory that generates food for wildlife and humans.

The white oak community, as the list shows, is loaded with berries. Serviceberry (also called

A Los Osos, California, hillside that was once covered in iceplant is transformed into a terraced food-forest a few steps away from the front door. Inspired by the Asian design of the surrounding buildings, the garden includes Indian Banana surrounded by a living perennial mulch and groundcover of Vietnamese cilantro (*Polygonum odoratum*), Japanese sweet Potato (*Ipomoea batatas*), and nasturtiums. Nearby broomcorn (*Sorghum* sp.) balances the height of the banana. Various thymes knit the stepping stone pathway together with aromatic herbs. DESIGN AND PHOTO BY LARRY SANTOYO.

juneberry or saskatoonberry) has been domesticated into varieties that yield excellent fruit, so let's plug in some of these. Thimbleberries are a treat known to all Northwest hikers; they rival raspberries for flavor. Two species of blackberry twine among this community; but, for the sake of your skin's integrity, I'd substitute the thornless variety. Snowberry doesn't taste very good to humans since the fruits contain soapy saponins, but birds savor the plant. Snowberry is related to honeysuckle, which suggests a possible ornamental and wildlife-attracting substitute. And, finally, wild strawberries are an obvious choice for a tasty ground cover.

Why on earth, you ask, did I include poison oak? This rash-producing shrub and its relative, poison ivy, remind me of the "Police Line—Do Not Cross" ribbons that cordon off crime scenes. The plants move into abused, chewed-up land and cloak it with a protective, human-deterring barrier. Poison oak seems to say, "You humans messed this up; now stay away while it heals." Gardeners obviously won't want to plant poison oak, but a harmless relative, lemonade berry *(Rhus integrifolia)*, bears flowers that can be steeped in boiling water to make a tangy drink. The flowers secrete nectar for insects, and birds enjoy the berries. A Southwest native, lemonade berry is hardy enough (USDA Zone 7) to survive in my Oregon yard. One drawback: Lemonade berry even looks like poison oak, so a gardener might accidentally grub it out during a robotic weeding frenzy.

Sweetbriar rose illustrates the line we're trying to tread between wild and domestic. You could use the native species or select a different variety, such as *Rosa rugosa*, that bears large, edible hips for both you and animals. But I recommend that you shun the heavily domesticated hybrid roses; their pollenless blossoms lack wildlife value, and they demand incessant care. For guild plants in general, choose the less domesticated varieties. Humans, adaptable generalists that we are, can learn to savor new, wilder tastes. Animals are often less flexible and have nutritional or taste requirements that are missing from highly bred cultivars.

The remaining shrub, oceanspray, is also called ironwood because its stems are steel hard and slow to burn. Native people fashioned arrow shafts, digging sticks, and eating utensils from the wood, which suggests potential carving projects to me. Also, the shrubs swarm with birds, which eat the seeds and hide among the dense twigs.

Three small plants finish our list. Sweet cicely *(Osmorhiza chilensis*, not to be confused with an eastern plant called sweet cicely, *Myrrhis odorata*, which also has edible leaves, seeds, and young roots) has an anise-flavored root used for seasoning, and the flowers attract butterflies and other insects. Yerba buena is a trailing, aromatic herb with leaves that produce a mild sedative effect when steeped as a tea. American vetch fixes nitrogen, but I might swap it for the more readily available common vetch.

Our white oak guild now contains plants for food, birds and mammals, insects, herbal medicine, and nitrogen fixation, which covers most of the necessary roles of any guild. The only obvious omission from the list is a heavy-duty mulch plant such as comfrey or artichoke. I'd recommend a few mulch plants initially to jump-start biomass production and then eliminate them later when the guild fills in. The guild will accumulate plenty of leaf litter once it's mature. Also, my intuition tells me a few more insectary plants (herbs such as dill or fennel or suitable natives) and more nitrogen fixers (perhaps beans and clover or the native, insect-attracting ceanothus) are also in order. The insectary plants will ensure good pollination and fruit set, which is important because we'll be harvesting this guild's products intensively. Also, we're pulling products out of the ecosystem's loops; thus we need to replace what we've withdrawn by importing nutrients via nitrogen fixers as well as mulch and nutrient accumulators.

In summary, the armchair method of guild construction begins with a library or Internet search to identify a plant community that suits your region, soil, and climate. Then, list the component species and gather either these native varieties or domestic cultivars. Try to balance both your own desire for food and other products with the needs of the wild creatures that will also depend on your guild. If you're not familiar with the plants you've listed, consult native-plant books, websites, and nursery catalogs to become acquainted with them. If the new guild lacks any of the elements listed in the above section on the apple-centered guild, fill in the gaps with species listed in this chapter and in the appendix. Also, I strongly urge that you trek out into nature and find a living example of the native community, if only to get a cursory feel for its patterns and structure. Then plant the guild, stand back, and wait to see what connections emerge.

Function-Stacking in Guilds

In the last chapter I described the major functions needed in a fruit-tree guild: nutrient accumulators, barrier plants, insectaries, and so on. That list is really just a compilation of the basic needs of a fruit tree. We can expand upon this approach by imagining other functions that might be needed or desired in a guild. Table 9-2 lists some of the possible roles that plants can play, both as supporting actors in the ecological theater and as bearers of many gifts for humans. The fruit-tree guild was designed by observing what jobs support an apple tree. In our landscapes there are plenty of other functions that need to be fulfilled to create a healthy ecosystem, and we can also envision activities (such as air cleanup or erosion control) and products that people desire. Guilds can be designed so that its members fill a variety of roles that are needed by the site or designer, as in the apple-tree guild.

Alternatively, a guild can be created to have one main function. For example, let's design a guild for attracting birds. We can begin by selecting several shrubs or small trees known as stellar bird-food and shelter species and that not-so-incidentally have other functions. Examples are:

- Red-osier dogwood *(Cornus sericea)*, for its protected perching sites—while also offering basketry supplies and dye and cordage from the bark.
- Bayberry *(Myrica pennsylvanica)* for both habitat and food. The berries hang on into winter, which extends the food-bearing season of this guild. The leaves are a bay-leaf substitute and the berries yield a fragrant wax used in candles.
- Highbush blueberry *(Vaccinium corymbosum)* for shelter and food, plus sweet berries for us, and a host of mycorrhizal associates for soil-building.

These can form the core of the guild. We'll want some smaller plants, perennial flowers that bear seeds and attract bugs for birds. Of thousands to choose from, we could select:

- Maximilian sunflower *(Helianthus maximilianii)* with its fall seeds and dense, sheltering foliage, as well as shoots we can eat and late-season blooms.
- Asters of all kinds *(Aster* spp.) provide seeds and attract tasty insects for birds to munch.
- Purple coneflower *(Echinacea purpurea)* also offers seeds, as well as having medicinal properties and attracting beneficial insects.

These six form a nucleus that we can build on. We've got bird attracting in the bag, extended over

Table 9-2. Guild Plant Functions	
Ecological Function	**Description**
Air Purifier	Cleans pollutants from the air. Sample plants include English ivy, common milkweed, and chrysanthemum (known to remove benzene).
Animal Forage	Provides food for domestic animals. Sample plants include Siberian pea shrub, buffalo grass, and buckwheat.
Erosion Control	Holds soils in place with fibrous root systems. Sample plants include sea buckthorn, bamboo, sumac, and many salvias.
Fire Retardant	Sagebrush (*Atriplex* spp.), white rockrose, jade plant, aloe vera, lavendar, salvia species.
Flood Management	Can stand submersion in water, and promote percolation to water table. Includes many native aquatic plants, annual ryegrass, feather reed grass, and fountain grass.
Fortress/Barrier	Provides a barrier to unwanted plant and animal species. Sample plants include oats (good smother crop for weeds), buckwheat, and gooseberry.
Insectary	Supports beneficial insects. Sample plants include golden marguerite, toothpick ammi, dill, and angelica.
Mulch Maker	Decomposes quickly providing "on-site" mulching. Sample plants include comfrey, cattail, and cardoon.
Nitrogen Fixer	Hosts nitrogen-fixing bacteria. Sample plants include wild lupine, sweet pea, and bladder senna.
Nitrogen Scavenger	Removes excess nitrogen from soil. Examples include berseem clover, barley, and oats.
Nurse/Scaffold/ Chaperone	Hardy pioneer plants that support establishment of other plants. Sample plants include alder, flowering quince, and Spanish broom.
Nutrient Accumulator	Deep-rooted plants that draw nutrients from soil, concentrating them in tissue. Sample plants include stinging nettle, yarrow, and sunflower.
Pest Repellent	Repels pests, eliminating pesticides. Sample plants include peppermint (repels insects and mice), lemon balm (repels flies and ants) and garlic (repels aphids, deer, and rabbits).
Soil Builder	Produces organic matter and improves soil structure. Sample plants include rape, Sudan grass, and crotolaria.
Soil Cultivator/Spike-Root	Deep-rooted plants that penetrate, loosen, and aerate the soil. Sample plants include little bluestem, daikon, and fava bean.
Toxin Absorption	Sample plants include black nightshade (removes PCBs from soil) and curlytop-gumweed (absorbs selenium).
Water Purification	Sample plants include cattail, common rush, canna lily, and ostrich fern.
Wildlife Food	Examples include blackberry (small birds) witch hazel (ruffled grouse, pheasant), and elderberry (many bird species).
Wildlife Habitat	Sample plants include barberry, high-bush blueberry, hazelnut, and cornelian cherry.
Windbreak	Examples, from small to large, are Jerusalem artichoke, elaeagnus, and hybrid poplar.

a long season. We want to make sure that the basic needs of this plant community are taken care of, too, so we don't have to trade our labor for what nature can provide. Obvious holes in this guild include nutrient accumulation and mulch-making. For the first, how about a lupine, which not only is a nitrogen fixer but in fall offers seedpods enjoyed by songbirds? The stems are also a choice nest material. For mulch, we could fall back on our old reliable, comfrey, or continue with the bird-luring theme and choose flame acanthus, a red-flowered variety of bear's breeches, a perennial with thick, broad leaves. Depending on soil conditions, microclimate, and other environmental influences, we may want to add other species to round out our guild.

Thus we can design a guild to take on a needed role. These function-specific guilds are, as far as we know, not like communities found in nature, so we're in new territory here. However, we need not worry much that novel plant combinations won't work well together. After all, most landscape designs pay little regard to whether plants are

Table 9-2. Guild Plant Functions (continued)	
Human Use	**Description**
Aromatic/Fragrance	Scented plants for their fragrance alone or to mask other smells. Sample plants include lavender, rosemary, and jasmine.
Basketry and Weaving	Shoots are straight and flexible. Sample plants include common reed, prairie willow, and fragrant sumac.
Cleanser/Scourer	Examples include pennyroyal, cranberry, horsetail rush, and potato.
Compost	Examples include comfrey, chicory, yarrow, and stinging nettle.
Cut Flower	Sample plants include black-eyed Susan, cosmos, yarrow, and daffodil.
Dried Flower	Typical are lavender, milkweed, and sunflower.
Dye	Sample plants include goldenrod (mustard, brown, and yellow dye), carrot (orange dye from roots), and red raspberry (purple dye from fruit).
Essential Oil	Contain essential oils that can be extracted. Sample plants include sage (used in perfumes and shampoos), dill (used in soaps and medicines), and creeping thyme (used in perfumes and mouthwashes).
Fiber	Used for fiber. Sample plants include New Zealand flax (for rope and simple ties), swamp milkweed (bark is used for twine or cloth), and oats (hulls used in construction board).
Food	Edibles. Includes fruits, nuts, greens, vegetables, edible flowers, herbs, and so on.
Insect Repellent	Sample plants include rosemary (sachets used in cupboards), parsley (juice used to repel mosquitoes), and lavender (repels mice).
Medicine	Plants traditionally used for healing. Sample plants include comfrey (used for wound healing), purple milkweed (to treat warts), and burdock (as a general tonic).
Oil, Wax, Resin or Polish	Sample plants include bitternut hickory (oil from seeds used in oil lamps), Japanese stone pine (pitch is obtained from rosin and used in waterproofing), and hazelnut (seed used for furniture polishing).
Soap	Sample plants include snowberry, New Jersey tea, and wild lupine.
Wood	Used for wood products. A few examples are sugar maple (for furniture and musical instruments), Amur corktree (for cork substitute), and walnut.

compatible beyond whether the assemblage looks good, and the plants usually survive. As long as the basics such as soil, light, and water are suitable, the guild members ought to flourish. Only rarely do plants have negative interactions that could cause discord in the guild. So the downside of guild innovations is slight, while the upside—brilliant synergies, serendipitous benefits, superb habitat—is enormous.

Creating a Superguild

A single apple or walnut tree—let alone an oak—isn't going to provide a terribly varied diet, even as part of a guild. There's a limit to how many apples or nuts a gardener will eat. However, several different tree-centered guilds can be combined to boost both the food choice and the overall biodiversity that a garden provides. One obvious solution is to substitute other types of fruit and nut trees—peaches, almonds, plums, persimmons—for apple and walnut trees in guilds. This creates an orchard made of guilds. But any orchard, even one with a remarkably diverse understory such as ours, acts as a beacon to summon fruit-chomping pests. Also, if the only trees in our yard are fruit-bearers, neatly pruned into open form, uniformly blossoming, all looking like—well, fruit trees—then the landscape will be visually boring and will lack the biodiversity that's possible and necessary for a thriving ecosystem.

If the garden is large enough, we can be more subtle than simply growing a bunch of fruit trees. Just as we combine nitrogen fixers, insectary plants, and other multifunctional florae to create dynamic guilds, we can weave together trees of diverse uses to create a "superguild." Guilds, each based on a different type of tree, can act as subunits of a larger, multitree superguild and be integrated to create a more deeply connected community. Our backyard ecosystem will then shift to a higher level of complexity. Think of the various guilds as organs in a body, combining to form a healthy and long-lived organism that is capable of much more elaborate behaviors than the components alone. Our guilds can do the same, altering microclimates, attracting new species, changing the look and feel of our landscape, and restoring it to health.

How can we assemble a set of guilds that will create a complete landscape? The walnut/hackberry guild developed by Tim Murphy hinted at a method. Tim's suggestion of using "buffer plants" to protect fruit trees from the effects of a walnut tree's toxic secretions pointed at one route for extending and connecting guilds. Bill Mollison, in *Permaculture: A Designers' Manual*, elaborates on the value of buffer plants. If we planted a walnut guild next to an apple guild, the apple tree would suffer from juglone poisoning. Instead, Mollison says, we can select useful buffer trees to fit between and link incompatible species.

What makes a good buffer tree? First, buffer trees should (obviously) be compatible with the trees we're trying to link. A tree harmed by juglone isn't a good choice for a walnut buffer (a few trees

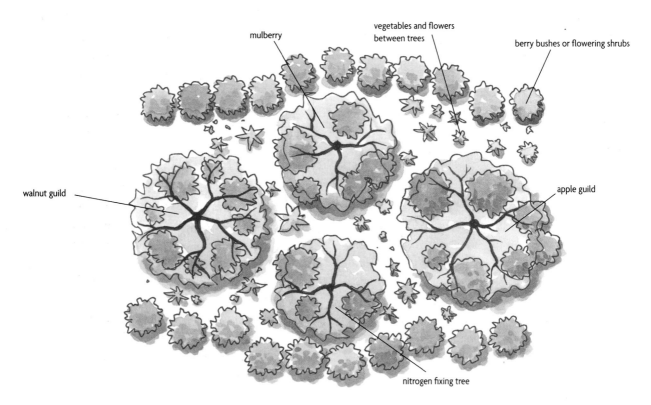

An orchard superguild. The nitrogen-fixing tree (black locust, acacia, tagasaste, alder, or the like) and mulberry are underplanted with useful shrubs and flowers (such as mulch plants and insectary plants). Rows of berry bushes and flowering shrubs fill the alleys between the trees, and any open space holds vegetables and flowers.

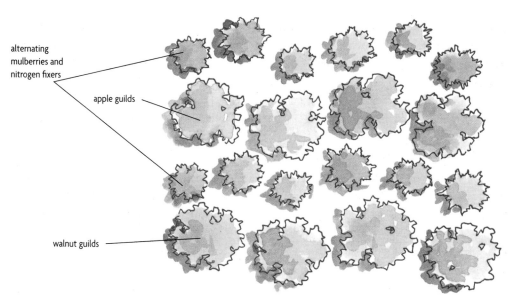

alternating
mulberries and
nitrogen fixers

apple guilds

walnut guilds

An orchard made up of repeated superguilds. Here, apple and walnut guilds are blended together using mulberries and nitrogen-fixing trees for buffering, diversity, animal feed, and soil building. As with the single superguild shown on page 204, spaces between trees could be filled with berry bushes, flowering shrubs, vegetables, and flowers.

unfazed by walnuts are listed below). Second, in keeping with our desire to find beneficial interactions among and within guilds, we should keep an eye out for buffer trees that have a positive effect on one or both of the guilds to be linked. Nitrogen fixers, mulch-producers, and bird- or insect-attracting plants come to mind. Third, species that offer food, animal forage, lumber, or some other useful product should be among our candidates. We want to stack as many functions as possible into our buffer plants. Some species to connect walnut and apple guilds (and, potentially, many other guilds) that satisfy one or more of these criteria include:

- *Mulberry trees.* Unharmed by walnut exudations, mulberries come in many attractive cultivars (white, Russian, Illinois, Olivett). Some home owners complain that mulberry fruit creates a gooey, staining mess, but intelligent placement (avoiding the driveway and play areas) will minimize this draw-

back. Also, if the backyard ecosystem is in good health, the abundant wildlife will greedily consume extra berries. Mulberries are quickly gobbled by domestic fowl as well, thus a few chickens or ducks in the yard will quickly clean up any dropped fruit.

- *Nitrogen-fixing trees and large shrubs.* Most nitrogen fixers tolerate walnut toxins. Black locusts work well here, having attractive foliage, generous blossoms that bees love, and rot-resistant timber for fence posts. Other attractive trees that add fertility to soil include acacia, red or black alder, golden-chain tree, silk tree, and mountain mahogany. Large nitrogen-fixing shrubs, such as Russian olive and wax myrtle, also make good buffer plants.

A combination of fruit, nut, and buffer trees— for example, apple, walnut, mulberry, and a nitrogen-fixer—creates an array that maximizes beneficial interactions and minimizes the negative. Here are some of the benefits: A nitrogen fixer boosts the growth of all three other trees by adding fertility to the soil. Mulberries not only buffer apples from walnut toxins, but research indicates that apples actually profit from mulberry companionship. The guilds-cum-buffers offer a liberal assortment of food that won't bore human palates, and the blossoms, fruit, and shelter will attract many species of wildlife.

The illustration on page 204 provides a layout that places each tree-based guild to best advantage. How will this pattern play in suburbia? Ten to twenty medium-sized trees can be tucked into a typical suburban quarter-acre without shrouding the inhabitants in a gloomy Black Forest. Two iterations of our four-tree "superguild" gives us eight trees, which leaves ample space in the yard for other species that will raise biodiversity still further. The illustration on page 205 shows one way of creating a larger superguild orchard.

There is a tangible contrast between a sterile yard that is studded with isolated, out-of-place specimen trees in ecological disconnection and this thriving semitamed woodland that is vibrant with wildlife, dripping with fruit and nuts, and echoing with the voices of children playing hide-and-seek among flower-spangled shrubs.

Guilds Aren't Perfect

I won't claim that guilds are the answer to all gardening problems. The advantages of guilds—reduced human intervention, less fertilizer and other inputs, a harmony between people and wildlife, and the magical synergy of plant communities—are obvious. The drawbacks are more subtle. First, guilds can consume a lot of space. Two or three guilds could fill much of a small city lot. In addition, guilds

are slower to establish than an annual bed. A fruit tree takes several years to bear. Even shrubs need a few seasons to mature. To nudge a guild into early productivity, annual vegetables and flowers can be planted between the young, more permanent guild elements. As the perennial plants begin to bear, both the space and the need for annuals will diminish, and we can simply stop reseeding them.

Another weakness: Since a guild's many plants act in close concert, tracing the source of a difficulty—say, stunted fruit on an apple tree—can be challenging. Is the problem due to root competition? An allelopathic interaction? A pest harbored by another guild member? In a guild, plant A may aid plant B, which benefits C, which inhibits A, so where do you start tracing a negative interaction?

Permaculture teacher Tom Ward has experimented with guilds and knows their complexities. "Guilds were first developed in the tropics, where there is little soil," Tom notes. "Allelopath toxins are harbored in the soil, but because tropical soils are shallow, allelopaths can't build up to toxic levels and are rarely a problem there. Negative interactions seldom occur. Without allelopaths to worry about, guilds are simpler to design in the tropics than they are here in the temperate zone."

In contrast to the tropics, temperate forests and prairies have deep soil. In the thick temperate soil layer, toxins secreted by microorganisms and allelopathic plants can accumulate. Thus, a diverse array of plant species may be shuttling among their roots an equally complex chemical freight. This varied assortment of sugars, lignins, alkaloids, and whathave-you can have unpredictable effects on nearby plants. Soil-borne toxins make temperate guild design more difficult.

Also, guilds are often site-specific. What works in New York may be completely inappropriate for California. Tom Ward points out that there is no handy list of guilds for every garden. "You're given an example or two," Tom says. "Nobody has ever put together a book of generic guilds because they are so specific to site. You have to use observation to figure out what plants grow well together in your region."

Several of the guilds cited in this chapter—the Three Sisters, the apple guild, and the walnut guild—are attempts at "universal" guilds that should thrive in most North American conditions. The Oregon white oak guild is a more site-specific guild, presented as an exercise in design based on local native plants. However, white oaks and their associates are found over much of the continent, so many readers can try something similar if oaks grow near them.

No, there isn't a "Book of Guilds" for every site. For the most part, temperate-climate guilds are a recent invention, only about twenty years old, and much remains to be learned and attempted. Perhaps readers of this book will help advance this young and very promising field.

Gardening with guilds forces a different attitude toward harvesting as well. You don't traipse down a row of clean-cultivated zucchini, filling a bushel basket with one crop. Guild harvests are reminiscent of the hunter-gatherers: You pluck a few greens, some peppers and tomatoes, a few herbs, a handful of nuts, and a small basket of fruit and berries for dessert.

Some plants aren't appropriate for guilds, particularly sprawling winter squash that can smother nearby plants, and a few vegetables that insist on a full day of sun. Most guild-gardeners have small beds of annual vegetables for bulk harvesting tucked here and there. However, gardeners who grow a significant portion of their own food have found that guilds, supplemented with annual beds, can approach the ecological ideal of minimal inputs and maximum diversity.

Nature-based growing systems such as guilds do entail a change in thinking. Tom Ward cites a story told about Masanobu Fukuoka, the sage-like founder of the Natural Farming movement. Fukuoka's method involves permanent cover crops interplanted with vegetables and perennials, all with minimal tending. "One day," Tom relates, "Fukuoka was asked, 'If we grow our fruit trees the way you recommend, with no pruning, how do we harvest the apples and what do we do with them?' Fukuoka's answer was, 'You shake the apples out of the tree and make cider, or feed them to pigs.' His point was, you go in a whole other direction."

Though not to that extreme, guilds ask for a subtle adjustment of our relations with our environment. The order of a conventional row-crop garden is the order of the machine. This regimentation invites us to view plants as mechanical food factories. We fuel them with fertilizer, service them with rakes and hoes, and measure their production in bushels, bins, and tons. We view the plants as part of our dominion. In a guild, we are but one living being among many others; and, like all the other animals enfolded by this community, we nurture and are nurtured by an almost-wild place. We prune and cull, as do the deer and mice. The fruit we leave does not rot on the ground to breed disease; it is gladly devoured by our many companions. We turn over a bit of soil, and the worms turn over yet more. We participate rather than rule. With guilds, we can begin to shed the mantle of command and return to nature the many responsibilities we have unnecessarily assumed.

CHAPTER 10

Growing a Food Forest

Gardening with guilds brings us one step closer to landscapes that look and act like natural ones but that have been tweaked to benefit people as well as the rest of nature. However, even guilds are just pieces of a larger whole. Now it's time to tie guilds and the other ideas presented in this book into a unified, ecologically sound landscape.

In Chapter 2, I described the process of succession, the evolution of a landscape over decades from bare ground through fast-growing pioneer species to a mature ecosystem. When not interrupted by fire or other disaster, the end result of succession nearly everywhere is forest. Even in the arid Southwest, dryland forests of ironwood, mesquite, and saguaro cactus blanketed what is now desert, until the sheep-grazers' depredations and the lumbermen's axes destroyed them. Given twelve or more inches of annual rain and the respite of a handful of years between wildfires, tree and shrub seedlings will sprout on almost any ground, patiently outwait the other vegetation, and create a woodland. This is why, as noted earlier, suburbanites must constantly weed and chop out woody seedlings from their well-watered lawns and garden beds. The typical yard, with its perfect regimen of irrigation and fertilizer, is trying hard to become a forest. Only the lawn mower and pruning shears prevent the woods from taking over.

So why fight this trend toward woodland? Instead, we can work with nature to fashion a multistoried forest garden, a food- and habitat-producing landscape that acts like a natural woodland. In a forest garden, the yard is a parklike grove of spreading fruit trees, walnuts, chestnuts, and other useful trees. In the bright openings are smaller persimmon trees, plums, cherries, pawpaws, and a few ornamentals such as golden-chain trees and pink-flowered silk trees (which just happen to fix nitrogen). Catching the sunlight farther down, dancing with birds, are flowering shrubs and berry bushes. Occasional honeysuckle and hardy kiwi vines wind up tree trunks, leaving a trail of blossoms and fruit. Beneath all this and in the bright edges are beds of perennial flowers, vegetables, and soil-building mulch plants. Plant guilds weave this many-layered garden into a cohesive whole, and the many-functioned flora extends a welcome to helpful insects, birds, and other wildlife, as well as to people.

A food forest such as this isn't as unconventional as it may sound. I'm not talking about a gloomy mass of light-blocking trees, but an open, many-layered edible woodland garden with plenty of sunny glades and edges. Many yards already contain most of the elements of a forest garden: a few tall trees in front or at the back edge, some shrubs for a hedge or berries, a vegetable patch, a few herbs, and a flower bed. But in the typical yard these elements lie separate and disconnected. A forest garden simply integrates all these pieces into a smoothly working whole.

At its essence, a forest garden has several layers, as does a natural forest. A simple forest garden contains a top layer of trees, a middle level of shrubs, and a ground layer of herbs, vegetables, and flowers. Each plant is chosen for the roles that it will play, whether for food, wildlife habitat, herbal medicine, insect attraction, soil building, or any of the other functions that we've covered throughout this book. The major trees and shrubs are spaced to let sunlight fall between them, and plants in the lower layers are placed in sun or shade according to their appetite for light.

A forest garden has a different feel from other garden styles, in large part because trees are a major element, integrated into and defining the other layers. Certainly, conventional gardens mingle shrubs and nonwoody perennials of varying heights in the traditional mixed border. And nearly every yard contains a few trees. But in a forest garden, trees—their leaves arching overhead, trunks thrusting skyward, branches enfolding the space—control the landscape's character. We're not strolling in an exposed group of bushes and flowers, our heads above most of the foliage; instead, we're nestled within a sheltering yet open canopy of trees of all heights. The trees dominate, yet without smothering other plants.

With a tree-filled forest garden, we have enlisted as our allies the most powerful and productive vegetation on the planet, the aristocrats of the plant world. In Chapter 6 I briefly described the many and important roles that trees play. I believe that trees—as full, integrated partners, not merely as scattered specimens—are a prerequisite for a healthy, sustainable landscape.

Trees' ability to produce soil-enriching leaf litter, fill the earth with humusy roots, quell temperature swings, hold moisture, arrest erosion, and offer tiers of habitat for animals is unparalleled, and in the forest garden they're on our side. And for productivity you can't beat trees. An acre of wheat provides a mere one to two tons of grain, while an acre of chestnut trees yields up to three tons of nuts, and an acre of honey-locust trees explodes with fifteen tons of protein-rich pods—without annual replanting. Apple and other fruit tree yields can reach seven tons per acre, although much of this is water weight. But even dried apple yields can match those of dry wheat. Compared to grains and other annuals, the vastly greater expanse of energy-harvesting greenery of trees gives them an unbeatable advantage.

Trees reach deep into the earth for nutrients and water, and far and wide into the sky for solar power. They are life's largest, most effective natural collectors of energy and matter. So, by incorporating trees as integral elements of the garden, we're putting heavy hitters on our team. Trees, though they share the space with many other species, define the forest garden and distinguish it from other landscape styles.

The wealth of trees, shrubs, and other florae we have to choose from means that the forest garden can be as varied as a forest itself and as individual as its owner. Some gardeners will want a veritable food forest, where the constant rain of ripe fruit and luscious berries almost warrants wearing a hard hat. Others will pitch their miniforest toward blossom and beauty, selecting plants to create a tall, thick cascade of color and many-textured foliage. Utilitarian souls may sculpt a garden that yields income from medicinal tinctures, craft wood, bamboo poles, rare seeds, nursery plants, or grafting stock. Or the gardener can mix and match the styles to tailor a garden that combines food, beauty, habitat, species preservation, and income.

A garden that uses trees and shrubs to reach far into three dimensions offers maximum wildlife habitat, the largest possible crop yields for the space, and the greatest possibilities for edge and diversity. It won't hurt property values either, as the most desirable neighborhoods are always those with well-developed trees. On hilly land, forest

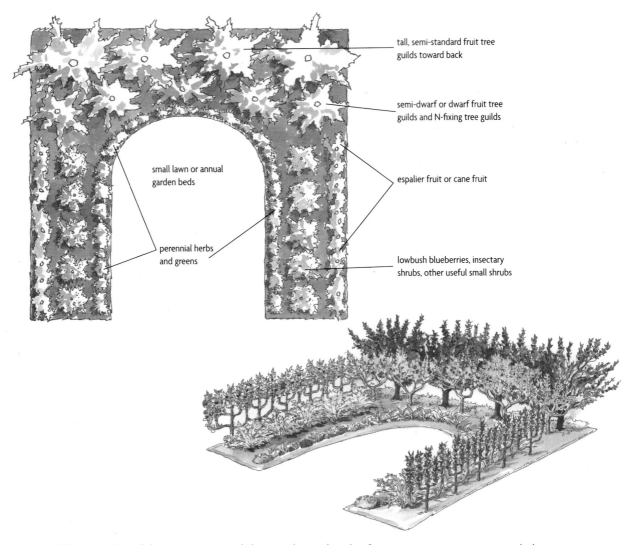

tall, semi-standard fruit tree
guilds toward back

semi-dwarf or dwarf fruit tree
guilds and N-fixing tree guilds

small lawn or annual
garden beds

espalier fruit or cane fruit

perennial herbs
and greens

lowbush blueberries, insectary
shrubs, other useful small shrubs

A U-shaped forest garden. If the U opens toward the sun, the garden also forms a sun-trap. A symmetrical planting arrangement gives a more formal appearance, less symmetry makes the garden feel wilder. REDRAWN WITH PERMISSION FROM *HOW TO MAKE A FOREST GARDEN*, BY PATRICK WHITEFIELD (PERMANENT PUBLICATIONS, 1997).

gardens are also the most ecologically sound way to develop steep slopes because the trees and other perennial plants hold soil in place and eliminate the need for erosion-producing tillage.

The illustrations on this page and the next show some of the possible forms that a forest garden can take. Shapes, heights, spacing, and overall size can be altered to suit the site conditions and gardener's preferences. A large yard provides enough room for full-sized trees, while in a smaller property, dwarf and naturally small species can fit together to provide biodiversity. Northern gardeners will want a more open array of trees to allow the not-so-strong sunlight to reach the ground layers, but southerners may desire dense spacing to provide needed shade.

Forest gardens raise the obvious question: Don't the upper layers cast too much shade for the lower

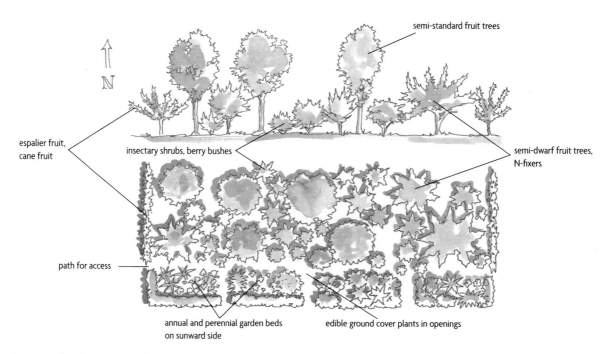

semi-standard fruit trees

espalier fruit, cane fruit

insectary shrubs, berry bushes

semi-dwarf fruit trees, N-fixers

path for access

annual and perennial garden beds on sunward side

edible ground cover plants in openings

A forest garden for a rectangular yard. Large trees are placed far apart so that light can reach shrubs and smaller trees. Vegetable or flower beds are located on the sunward side.

plants? Part of the answer is that proper tree spacing and shade-tolerant plants will keep lack of light from being a problem. But to be perfectly honest—especially for northern gardens where the sun is weaker—fruit yields and flower density won't be as large in the shady parts of the understory as in full sun. I have grown currants and gooseberries, two shade-tolerant bush fruits, in both full sun and under some pear trees, and the sunnier plants bear more fruit. But the shade-grown shrubs require less water, have lusher, darker foliage, and are still packed with plenty of berries. Plus, the shrub-filled, sun-dappled margin under the pear tree offers far more diversity and value—ecologically, aesthetically, and for my palate—than if I were just growing grass.

Forest gardens offer the same advantages as guilds, and then some. Nearly every cubic inch is filled with greenery, flowers, or fruit. This riot of vegetation into three dimensions furnishes vast amounts of habitat for birds, small animals, and beneficial insects. Pest problems dwindle. And,

once established, forest gardens are low-maintenance because the thick vegetation cover reduces water needs, smothers weeds, and renews soil through self-mulching and natural soil building. Because the forest garden holds mostly perennial and self-seeding plants, it also needs no tilling and little seasonal replanting.

At the Bullock brothers' several-acre food forest on Orcas Island, Doug Bullock listed some other access benefits of forest gardening. "Sheer biodiversity is part of it," he told me. "We get birds and other animals here that no one else has seen for years. But the best part is the food—it's unreal!" We stood beneath a plum tree bent nearly double with fruit, and I nodded as Doug continued. "Every summer we have about twenty students here for three weeks. And there's enough fruit right here to feed them. Think about it: Twenty people grazing for weeks on plums, peaches, and berries, and when they're gone there's still tons of fruit on the trees for us."

Because Doug and his brothers have populated their food forest with a wide variety of plants, every month of the year brings fresh fruit or vegetables: cool-season salad greens in midwinter, berries in late spring, and branch-breaking loads of fruit in summer and fall. Even in December, their exotic medlar trees bear a fruit that tastes like cinnamon-spiced pear butter.

Experimenting with Forest Gardens

Temperate-climate forest gardening is a new field, and only a few mature forest gardens exist on this continent. However, many more are old enough to have begun producing, and hundreds more are currently being planted. I visited several established food forests while researching the first edition of this book and have returned to some of them in the intervening years.

One site that illustrates the transition from raised-bed to forest garden is that of Jerome Osentowski, near Aspen, Colorado. Jerome faces some tough gardening challenges, as he lives 7,400 feet above sea level. Frosts can hit during any month. When I first visited him, in September of 1999, his one-third-acre garden was still lush and green, but he expected the first killing frosts of autumn soon.

A Brief History of Forest Gardens

Forest gardening is a young field for North American gardeners, but it has a long history. Food forests have existed for millennia in the tropics, though early anthropologists didn't recognize them as gardens at all. Accustomed to row crops and annual vegetables, the first white visitors to tropical home-gardens assumed that the small plots of manioc, beans, or grain near African, Asian, and South American houses provided most of the inhabitants' food. The surrounding tangle of vegetation was assumed to be untamed jungle, and these people were branded as practicing only primitive agriculture.

Only after prolonged and unprejudiced observation did anthropologists comprehend that virtually every plant near the dwellings was useful in some way. The tall trees were timber and firewood producers or nitrogen fixers, while the shorter ones bore mangoes, papayas, avocados, and other marvelous fruits. Beneath these were shrubs for food, fiber, and wood products. The herb layer was filled with medicinal, edible, and ornamental plants. Rampant growth was slashed back several times each year and used for mulch or animal fodder. But because these plants were arranged in guilds and by function, rather than in neat lines and beds, scientists had no idea that they were looking at an ecologically sound, carefully worked-out scheme for producing nearly everything the occupants needed. Sadly, many of these wonderful food forests have been replaced by Western-style cash-crop agriculture, making the once self-reliant inhabitants dependent on fertilizers, pesticides, and imported, processed food and other goods.

Fortunately, a number of visionaries saw the immense value of these tropical forest-gardens. One was Robert Hart, an Englishman who not only studied tropical food forests but transplanted many of their concepts to temperate gardens. His book, *Forest Gardening,* was the first to describe the subject for the Northern Hemisphere. A second useful book is *How to Make a Forest Garden,* by Patrick Whitefield. Both books are written primarily for a British audience. The new bible for food forest enthusiasts is *Edible Forest Gardens,* by David Jacke and Eric Toensmeier. This magisterial two-volume set, eight years in the making, thoroughly covers the theory and practice of forest gardening for temperate climates. It includes extensive plant lists and design ideas and is a comprehensive guide that has no equal. See the bibliography for more information on these books.

For years, much of Jerome's income came from growing organic salad greens for the upscale markets and restaurants of Aspen. Supplying this finicky market year-round supported Jerome for a decade or so. But it took arduous labor, and Jerome was dismayed by the mountains of hard-to-find compost materials that he was importing, and then exporting from his land as salad greens. This open loop disturbed his permacultural sense of propriety. Finally, California salad growers 1,000 miles away began offering produce to local stores more cheaply than Jerome could. After ten years, Jerome began shifting to food forestry. Now, many of the former salad beds held small trees and shrubs.

We stood by one bed in which celery and a few heads of lettuce dotted a sunny edge below some young trees. "The food forest was a natural evolution of this place," Jerome said as I admired the heat-holding rock terraces of his young forest garden. "After years of growing annual vegetables, a lot of fertility had leached down to where the short roots of the salad greens couldn't get it. So I went to fruit trees, with their deep roots, to get at all those nutrients."

I asked Jerome what species he had planted. Swinging his arm to encompass the slope, he said, "Let's start with the trees. We've got apples—there's one with five different varieties grafted onto it. Apricots, plums, some native Douglas firs, and New Mexico locusts for nitrogen. The trees are young, not really in production yet. But the shrubs are really giving us a lot of food now." He pointed out the understory of black and white currants, gooseberries, bush cherries, cranberries, and Siberian pea shrubs. Bamboo and willow were sprouting vigorously, and several varieties of grapes, along with scarlet runner beans and squash, entwined the other vegetation. Strawberries and claytonia (miner's lettuce) swarmed over the rock terraces.

"We've got a lot of medicinal herbs, too," Jerome continued. "A nice market crop if we want it. Echinacea, St. John's-wort, astragalus, artemisia, lots more." The lush cascade of greenery nearly filled the hillside garden. "What makes this place work, though, are what I call the *compañeros*, all the guild companion-plants." He showed me the rich array of soil-building and insect-attracting species: nitrogen fixers such as pea shrubs, fava beans, clovers, fenugreek, and alfalfa; bee plants such as borage and comfrey; other insectary species, including fennel, celery, dill, and coriander; and strongly scented pest-confusers such as horseradish, Mexican marigold, garlic mustard, and walking onions. These many-functioned plants reduce Jerome's share of the pest control and fertilization duties and augment the web of ecological connections among the forest garden's inhabitants.

The rock terraces don't just give Jerome more flat ground for his garden. They are essential to mitigating the volatile mountain climate. The mass of the stones absorbs heat, softening temperature swings, warming the plants at night, and blocking frost. "The rock terraces were important in helping the young plants survive," Jerome told me. "They get shaded now in the summer, but they still store heat in winter and especially in spring when the plants need it most." During winter, the rocks, snow cover, and mulch combine to prevent the ground from freezing, even when temperatures plunge below zero. This allows slug-eating snakes and other beneficial wildlife to survive the cold season.

The garden is surrounded by a tall deer fence, and a complete guild was designed to grow on it. Hops and sweet peas trellis up the woven wire, and Russian olive and gooseberry form a green shrub layer. Sunflowers stretch skyward. Clover and strawberries cascade along the ground, interspersed with garlic in the root zone. In a forest garden, every site offers new opportunities for creative design.

Though food is one obvious benefit here, Jerome explained the forest garden's compounding value. "As I phase out the salad-green operation, I can get income from the medicinals and tinctures, and from nursery stock and scionwood for grafting. But I've found that's not the most valuable part. I learn from all this. And so do my students who come up here for the classes at Central Rocky Mountain Permaculture Institute." The real value-added product of the forest garden is the inspiration, knowledge, and renewal that comes when humans and the rest of nature mesh in a healthy, vigorous, and diverse setting.

A few years later I returned to Jerome's garden to find a mature food-forest in lavish abundance. It was mid-August, and sturdy peach trees stood guilded with Siberian pea shrubs, sunflowers, cabbage, clover, comfrey, and cosmos. Lunch for

Jerome Osentwoski's forest garden at Central Rocky Mountain Permaculture Institute. The rock terraces and pond both store daytime heat and release it during the cool Colorado nights, which aids plant growth and fruit production. PHOTO BY JEROME OSENTOWSKI.

Jerome's Guilds and Guild Plants

- *Deer fence guild:* hops, sweet pea, Russian olive, gooseberry, sunflowers, clover, strawberry, garlic.
- *Apple-tree guild:* red currant, Siberian pea shrub, red and white clover, borage, garlic, fava bean, dill, lupine, astragalus, native wildflowers, mint, basil.
- *Peach-tree guild:* Siberian pea shrub, sunflowers, cabbage, clover, comfrey, horseradish, calendula, nicotiana, cosmos.
- *Douglas-fir guild:* currant, Siberian pea shrub, salad burnet, crotolaria, Mexican marigold.

Other plants used in Jerome's fruit tree guilds

- *Shrubs:* black and white currants, gooseberries, Hansen's cherry, Nanking cherry, elderberry, cranberry.
- *Vines:* grapes, hops, sweet pea, scarlet runner bean, nasturtium, squash.
- *Ground covers and herbs:* strawberry, claytonia (miner's lettuce), salad burnet, celery, arugula, mustards, amaranth, chrysanthemum, parsley, cumin.
- *Nitrogen-fixers:* Siberian pea shrub, Russian olive, fava beans, clovers, lupine, bird's-foot trefoil, fenugreek, alfalfa.
- *Insectary plants:* borage, buckwheat, comfrey, fennel, celery, dill, coriander, oregano, chamomile.
- *Pest fumigants and repellents:* horseradish, Mexican marigold, garlic mustard, walking onion.
- *Medicinal plants:* astragalus, echinacea, mullein, St. John's-wort, artemisia, spilanthes.
- *Root plants:* garlic, walking onion, Jerusalem artichoke, carrot, potato.

twenty students came almost exclusively from the garden, day after day. No longer does Jerome import truckloads of organic matter. The garden generates almost all the mulch and compost materials it requires. Much of the mulch is from woody plants, to create nourishment that favors fungi, which predominate in forest soils, as opposed to the bacteria that prevail in annual garden soil and turf lawns. The fruit-tree guilds also yield horseradish, astragalus (a nitrogen-fixing medicinal herb), mint, basil, and other culinary herbs that Jerome sells to three local supermarkets and two farmers' markets.

The conditions have given Jerome a graduate education in food forestry. Dwarf fruit trees, the usual choice for small spaces and high production, fared poorly. They are bred to have feeble root systems, which keeps them small. But in these nutrient-poor soils and harsh conditions, the skimpy roots meant starvation. Standard-size fruit trees, with expansive roots, survived, and in Jerome's environment haven't grown much larger than dwarfs.

Osentowski has invented what he calls "Polish swales." Instead of digging swales into the rocky soil, he does it backward: he piles up small branches along the contour lines, adding compost and discarded greenery, along with stones and other available debris. This forms berms that trap soil, leaf litter, manure and bird poop, and anything else sluicing down the steep slopes. The berms of these inverted swales slow down water and force it to percolate down into the food forest's root zone.

What inspired me the most on my later visit was Jerome's integration of two large greenhouses into his home and garden. One, which he has christened Mana after the Hawaiian spiritual force, grows like a gossamer bud from his house. It's dual purpose, heating air that is circulated through his home and also sheltering a semitropical food forest. The second greenhouse, also with a name from the tropics, Pele, for the Hawaiian fire goddess, holds a sauna amid the greenery as a backup heat source. I was astounded to see bananas, figs, pomegranates, jujubes, chayote squash, and other plants not often found north of Los Angeles. Yet here they thrived at 7,400 feet in winter temperatures that can dip to twenty below zero. One key to his success is an inflatable double-walled clear plastic that insulates far better than glass and is much less expensive. Also, the thermal mass of the soil and the rock walls capture daytime heat. A fan pushes warmed air through a set of underground pipes to distribute this heat where it is needed, which includes the house. In the high Rockies, Jerome is developing methods that will allow people in virtually any climate to enjoy tropical food, without massive energy use. This immensely expands the possibilities of forest gardening and might offer us clues to dealing successfully with climate change.

The Seven-Story Garden

It's time to look at forest garden design. A simple forest garden contains three layers: trees, shrubs, and ground plants. But for those who like to take advantage of every planting opportunity, a deluxe forest garden can contain as many as seven tiers of vegetation. As the illustration below shows, a seven-layered forest garden contains tall trees, low trees, shrubs, herbs, ground covers, vines, and root crops.

Here are these layers in more detail. Table 10-1 suggests plant species for each layer.

1. *The Tall-Tree Layer.* This is an overstory of full-sized fruit, nut, or other useful

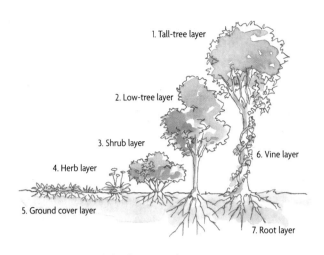

The seven layers of the forest garden.

trees, with spaces between to let plenty of light reach the lower layers. Dense, spreading species—the classic shade trees such as maple, sycamore, and beech—don't work well in the forest garden because they cast deep shadows over a large area. Better choices are multifunctional fruit and nut trees. These include standard and semistandard apple and pear trees, European plums on standard rootstocks such as Myrobalan, and full-sized cherries. Chestnut trees, though quite large, work well, especially if pruned to an open, light-allowing shape. Chinese chestnuts, generally not as large as American types, are good candidates (see Table 10-1 for botanical names of all species mentioned here). Walnut trees, especially the naturally open, spreading varieties such as heartnut and buartnut, are excellent. Don't overlook the nut-bearing stone piñon and Korean nut pines. Nitrogen-fixing trees will help build soil, and most bear blossoms that attract insects. These

Table 10-1. Plants for the Forest Garden
The herb layer has been omitted from this table, as there are thousands of suitable species and many of them are listed elsewhere in this book.

Tall-Tree Layer

Common name	Botanical name	N-fixer	Wildlife value	Insectary	Edible	Hardiness zones
Acacia	*Acacia* spp.	•		•		7-10
Algoroba	*Prosopis dulcis, P. juliflora*	•				7
American chestnut	*Castanea dentata*				•	4
Apple	*Malus pumila*			•	•	4-9
Asian pear	*Pyrus pyrifolia*				•	4-9
Beech	*Fagus grandiflora, F. sylvatica*			•	•	4
Black locust	*Robinia pseudoacacia*	•		•		3
Black walnut	*Juglans nigra*				•	4
Buartnut	*Juglans × bisbyi*				•	5
Bur oak	*Quercus macrocarpa*		•			2-8
Butternut	*Juglans cinerea*				•	3
Cherry	*Prunus cerasus, P. avium*		•	•		5-9
Chinese chestnut	*Castanea mollisima*				•	5
European pear	*Pyrus communis*				•	4-9
Heartnut	*Juglans ailantifolia cordiformis*				•	5
Hickory	*Carya* spp.				•	6
Honey locust	*Gleditsia triacanthos*		•	•		4-9
Mesquite	*Prosopis* spp.	•		•		7
Peach	*Prunus persica*				•	5-9
Pecan	*Carya illinoensis*				•	6-9
Piñon pine	*Pinus edulis*				•	5
Plum	*Prunus domestica*				•	4-9
Stone pine	*Pinus pinea*				•	4
Tagasaste	*Chaemocytisus palmensis*	•				8-10
White oak	*Quercus alba, Q garryana*		•			4-9
Yellowhorn	*Xanthocera sorbifolium*				•	5-7

Low-Tree Layer

Common name	Botanical name	N-fixer	Wildlife value	Insectary	Edible	Hardiness zones
Almond	*Prunus dulcis*			•	•	6-9
Apple, dwarf or semi-dwarf	*Malus pumila*		•	•	•	4
Apricot	*Prunus armeniaca*			•	•	5-9
Bamboo	*Phyllostachys* spp., *Fargesia* spp.		•	•	•	6
Chinkapin	*Castanea alnifolia, C. pumila*		•		•	
Cornelian cherry dogwood	*Cornus mas*		•		•	4

(continues)

Table 10-1. Plants for the Forest Garden (continued)						
Common name	Botanical name	N-fixer	Wildlife value	Insectary	Edible	Hardiness zones
Crabapple	Malus spp.		•	•	•	3
Fig	Ficus carica				•	6
Filbert/hazel	Corylus spp.		•		•	4
Golden-chain tree	Laburnum spp.	•				5
Hawthorn	Crataegus spp.		•		•	4
Jujube	Ziziphus jujuba				•	6-9
Loquat	Eriobotrya japonica				•	8
Mayhaw	Crataegus opaca, C. aestivalis		•		•	6-9
Medlar	Mespilus germanica				•	5-9
Mountain ash	Sorbus spp.		•		•	3
Mulberry	Morus spp.		•		•	5-9
Osage orange	Maclura pomifera		•			5-9
Pawpaw	Asimina trilobata				•	5-7
Peach, dwarf or semi-dwarf	Prunus persica			•	•	5-9
Pecan	Carya illinoensis				•	6-9
Persimmon, American	Diospyros virginiana				•	5
Persimmon, Asian	Diospyros kaki				•	7
Pomegranate	Punica spp.				•	8
Quince	Cydonia oblongata				•	5-9
Silk tree	Albizia julibrissin	•	•			7

Common name	Botanical name	N-fixer	Wildlife value	Insectary	Edible	Hardiness zones
Shrub Layer						
Serviceberry (saskatoonberry)	Amelanchier alnifolia		•	•	•	2
False indigo	Amorpha fruticosa	•	•			3
Aronia (chokeberry)	Aronia melanocarpa		•		•	4
Japanese barberry	Berberis thunbergii		•			4-8
Siberian pea shrub	Caragan arborescens	•				2-8
Hackberry	Celtis occidentalis		•			3-7
Summersweet clethra	Clethra alnifolia		•		•	3-8
Red azarole	Crataegus azarolus		•		•	4
Russian olive	Elaeagnus angustifolia	•	•		•	4
Goumi	Elaeagnus multiflora	•	•		•	5-8
Autumn olive	Elaeagnus Umbellata	•	•		•	4
Pineapple guava	Feijoa sellowiana				•	7
Salal	Gaultheria shallon		•		•	6-8
Witch hazel	Hamamelis virginiana		•			4-8

Table 10-1. Plants for the Forest Garden (continued)						
Common name	Botanical name	N-fixer	Wildlife value	Insectary	Edible	Hardiness zones
Sea buckthorn	*Hippophae rhamnoides*	•			•	3-8
Indigo	*Indigofera tinctoria*	•				6
Hansen's bush cherry	*Prunus besseyi*		•	•	•	4
Nanking cherry	*Prunus tomentosa*		•	•	•	3-8
Gooseberry	*Ribes hirtellum*		•		•	3
Currant	*Ribes* spp.		•		•	3
Jostaberry	*Ribes × Rubus hybrid*		•			3
Rugose rose	*Rosa rugosa*		•		•	2-8
Raspberry	*Rubus idaeus*		•		•	3-9
Blackberry	*Rubus* spp.		•		•	5
Elderberry	*Sambucus* spp.		•		•	3
Buffaloberry	*Shepherdea argentea*	•	•		•	2
Highbush cranberry	*Vaccinium macrocarpon*		•		•	4-8
Blueberry	*Vaccinium* spp.		•		•	4
American cranberry	*Viburnum trilobum*		•			2
Common name	Botanical name	N-fixer	Wildlife value	Insectary	Edible	Hardiness zones
Vine Layer						
Kiwifruit	*Actinidia deliciosa*				•	7
Kiwifruit, hardy	*Actinidia arguta, A. kolomikta*				•	4-8
Clematis	*Clematis* spp.			•		5
Melon	*Cucumis melo*				•	Annual
Cucumber	*Cucumis sativus*				•	Annual
Squash	*Cucurbita* spp.				•	Annual
Hops	*Humulus lupulus*		•	•	•	4
Jasmine	*Jasminum* spp.		•			6
Honeysuckle	*Lonicera* spp.		•	•		3
Passionfruit	*Passiflora* spp.			•		6
Scarlet runner bean	*Phaseolus coccineus*				•	Annual
Pea	*Pisum sativum*				•	Annual
Magnolia vine	*Schisandra chinensis*		•		•	4
Nasturtium	*Tropaeolum majus*			•	•	Annual
Grape	*Vitis* spp.				•	6
Common name	Botanical name	N-fixer	Wildlife value	Insectary	Edible	Hardiness zones
Ground Cover Layer						
Ajuga	*Ajuga reptans*			•		3

(continues)

Table 10-1. Plants for the Forest Garden (continued)

Common name	Botanical name	N-fixer	Wildlife value	Insectary	Edible	Hardiness zones
Bearberry (kinnickinnick)	*Arctostaphylos uva-ursi*		•		•	6
Clover	*Trifolium* spp.	•		•		3
Creeping phlox	*Phlox stolonifera*			•		4
Creeping thyme	*Thymus praecox, T. vulgaris*			•		4
Lingonberry	*Vaccinium vitis-idaea*				•	4-7
Miner's lettuce	*Montia* spp.			•		4
Nepalese raspberry	*Rubus nepalensis*				•	6
Prostrate verbena	*Verbena peruviana, V. tenera*			•		5
Stonecrop	*Sedum* spp.			•		3
Strawberry	*Fragaria* spp.			•	•	5
Sweet violet	*Viola odorata*				•	6
Thrift	*Phlox subulata*			•		4
Trailing bellflower	*Campanula poscharskyana*			•	•	3
Wild ginger	*Asarum canadense*				•	3

Common name	Botanical name	N-fixer	Wildlife value	Insectary	Edible	Hardiness zones
Root Layer						
Camas	*Camassia quamash*			•	•	5
Biscuit root	*Lomatium* spp.		•	•	•	5
Earth chestnut	*Bunium bulbocastanum*				•	5
Garlic	*Allium sativa*				•	4
Garlic chives	*Allium tuberosum*				•	3
Groundnut	*Apios americana*	•			•	3
Hardy ginger	*Zingiber mioga*				•	6
Horseradish	*Armoracia rusticana*				•	5-9
Hog peanut	*Amphicarpaea bracteata*	•		•	•	3-9
Licorice fern	*Polypodium glycyrrhiza*				•	6
Jerusalem artichoke	*Helianthus tuberosus*		•	•	•	2
Mashua	*Tropaeolum tuberosum*			•	•	7
Mountain yam	*Dioscorea batatas*				•	5
Oca	*Oxalis tuberosa*				•	7
Peanut	*Arachis hypogaea*	•			•	6
Potato	*Solanum tuberosum*				•	Annual
Ramps	*Allium tricoccum*				•	4-8

include black locust, mesquite, alder, and, in low-frost climates, acacia, algoroba, tagasaste, and carob.

Since much of the forest garden lies in landscape zones 1 and 2, timber trees aren't appropriate—tree felling in close quarters would be too destructive. But pruning and storm damage will generate firewood and small wood for crafts.

The canopy trees will define the major patterns of the forest garden, so they must be chosen carefully. Plant them with careful regard to their mature size so enough light will fall between them to support other plants.

2. *The Low-Tree Layer.* Here are many of the same fruits and nuts as in the canopy, but on dwarf and semidwarf rootstocks to keep them low growing. Plus, we can plant naturally small trees such as apricot, peach, nectarine, almond, medlar, and mulberry. Here also are shade-tolerant fruit trees such as persimmon and pawpaw. In a smaller forest garden, these small trees may serve as the canopy. They can easily be pruned into an open form, which will allow light to reach the other species beneath them.

Other low-growing trees include flowering species, such as dogwood and mountain ash, and some nitrogen fixers, including golden-chain tree, silk tree, and mountain mahogany. Both large and small nitrogen-fixing trees grow quickly and can be pruned heavily to generate plenty of mulch and compost.

3. *The Shrub Layer.* This tier includes flowering, fruiting, wildlife-attracting, and other useful shrubs. A small sampling: blueberry, rose, hazelnut, butterfly bush, bamboo, serviceberry, the nitrogen-fixing *Elaeagnus* species and Siberian pea shrub, and dozens of others. The broad palette of available shrubs allows the gardener's inclinations to surface, as shrubs can be chosen to emphasize food, crafts, ornamentals, birds, insects, native plants, exotics, or just raw biodiversity.

Shrubs come in all sizes, from dwarf blueberries to nearly tree-sized hazelnuts, and thus can be plugged into edges, openings, and niches of many forms. Shade-tolerant varieties can lurk beneath the trees, sun-loving types in the sunny spaces between.

4. *The Herb Layer.* Here *herb* is used in the broad botanical sense to mean nonwoody vegetation: vegetables, flowers, culinary herbs, and cover crops, as well as mulch producers and other soil-building plants. Emphasis is on perennials, but we won't rule out choice annuals and self-seeding species. Again, shade-lovers can peek out from beneath taller plants, while sun-worshiping species need the open spaces. At the edges, a forest garden can also hold more traditional garden beds of plants dependent on full sun.

5. *The Ground-Cover Layer.* These are low, ground-hugging plants—preferably varieties that offer food or habitat—that snuggle into edges and the spaces between shrubs and herbs. Sample species include strawberries, nasturtium, clover, creeping thyme, ajuga, and the many prostrate varieties of flowers such as phlox and verbena.

They play a critical role in weed prevention, occupying ground that would otherwise succumb to invaders.

6. *The Vine Layer.* This layer is for climbing plants that will twine up trunks and branches, filling the unused regions of the all-important third dimension with food and habitat. Here are food plants, such as kiwifruit, grapes, hops, passionflower, and vining berries; and those for wildlife, such as honeysuckle and trumpet-flower. These can include climbing annuals such as squash, cucumbers, and melons. Some of the perennial vines can be invasive or strangling; hence, they should be used sparingly and cautiously.

7. *The Root Layer.* The soil gives us yet another layer for the forest garden; the third dimension goes both up and down. Most of the plants for the root layer should be shallow rooted, such as garlic and onions, or easy-to-dig types such as potatoes and Jerusalem artichokes. Deep-rooted varieties such as carrots don't work well because the digging they require will disturb other plants. I do sprinkle a few seeds of daikon (Asian radish) in open spots because the long roots can often be pulled with one mighty tug rather than dug; and, if I don't harvest them, the blossoms attract beneficial bugs and the fat roots add humus as they rot.

Designing the Forest Garden

The forest garden design process largely follows the sequence laid out in Chapter 3: observation, visioning, planning, development, and implementation. As well, extra focus on a few points will be helpful:

- In an exposed site, wind barriers (fences and hedges) will greatly speed the establishment of the other plants.
- Trees and woody plants should go in first because these take the longest to mature and define the shape of the garden. Remember to design for the full mature size of trees—it's easy to place spindly seedlings too close together, leading to overcrowding and dense shade when they mature. Leave room for sunlight to penetrate between full-grown trees, rather than creating a closed tall-tree layer. The more northerly the garden, the weaker the sun will be, so more space will be needed between trees.
- Early on, include plenty of nitrogen-fixing and other soil-building plants. The dense plantings of the forest garden will demand lots of nutrients during their youth, so the soil must be in great shape. The fertile, organic-rich soil built by nutrient-accumulating plants will accelerate growth and speed succession along.
- Buying the plants for a forest garden all at once can get expensive, so those with a limited budget should consider setting aside a small area as a nursery for seed-starting, rooting cuttings, and general plant propagation. It's best to place the nursery in zone 1, so you can keep close watch on the tender youngsters. Here, you can start perennials for the herb, root, and ground-cover layers from seed en masse; propagate cuttings for trees, shrubs, and herbs; divide established plants to yield numerous progeny; and create a swelling population of plants to colonize the new garden. You

can nurture these for a year or two and then move them to their permanent homes. Those with the expertise can graft tree varieties, too. A nursery is invaluable for furnishing huge number of plants very cheaply.

- The open spaces between trees and shrubs can at first be filled with annual vegetables, flowers, nitrogen-fixing cover crops such as clover, and nursery stock. As the upper layers grow and the nursery plants become ready to transplant, these beds will shrink.

For a design example, let's look at the typical case of a homeowner wanting to take out a lawn and install a more ecologically sound forest garden. We'll select a U-shaped design, which provides a private, warm, and sheltered space in the center (see the illustration on page 210). Ideally the U would open toward the south for maximum sunshine.

This design will emphasize food—three dimensions of fruit, berries, vegetables, and herbs, with a minor emphasis on flowers. We want plenty of vegetables and flowers in the lower layers for the first few years, but we know that as time goes by, the upper layers will be the principal providers. With these goals in mind, we can begin the design.

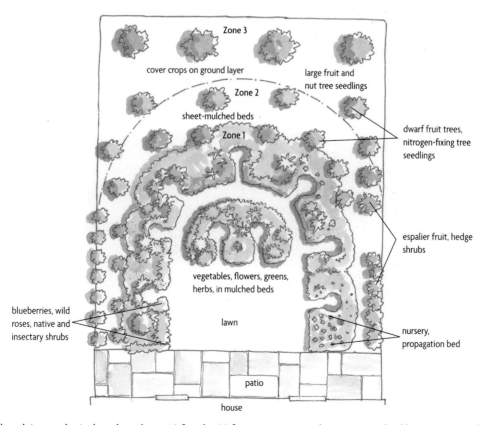

A freshly planted evolving ecological garden, about 40 feet by 50 feet. A nursery and propagation bed lies conveniently close to the house for regular care. Temporary, well-composted beds line the lawn in Zone 1 for fast, early food and flower production. Young trees and shrubs—as many as can be afforded—begin to fill the more distant Zones 2 and 3. Zone 2 is deeply sheet-mulched to quickly build soil, while the less-urgently needed Zone 3 is cover-cropped for long-term soil restoration.

First, map the area for the new garden and sketch in any existing foliage that will be saved. Then draw in the new plantings. The sunny, open area in the center of the U can be kept as lawn or converted to flower and vegetable beds. Many parents opt to preserve an expanse of lawn for children to play in, but once the forest fills in, I guarantee that the kids will abandon the open grass for the more enchanting shrubbery, a perfect place for hideaways and forts. The lawn can be kept just big enough for a little sunbathing.

For a windbreak and privacy screen, we'll create an edge of hedge and wall plants: espaliered or cordoned fruit trees, berry bushes, shrub willows, roses, dogwoods, elderberries, and useful native shrubs.

Then sketch in the tree layers. Tall trees are best placed to the north to reduce the shade cast on other plantings, but wide spacing will also allow ample sunlight to fall between trees. The spacing reflects the mature size of the tree. Since this is a fair-sized suburban property, we have room for some full-sized trees: apple, pear, walnut, plum, and cherry. We want some nitrogen fixers, so we'll add black locust and golden-chain tree. In the low-tree layer are dwarf and semidwarf fruit trees plus, under the taller trees, naturally small persimmons, pawpaws, and mulberries. In this example, no tall trees are close to the house, which will allow ample light for the zone 1 understory.

The shrub and lower layers require some thought because we want to have constant food production while the upper layers mature. To give the owners lots of zone 1 and 2 vegetables and herbs until the

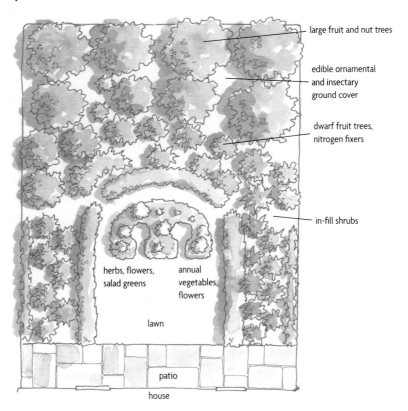

large fruit and nut trees

edible ornamental and insectary ground cover

dwarf fruit trees, nitrogen fixers

in-fill shrubs

herbs, flowers, salad greens

annual vegetables, flowers

lawn

patio

house

After five to ten years, the garden has filled in. Since the perennial shrubs and trees are now producing abundantly, the temporary keyhole beds have shrunk to narrow, edge beds. A ground cover of edible, flowering, and insectary herbs and shrubs fills in the gaps between and below major trees.

trees begin to bear, we'll design some keyhole beds near the house: temporary ones under the low trees and permanent beds in the open center. One of the short-term beds is reserved for plant propagation. This arrangement means that the low trees near the house won't be underplanted with perennials as densely—yet—as those farther away.

Three factors interact to mold the design of the more distant parts of this forest garden. One is the zone effect: The farther-off places—zones 2 and 3—won't be visited as often as the nearer zones, so they can't demand as much care. A second factor is that of time: The young plantings will start small and need one or more years to mature. And the third is budget: Many gardeners won't want to spend the large sum necessary to plant the entire yard densely all at once, and this far-off zone is the best place to plant sparsely until more stock is ready. So we need to develop a planting strategy that reflects these constraints. This less-maintained zone will sport only a few small specimens at first, thus it is prone to weed invasion and neglect while the woody plants mature and the low layers fill in.

My recommendation is this: In zone 2, mulch heavily between the young trees and shrubs and plant the herb, root, and ground-cover layers as time, nursery stock, and money become available. Renew the mulch once or twice a year to build the soil quickly and smother weeds. To try to cultivate and plant this large area would probably be biting off too large a chunk at once. Remember, the wisest strategy is to get zone 1 established first and then expand outward. With the above approach, the shrubs, trees, and soil of zone 2 will be ready when zone 1 is up and running.

The farthest reaches of this yard elicit yet another approach. It's doubtful we can conjure up enough mulch to cover the entire forest garden, and since the full-sized trees and large shrubs of zone 3 will take longest to mature, soil-building isn't as urgent a task. Once the trees and major shrubs are in place in this more distant zone, I'd advise planting a soil-building, habitat-providing cover crop mix. This will keep weeds at bay and boost fertility until we're ready to plant the lower layers. One choice for a cover crop is clover and annual rye mixed with beneficial-insect-attracting herbs such as yarrow, dill, and fennel, and maybe a little subsoil-loosening daikon thrown in. This lush mix need be mowed only once or twice a year, so it needs very little maintenance while it boosts fertility. Cover crops are a good strategy for less-visited parts of a garden.

Thus, we have created three zones in this forest garden: an intensively cultivated zone 1, a well-mulched but lightly planted (for now) zone 2, and a long-term set of soil-building cover crops beneath the young shrubs and trees of zone 3. Of course, the lucky gardener with sufficient money and access to labor and materials might, if confident enough in the design scheme, just joyously install the whole design at once, with dense plantings and mulch in place of the cover crops.

Guilding the Food Forest

Let's look at the possibilities for guilds that will connect the pieces of our food forest design. Creating guilds based on the major fruit trees is fairly straightforward; we can plug in many elements from the apple-tree guild described in Chapter 9 or from Jerome's list earlier in this chapter. This means placing grass- and rodent-suppressing bulbs near the tree trunk, insect-attracting and soil-building plants in the herb and shrub layers, and additional food-providing plants and other useful species.

Remember, though, that this guild doesn't stand in isolation—it's nestled among other trees and large shrubs, so the pattern of planting is tugged and shaped by the neighboring vegetation. One lone guilded tree could be surrounded by concentric circles of its companion plants, but not in the forest garden, with its numerous trees. Concentric

In this Santa Barbara, California, garden, black sage *(Salvia mellifera)* and California poppy *(Eschscholzia californica)* in the foreground represent the drought-tolerant vegetation of the area's native chaparral landscape, while figs, citrus, persimmons, bananas, with a backdrop of a date palm, illustrate the wide variety of fruit trees that can be grown in this arid California climate by adding water. Contour pathways that help percolate water into the soil are lined with locally collected stone. Design by Larry Santoyo of **Earthflow Design Works.** PHOTO BY LARRY SANTOYO.

rings of mulch plants and others beneath the tree's dripline are no longer the right pattern now that other shrubs and trees are close by. Instead, mulch plants, insect-attractors, and other guild members—depending on their need for light— should be tucked into openings between neighboring trees and shrubs, nestled into pockets under the branches, or lined alongside paths to allow access for picking and pruning. Plants that suppress weeds—bulbs and some of the thick mulch plants— can form, instead of a circle under one tree, a natural boundary around a whole cluster of trees and shrubs, or can define the outline of a clearing or a sunny edge.

In addition to fruit-tree guilds, we can also design a walnut-tree guild for this garden. Remember, though, that walnuts are allelopaths, whose mildly toxic root secretions will stunt the growth of many other plants. This is where the use of buffer plants, described earlier, is essential. The lofty walnut, together with its guild of hackberries, currants, and solanaceous annuals such as peppers and tomatoes, will go at the north end of the yard. Then we can insert buffering black locusts, mulberries, and Russian olives between the walnut and any fruit trees.

The semidwarf fruit trees closer to the house can also be guilded, but we'll underplant these trees with smaller shrubs and fewer of them because the central trees aren't very large and we want plenty of light and edge for the zone 1 herb, root, and ground-cover layers. Good candidates for these guilds are nitrogen-fixing small shrubs such as buffaloberry, ceanothus, and indigo; weed-suppressing and mulch plants including comfrey, borage, and nasturtium; and any of the wealth of smaller insectary plants.

A guild next to the house will have a different composition than one that's located farther away. Guilds very near the house should emphasize plants for food, medicine, and other human use, with less florae for wildlife, mulch production, and the like. Our own labor can substitute for the natural mulching, weed-prevention, and other guild functions that we give up in exchange for having enhanced yields right outside our door. It's no problem to add a bit of compost and squish a few cucumber beetles right off the back porch, but I'd rather that out in zone 3, seventy-five feet away, nature did those jobs.

To install the forest garden, first eliminate most of the grass, preferably without toxic herbicides. This means either stripping the sod by hand and composting it, power-tilling the sod at intervals a few weeks apart to kill emerging grass remnants, throwing a giant sheet-mulch party to smother the lawn, or a combination of all three (for a review

of creating and planting sheet mulch, check back to Chapter 4). This is the best time to amend and improve the soil with lime, organic matter, and long-term fertilizers, because much of the yard will soon be covered in perennials, which makes digging-in fertilizer less easy. As mentioned, the center of the U-shaped garden can be left in grass for a play and relaxation space.

Next, plant the trees. The back one-third of the yard (zone 3) should then be planted with the cover crops and green manures mentioned above. Zone 2 and much of zone 1 now receive a soil-building layer of deep sheet mulch, with some of the closest zone 1 beds getting a topping of rich compost to get them ready for immediate use. Keep the mulch pulled back from the tree trunks to discourage bark-gnawing rodents.

Finally, plant shrubs and other perennial plants, bulbs and other members of the root layer, and ground covers right into the sheet mulch.

How the Food Forest Evolves

Besides bringing food and blossom nearly all year, the many rhythms and cycles of a forest garden can fascinate and inform. In a garden full of annuals or even in a single-layer perennial garden, most plants follow a simple yearly cycle: growth in spring, dieback in fall, and renewal—or replanting—the next spring. But in a forest garden, the life spans of many of the occupants are measured not in one year but in decades or more. Thus, the garden's character will constantly change over its entire existence. Besides the regular annual cycle of all florae, the trees, shrubs, and perennials have different life spans and growth rates, and varying responses to the seasons and to each other. Complex natural rhythms play off one another, interlocking and contrasting in varied syncopation.

Even the seasonal cycles are more complex than in a conventional garden. In a staggered sequence of green that ripples from the garden floor to the canopy, each layer of the garden shares light and nutrients with the others. Each spring, the lower layers of a forest garden are the first to leaf out and drink in the early sunlight, just as in a natural woodland. Next, the shrubs put on their green covering, followed in a few weeks by the trees overhead. Many of the plants also reach peak size at different times of the season, further sharing resources. This cooperative aspect of the forest garden is balanced, however, with a little competition. The plants, particularly in the lower layer, do a little jostling of each other, spreading and shrinking as they compete for light, water, and nutrients. The gardener also affects these cycles, with trowel, pruners, and harvest basket.

These rhythms and diversity are augmented by the movement of wild plants into the forest—both so-called weeds and unusual natives—and the gardener, after observing the newcomer, can vote on whether it should stay or go. Birds, insects, snakes, lizards, and small mammals will also find safe harbor here, further adding to the complexity and interest. Watching and learning these varied rhythms provides the best possible introduction to ecology and the natural world. Yet we can do a little intelligent tinkering, too, favoring a useful or attractive species here, encouraging a nascent guild there.

The evolution of the forest garden over the years—not just over the seasons—offers its own benefits. Though the beauty and value of a mature landscape can't be denied, we're not just idly passing time until those tiny seedlings and baby shrubs grow up. Each phase of the garden carries a new set of rewards. When the garden is young, and the scattering of freshly planted trees is at the "twig farm" stage, the sunny spaces between seedlings can be filled with annual and perennial vegetables and flowers. In a year or three, the shrubs and berry bushes will begin to show their true colors and fruit, and for the next five to ten years, before the trees cast much shade, they will be at peak form. Meanwhile, the open ground for annual beds will slowly shrink, soil fertility will grow from the thickening leaf litter, and niches for wildlife will compound by the minute.

After three or four years, the fruit trees will begin to bear, and the backbone of the garden will be apparent. By the fifth year, as trees and shrubs fill out, the herb and ground layers will thin in the reduced light, and herbs, flowers, and vegetables can migrate to the edges and deliberate clearings. In spots, flowering and fruiting vines will tie the upper layers together. The gardener won't need to import much fertilizer and mulch any more, as the forest, through the rain of leaves and the upward tug of deep-soil nutrients through roots, will be just about self-sufficient. In ten years, the trees will approach their full height, and the canopy will begin to close. The garden will take on the serenity and majesty of maturity but will continue to fill out for another ten or twenty years. By then, much of the original herb layer will have been renewed with new plantings, and some shrubs and small trees will have reached the end of their lives. The substitutes will continue the evolution of this garden. Even at maturity, the garden continues to change gracefully.

The changes in the evolving forest garden are mainly these:

- From most plants being in full sun in the early years to only the upper layers, clearings, and edges receiving all-day sunshine.
- From drought-prone and vulnerable to the vicissitudes of weather and neglect to evenly moist, self-regulating, and filled with mild microclimates.

- From windy and exposed to calm and sheltered.
- From most of the flower and food production, habitat, mulch, and biomass being created by the lower layers to much of these being produced by the shrub and tree layers.
- From needing imports of mulch and fertilizer to generating abundant fertil-ity and soil via leaf fall and deep-rooted nutrient collection.

Earlier, I've sung the virtues of extending the garden upward into the third dimension. The forest garden reaches yet further, into the fourth dimension of time. The long unfolding of this growing garden brings new opportunities and benefits into reach.

CHAPTER 11

Permaculture Gardening in the City

Much of what's been offered in earlier chapters assumes the reader has a fair-sized yard: not much less than a quarter-acre or so. But plenty of people live in cities, where yards are small or even nonexistent. And since I've returned to city life since writing the first edition of this book, I know that creating an ecological garden in the city carries with it some special challenges. Fortunately, they are matched by a pile of opportunities even larger.

Many of the urban gardener's dilemmas arise because city life puts a premium on space. The crush of people in cities makes every bit of ground heavily trafficked, intensely used, and fiercely sought for a host of competing uses. What you are eyeing as a sweet garden spot, your kids will deem their playground, your spouse as perfect for the comfy chaise lounge, your dog as an ideal site for digging (or worse), and the letter carrier as the quickest path to the next yard. Right off, it's obvious that urban yards need to be exquisitely multifunctional. In keeping with the principles of permaculture, though, rather than viewing this as a liability, we can think of the necessity for multiple-use yards as a spur to greater creativity and a more engaging landscape.

In case any suburbanite readers are thinking "this won't apply to me" and are ready to skip ahead to the final chapter, I'll suggest that these space-saving, high-intensity design approaches will apply to everyone. As houses both urban and rural have

swollen in size since World War II—the average square footage has doubled—they've left less room around them to garden. Yards have shrunk, too: Many recent suburbs offer lots that are no bigger than those of urban houses, 5,000 square feet or less. Not only are these yards small, they are usually fragmented by the house, driveway, walks, and other hardscapes into even littler spaces. Those yard splinters won't hold many large guilds, so we'll need to come up with other options. Doing more in the small spaces of any metropolitan area, urban or suburban, is one focus of this chapter.

The techniques for creating life-filled home ecosystems in urban settings are similar to what we would use in any ecological landscape, but the strategies that guide how we assemble and organize those techniques are different. To garden ecologically in metro areas, a smart strategist will play to the city's strengths and mitigate the weaknesses. The great strength of any city—the reason people go there—is the social capital: the synergies and opportunities generated by creative people working together. As I've noted, a major weakness, especially for gardeners, is the paucity of land. Fortunately, if we play it right, the social resources are exactly the force needed to make up for the scarcity of land.

Here's an example. In moving to Portland, Kiel and I traded our ten rural acres for a fifty-by-one-hundred-foot lot. My first thought was, "How am I going to fit all my favorite fruit trees into this tiny space?" The yard was almost a blank slate: mostly grass, some bark mulch hastily installed by the seller to mask formerly weedy spots, and a dog run. The sole trees were a sapling Japanese maple and a mature European prune plum that straddled the property line. The plums came ripe just after we arrived. One morning I was chatting with my next-door neighbor, a retired electrician and fervent gardener named Johnny, while we harvested plums on our respective sides of the fence. Johnny asked me if I liked figs. My strong affirmative resulted in a plastic tub brimming with ripe Mission figs wobbling my way from his side of the fence. For the next few weeks, whenever I returned the empty basin to Johny, it come back moments later loaded with fruit.

I had also met my neighbor Theressa, who lived across the street, and because I had a surfeit of plums, I carried a bag of them over to her. She smiled ruefully and said, "Sorry, I don't need plums—I've got a tree of my own." Theressa then told me that I had just missed peach season, when she had been giving fruit away. But in a few weeks, she said, her Granny Smith apples would be ready, so I should load up on those. The neighbor next door to Theressa, a computer guy named Will, overheard us and said if I needed fruit, I should come right over and help him harvest the enormous Bartlett pear tree in his backyard. Will got my bag of plums, and I came home with twice as many pears. My neighbors' yards had become my orchard.

I realized that I didn't need to plant all my favorite fruit trees. I just needed to plant the ones that were missing from the neighborhood. The next spring I bought an Asian pear, a Hachiya persimmon, and a sweet Stella cherry to fill our community's gaps. I added an espaliered apple grafted with four varieties, even though there were a few apples in my neighbors' yards, since the tree could provide storage and pie apples that we lacked, as well as acting

A plum tree in front of Will Hooker's Asheville, North Carolina, yard, planted through a street-tree improvement grant. Will says that neighborhood children love riding their bikes under the tree to grab free fruit. PHOTO BY WILL HOOKER.

as a hedge. The four-way apple also taught me how to maintain an espalier. With those plantings, most of the tree niches in our yard were filled.

Urban yards are rarely big enough to encompass more than permacultural zone 1 and a modest zone 2, the areas of intensive use. Larger zone 2 and zone 3 functions such as orchards and woodlots usually won't fit. But your neighbors' yards can be your zones 2 and 3, just as your yard can be part of theirs. Most mature fruit trees bear too heavily for any but the most fanatical fruit lovers to consume, leaving most of us with the choice of letting fruit rot or giving it away. As Bill Mollison says, where you have fruit, you have friends. For millennia, food has been at the center of community creation and rituals of friendship, and sharing it is one of the most natural ways for neighbors to meet and trust each other.

The sharing goes well beyond food. Resources such as mulch and firewood, normally grown in zones 3 and 4, can come from your neighborhood and nearby parts of the city. These places are the city-dweller's outer zones.

I was surprised to find that mulch, fertilizer, and other organic matter are more abundant and easier to come by in cities than in rural areas. To get manure when we lived in rural Oregon, I had to drive to a stable three miles away or to a more distant chicken farm, load the manure myself, and pay the farmer. The supply was hit-or-miss, as neighboring farmers and gardeners competed for it. Mulch was equally hard to find because anyone generating wood chips, leaves, or clippings would simply dump it on their back forty, where no one could use it.

But in the city, I don't even have to leave home to get organic matter—I can have vast amounts of mulch, manure, and compost materials delivered right to my door. That's because organic matter in a metropolis is considered waste. It is a surplus that must be disposed of. It can't just be piled up in a tiny yard; there would soon be no yard left. Anyone creating more than a modest amount has to pay to haul it to the dump. So a person or business that generates organic matter is usually pleased when someone will dispose of it for free. When my neighbors and I, hearing the clash and roar of the wood chipper, ask the tree-trimming crew if we can have this fresh mulch, the arborists smile with relief. We've just saved them a hundred-dollar dumping fee, and they will gladly drop ten cubic yards of freshly chipped wood and leaves in our driveway.

We also get free manure from a rabbit-rescue nonprofit agency in town. Zoos are another source. Restaurants and grocery stores disgorge food scraps by the cubic yard. And don't get me started on the volume of coffee grounds in cappuccino-crazed Portland. Spent coffee is excellent compost fodder, particularly for a worm compost bin, which is a space-saving soil technique perfect for urban houses and even apartments.

The flow of free and cheap resources of all types in the city is vast. Websites such as Craigslist and FreeCycle can apprise us of the abundance out there in urban zones 3 and 4. Now we begin to see that in urban zones and sectors, elements and flows are dictated more by humans and commerce than by biology and landscape, and their cycles are at least as complex and productive as those of large yards and farms.

My own introduction to the uniqueness of city zones and sectors came at a workshop I gave at the Los Angeles Ecovillage, an ecologically based community in a neighborhood of apartment buildings, freeways, and stores in East Los Angeles, on the edge of the downtown core. After introducing the concepts of zones and sectors to the class, I asked them to think of some specifically urban sectors. (Remember that sectors are forces and influences coming from off the site, such as wind and sun, that affect a landscape design.) Someone immediately described the "billboard sector." Behind the ecovillage yard loomed an enormous billboard that faced nearby Highway 101. It cast deep shadow over the backyard for much of the day, and at night was ablaze in a battery of sodium-vapor lamps. Because of the billboard sector, the student explained, they had been forced to garden in the front yard.

Another student piped up, "That makes me think of another sector!" She explained that when the community moved their vegetable garden to the front yard, they had planted tomatoes along the sidewalk. But an elementary school sat across the street, and a half-dozen times a day, hundreds of children would boil out of their classrooms and swarm past the yard. Every tomato showing the slightest blush of red was snapped up. The ecovillagers rarely got tomatoes. "We forgot about the schoolchild sector," the woman announced.

In response the ecovillagers evolved a clever strategy, which was to plant tomato varieties such as Green Grape, which never turns red but sports delicious green fruit. Black Krim, which ripens to an unappealing green-purple with black stripes, was another choice, along with White Wonder, Kentucky Yellow, and others that won't display the iconic tomato redness. The kids remained clueless,

A suburban front yard in southwest Houston, Texas, designed by Kevin Topek of Permaculture Design, LLC. Plantings between side-walk and street to create habitat and privacy. These native and drought-adapted species need little maintenance and a minimum of water. Species in the foreground include Mexican Turk's cap, almond verbena, bulbine, rudbeckia, ruby grass, cassia, and thryallis.
PHOTO BY KEVIN TOPEK.

and the tomato harvest was safe. In this way, the schoolchild sector was deflected, just as any sector's energy can be blocked by good design.

Other sectors that the Los Angeles class identi-fied were:

- The bad-smell sector, coming from the fast-food joint around the corner.
- The noise sector, primarily the nearby freeway, but also the schoolyard and street.
- The workshop sector, because holding events at the ecovillage brought many people to their site, with concomitant activity, excitement, and disruptions.
- The crime sector, which was the alley behind their buildings, an unsafe place at night. A student pointed out that the crime sector at intervals became . . .
- The police sector because two beat cops patrolled the alley periodically after dark.

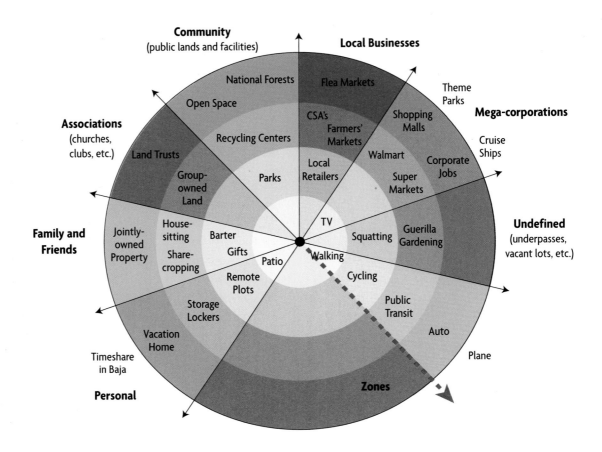

Zones and sectors in an urban context. Here, the zones, instead of being defined by their distance from your doorstep, represent places reachable by foot, bicycle, public transit, car, and plane. Sectors are the influences and forces that affect a city-dweller, such as family, community, multinational corporations, and local businesses. REDRAWN WITH PERMISSION FROM "ADAPTING ZONES AND SECTORS FOR THE CITY" BY BART ANDERSON, WWW.ENERGYBULLETIN.NET/12052.HTML

Viewing zones and sectors through an urban filter lets us see the influences on our landscapes, as well as our lives, in a new perspective. When Bart Anderson, a former reporter and current coeditor of the website EnergyBulletin.net, took a permaculture design course, he was inspired to expand the use of zones and sectors. Many of the traditional elements, such as fire sectors or zones for timber crops, didn't apply at all to his urban life. But he realized that the concept was a powerful tool for viewing his home and habits in the context of an entire city and social network.

Bart saw that when looking at a city person's movements as a whole, zone 1 could define places accessible by walking. Zone 2 encompassed destinations reached by bicycle; zone 3, by public transit; zone 4, by car; and zone 5, by plane. Sectors, in turn, became the social and economic influences on an urbanite's life. In Bart's plan, sectors could be divided into family and friends, personal activities, associations such as churches and nonprofits, community and local government, local businesses, and non-local corporations. A zone, such as the area reachable by public transit, may intersect with a local business sector at a farmers' market, with the community at a recycling center, and in the friend sector at a buddy's garden. The figure shown above shows how Bart defined the zones and sectors for his own metropolitan life.

This way of viewing zones and sectors makes explicit many of the differences between urban and nonurban landscapes. In rural life, many activities, such as socializing, meal preparation, and relaxation, most often occur on a home owner's property. Rural people are more likely to have orchards, large production gardens, and firewood trees and may even homeschool their children and do maintenance such as car repair at home. In the city, much of this occurs away from home, and so urbanites do more activities in "zones" that are not owned by them and are commonly businesses or public places instead of private homes. Thus for urbanites, their "site" frequently expands beyond the boundaries of their property line. Just as I discovered my urban orchard in Theressa, Johnny, and Will's yards, I find my office is sometimes in a coffee shop, and my firewood comes from city parks. Even food harvesting can occur away from home, as many fruit trees are on public property or are otherwise open to our use. Tools like the Internet have made these resources even more available. One website, urbanedibles.com, is a user-created database of harvestable fruit trees and other edible species throughout my city of Portland, with addresses and hints for making best use of the plants.

For the idea of zone and sector to be a useful tool for design and efficient resource use, in urban spaces it must encompass a different set of places and forces than in wilder lands. The roles of large natural elements such as fire and wind lessen, while the importance of human influences such as traffic, billboards, neighbors, authorities, and businesses enlarges.

The Edge of the City

In proper permaculture assessment style, let's look at some influences that affect metropolitan dwellers who want to garden ecologically and find ways to turn them into productive assets rather than destructive liabilities.

We've seen in Chapter 3 and elsewhere that understanding and working with edges in the permacultural sense—the boundary between two environments—lets us create microclimates, increase yields and biodiversity, and better manage our landscapes. Viewing the urban environment from the perspective of its edges gives us a powerful tool for adapting our gardens to these challenging places. As a general rule in metro areas, edges are often sharp and abrupt. In contrast, natural and even rural boundaries are frequently gradual, soft, and often permeable. We can learn a great deal by examining the different types of edges found in city landscapes. These include:

The sun/shade edge. Moving from sun to shade in nature, we amble from open, full daylight to speckled dappling beside a tree and finally to deep shadows under the shroud of the canopy. We've traversed a gentle edge from light to relative dark, but even the shady places are bright enough for many plants to grow. Out between the trees, and even beneath branches, we find light gaps that shift daily and by season. At some time of day or year, almost every spot in the wild receives direct sun.

In the built environment, though, the north sides of buildings are in eternal shade, something almost never experienced in nature. In the city, we can step with no transition from glaring white light into inky shadow. Changes in *albedo*, or the amount of reflected light, are extreme: A city can be a checkerboard of reflectivity contrasts, shifting in a fraction of an inch from light-devouring black asphalt to glaring whitewashed walls. Those are serious design challenges. And if that dark north edge is under the eaves of a house, it becomes the garden-er's nemesis: dry shade, a place where few plants can thrive. So these edges guide our choices. We can select plants from the short list of dry-shade lovers, or perhaps this confluence of tricky sectors is telling us to consider the spot for some function other than planting, such as storage or socializing. After all, it's shady, which in summer heat can be a fine place for a deck or patio, and humans, unlike plants, don't require moist soil.

Moist/dry edges. Dense settlements spawn wild variations in soil moisture. Soil under a building's eaves may stay dry all year, while inches away the downspout might create a permanent bog. That's a harsh habitat transition that few plant species can bridge. Moisture gradients also exist in time as well as space. Some places dry out instantly, such as soil alongside a blacktopped driveway that's baking in the sun. A few feet away, though, a low spot in shade may seem to stay soggy forever.

These observations shape our planting. Once we've assessed the conditions, we can choose solutions from many possibilities. We could select plants that thrive in the existing conditions, whether by finding species flexible enough to span the broad moisture gradient, or putting water-lovers in the wet soil and xeric plants in the dry areas. We could soften the harsh edges in several ways, such as by creating better drainage in the wet spots through raising them, incorporating sand or gravel in the soil, or creating a physical drain. In the dry places, we can increase organic matter so they'll absorb and hold more moisture. Another edge-blurring tech-nique is to redirect excess water away from the wet spots and into the dry ones, using swales, berms, or other earth contours.

Warm/cold edge. Urban temperature gradients can be harsh because the built environment contains impermeable objects that block wind and dense

ones that hold heat. That means shockingly abrupt changes between microclimates. The west side of a house will cook in afternoon sun, while just around the corner, the permanent shade of the north face is cool. Dryer vents, air conditioners, car exhausts, and other machinery pump out heat in sporadic blasts, sowing confusion among plants trying to guess what season it is. With all this heat being generated, spread about, and absorbed, the entire metropolitan belt is usually several degrees warmer than the surrounding countryside. That heat evap-orates soil moisture quickly, creates wind, and dries the air, stressing plants.

Again our task is to temper the harshness or, if that's impractical, find landscape elements, living or inanimate, tough enough to take the punishment. In the sun-baked hot-spots, we can create shade; or, if sun and its accompanying warmth are rare commodities, we can capture and enhance those sunny microclimates through U-shaped hedges, walls and rocks that store heat.

Soil edges. Urban soil profiles yield another puzzling hodgepodge of conditions. Let me describe our yard as an example. Most of it is rich Willamette Valley loam, one of the finest agricultural soils in the world. But on the edges of the backyard lies orange clay mineral soil that is probably fill, from who knows where. Two perennial collards, planted just a few feet apart in these contrasting soils, display disturbingly different characters, the one in the loam being robust and deep green while the other, in clay, is anemic and small. In the front yard, a brown clay was used as fill, different in pH and drainage from the backyard's fill dirt. The parking strip contains a grayish silty soil covered with about two inches of black commercial topsoil. That's four soil types in a fifty-by-one-hundred-foot lot.

The pH of our urban yard varies from very acidic to roughly neutral, which I discovered when acid-loving blueberries did poorly in the backyard but were thriving in front. I've also found one patch that is toxically alkaline. A little probing there revealed a deep layer of debris-filled ash, where a trash burner had stood for perhaps decades.

The drainage on our lot is irregular. The loam holds moisture but drains well; it's great soil. But in one strip the soil is underlain with loose pebbles, perhaps an ancient drainage ditch, while elsewhere is a subsurface belt of tightly compacted gravel, marking an abandoned driveway. In one patch, next to thriving vegetation, plants withered quickly after only a few days without rain. My shovel revealed that eight inches below them was a buried sidewalk. After another archaeological exploration, a subterranean brick walkway appeared. The house was built in 1885, so time and many owners have left a deep and varied legacy.

Let's move on to toxics. Soils in cities often contain lead, deposited in a light dusting everywhere during the era of leaded gasoline and in concentrated bands along the foundations of most houses built before 1960, when lead-based paints were the rule. Backyards were once the traditional place to change oil, dump paint thinner, and generally treat as a petrochemical refuse site. All these remnant hazards may lurk beneath an innocent-looking lawn.

As cities have gentrified, neighborhoods that were formerly industrial have been converted to residential uses, and unknown poisonous residues from manufacturing may fester in the soil beneath. Samples of groundwater downhill from cemeteries show high levels of mercury and other compounds used in embalming. Rainwater running down road gutters could be an abundant resource for irrigation when shunted onto yards via curbcuts and bioswales, but since it is blended with petroleum drippings, it must be cleaned up first. In colder regions, yards can be salted along the edges where road deicers have washed onto them. Concrete itself is alkaline, thus runoff from streets, sidewalks, and foundations raises soil pH.

Urban soils in general have less organic matter and soil life than their country counterparts. High densities of people, pets, and the occasional parked car means compacted ground, causing shallow roots in plants, with attendant poor drought tolerance and nutrient uptake, sluggish drainage, and lack of aeration.

All this adds up to abrupt and unpredictable edges between patches of soils that are acid or alkaline, compacted or aerated, well-drained or boggy, fast-drying or eternally damp, clay or silt or sand, toxic or safe, dead or life-filled, fertile or impoverished. No rural property is apt to offer such a diverse set of soil conditions.

The correction for most of these soil difficulties begins with a simple assessment. I'm a big fan of urban archaeology: digging test pits a foot or two deep at intervals, just to see what's there. This will detect old driveways, walkways, dump sites, ash pits, and an astounding number of children's toys from bygone eras. Of course, holes dug in the course of planting trees will yield this information, too, but it's preferable to make shocking discoveries such as buried sidewalks when you don't have a rapidly drying root ball to worry about.

You could spend a small fortune doing complete soil tests in a regular pattern around the yard, but much of what you need to know will be told simply by checking the pH. A basic pH meter is inexpensive and comes with instructions. Or pH-testing paper from garden or aquarium supply stores will do; just thoroughly mix soil and water in equal proportions, let the soil settle out, dip the pH paper in the water, and compare the color to the chart in the kit. Soils that are outside a pH range of 6.5 to 7.5 can be corrected with lime (for acid soil) or gypsum (for alkaline soil).

It's wise to test urban soils for lead and perhaps for other metals if they are known to be a problem in your neighborhood. Many city governments provide lead test kits. In most of these cases, the

Newly installed earthworks including swales, berms, permeable pathways, French drains, and keyhole planting in this Willits, California yard. The standing water seen in the foreground was common throughout the site before the earthworks, compost, and mulch were installed. Posts for trellising the mini-food forest can be seen where the lawn once was. In the background is the down-spout leading to the water storage under the house and to the left the garage/guest room features trellises for vertical gardens in front of it. Design by Maximillian Meyers of the Mendocino Ecological Learning Center. PHOTO BY MAXIMILLIAN MEYERS.

cure is that old refrain: Add organic matter. Where lead levels are high, such as along house foundations, we can use a multipronged strategy. First, have the soil tested and, if lead is present, ask an expert (often a city employee) about the relative risk it poses. Lead is relatively immobile and won't drift too deep into the ground. Because of that, if lead levels are high, the usual course is to remove the top six to twelve inches of soil. Replace the soil with a healthy topsoil covered by deep mulch, totaling at least as thick as the former soil.

If you are still concerned about residual lead after this, options abound. One is to grow no food-producing plants in those areas. But if those spots are some of the only places available for food production, to further clean the soil use plants that specifi-

cally accumulate lead (see Table 6-2 for a list). Also, fungi such as oyster mushrooms (*Pleurotus ostreatus*) sequester heavy metals, so you can grow these in the mulch as well. Kits for growing oyster mushrooms can be bought via the Internet or from many garden-supply stores. The mushroom spawn can then be inoculated straight into a mulch of fresh, moist wood chips. The resulting plants and mushrooms are lead contaminated, so dispose of them as your city directs and then test the soil again.

Mushroom guru Paul Stamets has accumulated research showing that fungi are superb at pulling both metals and petroleum-based pollutants out of soil. In his revelatory book, *Mycelium Running*, Paul proves that mushrooms can remove petroleum products and other toxins from soil, improve

The same view 10 months later showing the developing mini-food forest with deciduous fruit trees and guild designed to provide food, medicine, mulch, fertility, beneficial insect and wildlife habitat, micro-climate creation, beauty, water harvesting, conservation and more. Plans include peaches, nectarines, plums, pluots, persimmons, apples, pears, Maximilian sunflowers, artichokes, asparagus, lupines, comfrey, fennel, lovage, rudbeckia, Russian sage, alyssum, chamomile, yarrow, leonotis, calendula, lavender, teucrium and many others. Design by Maximillian Meyers of the Mendocino Ecological Learning Center. PHOTO BY MAXIMILLIAN MEYERS.

fertility, and boost soil's ability to hold water. Mushrooms fill a crucial and neglected niche in the urban garden. Fungi can knit together mulch and buried organic matter into what Stamets calls "nature's Internet," shuttling nutrients, water, antibiotics, and other compounds from where they are abundant to where they are needed and scarce. A further boon from mushrooms is that, once all toxicity is gone, many of the cleanup fungi are delicious edibles and so can be grown for food. The powerful combination of organic matter, fungal abundance, and accumulator plants can quickly turn unhealthy city soils into clean bastions of fertility.

Most other soil-edge difficulties can likewise be solved, or at least abated, by adding organic matter, whether by compost, mulches, or cover crops.

Organic matter buffers pH problems, restores nutrient balance, lightens clay soils, helps sandy and silty soils hold moisture and nutrients, fluffs and aerates compacted earth, and I believe it can leap tall buildings with a single bound, too.

Windy edges. Average wind speeds in cities are less than in the country because the skyline acts as an immense windbreak. But, paradoxically, in cities we find more air turbulence and extremes of wind speed. That's because the urban windbreak isn't exactly well designed. The buildings vary enormously in height, spacing, and bulk, which is a recipe for roiled air. One result is the so-called *Venturi effect:* Wind is "squeezed" and speeds up between buildings, which creates near-permanent gales of chilly or dry air. This can cool and desiccate soil and plants. Yet around the corner from those howling, drying gusts, wind blockage from the same building might create a hot, still microclimate.

Here, vegetation provides most of the answer. Trees and shrubs will calm the air in turbulent zones and offer shade in sun-seared microclimates. Where the Venturi effect has created near-permanent blustery spots, thick rows of evergreens may be necessary to soften the winds. But most everywhere else, shrubs and small trees separated by gaps roughly the width of their mature-growth canopies will ease those turbulent winds.

Edges of all kinds in cities, then, are extreme: abrupt, highly contrasting, and often spanning a wider range of conditions than in less built-up places. Much of the work of ecological design in cities is to soften the harshness of these sharp edges.

Small Space, Big City

So many souls competing for space in cities has jolted urban land prices into the stratosphere, thus yards—for those lucky enough to have one—are small. Simply acquiring enough land for a garden is a challenge for many urbanites. The fact that land is so precious in cities suggests two broad strategies for gardeners, and each offers many options. One approach is to make the most efficient use of the land available through space-saving garden techniques. The second is to find more land to garden on. We'll explore both.

Making the Most of Space

Lack of space isn't a new problem for gardeners; thus, many garden writers and thinkers have cogitated on the question of getting more from less. Strategies for growing in a small space abound. A permacultural assessment of these strategies leads us down two possible design paths. Our choices are to make better use of the space, and/or to get more from the time available. Thinking in terms of space, we have techniques to pack more plants into a horizontal area and ways to stack more in vertical space. But how can we expand our options in time? Well, for one thing, we can extend the growing season by protecting our plants from extremes of cold and heat, and we can choose plants that are able to tolerate the less hospitable ends of the growing season. We can also devise ways to make the most efficient use of our own time. In combination, these diverse strategies yield options galore. Here are some of them.

Horizontal Packing Techniques

1. *Keyhole beds.* In Chapter 3 and elsewhere I have described this space-saving garden-bed pattern. It's perfect for urban yards since it minimizes path area and maximizes growing space. One strategy is to use this single shape to hold groups of plants with similar functions. One keyhole bed could be dedicated to herbs and salad greens, another to production vegetables such as canning crops, another to berries and perennial food plants. Or, for the polyculturally inclined, all those types of plants, along with insect-attracting flowers as well as soil-building mulch and nutrient-producing species, could be combined in one or more beds. To give order to such a complex polyculture, place the plants used most often, such as greens and herbs, nearest the path and less frequently harvested varieties, such as beans, onions, peppers, and storage crops, farther back. Soil-building, insectary, and habitat plants can go along the outer edges or in margins between beds.

2. *Interplants and polycultures.* Chapter 8 described interplanting, a technique for combining in one place several plant species that physically fit together well. One example of a space-efficient annual vegetable interplant is carrots, onions, and lettuce. Another is bush beans and lettuce. Radishes and young salad greens can be tucked in among other plants to boost yield and fill bare spots. An out-of-print book by Marjorie Hunt, *High-Yield Gardening*, lists many more interplanting strategies.

The dense polycultures developed by Ianto Evans and by Jajarkot Permaculture, also described in Chapter 8, are ideal for small gardens. My urban yard contains perennial polycultures of sea kale and bush collards underplanted with a ground-cover of strawberries and Nepalese raspberries, with chives, parsley, and garden sorrel in the openings. Self-seeded arugula and chard have packed into any remaining bare patches, and these I harvest young, while the leaves are tender and mild.

3. *Square-foot gardens.* Mel Bartholomew's popular book, *Square Foot Gardening*, offers a high-density approach ideal for urban yards, even those limited to balconies and rooftop gardens. However, his recommended soil mix uses vermiculite and peat moss—two ingredients that are very fossil-fuel intensive—and he focuses on annuals. I've altered his method in my own yard to reduce the oil-gobbling inputs by using well-prepared native soil and homemade compost, and my beds contain many perennial greens and vegetables. The essence of his technique—dividing a raised bed into individual one-square-foot compartments and planting each separately—is an efficient approach to intensive garden management that may appeal to slightly compulsive urbanites with a penchant for organization.

My experimental urban variants on Mel's square-foot beds show great promise in the yard's zone 1. The high yields are matched by fairly high inputs (wood for the bed walls, lots of compost, and the optional vermiculite and peat moss), so I have reservations about the relatively large ecological footprint of this method. But organic matter and used lumber are easy to procure in many cities, and as long as that is true, using often-wasted resources assuages my guilt over this high-input method. Square-foot gardening really cranks out the crops in a tiny space.

4. *Biointensive gardening.* Evolving far beyond its origins in the intensive techniques developed for Paris market gardens, this method is covered in detail in John Jeavons's practical book, *How to Grow More Vegetables*. It relies on deep double-digging and regular infusions of compost to create loose, rich soil and boasts extremely high yields. John and his team are fanatical about data and have compiled numbers for planting densities, seed requirements, yield per square foot, and much more. For those with the energy to turn large volumes of soil, it's a useful zone 1 technique, where intensive management is the rule. Jeavons

recommends double-digging all beds each time a crop is planted, but I know many, including myself, who have relaxed into engaging in this strenuous task only once every few years or when yields seem to decline. Besides, if beds contain perennials, double-digging is nearly impossible. Instead, after an initial double-dig when I first prepare the bed, in subsequent seasons I surface-cultivate compost and other amendments into the soil.

Unlike most authors of books on high-density techniques, John carefully accounts for inputs. He calculates how much of a garden should be dedicated to crops for compost because a true accounting of yield must include land needed to provide fertilizer for the plants. John has found that the necessary compost crops take up three or four times as much land as the production beds. This finding reveals the heavy ecological impact of high-density vegetable gardening. This isn't to say *you* must grow all your own compost plants, only that these resources are part of any garden's ecological footprint. Somewhere, land is being used to produce your fertilizer, and the people doing that may not share your high ecological standards. However, an alternative for urbanites to sacrificing precious yard space for compost crops is to harvest the urban waste streams. As mentioned, in urban areas organic matter is often surplus, so diverting landfill-bound compostables toward a productive yard pares down your garden's impact while shrinking landfills and the energy they use.

Jeavons's biointensive method specifically includes fruit trees, berry bushes, flowers, and compost crops; thus the technique has already been designed for a broad palette of perennial and annual plants that serve many functions. It fits well in urban permaculture strategies.

Any of these four approaches to high-density gardening, or a mixture of them, can bring productivity and biodiversity to an ecological gardener's landscape. Their focus on big yields in small spaces makes them ideal for city yards.

Vertical Stacking Techniques

I've mentioned how extending plants into the third dimension opens up new niches and possibilities for more diversity and complexity, richer food webs, and beauty. Natural ecosystems are almost always densely stacked and layered. By mimicking this quality of the wild landscape, we can make our yards behave more like nature while making the best use of our limited land. Techniques for doing this include the following.

The stacked food forest. Chapter 10 described ways to arrange up to seven tiers of plants in vertical space: tall and small trees, shrubs, herbs, ground covers, root crops, and vines. Paul Stamets, the fungi expert mentioned earlier, exhorts us to interweave an eighth layer, edible mushrooms. With seven or eight densely stacked, food-producing, habitat-offering, fertility-enhancing, and otherwise multifunctioning layers, we would be hard-pressed to come up with a more vertically efficient way of creating an ecological garden. In smaller urban yards, the tall-tree layer may need to be omitted or scaled down to a more modest size, using a semi-dwarf or naturally small fruit tree. This, in turn, will shrink the small-tree layer; but, fortunately, recent breeding work has expanded the array of semidwarf, dwarf, and minidwarf trees available, so there is much to choose from.

Trees such as pears and plums, formerly only available in larger sizes, now exist in petite proportions. Quince rootstocks have long been used to dwarf pear trees but are known for their frequent graft failures because the two species are not always compatible. Now, a series of true dwarf pear rootstocks have come to market, including Pyrodwarf, Pyro 2-33, and BP1. For plums and other stone fruit, Pixy, Krymsk #1, and Mariana 26-24 are a few of many dwarfing rootstocks. Since dwarf apple varieties abound, and most other fruit trees, such as persimmons, Asian pears, peaches, and apricots are naturally small, we have a near-complete selection of diminutive fruit trees for the urban garden. Nut trees are more challenging because most of them are towering. Walnuts and pecans that are both small and bear tasty nuts aren't widely available. A pecan/hickory cross called a hican is both smaller (to twenty-five feet) and more cold-tolerant (to USDA Zone 4) than the pecan itself. Filberts, or hazelnuts, form a large bush that can be pruned to a treelike shape, and variants of the hazelnut, called trazels, tree hazels, hazelberts, and filazels, also develop into diminutive trees. Pine nuts can be had via the Siberian dwarf pine, which reaches only ten feet in height. Thus our selection of city-scaled food-producing trees is wide enough to give us room to experiment.

Urban guilds. Guilds in cities, too, will often need to be based around smaller central elements. Again, a dwarf tree is a natural here, but using a shrub or large herbaceous plant as a guild focus is another way to shrink a spatial footprint while preserving vertical density. The Three (or four or five) Sisters offer one inspiration. This combination stacks a central grain crop, a climbing nitrogen-fixing bean, a weed-smothering squash, and possibly some insect-attracting food-producers into a space-conserving pattern that is further tied together by the multiple interactions among its member species.

Urban guilds often contain fewer species than their more expansive large-yard counterparts. In my Portland yard I've experimented with two small-tree guilds. One holds a persimmon tree, which, when planted, had a nitrogen-fixing bladder senna inserted into the same hole. I trim down the vigorous N-fixer two or three times a season, and the persimmon appears to be thriving on the regular shots of nitrogen, and mulch from the feathery branches, that this clipping yields. The persimmon is in a tight nook against a fence and beside a small sauna, so there is little room for much else. But I've packed a few dozen daffodil bulbs around the trunk and ringed the small space with edible daylilies and a perennial onion relative called ramps (*Allium tricoccum*). The guild could hold a bit more, once the sauna construction is over, and I will inject a few insectary plants and some perennial greens into the openings.

The second guild is based on a peach tree. Beneath the peach is a goumi, mentioned in Chapter 6 as a nitrogen-fixing shrub with edible berries. Also tucked under the peach are a honeysuckle bush, sea kale with its edible greens and shoots, a couple of purple-flowered *Veronica spicata* (speedwell) plants to attract insects, and a ground cover of Himalayan raspberry. I've pruned the peach to an open form to allow plenty of light to reach the plants beneath.

Espalier, cordon, and related pruning techniques. Fruit trees in small spaces have long been pruned into forms such as *espalier*, where branches are grown horizontally in a single, flat plane; *cordon*, in which a single stem is planted at a 45- to 60-degree angle and pruned down to short side shoots or fruiting spurs; and *fan training*, for vigorous trees such as peaches and plums, where branches are made to radiate in a fan shape from a short trunk. Sensitive but ironic New Age types sometimes call these severe pruning techniques "hortitorture." Yet they are ideal for jamming an immense amount of fruit production of many varieties into a tiny space. My four-variety espaliered apple also doubles as a barrier to persuade our dog to stay out of a raised bed. Under the espalier I have tucked small greens and herbs. Lettuces and other cool-season greens enjoy the shade of the apple in the heat of summer. Espalier and related methods require frequent pruning and attention to preserve the form, but they reward this labor with vast productivity. The regular management and observation needed is not difficult when the trees are in a small yard's zone 1.

Trellises and other stacking tactics. Arbors, trellises, fences, walls, hanging planters, stakes, tepee frames, suspended netting, tree trunks, and almost any other vertical surface can be used to train plants upward (or downward), conserving space. Obviously, any vining perennial such as grape, jasmine, wisteria, or kiwi, as well as annuals like beans and peas, should be boosted into the air to take up less room. But I see a surprising number of other plants sprawled across expanses of precious earth when they could be stacked skyward. Winter squash, melons, and cucumbers are often left to ramble, yet their natural habit is to climb. For these, some people fashion slings from netting and old pantyhose to hold the fruits, believing squashes and such will break off if left hanging unaided. I stopped making slings after a Hubbard squash ran a furtive tendril up a lilac bush and, before I noticed it, had dangled an unsupported 30-pound squash from a straining branch. I concluded that nature could build tough enough hangers without my help, and since then our melons, cucumbers, and squash have hung on their own successfully.

Less obviously vining plants can also be coaxed into the vertical dimension. Indeterminate tomatoes can be trained to grow up a single string if side shoots are religiously trimmed. I've seen zucchini, normally a floppy bush, carefully taught to climb. The key to maintaining climbers is to locate them where they are noticeable, in zone 1 or inner zone 2, and spend a moment every few days in gentle training, instead of launching a panicked prune-a-thon once a month, after the plant form is established wrongly.

Examples of high-density pruning technique for small yards, which allow multiple varieties of fruit tree to fit into tight spaces or against walls and fences.

Almost any garden site can be stacked. Rounded spaces such as keyhole beds can be edged with a flexible trellis made from concrete reinforcement panels or stiff wire mesh. Rectangular raised beds can receive trellises along their northern edges, where they won't shade other plants. Tepee frames

Dwarf apple trees grown in a variation of espalier called a Belgian fence, in the Asheville, North Carolina, yard of Will Hooker, a professor of landscape design at North Carolina State University. This high-density technique allows several varieties of fruit trees to produce an enormous amount of fruit in a tiny space. PHOTO BY WILL HOOKER.

can be set over small mounds and odd spots. And poles can be tucked anywhere.

Stacking tactics can themselves be stacked, such as suspending plant baskets from the edges of an arbor, or directing snow peas, mashua, or another short vine up a fence while a grape is trained horizontally onto supports along the top of the fence. Ideally the under-crop will leaf out before the late-budding grape casts its shade, just the way, in a forest, the understory and herb layer green up before the canopy does.

Most of these vertical aids serve other functions as well. A leafy arbor or trellis casts cool shade on hot days. Our west-facing deck would otherwise be uninhabitable on summer afternoons, but an overhead wisteria blocks the sun until midafternoon.

When the sun drops lower, beans and squashes climbing the deck railing and a trellis above it protect us from the slanting but still fierce rays. This plane of annual vines also forms a perfect privacy screen, turning the deck into an intimate room with living walls and roof. How many functions can we create by stacking plants into the vertical? Shade, cooling, privacy, higher and more varied yields, habitat, visual interest, screening of ugly views, pet barriers, windbreak—and I'm sure I've missed a few.

Expanding Gardens in Time

To make better use of limited garden space in cities, we need to make the best use of the time for growing. Adding a few weeks to either end of the garden-friendly season and growing more in the allotted season gives us the same benefits as having more room: larger harvests, more biodiversity, richer habitat, and so on. Strategies for making better use of time fall into two categories. The first comprises time- and labor-saving tricks, and the second covers ways to create microclimates that lengthen the growing season or let us grow plants from outside our climate regime.

Saving Time in the Garden

Much of this book, and permaculture itself, is really about making efficient use of time and labor. That's one way to think about many of the design techniques covered in these pages. The permaculture concept of zones tells us how to arrange the plants, hardscapes, and other elements in our design in relationships that let us spend the least time and effort caring for them. What we use most or needs our closest attention goes nearest us, which conserves effort.

Using sectors in the permacultural sense likewise saves time by creating conditions, such as shade or still air, that shrink our need to be watering or waiting for that deck to cool off so we can relax. And the strategy of matching needs to yields places the pieces of a landscape in relationships to provide more for themselves. We don't have to fertilize, spray, mulch, or water if these tasks are being done automatically through good design. Guilds, too, save time in the same way, by tying together plants that serve each other. A review of the strategies and techniques in this book reveals that nearly all, at heart, are ways of giving us less weeding time and more hammock time. So I won't expend more verbiage on time-saving techniques here—they fill most of this book already.

Expanding Time with Microclimates

We can also coax time to stretch by expanding the length of the growing season. This also broadens the palette of plants we can raise by letting us grow species usually found in warmer or cooler climes than ours. Both of these enlargements are achieved by creating the right microclimates for our plants. Microclimate management also offers some side benefits because the conditions that most plants prefer boil down to "not too hot, or cold, or wet, or dry," and these are the conditions that we like, too. Plus, benign microclimates can lessen our need to heat or cool our homes and can otherwise protect them from harsh weather.

The what and how of microclimates were covered in Chapter 6, so here we'll dive into the topic in specifically urban ways. Because urban lots are so small, often our efforts can improve the climate of the entire yard—the "macromicroclimate," if you will. In hot parts of the country, that means creating cooler conditions over much of the yard. In northern regions, we'll want a landscape that warms up sooner in spring and preserves heat into the late fall and beyond. In places with wild seasonal swings, such as the high desert, our challenge is to cool off the summer highs without exacerbating the bitter winter lows. In other words, microclimate manage-

ment is about creating the Goldilocks effect: not too much of anything—just right.

We create that happy medium by shaving off the city's extremes. In small urban spaces, one seemingly modest area that generates a harsh effect can push the entire site into unpleasantness. A baking south-facing wall, asphalt driveway, or shaded and breezy corner can bleed its effect over tens of feet—too much for us and our plants to escape when the backyard itself spans no farther. Those are the places to tackle first. Once the swings in these high-impact spots are damped down, we can identify and enhance smaller climate zones and even aid individual plants. Thus, begin by observing. Perhaps the extreme places in the yard are already obvious, such as that immense black driveway that cooks the plants on either side in summer. If you don't know where your yard's extreme climates are, walk around on a day when conditions are leaning toward, but not fully at, the ones you hope to avoid. In other words, where heat is the enemy, walk around and find the unpleasantly toasty spots on a warm sunny day, but not on the hottest day of the year when the heat is so miserable you can't sense where hotter places are. Where cold is the problem, a morning after a light frost is ideal for finding the trouble spots. See where frost remains the longest as the day warms up. Those are potential chill zones that you'll want to modify.

Creating Warm Microclimates

Where the cold season is long or harsh, catching and storing heat in the small yard is crucial. Doing this begins by remembering that, in microclimates, heat moves around in two principal ways: by radiating from a warm place to a cooler one and by air mixing. So, to warm up a yard, we want to catch heat when it's coming in, keep it from radiating out, and stop breezes from carrying it away.

Usually, heat arrives from the sun. Thus creating sunny openings, permanent or seasonal, is where we begin. Observe where shade falls in the yard and how it changes over the year. High pruning, pruning to an open shape, and trimming back of trees will let in more light. Another strategy is to favor deciduous plants with seasonally bare branches that allow winter sun to warm cold ground. This doesn't mean we need to eliminate evergreens, but they should be placed where their chilling via shade won't be a problem, such as on the north side of a yard. (They may then shade your northern neighbor's yard or house, which is something else to consider.)

Now we need to store the sunlight we've allowed in. Note that, even under trees, sun reaches the east, south, and west sides at some time of day or year. Sun-loving plants can be located in these places, and they will often be warmer than if they are in the open. That's because plants, and the ground around them, catch the sun's heat during the day but radiate it back out at night. Under branches and leaves, this heat can't escape as quickly as in the open, will be reflected back down or absorbed by the tree, and then will radiate out again to warm what is near it. The south and west sides of any object will usually get warmer than the east side, so those are the best places for storing heat.

Once the sunny spots are created or enhanced, we need to catch and store that heat. Here the answer is thermal mass, that is, dense objects such as rock and concrete that don't cool quickly once warm. We've all noticed that after a sunny day, a brick or stone wall stays warm into the evening longer than a light metal railing. That's because the wall, being more dense, can store more heat. Thus rock terraces and walls in sunny spots are a great way to create warm microclimates, by storing up the day's heat and slowly releasing it at night. In cities, we can build terraces from broken concrete, known to natural builders, because it is the city's most abundant rock type, as "urbanite." Urbanite, when arranged in evenly thick chunks and smothered by plants, is almost indistinguishable from rock, and it can be stained with iron oxide or other natural pigments to further disguise its origin. Many design clients, skeptical that urbanite can ever be made attractive, have quickly seen that, when installed neatly, it becomes a natural part of even a formal landscape.

Having captured and stored radiant heat with thermal mass, we can tackle the other factor in microclimate creation: air mixing. A greenhouse warms up because sunlight's energy is converted to heat inside the structure, but it stays warm because there is no breeze to carry off that heat. So, to warm a cool place, we want to slow or stop the wind from stealing our heat. Large-scale strategies for doing this include fences and walls, dense plantings of trees and shrubs, enclosed courtyards and gardens, and, in general, fashioning cozy, enfolding spaces that let in light but not wind. On a smaller scale, we can use cold frames, cloches (small enclosures of glass or transparent plastic), and spun row covers known by trade names such as Reemay.

Again, this kind of intensive management, potentially overwhelming in a large lot, is very feasible in the intimacy of an urban yard. For details on building heat-trapping devices both large and small, as well as a clear explanation of strategies for gardening well into the cold seasons, I recommend Eliot Coleman's book, *Four-Season Harvest*. Coleman lives in Maine yet grows vegetables year-round. For techies and tinkerers, another fine book on sun-capturing techniques and structures is *Solar Gardening* by Leandre and Gretchen Poisson. The Poissons have delved deep into what they call "solar architecture," inventing a set of sun-trapping devices such as solar cones and solar pods that push the growing season through frost and beyond.

Creating Cool Microclimates

If catching and holding heat is the strategy for nurturing warm microclimates, in hot regions we want to do precisely the opposite. Here we avoid letting warmth build up, use air mixing to carry

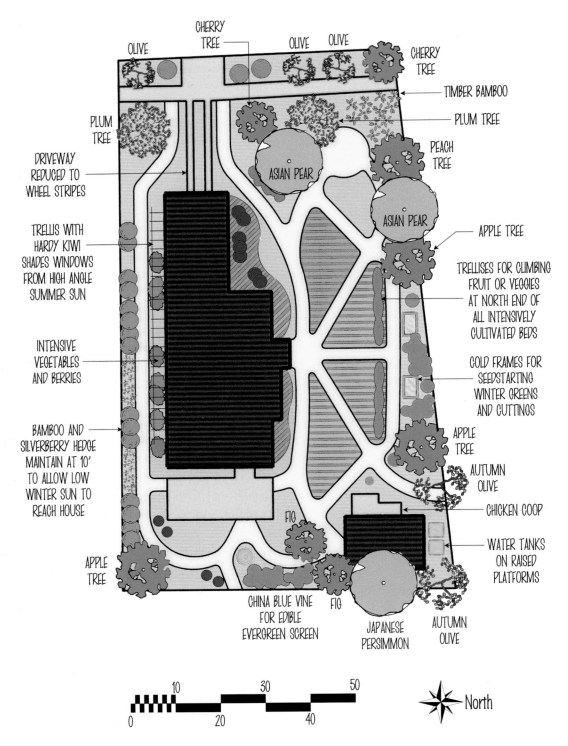

OLIVE

CHERRY TREE

OLIVE   OLIVE

CHERRY TREE

TIMBER BAMBOO

PLUM TREE

PLUM TREE

DRIVEWAY REDUCED TO WHEEL STRIPES

ASIAN PEAR

PEACH TREE

TRELLIS WITH HARDY KIWI SHADES WINDOWS FROM HIGH ANGLE SUMMER SUN

ASIAN PEAR

APPLE TREE

TRELLISES FOR CLIMBING FRUIT OR VEGGIES AT NORTH END OF ALL INTENSIVELY CULTIVATED BEDS

INTENSIVE VEGETABLES AND BERRIES

COLD FRAMES FOR SEEDSTARTING WINTER GREENS AND CUTTINGS

BAMBOO AND SILVERBERRY HEDGE MAINTAIN AT 10' TO ALLOW LOW WINTER SUN TO REACH HOUSE

APPLE TREE

AUTUMN OLIVE

CHICKEN COOP

FIG

WATER TANKS ON RAISED PLATFORMS

APPLE TREE

CHINA BLUE VINE FOR EDIBLE EVERGREEN SCREEN

FIG

JAPANESE PERSIMMON

AUTUMN OLIVE

10   30   50

0   20   40

North

In this design for a Portland, Oregon, garden, designer Leonard Barrett of Barrett Ecological Services oriented paths to radiate outward from the front door, creating a sense of expansiveness and possiblity and allowing efficient movement between the kitchen garden and the house. REDRAWN BY KRISTA LIPE.

it off, and treasure and enhance cool places and times. In hot climates, shade and breezes are your friends. Arbors, roof overhangs, and the canopies of large trees and shrubs should cover as much ground as is practical. South of roughly 40 degrees latitude, summer sun is intense enough to super-saturate plants' ability to photosynthesize. The green engines of vegetation can only whirl so fast, and this limit is quickly reached by the power of strong sunlight, so in low latitudes, most plants can be fully productive in partial shade.

Fences and privacy screens may be necessary in city lots, but in hot climates, make them permeable rather than solid so wind can flow through them. Avoid dense materials like stone and dark-colored objects, unless they are in shade during much of the day. At high altitudes and other places where nights are much cooler than days, large massy objects such as rocks, masonry walls, and even tree trunks—which are mostly water—will chill down at night and keep the surrounding area much more comfortable during the day as long as they are kept in shade. Structures in sun should be thin and light—boards or thin metal rather than rocks, say, for edging beds or for fences—so they will lose their heat quickly when the sun is gone.

Finding Your Urban Garden

We've explored ways to grow more in the small spaces available in cities, but what can we do for apartment dwellers, renters, and others who have no land at all? Once again, knowing that the most abundant resource in the city is people and that our outer zones are not necessarily on our own land, we can find some answers. Land that is ripe for garden-ing turns out to be surprisingly available in many cities, especially outside of the downtown core. The first place that many landless urbanites look is often the community garden program. These are usually run by the municipal parks department and can be found by contacting them. If your city doesn't have a community garden program, why not suggest starting one? Be forewarned, though, that the small plots in these great programs often have long waiting lists, so a bit more cunning may be necessary to scare up arable urban soil.

To find garden space in cities, a good permac-ulturist starts with assessing resources. Who owns land in cities? Schools, churches, senior residences, and community centers increasingly offer garden programs that are in search of gardeners and mentors. Enterprises such as the Edible Schoolyard and Farm-to-Cafeteria projects have cropped up in many cities, and blueprints for establishing them in your city can be found at websites such as www .edibleschoolyard.org.

Vacant lots and margins of commercial property can be gardened. My neighbors and I raised vege-tables and berries at an empty lot down the street—with the owner's permission—until it was sold to a developer.

I've known of a few guerrilla gardens, too, estab-lished on vacant property or park edges with-out consent. The risks here are obvious. Some of the more anarchical garden fanatics I know have installed guerrilla gardens in empty lots or unused commercial property or parks and then walked away from them, partly in hopes that neighbors or local homeless people would adopt them, but partly from a "stick it to the Man" attitude, simply enjoying the knowledge that they have gotten away with something. Virtually all of these gardens that I know of have vanished. Just building a guerrilla garden and leaving it to unknown others to take over rarely works. It takes people to keep a garden.

Many property owners, especially older and retired people, unable to garden as easily as they once did, often respond happily to offers to garden in their yards, especially when the request is sweetened with the offer to share the produce.

As proof that there are many homeowners willing to share their gardens, urban farms based in multiple lots are springing up in many cities. Near me, an enterprising urban farmer named Kollibri Sonnenblume raises vegetables for market in plots spread over twenty different yards across southeast Portland. Much of his travel among these plots is on a bicycle, and he hauls produce and supplies in a bike trailer. If Kollibri can find twenty households willing to open their yards to other gardeners, that points to an abundant resource and generous people.

Farmers' markets have sprung up by the thousands in many cities, and often this produce is grown locally. Talk to some of the farmers at these markets. Many of them—who are often large-scale gardeners rather than full-fledged farmers—tend small plots of land nearby and may be willing to share a bit of one in exchange for help with farm or market chores.

Rooftops are increasingly sprouting gardens, both because land is expensive and because covering the dark, heat-absorbing surfaces of urban roofs helps cool our cities and reduce stormwater runoff. Cities from Boston to San Diego are stacking functions via gardens on the flat roofs of schools, offices, warehouses, and apartment buildings. Often these require light soil mixes using vermiculite or perlite to minimize weight, but, to my mind, the benefits of cooling, carbon sequestration, and local food production offset these high-energy inputs.

A few progressive businesses are creating employee gardens on company property, converting those sterile expanses of immaculate office-park grass to more useful food, flowers, and habitat. Perhaps your employer is willing to join these visionaries. I look forward to the day when businesses, eschewing the wasteful, life-denying grass that often surrounds offices, point proudly to the carbon-sequestering, water-purifying, habitat-rich food forests thriving on their grounds.

As city governments and citizens begin to feel the pinch of high energy prices, they are increasingly aware that food often comes from thousands of miles away. A far-off food supply is a tenuous one, and this realization has spurred many cities, from my own Portland to Rochester, New York; to Santa Cruz, California; and to countless cities in between to establish food-policy councils and other efforts to develop a secure, local foodshed. These groups are quickly creating a farm- and garden-friendly environment for urbanites. Local laws are toppling that once made urban food growing difficult, such as prohibiting certain plants—often vegetables—from the front yard. Some cities have begun inventorying land that could be used for food growing, and this, too, will expand the real estate available for gardening. So think creatively about urban land: almost any space not covered by pavement and buildings is potentially a garden spot, if the owner can be shown the benefits—for them, for the city, the planet, and you—of life- and food-giving plantings.

Roadside Attractions: The Parking Strip

One oft-overlooked bit of potential garden space in cities is the parking strip, also known as the right-of-way or, indicative of its landscape challenges, the hell strip. Not only is it the most distant piece of ground from where we usually hang out in the backyard, it is across the sidewalk, making it difficult to plumb with irrigation lines, and it's not a pleasant place to be, near the street's traffic and under the view of every house on the block. It's also not really under the homeowner's control: Although the homeowner must maintain it, it's usually encumbered with a file-full of easements to the power utility, the phone and cable companies, and the city, often with restrictions on what can be planted there. Plus, it's the public right-of-way. Any citizen has the right to freely pass across this strip of ground, for access to parked cars, for relieving dogs, and for anything else on the legal side of loitering and vandalism. Yet at current land prices and scarcity, it's a shame not to use it to the fullest.

To pull the parking strip into the home ecosystem, start by learning what your city will allow there and how those ordinances are enforced. My own decidedly unscientific survey of several cities suggests that the most common restrictions are on tree size beneath power lines. Fortunately, many useful trees are small. Another common rule prohibits fruit trees along streets since the fruit may drop on cars. (How rich we must be to value automobiles more than food!) And some cities insist that any plants other than trees and shrubs must be shorter than one foot, to allow easy access to cars. However, every official I spoke to, when pressed, said that these rules were almost never enforced, even after complaints. Cities simply lack the resources to pester residents about their plantings unless they are creating a fire hazard or reducing property— and thus tax—values. Thus, without encouraging anyone to violate local ordinances, I think there is leeway in streetside planting possibilities.

Soil on hell strips is often badly compacted. A first step is to fluff it up by adding compost and mulch. Grass can be quickly eliminated via sheet mulch, although the long edges along sidewalk and curb need to be done carefully so that underlying cardboard or newspaper doesn't protrude, which is both unsightly—we want to stay friends with neighbors here—and slows decomposition.

The parking strips in locales with ample rainfall are often soggy because the rain captured by the sidewalk usually runs onto it, doubling or tripling the water load. Applying a deep mulch or otherwise raising soil levels to shed water helps here. Raised beds on the parking strip will also help direct foot traffic away from planted areas. We can't stop passers-by from trampling the public right-of-way, but we can guide their feet to safe places via soil contouring, paths, and hardscapes such as flagstones and brick. Excess water can also be deliberately guided to swales and shallow depressions lined with water-loving plants.

In arid regions, we go down rather than up: A sunken parking strip will hold precious rain and can harvest runoff from the sidewalk, so here we want to dig basins and swales. These depressions don't have to be caverns, just an inch or two below sidewalk level. These can be mulched, too.

With broad-scale soil preparation taken care of, we can consider plantings. Parking strips in cities are dosed with pollution from car exhaust, runoff water from dirty pavement, and dog feces, which raises questions about how safe it is to grow food there. Studies suggest that plants on less busy streets, those with fewer than 1,000 cars per day (about one per minute during the daytime) don't accumulate worrisome levels of pollutants from cars. Some authorities put the limit at 2,500 cars per day. My own preference is not to grow food on the parking strip, but then, I have the rest of my yard for that. If it's the only place you have for growing food, and you don't live on a busy street, go for it. But there are many other useful roles the parking strip can play: a place for bird and beneficial-insect habitat, carbon sequestering, soil building, and ornamental plants.

The hell strip lends itself to small guilds. A shrub or small tree accompanied by a few smaller insectary, nutrient-accumulating, and other functional plants will need little care once established. Envision the magic of a street edged with guilds of bird-habitat plants, or scented herbs and flowers. Parking strip enhancements can attract another important species, too: people. On rights-of-way from Seattle to Tucson and Atlanta, I've seen benches installed on once-sterile strips, encouraging passers-by to tarry a bit and chat with their neighbors. In this way, empty neighborhoods of strangers who never see each other become welcoming communities of friends again.

This Houston, Texas, parking strip eliminates resource-guzzling grass and instead harvests valuable rainwater, which relieves overtaxed storm drains and grows carbon-sequestering plants that also offer beauty and habitat for birds and insects. The design is by Kevin Topek of Permaculture Design, LLC. PHOTO BY KEVIN TOPEK.

In designing for the parking strip, keep proportion in mind. On narrow parking strips, or those overhung by power lines, trees must be small to avoid eventually buckling sidewalks or inciting the electric company to cut them down. There is, however, one big incentive for planting the largest practical trees on parking strips: They raise property values. A California realtor's association estimates that a mature street tree adds $6,500 to the sale price of a house. The most appealing, and expensive, neighborhoods in any city are those with tree-lined streets. Cutting street trees takes money out of your pocket.

I invite you to think of plantings in the city as creating the urban forest. What kind of city forest do we want? Too often, street plantings are chosen for what they won't do: not crack pavement, not reach power lines, not choke on pollution, not drop messy fruit. Instead, we can envision positive roles for our city's forest and design it not for what it won't do but for how it can serve our needs and nature's. The forest created by street-side trees can cool the air; regulate humidity; shelter birds, bats, and helpful insects; reduce heating and cooling bills; feed the poor; provide income for homeless through harvesting, compost-making, craft materials, and wood gathering; preserve biodiversity and endangered species; quiet the bustle of the city; offer food and enjoyment to passersby; and create neighborhood cohesion by giving us beauty, comfort, and a lovely place to be with one another. City forests, often an unproductive by-product of random plantings, can be designed to serve many needs, instead of being simply accreted.

Urban Animals: Domestic, Wild, and Feral

Most of the techniques and suggestions in Chapter 7 for involving birds, insects, and other useful animals in the landscape apply to urban yards as well. One difference is that, in cities, there are fewer problems with large animals and more with small ones. Rat-proof compost bins are needed, but eight-foot deer fences aren't. However, most of the animals that enhance the quarter-acre and larger lot can also be attracted to or raised in a small city yard. Even apartment dwellers can have worm bins and bird feeders.

Tying cities back into natural ecosystems is important, and creating habitat for birds and insects is one of the best ways to do this. These small creatures weave connections among individual species, plant communities, and whole ecosystems by transporting seeds, pollen, and nutrients. Their presence makes those flows possible and is also an indicator of the health of any environment. Plantings of multifunctional species that proffer habitat for animals can prevent cities from becoming ecological deserts and barriers between biomes. If, one yard at a time, we refashion our cities and suburbs to be forests and greenscapes, they can tie together wild areas and serve as corridors for species that migrate or have large ranges. A yard planted to animal-friendly species, whether natives or exotics, becomes an important link among natural communities. To dispel the grayness that can creep into urban life, there are few sights better than that of a bright-winged butterfly or colorful songbird.

Cities are also becoming friendly again to small livestock and poultry. Many towns have dropped their prohibitions of poultry in urban yards. The revised ordinances usually exclude roosters and limit hens to three or four. However, I've known many city chicken raisers who began with the legal number of birds, got their neighbors addicted to the taste and farm-bright color of fresh eggs, and quickly increased the size of their flocks to meet local demand. Ordinances covering chickens are usually complaint-driven (we rarely see black helicopters in search of too-full henhouses), and when neighbors are happily breakfasting on your chickens' offerings, they won't gripe. But even three hens will provide a dozen or more eggs per week during warmer months, enough for a family.

Rabbits are another natural for city yards. Urban permaculturist Connie van Dyke raises rabbits for meat in her backyard, and she offers instruction to those who want to take responsibility for their carnivory in this way. This gentle woman has shocked more than a few people when they learn that she butchers her bunnies, but Connie is honestly addressing one of the most challenging problems for the urbanite wishing to become less dependent on shipped-in food: How do you obtain protein? For those reluctant to pick up the knife themselves, rabbits have many other uses besides meat. The sheared or naturally shed fur of breeds such as Angoras makes soft and supple fiber for weaving and spinning. Plus, all rabbits trim grass and weeds and produce a manure that is high in nutrients but less liable to burn plants than chicken droppings. And the urban livestock spectrum can expand beyond poultry and bunnies: Some cities allow pygmy goats and pot-bellied pigs as well.

How can we integrate pets into urban permaculture? In the confined space of a small yard, a dog becomes a significant force. When we lived on rural acreage, our dog had plenty of room to roam and rarely bothered our plantings. But in our small city lot, Bella can wreak havoc. Some of my first plantings were along the fence—I was getting my edges under control—but I soon found that Bella took her watchdog duties seriously. She patrolled the yard perimeter relentlessly, pounding young seedlings and baby shrubs into green mush and splinters. In places I have pulled back from the fence, leaving a narrow path for her reconnoiters. In others my strategy was to buy large plants or put up temporary barriers of bamboo or stakes. These latter are only marginally effective, as a large dog excited by a squirrel or passing rival will barrel through flimsy stakes. In dog-occupied yards, some edges must simply be designated sacrifice zones, or they'll be sources of eternal frustration for the pet owner.

As with any design element, understanding the habits of your dog will help solve the problems. Different breeds have varying characters. Ours is a digger and the neighborhood cop, but she's not a ball or Frisbee chaser. I've dedicated a small patch of soil as a digging spot, and to redirect her when she's in hot pursuit I've used raised beds with wooden sides and low railings for annual vegetables and moved some of my garden to the front, outside of the fenced backyard.

Cats, too, can be a challenge in multifunctional landscapes. To have joyfully created some enticing bird habitat and then see a cat convert it into a private killing ground brings on both horror and guilt. In some cases it comes down to a stark choice between having either birds or outdoor cats, but often it's neighboring cats that are the problem. Frequently, the solution to an animal problem is another, competing animal. Our dog will tolerate only our own mostly indoor cats in our yard, so the neighbors' cats give our yard a wide berth. But not everyone wants to own a dog. I know a few people who have meticulously cat-proofed their fencing, which is tedious but effective. Commercial cat repellents are moderately useful. Another solution is to concentrate bird habitat well off the ground by limbing up trees and thinning shrubs, so that ground-feeding birds are not attracted.

Cats will also use bare soil as their litter box, which is yet another reason to mulch. I've also used floating row covers specifically to thwart cats. Other gardeners spread bramble branches on newly seeded beds, or lay a pattern of bamboo poles a few inches above the beds.

Form, Function, and City Permaculture

Urban sites inspire a complex array of challenges and opportunities for permaculture design. There's a lot to fit into a small space. I haven't mentioned graywater reuse (covered in Chapter 5) in this chapter, but it, too, is ideally suited to urban yards, as a way to conserve water and also to recycle wastes into nutrients, turn them into greenery, and hold them in the home landscape. A graywater wetland in a

city lot not only purifies water that can then flow into a pond and be used for irrigation, but it can double as a productive bog garden. Water harvesting and storage in tanks and small ponds also is a perfect city strategy. I know of many city gardeners who have weaned themselves from outdoor use of municipal water with just one or two 55-gallon rain barrels to irrigate their small gardens.

When the many strategies and techniques of permaculture are packed into a tiny urban lot, it becomes an exciting and dynamic place. In a few thousand square feet, we can fit dozens or hundreds of plant species that feed us as well as the helpful birds and bugs and that nourish the life of the soil. Rainwater caught by rooftop and pavement and graywater from sink and shower courses through swales, wetlands, and ponds, nurturing plants and critters above and below the soil line. Plants and water themselves cycle through chickens and other small animals, and these in turn offer eggs and manure in their own cycles. The harsh forces of weather, noise, traffic, wind, and sun are caught by these nested loops and transformed into gentle oases of life and welcoming microclimates. Though an urban ecological garden feels like a welcome island of tranquility in a busy city, beneath its green and lush surface is a complex web of dynamic life. Good ecological design lets us fit a lot into a tiny yard.

Although one trajectory of this book has been toward the forest garden and a natural-looking landscape that also serves people, much of what I've described in this chapter won't give a forestlike feel to the yard. Raised beds and espalier fruit trees, rain barrels and graywater wetlands, dog paths and water-harvesting curbcuts are not elements found in wild forests. This points us to a broader understanding of what permaculture can be. It is not simply forest gardening or mimicking the look and feel of a natural ecosystem.

Permaculture is a design approach to create landscapes that function like ecosystems, but that doesn't mean they must always look like what we see in nature. The essence of permaculture is to nurture the same processes that occur in the wild. An native oak and an espalier fruit tree both perform similar roles in the environment, offering habitat, breaking the force of rain, holding and building soil, and all the rest. A graywater wetland lined with butyl rubber purifies water and grows cattails and rushes just as well as the ancient swamp forty miles downstream of town. In the end, it is the ecological function we are after, not the appearance.

It is probably easier to design a landscape that functions like nature if it looks like nature, particularly for the less experienced designer. For most of us, appearance and process are deeply interlinked, as we are told in the timeworn architectural adage that form follows function. But, at heart of the ecological garden, we not mimicking the form of nature. We are cultivating the conditions for natural processes to occur, so that our landscapes behave like ecosystems and tie into the rest of the harmonious relationships that knit this planet together. By realizing that form and function can be distinct, new and broader avenues of design open up to us.

A well-mulched raised bed and a forest floor, though looking very different, are both homes for the talented microbial alchemists that decompose dead tissue and stitch it back into the dynamic flows of life. A mandala-like labyrinth of keyhole beds looks unlike anything in wild nature. But in the way it maximizes planting area yet shrinks path edge to a minimum, it is following the same rules that guide the natural creation of the bubble-shaped alveoli of the lungs and the lobelike homes of coral reef inhabitants. That is, mandala garden, lung, and coral are all choosing a pattern that stretches surface area to the utmost to catch and move resources, whether those resources are sunlight and soil, oxygen and carbon dioxide, or nutrients dissolved in seawater that pass by. When we learn

to recognize the patterns of life, at whatever scale and in their many and often cryptic manifestations, and become adept at speaking their language, we can design with those patterns in many forms. We are no longer limited to copying appearances because we have discovered deeper resonances with nature.

In a permaculture design, we may want the ecological functions and wholeness of a forest edge, but in the city we don't have room for tall trees and six or seven other layers stacked underneath them. But once we grasp the pattern of a gentle edge that arcs to the ground in a graceful curve instead of a harsh right angle, and as we understand how nature nests shapes inside each other like Russian *matrioshka* dolls and orders them so each can catch light, water, and fertility, we can incorporate the essence of these patterns, instead of relying on an uninformed mimicry of form.

Permaculture author and designer Patrick Whitefield points out the difference between what he calls "original permaculture," meaning designs that look like natural landscapes, and "design permaculture," which he says focuses on processes and the connections among them. Though I think the distinction is very useful, Whitefield's terminology is less so, since many "original" permaculture sites, such as Mollison's and Holmgren's own early designs, don't resemble nature at all, with their keyhole beds, on-contour rows of trees, and deep straw mulches. And all permaculture uses design to create connections. The distinction is not between original and later designs but between what is better captured in the terms *form permaculture* and *function permaculture*.

In form permaculture, mimicking the shape and visible arrangements of nature allows us to more easily capture her processes as we design. In function permaculture, our deeper understanding of process allows us to work directly with natural functions in a way that may not look like nature.

Ecological urban landscapes will more often use function permaculture than form permaculture because small urban spaces don't easily allow the grand arrangements found in the wild but force us to concentrate on processes and functions. In the city, adhering to a natural form is not critical as long as the shapes and patterns we use work well and appeal to us.

Thus city permaculture gardens will rarely look like wild land, and the appearance of both the overall design and the pieces within it may have novel forms, such as spiral or branching garden beds that hold stacked arbors, and curbside swales paralleling dwarf tree guilds. Although city yards are still influenced by sun and wind just as wild land is, their design and function is also shaped by children, pets, local ordinances, your social life, traffic noise, easements, the neighbors' comments, and a host of other forces not felt in any native forest. They won't look just like nature; but, with an understanding of nature's pattern and process, they can act like it.

CHAPTER 12

Pop Goes the Garden

In the previous eleven chapters I laid out a tool kit for assembling an ecologically sound garden. Here I'll quickly review where we've been and describe what happens when theory meets practice: how real ecological gardens work, what the limitations are, and what to expect as the garden matures. For those who like the big picture, I'll also discuss some of the underlying principles that make ecological gardens tick—why connections, not just pieces, are so important—and suggest some directions for further exploration.

At the heart of any garden or landscape, at the base of the ecological pyramid, is soil. Create healthy soil, and the rest of gardening simplifies. Because of techniques such as composting, deep mulches, cover crops, and nutrient-storing plants, the ecological gardener's soil teems with worms and beneficial microorganisms that shunt fertility to plant roots. This rich, humusy earth supports a broad array of soil life, which in turn nurtures diverse plant species and the wide spectrum of helpful insects, birds, and other animals that come to share in the bounty.

Healthy soil ensures that the second element of a self-sustaining garden, water, is in abundance. Deep, spongy humus will hold every drop of rain and irrigation water better and more cheaply than any other medium. Deep mulches slow evaporation. To weather long droughts, we can also store water in ponds and tanks that are filled by rain, recycled through graywater systems, or, less sustainably, piped from a well or municipal source. All this means that the natural condition of this garden is abundantly moist.

Soil and water are the behind-the-scenes elements that make the garden work. A third element, on center stage, is the vegetation. Chosen to play many roles, the useful and beautiful species have here been selected from native plants, naturalized varieties, noninvasive exotics, indigenous and foreign rare species needing preservation, heirloom crops, and cuttings from neighbors' and friends' yards—in short, from as many sources as are available and ethical. Each plant serves at least two functions—oh, perhaps a handful of them just look pretty; we're human, after all—and in combination they offer benefits both people and the rest of nature.

Finally, by choice and by serendipity, the garden extends a home to many animals. In the right circumstances, rabbits, chickens, ducks, or even a pot-bellied minipig may be at work here, tilling and manuring soil, converting weeds and waste to fertilizer, and connecting us to a more-than-human nature. But even without domestic animals, an ecological garden swarms with niches for pollinators, pest controllers, and scavengers that work the blossoms, nibble the ample foliage and wild berries, or search for prey. The garden is alive with buzzing, fluttering, soaring, scampering allies.

Soil, water, plants, and animals are the four dynamic components of the ecological garden. To this list I might add a fifth, the designers and occupants, who will interact with and shape all the others. The garden also contains a sixth, static element: the structures. Though inert, greenhouses and other buildings, fences, trellises, compost piles, paths, and gates shape the flows that move through the garden.

But, as I've said before, these are just pieces. The beauty and effectiveness of the ecological garden is in how the parts are connected. It is the flows between objects, not the objects themselves, that define a natural, sustainable environment.

This garden combines many strategies to create a dense web of connectedness. Stacking functions is one method we use to ensure that everything is linked to one or more other elements. Here, elements serve multiple functions. A Maximilian sunflower hedge at one edge of the garden, for example, provides an impenetrable weed barrier, edible shoots, late fall color, seeds for birds, and plenty of mulch material. These uses tie the sunflower to many other parts of the garden and reduce work and imports such as fertilizer.

Also, each function is performed by multiple elements. The sunflower hedge reduces cold fall winds and could be combined with other hedges and trees, a carefully placed greenhouse, a rock wall, and even an earth berm to form a sheltered place for tender plants or a little sunbathing. Combining several techniques that serve the same purpose provides backups in case one method fails and often yields unexpected synergies. Look: That combination of windbreaks has also blocked noise from the nearby highway and screened the view from the neighbors. Now we have a perfect sanctuary or a hot-tub site.

The garden's pieces are also connected by careful use of the zone-and-sector method, which locates each plant or other feature by how often it needs attention and how it interacts with sun, wind, a view, or other energies from outside the site.

Patterns from nature shape the garden's design. Paths and plantings curl into mounded spirals to save space, bend into keyhole beds for easy reach, and use branch, net, lobe, and other patterns to catch and save energy. The right balance of edge and interior gives both diversity and protected habitat. The garden is stacked in layers to broaden its reach into the third dimension, where it can reap sunlight effectively and also supply many niches for wildlife.

Here, plants harvest and store sunlight, ponds catch water, graywater wetlands capture and use wastes that would otherwise be lost. All these pieces link together to forge a complete and harmonious whole that replenishes and enlarges itself. The garden is a net, a sieve, sifting and sorting energy and nutrients from whatever passes through it and transforming them into a community of flowers, birds, insects, food, and healthy people.

The diversity of this landscape makes it flexible and resilient. With so many inhabitants, connected by such a multitude of interactions, there are many pathways, loops, and possibilities. Cycles ebb and flow with changes in the environment, adapting to new conditions. Too many aphids in one corner are met with a sudden surge of ladybugs that have lain semidormant amid yarrow and fennel, waiting for such a feast. A heavy load of fallen fruit, rotting because the owners are on vacation, is pounced on hungrily by birds, insects, and soil life, to be reincarnated as soil and more life before the owners return, unaware of the janitorial frenzy that's gone on in their absence. Small miracles like these are commonplace here.

Ecological gardens are constantly evolving, and the process of their evolution—not just the final product—is fascinating to watch. It's exhilarating to see once sterile soil enrich and heal itself each year, to watch new birds or insects find a home, to

Terraces made from broken concrete ("urbanite") hold perennial food and habitat plants in the Los Alamos, New Mexico garden of Mary Zemach, designed by Ben Haggard and Nate Downey, Santa Fe.

taste the first lingonberry, grape, or heirloom apple. Each year brings new treats and is an endpoint in itself, rather than some stage to be impatiently hurried through.

Choosing the Right Pieces

Providing the right pieces and getting important cycles going is most of the work in creating an ecological garden. And once again, by "pieces" I don't mean simple objects—trees, shrubs, fences— but pieces that do things: soil builders, sunlight harvesters, and the like. So here I'll summarize much of what is spread over the pages of this book by listing the key functions (the roles for plants and ways to harvest and store resources) and relationships (the nutrient cycles and other important interactions) that make up a successful ecological garden. Some of this section will be simple recap, but I'll also present some ideas in new or larger contexts. With these elements in the right places, the garden is almost guaranteed to coalesce into a miniecosystem.

Building Fertility

Catching and holding resources is the key to a sustainable garden (or society, for that matter).

All plants harvest carbon and minerals and, if left to compost in place, will add them to the soil. Some plants are better at this than others, though. Particularly in the young landscape or in gardens that are harvested regularly, fertility-building plants are critical to create and maintain healthy soil because they channel nutrients to impoverished earth and replenish what is taken by the harvest basket. Fertility builders can make up as much as half of a young garden. These plants, many of whom we met in Chapter 6, can be divided into three groups (species are listed in the appendix).

Nitrogen fixers. Nitrogen is often the limiting nutrient in a garden, thus N-fixing plants like legumes and the many others listed in the appendix will slash the need for fertilizer and at the same time pour more organic matter into the living soil than fertilizer ever could. This is perhaps the most important class of plant to have in a young garden. In poor soils, having 25 percent N-fixing plants to begin with is not too many. They can be culled as the garden matures. Remember to use nitrogen-fixing trees and shrubs, too, not just perennial and annual herbs.

Nutrient accumulators. These deep-rooted plants mine minerals from the subsoil, ferrying nutrients into the garden where they can be swept into the intermeshing cycles of matter and energy by other plants, microbes, and animals. They balance the nitrogen and carbon added by other soil builders.

Mulch plants. All plants add mulch to the soil at leaf fall, but some excel at this. Plants with large leaves and dense canopies that can tolerate heavy pruning are the best choice. Initially, most mulch will come from the herb layer, but as the garden matures, trees and shrubs will take over much of this role.

Including Life's Other Kingdoms

Though plants are the central feature of a garden, to truly thrive a backyard ecosystem must extend its connections into the rest of nature. These links draw energy and nutrients into the garden in ways that the flora and the gardener can't and create more complex and resilient cycles. When a bird flies into the garden, it often carries new seeds from elsewhere that will broaden diversity or fill an unused niche. Also it will likely plop a small offering of manure that it harvested from outside the garden. To some this may just be bird poop, but from the ecological viewpoint it's a useful input that the gardener didn't have to work for. Each visitor to the garden shuttles in energy and nutrients garnered from elsewhere. Plus, every arriving bird, insect, or other animal creates new links in the food web, reaping unused resources, providing food for others, and adding to the dynamic balancing act that is an ecosystem.

To attract beneficial visitors and encourage them to stay, we need plant varieties that forge partnerships with the other kingdoms of life. Here are some classes of vegetation that will do this.

Insectary plants. Familiar by now, these are species that offer nectar or pollen, attract prey species (such as aphids and caterpillars), or furnish homes for insects. The category should include native plants to attract indigenous beneficial bugs but exotics as well since a huge proportion of the insects around us are imports that have become naturalized and need nonnative hosts. A wide variety of insectaries should be included so they'll bloom and otherwise work their magic over a long period. This way pollinators and pest fighters will always be ready to buzz in when needed.

Wildlife attractors. Herbs, shrubs, and trees that offer food and shelter for birds, mammals, reptiles, and amphibians will bring layers of diversity to the garden and reduce pest problems. Again, variety is important. Choose plants of different heights, both woody and soft-tissued ones, having diverse fruit, flowers, leaves, and twigs to support the many types of feeding styles, with dense and open foliage and a selection that offers food at all seasons.

Feed and forage species. I've shown how small animals such as chickens, ducks, rabbits, and others can make us less dependent on imports such as fertilizer and do useful work in the course of their normal activities. So why not further close the loop and give our animal helpers their own feed and forage from plants that provide seeds, nuts, pods, fruit, fodder, and browse?

Plants for people. All gardens need to offer something for humans, thus we also tailor the flora to suit ourselves by including plants for food, income, crafts, fiber, medicine, building supplies, nursery stock, seed saving, and just plain beauty.

Harvesting and Recycling Resources

An ecological garden is like a net, sieving and holding whatever resources (minerals, organic matter, sunlight, water, and organisms) flow through it. And, just as important, these landscapes are consummate recyclers, shuttling each bit of matter and energy from soil to plant to animal and back again, over and over until every last bit of benefit has been extracted. This careful stewardship of all resources is one key to a sustainable garden. So we employ a spectrum of techniques to grab and recycle as many of the resources entering the garden as possible. The best of these methods are passive, needing no work from the gardener beyond setting them up, after which they harvest resources and cycle them in the garden, day in, day out. That's a simple way to build abundance. Here are several strategies, and their related techniques, for resource gathering and recycling.

Harvesting water. Digging swales and channels to catch runoff, adding humus to soil, using deep mulches and dense plantings, and capturing rooftop rain in tanks and ponds are all good methods to catch and hold most of the water needed to keep the garden growing. This will reduce the demand on wells and other high-input, less renewable water sources.

Catching nutrients. A graywater system will net minerals and organic matter that would otherwise be lost down the sewer. Humus-rich soil will prevent that precious matter from leaching away in rains. Composting and mulching (as opposed to leaving trimmings at the curb for pickup) will keep fertility on the site. Neighbors will often happily part with their own yard waste (silly them!), a great free source of organic matter. And the plants themselves will pull nutrients out of rain and harvest dust and wind-blown debris.

Gardening in layers. The immense leafy area of a multistoried garden that mixes trees, shrubs, and low plants will capture sunlight and turn it into life far more effectively than a one-layer landscape. Multiple layers will also slow moisture loss from evaporation and perhaps even harvest fog to boost total precipitation. Plus, the three-dimensional garden will attract more birds and beneficial insects to its varied habitat, with all the bonuses they offer.

Using sectors. By locating plants, buildings, paths, windbreaks, and other elements in the right relationship to seasonal sun and wind patterns, views, fire and wildlife corridors, and other energies coming from off the site, we can harvest these forces' benefits and reduce their draining effects.

Adding animals. Animals are often overlooked as garden elements. But they have many roles. They will eat whatever is in excess and turn it into useful work, more animals, products, and manure. We can choose which of these multiple gifts we want. Techniques for drawing animals into the garden can be as simple as hanging a bird feeder where we want soil scratched and manure dropped or as complex as incorporating multispecies plantings that provide nutritious chicken forage and raising poultry for eggs and meat in chicken tractors.

Animals will chow down on surplus and unusable fruit and foliage, prepping it via their digestive tracts so that decomposers can easily pump it back into the garden ecosystem. They are the consumers that bind producer plants and decomposer soil life together.

Building Interconnections

In the rich interconnectedness of an ecosystem, small failures are shrugged off. The loss of a few plants or an outbreak of disease isn't the setback it would be in an orderly row-crop garden. That's because the connections and redundancy turn the garden ecosystem into a resilient net. Sever a few threads, and the whole remains. And in a living net, the breaks are quickly repaired by the shifting, breeding, swarming surge of life. It is this webwork, more than any other factor, that distinguishes the ecological garden from the more conventional, vulnerable forms. So creating these connections—deep, multiple, and strong—is a chief goal of the ecological gardener. Here are some strategies for forging this webwork.

Designing with zones. The first links to build are the ones that tie the gardener to the elements of the landscape. A garden that is not well connected to a gardener, that offers no reason to linger and nurture it, will speedily revert to vacant-lot wilderness. The zone system forges links whose length—the distance between the design element and the house—depends on how often that element needs attention. The busiest connections are the shortest,

which saves time and ensures that fussy or oft-used plants don't suffer from neglect. And, best of all, using zones means living in the center of a garden.

Offering niches for the gardener's allies. The vast majority of wildlife, whether bug, microbe, or vertebrate, is helpful or harmless to the garden. And in general, the more varieties of species, the less chance that any one will get out of control. I've described plants that attract wildlife. Other niche-enhancers include birdhouses and feeders, mulch to hide predaceous beetles and attract insect-hunting birds, rockeries for helpful lizards and snakes, brush piles for bugs and birds, and ponds to offer homes for fish and amphibians and drinking spots for other animals.

Enhancing survival and growth with nurse plants. Nurse, scaffold, and chaperone plants (Table 6-4) will help ensure that young or tender species will become established. They will also boost their protégé's growth rate far beyond what a young plant could achieve alone. Providing nutrient accumulation, shelter from wind and fierce sun, and natural mulch and often harboring beneficial insects and wildlife, nurse plants and others mediate critical connections between young transplants and the forces that can kill or aid them. Helper plants are one of the biggest factors that propel a garden toward behaving like an ecosystem. Use them liberally.

Community-building via guilds. Guilds, or plant communities that mimic those in nature while providing for people, let plants and animals pick up much of the gardener's work. A stand-alone fruit tree, for example, must be watered, fertilized, and sprayed, and its pollination chances and susceptibility to disease and pests are at the whim of the elements. But if we design a guild that connects the tree to plants and animals that will do these tasks, not only are the gardener and the tree happier, but the rich, multilayered webwork of the guild will harvest more resources, sculpt new niches, and boost biodiversity.

Stacking functions. Designing each element to have multiple functions—a nurse plant, for example, that provides shade and nitrogen to its young charge, nectar to hummingbirds, berries for wildlife, and fast-growing mulch—builds a dense network of connections. Each role played by a plant or other garden element connects it to something else. As this web grows thicker and more interlinked, the garden becomes easier to maintain because most of the tasks are done by the garden itself, and if one organism fails, another is there to pick up the slack. Also, a deeply interwoven landscape begins to act as a single being, with its own character and novelties. This makes the ecological garden a fascinating place.

Growing by chunking. Imposing an arbitrary, large, and untested pattern on a landscape all at once is a recipe for disaster. This often results in unsuitable plantings, disconnected elements that don't work well together, and constant rescue efforts. Instead, start small and close to the house, find out what works, get one area growing successfully, and then repeat this pattern (with appropriate variations for new sites). In time, these many small patches of fertility and thriving plants will link up, bonding into a resilient, healthy whole. Ecological designers call this approach "growing by chunking."

The Garden Gets Popping

Although every moment in the ecological garden is gratifying, there is one stage in a site's evolution that is particularly exciting. That's when, after an initial period of sluggish plant growth and imperceptible soil improvement, the garden suddenly explodes into life and seethes with greenery, fruit, blossoms, and wildlife. The early establishment phase can take a few years, but then look out! The whole place suddenly "pops" as if some critical mass has been reached. The garden surges into vital action, moving from near-desert to lush jungle in a seeming instant, bursting with living energy. Everyone who practices permaculture and ecological gardening for a few years has seen this amazing transformation. Let me describe one example.

In the first chapter, I introduced Roxanne Swentzell's garden in New Mexico. Remember that when she and her two young children moved in, the place was gravel desert. "At first, everything we planted died," Roxanne had said. "It was just too harsh." The plants would cook in summer and freeze or dry out in winter. "We'd bring in big old rocks or logs for protection and plant little trees behind them," she recalled. "That helped a little. But we still had to plant a lot of things over and over." They trucked in manure and mulch and built rock walls to hold heat on cold nights, trying to foster benign microclimates that would enfold tiny pockets of fertility.

On my second visit, permaculture designer Joel Glanzberg, who helped design and install the garden, arrived to show me around. Explaining their strategy for coaxing plants to survive, he told me, "In the beginning we'd find a sheltered spot, like along a swale. We'd mulch it and put in pioneer species, usually native and exotic nitrogen fixers like New Mexico locust, Russian olive, and Siberian pea shrub." In the shade of these, they planted fruit and nut trees that would eventually soar past the nitrogen-fixing nurse plants to form the canopy. "We'd work on creating a favorable spot, concentrating our resources there, and then grow out from those nuclei," Joel said. "And those nuclei started to link up. Rox figured out quickly that you get little areas under control, and once you're successful there, move on and repeat the pattern." This strategy, duplicating small successes rather than trying to do everything at once—growing by chunking—pares down the chance of failure by building on past successes.

The strategies worked. In about the fifth year, life began to take hold and gain momentum. The soil was rich enough, the shade amply dense, the leaf litter so abundant, the roots sufficiently deep, for the pieces to coalesce into a whole. The system "popped." Plants that had struggled in the harsh desert for several years suddenly were detonating, growing several feet in a season. The soil stayed moist through month-long droughts. Glistening fruit shouldered through the thick foliage. The most useful tools were no longer shovel and sprinkler, but bushel basket and pruning saw. Birds filled the new forest with song. And a nearly closed canopy of greenery now cast cool shade that offered refuge from the intense New Mexico sun and kept the soil from burning to dry powder. A completely different energy now suffused the place. Someone with a mystical bent would say that a spirit had come to inhabit the land and give it life.

As Roxanne described the garden's beginnings, I watched honeybees fly from a hive near the back door to a thick carpet of flowers ringing a small pond. Roxanne clipped more branches from a luxuriant Russian olive. "Our biggest problems now are too much shade and too much water," she said. "And I can't even throw a peach pit into the bushes, because next year there'll be a peach tree growing there." Yet only a few years back the place had been barren, as it remained outside Roxanne's fence. There the ground was still naked gravel, and the air blistering hot, while just inside, the temperature was ten degrees cooler. In winter, frosts were fewer and nighttime lows less severe. The garden's design had changed the merciless high-desert climate into something sweet and benign. That's a significant feat.

I looked over the surrounding bare, eroded hills

In just a few years, Flowering Tree Permaculture Institute grew from a sun-baked, barren desert into a lush oasis that hums with life.

and imagined the Southwest covered in a rich food forest such as this one. Each house could be a nucleus for an expanding net of green canopy and deep soil, eventually linking into a continuous carpet of lush, abundant nature.

The phenomenon I was seeing, the "pop" of a young ecological garden into a self-sustaining ecosystem, is well recognized. It's happened for the Bullock brothers, for Penny Livingston, for Roxanne, for Jerome Osentowski. It happened to me in southern Oregon. Kiel and I began improving our own zones 1 and 2 there when we arrived there, and in the fourth summer we watched once-struggling trees shoot skyward. Wildflowers we had not planted blossomed everywhere. The ground outside the house had been hard clay that baked to pavement in summer, broken only by a few tufts of grass burnt brown by July. After deep mulching and dense planting, that soil was black and full of worms and grew deeper each year. I went from having to fire up the irrigation system a few days after the rains ended in May, to not having to water anything until six weeks into the dry season. Many plants thrived without water through the entire hot, dry summer. The once-baked ground was shaded by fruit trees, a wealth of shrubs, and bush-sized perennial flowers interspersed with salad greens, herbs, and strawberries.

In the wilder, untended parts of our yard, where three or four stunted weed and grass species once labored to survive, a dozen or more wildflowers and native grasses soon grew tall and thick—and I didn't plant them. Without looking hard, I counted over fifteen bee and beneficial wasp species, innumerable beetles, and four different lizards. Birds that had once only visited briefly, such as western tanagers, took up residence. And each succeeding year got better.

In my Portland yard, the process is repeating. Our soil didn't need as much work as it had in southern Oregon, but the yard began as a badly compacted expanse of nothing but grass. Three years later, fruit trees, surrounded by thickly stacked guilds, are bearing; dense foliage cools us and the house on hot days; and wrens, flickers, jays, sparrows, chickadees, and a host of other birds spend much of their day here. Turning a shovelful of soil anywhere in the yard reveals black earth busy with worms. The once-empty yard froths up so much biomass that I am giving away compost and topsoil, else we'd be buried under it. The new trees are nearly big enough for Kiel to string her much-beloved hammock between them.

It's useful to ask two questions here: What's happening when a garden pops? And, how do we make it happen quickly?

The Garden as Organism

First, what's happening? For one thing, an ecological garden moves rapidly through the pioneer phase—full of fast-growing, low plants with limited habitat for other species, rather like conventional gardens—into a more mature, many-layered, high-biomass, high-diversity, closed-loop ecosystem.

Many of the techniques described in this book are designed to accelerate this natural process of succession and to make the connections among

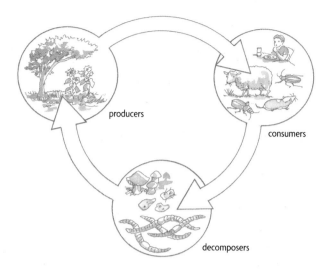

The producer-consumer-decomposer cycle. All three elements of this cycle are equally important. In most yards, the decomposers (worms, bacteria, fungi, and other soil creatures) are neglected, which starves the producers (plants), and in turn the consumers (animals), of resources. If each link flourishes, the others grow stronger, too.

organisms tight, many-layered, and efficient. Deep mulches, for example, quickly boost the amount of energy and food available for soil life. Thousands of species of soil organisms arrive with this mulch, drift in on air currents and raindrops, or are present but dormant. In the welcoming habitat, they spring to life. This rapidly enlarges the decomposer component in the all-important producer-consumer-decomposer cycle.

As I've said before, in most gardens, the decomposers are few and weak, able only to cycle and release low levels of nutrients. This poverty constricts the vigor and number of the producers (plants) and consumers (birds, insects, and you) that depend on the decomposers to provide raw materials for growth. Ramping up the activity of the decomposers by adding plenty of organic matter unchains the once-stunted plant and animal life. The vigorously cycling soil life pumps out an enormous surplus of nutrients, throwing off food and energy in wild abundance and in many forms, so that more plants and animals, both in terms of diversity and sheer numbers, can thrive. Deep mulch also generates humus, which becomes a capacious reservoir for water and for minerals like calcium, potassium, and others essential for plant growth.

Think of the whole garden as an organism. Deep-mulching the area around a house, combined with dense planting, creates an expanding circle of vigorous life and fertility. The densely interconnected soil, plant, and animal life are now surging with nutrients, water, pollen, chemical messages, and other "information flows." As the gardener gradually expands this intensely planted area farther from the house, the area of thick interconnections expands, nutrient and energy flows link up and fatten, new niches appear, and more species can thrive in this vibrant place. The living interconnectivity of the garden is so boosted that it becomes a fibrous knot of life, virtually impossible to wound, invade, or otherwise destabilize.

This resilience exists for many reasons. Having so many species from all of life's kingdoms provides a huge assortment of food types and habitat. This means each inhabitant of the garden has several places to feed instead of a single "all-eggs-in-one-basket" food supply that might fail. And with so many habitats present, every inhabitant has a good chance of finding the right microclimate, soil type, branch height, or other quality needed to survive. This high biodiversity—lots of species—means that if one species dies out, many others that play similar roles stand nearby to plug into the gap and keep the community functioning.

This garden is hard to damage. A new species may appear from the wild or the nursery, but rarely will it become invasive. The odds are high that it will find fertile soil and the right conditions to grow. But with so many other species present—potential competitors—it's not likely to find enough unused food or space to become a pest. If it spreads too fast, it becomes a delicious and abundant food source

for one of the thousands of species of insects, soil fungi, or other consumers that will keep it in check. Remember how muskrats at the Bullocks' bog were knocked back by the arriving otters? Be assured that this wasn't an isolated case. The brothers had a similar problem with slugs, too, until ducks moved in and munched the slimy invaders down to manageable numbers. This will happen in any balanced ecosystem.

Also, this kind of garden fills out quickly because nearly any potential resource that enters it will be grabbed by some waiting organism. That translates into fast growth and dense interconnections. Here's why. In conventional gardening, with expanses of bare soil and little variety, fertilizer can leach out of uninhabited ground, precious water evaporates, sunlight falls on empty space, and with many links missing in the producer-consumer-decomposer webwork, many resources—from dead branches to dried leaves to old corn cobs in the compost—go unused because the creatures capable of recycling and using them are missing.

But in a diverse garden, nothing goes to waste. Something is always there to use it. Any potential food or habitat source is seized on hungrily by one of the zillion species present and incorporated into the ever-building structure of the garden. It's another example of the "rich get richer" phenomenon, more formally called the law of increasing returns. Once an ample framework for harvesting wealth is built—in this case, wealth being sunlight, food, and incoming species, the framework being fertile soil and a multistoried assemblage of plants—the garden keeps getting richer and more diverse. The ever-enlarging wheel of life just gets better and better at harvesting and using nutrients and the constant stream of free energy from the sun, which powers yet further growth and interconnection.

Also, the design itself makes sure that little goes to waste. Using graywater means that nutrients that would otherwise go down the drain are captured and stingily held by the soil, then fed to plants and recycled in the garden. Designing with zones ensures that the places that need the most care are the closest to hand, making it easy to notice the little bare spot that needs mulching, the drooping ground cover crying for water, or the slugs perforating the lettuce. Taking sectors into account effectively uses free energy such as sunlight and damps down the battle against wind or fire, freeing our time for more productive work. Using insectary and wildlife plants extends the garden's reach beyond the plant kingdom into the realms of microbes, insects, and other animals. This lets us bring oft-overlooked allies and energy into the garden, filling it with busy workers while we sip lemonade in a hammock.

Another reason for the "popping" phenomenon is that we've mimicked natural plant communities. This takes advantage of a few billion years of groundwork done by evolution. A plant community's species have coevolved over eons and so are familiar partners. They know what to do with each other. The interconnections and flows of nutrients, chemical signals, and pollen, as well as the niches for the beneficial supporting cast of soil life, have already been worked out. This is why the guild approach is so much more successful than just planting blocks of a single species. Like a great sports team, the members have rehearsed their moves so many times that, when we bring them together, they blend into a smoothly performing ensemble and get to work. Ecologist Stuart Pimm, who has studied natural communities, described this process in an interview with author Kevin Kelly. Pimm said that in these communities, "The players have played many times. They know what the sequence is. Evolution not only evolves the functioning community, it fine-tunes the assembly process of the gathering until the community practically falls together." So putting together the members of an existing plant community fattens the chance of a successful and rapid meshing and shrinks the possible niches for invaders such as pest species.

In a garden this full of life, seething with complex food webs and a rich supply of nutrients, plenty of opportunities exist for successful, mutually beneficial links to form and thicken. That makes the system pop. Now let's look at how we can speed up the process to accelerate our arrival at that delightful popping stage.

Where to Begin?

I've described the process of designing the garden and given lots of techniques to use. But ecological gardening is a new field crammed with fresh information, so I wouldn't be surprised if you are looking at your design sketches, nicely drawn according to zones and sectors and full of multifunctional plants, and asking, "Yes, but what do I do first?" Sure, begin at your doorstep, but begin doing what? What are the very first things to do that will help a garden become an ecosystem?

The title of an excellent book by Grace Gershuny gives the answer: *Start with the Soil.* Not only is the soil the base of the ecological pyramid and thus the logical place to begin, but very shortly the soil will be stuffed with perennial plants and thus be much harder to work on. Bringing the soil to rich, loamy fertility will accelerate and invigorate all that succeeds it. So the first step is to create a small bed of rich soil near the front or back door or in other close-in site (how to choose the exact spot for this bed is explained in a few paragraphs).

Think of this luxuriantly fertile region as the heart of zone 1, the place that will support the first set of dense plantings and will probably be heavily harvested. So this soil needs to be immensely fertile. This will be the initial nucleus of high fertility and diversity, to later be linked up with others, just as Joel Glanzberg described.

To get the garden going, we want to build this startup bed's soil rapidly. If there's a source of

Ecological Compromises, or
You Can't Make an Omelet . . .

In a perfect, environmentally optimized world, we'd never power-till, all of our mulch supplies would come from nearby—ideally from our own property—and we'd find renewable sources of soil amendments instead of mined, exhaustible products such as rock phosphate and greensand. But it's not a perfect world, and I'm not going to be so dogmatic as to demand we create and use our gardens using only completely sustainable techniques. When it's time to get our hands dirty, idealism runs into the brick wall of practicality. I'd much rather see gardeners consume some nonrenewable resources to create eventually self-sustaining gardens than have them sit paralyzed by the fear of committing an environmentally incorrect act.

We do what we're comfortable with. David Holmgren, the cooriginator of permaculture's concepts, says, to the horror of purists, that he doesn't oppose a one-time use of herbicide to prepare land for tree planting, considering the energy used and destruction caused by the alternative: bringing in machines to clear the site year after year until the trees are established. And otherwise-organic gardener Doug Clayton now applies the insecticide Imidan once a year to his fruit trees. He believes a single dose of this effective pesticide is far less harmful than what he once used: almost-weekly sprayings of organically acceptable, yet very toxic, pyrethrum and rotenone.

If renting a power-tiller once, or buying peat moss from fossilized northern Canadian sphagnum beds, or bulldozing to grade a site, or some other method eschewed by the idealist is what it takes to get your backyard ecosystem up and running, then do it. Especially in the establishment phase, when we're working hard to restore abused land and heal broken cycles, we should be forgiving.

Use techniques that work for you. I've seen permaculture sites that mix conventional raised beds full of annual plants with semiwild forest gardens. The raised beds are efficient to harvest, plus it's easy to see what's going on. In a forest garden, plants occasionally get lost in the diversity. Mixing and matching an assortment of techniques is fine.

One rule of thumb for making these sorts of choices is to think long-term. Using nonrenewable resources to create a landscape is justified if, in the long run, that landscape will conserve or provide more resources than it took to build it. Using a less-than-natural technique that produces homegrown food and reduces the pressure on wild land is preferable to giving up in exhaustion. Overall, doing an imperfect something is better than doing a perfect nothing.

compost available, then the fastest method to boost fertility in a small space is to remove unwanted vegetation from this bed, and scratch in an inch or two of compost. Also add other necessary amendments such as lime, phosphate, and potassium (a soil test will show what's needed). If no compost is handy, then sheet mulching is the method I prefer.

As I mentioned in Chapter 4, I consider adding compost to be a short-term method, an emergency technique to quickly bring soil to decent fertility so that a patch of ground can be pushed into production fast. But to build soil that is truly surging with life, I like sheet mulching—composting in place—because it encourages multiple generations of soil life (ecological succession in the soil), fills the garden bed with the rich excretions of decomposer organisms instead of wasting them beneath the compost pile, and leaves the soil creatures undisturbed. Besides, it's much less work than building a compost pile in one place and then transporting and working-in full cartloads of the finished product. The downside is that the sheet-mulched bed won't reach maximum fertility for a year or two. But it still can and should be planted immediately by using soil pockets or a thin top-dressing of good soil.

How big should this first bed be? That depends on how much compost or sheet-mulch material—and labor—is available. A typical wheelbarrow, powered by a non-Herculean human, can hold one to three cubic feet of compost, enough to cover ten to thirty square feet of ground one inch deep. That's not much—it will take a lot of wheelbarrow loads to do a single garden bed. And, as I explained in Chapter 4, one pickup load of mulch material will cover about fifty square feet. Also, remember to cover a small area well rather than a large area thinly.

Where exactly to locate these precious first garden beds? Here's where knowing a little about microclimates comes in handy. Joel Glanzberg talked about placing their first plantings along swales, where water would collect and linger and where potential shelter from wind and sun already existed. In high-mountain Colorado, Jerome Osentowski built rock terraces that held heat in his frost-prone garden. And near cool, foggy San Francisco, Penny Livingston planted a peach tree amid a set of small ponds, where stored heat from the water as well as reflected light would speed growth. Finding (or creating) and using benign microclimates will boost the odds of success and accelerate plant growth, speeding the arrival of that happy day of system-pop.

Which microclimates to choose depends on the overall environment and climate. What's benign in the desert—a moist, shady, not well-drained site, for example—would be disastrous in a damp northern climate, where a sunny, fairly dry spot is far better. In general, look for sites that have no wild swings of temperature, moisture, or sunlight. Whatever the local climate extremes are in the region—brutally high or low temperatures, soggi-

ness or drought, leaf-crisping sun or months of kill-me-now gray skies—find a place that will counter or mitigate those extremes. Desirable in almost any location is lack of wind, so locate the heart of zone 1 in the still shelter of a house, earth berm, wall, or planted windbreak.

If favorable microclimates don't exist, as they didn't for Roxanne Swentzell, then make them. Pile up rocks or logs or build a wall for a windbreak. Dig a swale for wind protection and added moisture. Create a raised bed to improve drainage or a sunken one in dry climates to catch infrequent rain. Prune a tree to let in light. Find and create good microclimates to give the garden the edge that it needs for a successful start.

Design guru Larry Santoyo, after giving some specific advice to his permaculture students, will often warn them, "The opposite is also true." Without meaning to confuse my readers, I will now illustrate this. In seeming contradiction to the ecological adage, "start at your doorstep," Australian permaculturist Geoff Lawton suggests that another important early step in ecological design is to define and control a property's edges. Edge, after all, is where flows and energy enter a site. These are opportunities. If missed, they can become problems.

For example, where do weeds and pests come from? From off the site. We need barriers at the edges and predator habitat to intercept them. An icy north wind can stunt plant growth if left unblocked. An unpleasant sector energy like that needs to be identified early on and dealt with via a fence or other quick windbreak, and this feature most likely will be located at the edge of the yard. Handled intelligently, flows across edges can be translated into useful work or materials. Creating hedges, perimeter paths, edge plantings, and screens and simply defining the margins of activities will transmute potentially destructive dynamics into useful energies. Defining edges can sculpt and organize work patterns, planting areas, and materials flows. Not only do we want to harvest incoming resources like sun, water, and graywater, we want to make sure that nothing we generate on the site leaves unless we want it to. Edge definition, which melds zones of activity with sector energies, will keep our efforts from simply diffusing outward by reminding us where we need to focus our work and in what intensity.

Assembling the Garden Revisited

How hard is it to click together all the pieces of an ecological garden? It might sound daunting. On previous pages I've told stories of wild chiles that need particular nurse plants and hot-sauce–tolerant birds to thrive and saguaro cacti that depend on mesquites and white-winged doves for survival. If nature's assembly rules are that specific and complex, what are the chances that a humble gardener can collect all the right elements to make a landscape pop? What are the odds that we will have the species and conditions necessary to create a smoothly functioning set of plant communities?

Very good odds, as it turns out. Nature is very forgiving and resilient, as both its continued survival in the face of human damage and ecology research prove. A number of ecologists have looked into the assembly of natural communities, and what they've found is encouraging and useful for ecological gardeners.

Two of these scientists are Jim Drake at the University of Tennessee and Stuart Pimm of Duke University. Drake and Pimm studied how communities of organisms form. They added fifteen to forty species of bacteria, algae, and microscopic animals (a blend of producers, consumers, and decomposers) one at a time, in many different combinations and sequences, to tanks of nutrient broth. They were surprised to find how often

this random mixing resulted in a stable ecosystem. Instead of dying in what could have been an unsuitable home, the microbes connected with each other, building food webs, multiplying, and preying on each other in a well-linked ecosystem. Pimm remarked that, after making these random groupings, the organisms assembled a network that was much more structured than had been expected from such a haphazard collection.

Drake and Pimm also performed computer simulations to support their findings. They programmed a computer with 125 software "species" and, after creating an initial stable community of three electronic organisms in the machine, added new species one at a time. At first, each invading species made the grouping fluctuate in population and often bumped out other species in waves of extinction, but eventually the communities settled down, clicked into place, and became relatively impervious to new invaders. This showed that simply adding random species together could create invasion-proof communities of interacting members.

In both sets of experiments, many species would survive for a while and then die off. They didn't wind up as part of the final community. But they turned out to be important ingredients of a successful, stable ensemble. If these species were dropped from the assembly process, the community ended up with a different final composition; it took an alternative path. These short-term species played the same role as nurse plants, performing some useful job along the way, but weren't part of the end product.

These experiments confirm what many permaculture gardeners have learned: We don't know exactly how the assembly of successful guilds and ecosystems works, but if we begin with a wide array of plant types, nature will usually sort out something that clicks. A skimpy selection takes a lot more babying and often never "pops" at all.

These experiments, as well as the experiences of

A grassy path through the 25-year-old forest garden of the Bullock brothers, Orcas Island, Washington.

the ecological gardeners cited in this book, hint that assembling a backyard ecosystem is not as difficult as one might think. Nature adheres to a deep order. It is as if living beings "want" to come together to form coherent communities. Given half a chance, plants and animals will self-organize into a connected whole. Ecological gardeners, take heart; we don't have to master every detail of guild design or include every single native bacterium, beetle, and plant species of a community to get a garden to "pop." Nature will often supply the missing pieces, click together the right connections, and link up the important cycles. A holistic garden wants to happen. We just need to supply a reasonable selection of pieces and arrange them in a usable order. Nature will choose the ones that work.

I'm not saying that creating an ecological garden will take no work. Building soil, nurturing an array of useful plants to maturity, and awaiting the arrival of beneficial insects, birds, and other wildlife all require labor and time. And transforming our own viewpoint, from a static bits-and-pieces orientation to one based on the interconnectedness of nature, may be the biggest hurdle of all.

But that initial investment you make will pay off handsomely. You'll hardly even remember it as you lie in your hammock, overwhelmed by the choice of fruit, hypnotized by the array of scents wafting your way, and comfortable in the knowledge that your landscape is allowing some bit of farmland to go free.

This book can only be an introduction to an enormous subject, one that could easily consume a lifetime of study, observation, and puttering among the plants. The bibliography offers further resources that go into more depth. The best way to learn, however, is simply to take a good look at the natural world, roll up your sleeves, and begin to create a garden that will provide for you and for the many other beings with whom we live.

APPENDIX

A Sampling of Useful Plants

Thousands of useful plant species exist, thus the plants listed in the following tables represent only a small sample of what is available. I've chosen to highlight these species here because they are relatively common, exceptionally useful, and not too difficult to grow.

Sources for this information include the *Plants for a Future Database* (www.pfaf.org); Tilth, *The Future Is Abundant* (Tilth, 1982); and Christopher Brickell, *The American Horticultural Society Encyclopedia of Garden Plants* (Macmillan, 1990).

Key to Appendix Tables

USDA Zone

This refers to the USDA Hardiness Zone system, representing the lowest annual temperature range for a specific growing region and thus offering some general indication of where a particular plant can be reliably expected to survive. These zones are only approximations and do not take into account specific microclimates (either natural or created by the gardener).

Also, as of this writing, the USDA has not released new zone maps, which may indicate shifting zone boundaries as a result of global climate change. However, the minimum temperatures defining the zones remain the same, as follows:

Zone	Minimum Annual Temperature (°F)
2	−50 to −40
3	−40 to −30
4	−30 to −20
5	−20 to −10
6	−10 to 0
7	0 to 10
8	10 to 20
9	20 to 30

Type

Tr Tree (a woody perennial with a single erect stem and a substantial leaf canopy)

Sh Shrub (a woody perennial with multiple stems arising from the base)

Cl Climber (a vining or trailing plant with a flexible stem)

E Evergreen (retaining its foliage year-round)

D Deciduous (losing its foliage year-round)

HP Herbaceous perennial (a non-woody plant that grows for several to many years)

HB Herbaceous biennial (a non-woody plant that sets seed and dies in its second year)

A Annual

P Perennial

Light

○ Prefers full sun
● Prefers shade
◑ Tolerates partial shade

Edible Part or Use

Bark Bark
Fr Fruit
Fl Flower
Lf Leaf
Med Medicinal
Oil Seed or sap used for oil
Root Root
Sap Sap
Seas Used as seasoning or spice
Sd Seed
Sht Shoot
Tea Tea
Y Young

Animal Use

Chk Poultry forage
For Forage, browse, or other animal feed
Hab Provides habitat
Hum Attracts hummingbirds
Ins Attracts beneficial insects

Other Use

Biomass Plant produces large quantities of biomass
Bskt Stem, branches, or root used for basketry
Dye Some or all of plant used to prepare dye
Fiber Leaf, stem, flower parts, or root used in paper, cordage, or other fiber product
Fragrance Has exceptional fragrance, may be used as perfume base
Gourd Fruit used as gourd
Hr Hedgerow species
N-fixer Nitrogen-fixing species
Nutr Nutrient-accumulator species
Poles Stem or branches used for poles and support stakes
Polish Used as furniture polish
Repellent Used as insect repellent
Soap Leaves, sap, fruit, or other part used as soap
Soil stab Used for soil stablization
Wbr Windbreak species
Wood Woody parts used for lumber, firewood, or craft wood

Tall Trees, 50 Feet and Larger

Common Name	Botanical Name	Hardy to USDA Zone	Type	Light	Edible Part or Use	Animal Use	Other Uses	Comments
Beech	Fagus spp.	5	D Tr	○◑	Sd, yLf, Med	Hab, For	Wbr, Hr	
Black locust	Robinia pseudoacacia	3	D Tr	○	Fl, Sd	Ins, Hab, Chk, For	Wbr, Hr, Wood	N-fixer
Black walnut	Juglans nigra	4	D Tr	○	Sd, Med	Hab, For	Wbr, Wood	Allelopathic
Chinese chestnut	Castanea mollissima	4	D Tr	○	Sd, Med	Ins, Hab, Chk, For	Wbr, Hr, Wood, Soil stab.	
English Walnut	Juglans regia	5	D Tr	○	Sd	Had, For	Wbr, Hr, dye, Wood	Allelopathic
Honey locust	Gleditsia triacanthos	3	D Tr	○	Seedpod	Ins, Hab, Chk, For	Soil stab.	
Limber pine	Pinus flexilis	3	E Tr	○	Sd	Hab, For	Wbr, Hr, Wood	
Monkey Puzzle	Araucaria araucana	6	E Tr	○	Sd	Hab	Wbr, Hr, Wood	Large nuts
Madrone	Arbutus menziesii	7	E Tr	○◑	Fr	Ins, Hab, For	Wood	
Oak	Quercus spp.	4	E Tr	○	Sd	Hab, Chk, For	Wbr, Hr, Wood	White oaks have least tannin in acorn
Pignut hickory	Carya glabra	4	D Tr	○◑	Sd, Sap	Hab, For	Hr, Wood	
Piñon pine	Pinus cembroides	4	E Tr	○	Sd	Hab, For	Wbr, Hr, Wood	
Ponderosa pine	Pinus ponderosa	4	E Tr	○	Sd	Hab, For	Wbr, Hr, dye, Wood	
Shagbark hickory	Carya ovata	4	D Tr	○	Sd, Sap	Hab, Chk, For	Wood, Soil stab.	
Shellbark hickory	Carya laciniosa	6	D Tr	○◑	Sd, Sap	Ins, Hab, Chk, For	Wood	
Sour cherry	Prunus cerasus	3	D Tr	○	Fr, Tea	Ins, Hab, For	Wbr, Hr	
Stone pine	Pinus pinea	4	E Tr	○	Sd	Hab, For	Wbr, Hr, Wood	Many other species have edible seeds
Sugar maple	Acer saccharum	3	D Tr	○◑	Sap	Ins, Hab, For	Wood	Many other species good for maple syrup
Sweet chestnut	Castanea sativa	5	D Tr	○	Sd, Med	Ins, Hab, Chk, For	Wbr, Hr, Wood	
Tree of heaven	Ailanthus altissima	7	D Tr	○		Ins, Hab	Wbr, Hr, Soil stab.	Tolerates pollution
Yellow buckeye	Aesculus flava	3	D Tr	○◑	Sd, Sap	Ins, Hab, For	Wood, soap	

Shrubs and Small Trees, 3–50 Feet Tall

Common Name	Botanical Name	Hardy to USDA Zone	Type	Light	Edible part or use	Animal use	Other uses	Comments
Silk tree or mimosa	Albizzia julibrisin	6	D Tr	○ ◑	Lf	Ins, Hab	Hr, N-fixer	
Alder	Alnus spp.	3	D Tr	○	Med	Ins, Hab	Wbr, Hr, Dye, Wood	
Juneberry	Amelanchier spp.	4	D Sh	○	Fr	Ins, Hab, Chk, For	Wbr, Hr	
Angelica tree	Aralia chinensis	7	D Sh	○ ◑	Sht		Wbr, Hr	
Chokeberry	Aronia melanocarpa	3	D Sh	○ ◑	Fr, Med	Ins, Hab, Chk, For	Hr, Dye	
Strawberry tree	Arbutus unedo	7	E Tr	○	Fr	Ins, Hab, For	Wbr, Hr	
Manzanita	Arctostaphyllos manzanita	7	E Sh	○ ◑	Fr	Ins, Hab, Chk, For	Wbr, Hr, Dye	
Giant reed	Arundo donax	6	Grass	○	Root, Med		Bskt, Wbr, Hr, Soil stab	
Pawpaw	Asimina triloba	6	D Tr	◑ ●	Fr	Hab, Chk, For	Dye, Fiber	
Salt bush	Atriplex canescens	7	E Sh	○	Lf, Sd		Wbr, Hr	
Spotted laurel	Aucuba japonica	7	E Sh	● ○			Wbr, Hr	
Coyote brush	Baccharis pilularis	8	E Sh	○		Ins, Hab	Wbr, Hr, Soil stab	
Bamboo	Bambusa textilis	7	E Sh	○	Sht	Hab, For	Wbr, Hr, Poles, Fiber	
Blue false indigo	Baptisia australis	5	D Sh	○			Ins, N-fixer	
Barberry	Berberis vulgaris	3	D Sh	○ ◑	Fr, Tea	Hab, For	Wbr, Hr, Fiber	
Butterfly bush	Buddleia davidii	5	D Sh	○		Ins	Wbr, Hr, Dye	
Box	Buxus sempervirens	5	E Sh	○ ◑	Med		Wbr, Hr	
Bottlebrush	Callistemon citrinus	8	E Sh	○	Tea	Ins	Wbr, Hr	C. sieberi & C. viridiflorus can also be used
Scotch heather	Calluna vulgaris	4	E Sh	○	Tea, Med	Ins	Wbr, Hr, Bskt, Dye	Acid soil
Siberian pea shrub	Caragana arborescens	3	E Sh	○	Sd	Ins, Chk, For	Wbr, Hr, Dye, Soil stab, N-fixer	
American hornbeam	Carpinus caroliniana	5	D Tr	○ ◑	Sd	Hab, For	Wbr, Hr, Dye	
Bittersweet	Celastrus orbiculatus	4	D Tr	○ ◑	YLf, Med	Hab, For	Wbr, Hr	Leaves should be cooked
Hackberry	Celtis spp.	4	E Sh	○	Fr, Sd	Hab, Chk, For	Wbr, Hr, Dye	

Common name	Latin name							Notes
Redbud	Cercis canadensis	5	D Tr	○	Fl	Ins, Hab	Hr	
Japanese quince	Chaenomeles speciosa	5	D Tr	○●	Root, Med	Ins, Hab, For	Wbr, Hr	
Mexican orange	Choisya ternata	7	D Tr	○			Wbr, Hr	
Summersweet	Clethra alnofolia	4	D Sh	○●	Lf	Hab, For	Hr	Acid soil
Cabbage palm	Cordyline australis	8	E Tr	○	Sht, Root		Wbr, Hr, Fiber	
Chinese dogwood	Cornus kousa	5	D Tr	○●	Fr, YLf	Hab, For	Hr	
Cornelian cherry	Cornus mas	5	D Tr	○	Fr		Wbr, Hr, Dye	
Hazelnut	Corylus spp.	4	D Tr	○●	Sd, Oil	Hab, For	Wbr, Hr, Bskt	
Azarole	Crataegus azarolus	5	D Tr	○	Fr	Ins, Hab, Chk, For	Wbr, Hr	
Black hawthorn	Crataegus douglasii	5	D Tr	○	Fr	Ins, Hab, Chk, For	Wbr, Hr	Many other species have edible fruits
Persimmon	Diospyros kaki	8	D Tr	○●	Fr	Hab, For	Hr	
Date plum	Diospyros lotus	5	D Tr	○●	Fr	Hab, For	Hr	
American persimmon	Diospyros virginiana	5	D Tr	○●	Fr	Hab, For	Hr	
Mountain pepper	Drimys lanceolata	8	E Sh	○●	Fr (spice), Med		Wbr, Hr	
Winter's bark	Drimys winteri	8	E Sh	○●	Bark, Med	Hab	Hr	
Russian olive	Elaeagnus angustifolia	2	D Sh	○	Fr	Ins, Hab, Chk, For	Wbr, Hr, N-fixer	
Silverberry	Elaeagnus commutata	2	D Sh	○	Fr	Ins, Hab, Chk, For	Wbr, Hr, Fiber, N-fixer	
Goumi	Elaeagnus multiflora	6	D Tr	○	Fr	Ins, Hab, Chk, For	Wbr, Hr, N-fixer	Tolerates air pollution
Autumn olive	Elaeagnus umbellata	3	D Tr	○	Fr	Ins, Hab, Chk, For	Wbr, Hr, N-fixer	
Elaeagnus	Elaeagnus × ebbingei	6	E Sh	●	Fr	Ins, Hab, Chk, For	Wbr, Hr, N-fixer	
Escallonia	Escallonia spp.	9	E Sh	○		Hum, Ins	Wbr, Hr	
Pineapple guava	Feijoa sellowiana	8	E Tr	○	Fr, Fl	Ins, Chk, For	Hr	
Fig	Ficus carica	7	D Tr	○	Fr	Hab, chk, For	Hr	
Fuchsia	Fuchsia magellanica	6	D Sh	○●	Med	Hum	Wbr, Hr	
Maidenhair tree	Ginkgo biloba	2	E Tr	○	Sd, Med			
Kentucky coffee tree	Gymnocladus dioica	4	D Tr	○	Sd pod	Hab, For	Hr, Soap, N-fixer	
Witch hazel	Hamamelis virginiana	5	D Sh	●	Sd, Med	Hab	Hr	
Curry plant	Helichrysum italicum	8	E Sh	○	Spice		Wbr, Hr	

Shrubs and Small Trees, 3–50 Feet Tall (continued)

Common Name	Botanical Name	Hardy to USDA Zone	Type	Light	Edible part or use	Animal use	Other uses	Comments
Mallow	*Hibiscus syriacus*	5	D Sh	○	Lf, Fl, Oil, Tea	Ins, Hab	Wbr, Hr, Fiber	
Sea buckthorn	*Hippophae rhamnoides*	3	D Sh	○	Fr, Med	Hab, For	Wbr, Hr, Dye, N-fixer	
Oceanspray	*Holodiscus discolor*	5	D Sh	○◐	Fr	Hab	Hr, Wood	
Japanese raisin tree	*Hovenia dulcis*	6	D Tr	○	Fr	Hab	Hr	
Hyssop	*Hyssopus officinalis*	3	E Sh	○	Tea, Med	Ins	Wbr, Hr	
ligeri tree	*Idesia polycarpa*	5	D Tr	○	Fr			
Bachelor's button	*Kerria japonica*	4	D Sh	○◐	YLf			Drought tolerant
Golden-chain tree	*Laburnum anagyroides*	5	D Tr	○◐			Fragrance, N-fixer	Flowers toxic
Bay tree	*Laurus nobilis*	8	E Tr	○			Wbr, Hr	
Lavender	*Lavandula* spp.	5	E Sh	○	Med	Ins	Wbr, Hr	
Tree mallow	*Lavatera arborea*	8	D Sh	○◐	Lf	Ins	Fiber	
Bush clover	*Lespedeza thunbergii*	5	D Sh	○		Ins	N-fixer	
Honeysuckle	*Lonicera caerula* var. *edulis*	3	D Sh	○	F	Ins, Chk	Hr	Disperses easily
Chinese privet	*Ligustrum lucidum*	7	E Sh	●	Med		Wbr, Hr	
Boxthorn	*Lycium barbarum*	6	E Sh	○	Fr, Sht, Med	Hab	Wbr, Hr	
Amur Maackia	*Maackia amurensis*	4	D Sh	○	YLf	Ins	Hr, N-fixer	
Osage orange	*Maclura pommifera*	5	D Tr	○		Hab	Wbr, Hr, Dye	
Apple	*Malus sylvestris*	3	D Tr	○	Fr	Ins, Hab, For	Hr	
Medlar	*Mespilus germanica*	6	D Tr	○	Fr	Hab		
White mulberry	*Morus alba*	3	D Tr	○	Fr, YLf	Chk, Hab, For	Wbr, Hr, Dye, Fiber	
Black mulberry	*Morus nigra*	3	D Tr	○	Fr	Chk, Hab, For		Also: *M. australis, M. mongolica, M. rubra* and *M. serrata*
Myrtle	*Myrtus communis*	8	E Tr	○	Med		Wbr, Hr	
Heavenly bamboo	*Nandina domestica*	6	D Sh	○◐	Sht	Hab	Wbr, Hr, Poles, Fiber	
Tupelo	*Nyssa sylvatica*	3	D Tr	○	Fr	Ins, Hab		Alkaline soil
Oso berry	*Oemleria cerasiformis*	6	D Sh	○◐	Fr	Hab, For	Hr	

Common name	Scientific name		Type		Fr, Oil	Hab	Dye, Soil stab	Notes
Olive	*Olea europaea*	8	E Tr	○	Fr, Oil	Hab	Dye, Soil stab	
Devil's club	*Oplopanax horridus*	4	D Sh	●	Sht, Med	Hab		
Mock orange	*Philadelphus coronarius*	5	D Sh	○		Ins, Hab	Wbr, Hr	Also useful: *P. delavayi, P. pubescens, P. purpurascens* & *P. × virginalis*
New Zealand flax	*Phormium tenax*	8	E Sh	○			Wbr, Hr, Bskt, Fiber, Dye	
Bitter orange	*Poncirus trifoliata*	5	E Tr	○	Fr, Med	Hab	Wbr, Hr	
Cinquefoil	*Potentilla fruticosa*	5	D Sh	◑	Tea		Wbr, Hr, Soil stab	
Apricot	*Prunus armeniaca*	4	D Tr	○	Fr	Ins, Hab, For		
Mazzard cherry	*Prunus avium*	5	D Tr	○	Fr	Ins, Hab, For	Hr	
Laurel cherry	*Prunus caroliniana*	7	E Tr	◕	Fr	Ins, Hab, For	Wbr, Hr	
Chery plum	*Prunus cerasifera*	4	D Tr	○	Fr	Ins, Hab, For	Wbr, Hr	
Plum	*Prunus domestica*	3	D Tr	○	Fr	Ins, Hab, For	Wbr, Hr	
Almond	*Prunus dulcis*	3	D Tr	○	Sd	Ins, Hab, For	Wbr, Hr	
Fuji cherry	*Prunus incisa*	6	D Tr	○	Fr	Ins, Hab, For	Wbr, Hr	
Damson	*Prunus insititia*	5	D Tr	○	Fr, Med	Ins, Hab, For	Wbr, Hr	
English laurel	*Prunus laurocerasus*	6	E Tr	◕	Fr	Ins, Hab, For	Wbr, Hr	
Portuguese laurel	*Prunus lusitanica*	6	E Tr	◑		Ins, Hab, For	Wbr, Hr	
Peach/Nectarine	*Prunus persica*	6	D Tr	○	Fr	Ins, Hab, For	Hr	
Sloe	*Prunus spinosa*	4	D Tr	○	Fr, Med	Ins, Hab, For	Wbr, Hr, Dye	
Nanking cherry	*Prunus tomentosa*	5	D Sh	○	Fr	Ins, Hab, For	Wbr, Hr	
Bamboo	*Pseudosasa japonica*	6	E Sh	◑	Sht, Med	Hab, For	Wbr, Hr, Poles, Fiber	
California coffeeberry	*Rhamnus californica*	7	D Tr	◑	Fr, Med	Ins, Hab, Chk, For	Wbr, Hr	
Indian cherry	*Rhamnus caroliniana*	6	D Tr	◑	Fr	Ins, Hab, Chk, For	Hr	
Cascara	*Rhamnus purshiana*	6	D Tr	○	Med	Ins, Hab	Hr	
Lemonade berry	*Rhus integrifolia*	3	D Sh	◑	Fr, Fl	Ins, Hab, For	Hr	
Staghorn sumac	*Rhus typhina*	3	D Sh	○	Fr	Hab	Wbr, Hr, Dye, Soil stab	Also: *R. copallina* and *R. glabra*
Golden currant	*Ribes aureum*	4	D Sh	◑	Fr, Fl, Lf	Ins, Hab, For	Hr	
Wax currant	*Ribes cereum*	3	D Sh	◑	Fr	Ins, Hab, Chk, For	Hr, Dye	
Black currant	*Ribes nigrum*	5	D Sh	●	Fr	Ins, Hab, Chk, For	Hr	

Shrubs and Small Trees, 3–50 Feet Tall (continued)

Common Name	Botanical Name	Hardy to USDA Zone	Type	Light	Edible part or use	Animal use	Other uses	Comments
Red currant	Ribes rubrum	5	D Sh	○ ●	Fr	Ins, Hab, Chk, For	Hr	
Gooseberry	Ribes uva-crispa	5	D Sh	○ ●	Fr	Ins, Hab, Chk, For	Hr	
Rose	Rosa spp.	2	D Sh	○ ●	Fr	Ins, Hab, For	Wbr, Hr	Hybrids and cultivars are less useful
Rosemary	Rosmarinus officinale	7	E Sh	○	Seas	Ins	Ins, Hr	
Himalayan blackberry	Rubus discolor	5	D Cl	○ ●	Fr	Ins, Hab, Chk, For	Hr	
Red raspberry	Rubus idaeus	3	D Sh	○ ●	Fr	Ins, Hab, Chk, For	Hr	
Black raspberry	Rubus occidentalis	4	D Sh	○ ●	Fr, Tea	Ins, Hab, Chk, For	Hr	
Hooker's willow	Salix hookeriana	6	D Tr	○	Med	Hab	Wbr, Hr	Many species are useful
Purple osier	Salix purpurea	5	D Sh	○	Med	Hab	Wbr, Hr, Bskt	
Blue elderberry	Sambucus caerulea	5	D Sh	○ ●	Fr, Fl, Med	Ins, Hab, Chk, For	Wbr Hr, Dye	Leaves toxic
Black elderberry	Sambucus nigra	5	D Sh	○ ●	Fr, Fl, Med	Ins, Hab, Chk, For	Wbr, Hr, Dye	Leaves toxic
Sassafras	Sassafras albidum	5	D Tr	○ ●	Lf, Bark, Fr	Hab	Dye	
Buffaloberry	Shepherdia argentea	2	D Sh	○	Fr	Ins, Hab, Chk, For	Wbr, Hr, Dye, N-fixer	Drought resistant
Mountain ash	Sorbus spp.	5	D Tr	○	Fr	For	Wbr, Hr	
Spanish broom	Spartium junceum	8	D Sh	○	Med	Ins, Hab	Wbr, Hr, Fiber, Dye, N-fixer	
Lilac	Syringa vulgaris	5	D Sh	○	Med	Ins, Hab	Wbr, Hr, Dye	
Tamarisk	Tamarix gallica	5	D Tr	○	Med	Hab	Wbr, Hr	Also: T. africana, T. parviflora and T. ramosissima
Blueberry	Vaccinium corymbosum	2	D Sh	○ ●	Fr	Ins, Hab, For	Hr	Acid soil
Cranberry	Viburnum trilobum	2	E Sh	○ ●	Fr	Ins, Hab, For	Hr	Acid soil
Yucca	Yucca spp.	4	E Sh	○	Fr	Ins, Hab	Hr	
Jujube	Ziziphus zizyphus	6	D Tr	○	Fr	Hab	Hr	

Useful Plants for the Herb Layer

Common Name	Botanical Name	Hardy to USDA Zone	Type	Light	Edible part or use	Animal use	Other use	Comments
Alfalfa	*Medicago sativa*	5	HP	○	Lf, Sd	Ins, Hab, For	N-fixer	
American licorice	*Glycyrrhiza lepidota*	3	HP	○◐	Root, Med		N-fixer	Less sweet than *G. lepidota*; invasive
Anise hyssop	*Agastache foeniculum*	8	HP	○	Lf, Tea	Ins		
Asparagus	*Asparagus officinalis*	4	HP	○	Stem			
Balsamroot	*Balsamorhiza hookeri*	5	HP	○	Fl, Sd, Root	Ins		
Breadroot	*Psoralea esculenta*	7	HP	○	Root		N-Fixer, soil stab	Also *P. hypogaea*
Bugle	*Ajuga reptans*	6	HP	○◐	Lf	Ins		
Bulrush	*Scirpus* spp.	4	HP	○◐	Lf, Sd, Root, Med	Hab	Fiber	
Bunchberry	*Cornus canadensis*	2	HP	◐●	Fr	For		
Camas	*Camassia quamash*	3	HP	○◐	Root	Ins		
Cardoon	*Cynara cardunculus*	5	HB	○	Fr	Ins		Self-seeds
Cattail	*Typha angustifolia*	3	HP	○◐	Fl, Lf, Sht, Root	Hab, For	Fiber, soil stab	Bog plant
Cattail	*Typha latifolia*	3	HP	○◐	Fl, Lf, Sht, Root	Hab	Fiber	Bog plant
Chamomile	*Chamaemelum nobile*	4	HP	○◐	Tea	Ins	Dye	
Chicory	*Cichorium intybus*	3	HP	○	Fl, Lf, Root	Ins	Nutr	
Chinese artichoke	*Stachys affinis*	5	HP	○	Lf, Root			
Chives	*Allium schoenoprasum*	5	HP	○◐	Fl, Lf, Root	Ins	Nutr	
Collards	*Brassica oleracea viridis*	6	HP	○◐	Fl, Lf	Hab		
Columbine	*Aquilegia vulgaris*	4	HP	○	Fl, Tea	Ins		
Comfrey	*Symphytum officinale*	5	HP	○◐	Lf, Med	Ins, Chk	Nutr, biomass	
Common milkweed	*Asclepias cornuti*	3	HP	○	Fl, Lf	Ins	Dye, Fiber	
Creeping thyme	*Thymus serpyllum*	5	E Sh	○	Lf, Tea, Med	Ins	Repellent	Also *T. vulgaris*
Dandelion	*Taraxacum officinale*	5	HP	○◐	Fl, Lf, Root	Ins	Nutr	
Daylily	*Hemerocallis fulva*	4	HP	○◐	Fl, Lf, Root	Hum	Fiber	

Useful Plants for the Herb Layer (continued)

Common Name	Botanical Name	Hardy to USDA Zone	Type	Light	Edible part or use	Animal use	Other use	Comments
Egyptian onion	Allium cepa proliferum	5	HP	○	Fl, Lf, Root		Nutr, Dye, Repellent	
European licorice	Glycyrrhiza glabra	7	HP	○◐	Root, Med		N-fixer	
Fairy thimble	Campanula cochleariifolia	6	HP	○◐	Fl, Lf	Ins, For		
Fennel	Foeniculum vulgare	5	HP	○◐	Lf, Sd, Root	Ins, Hab, Chk	Nutr	
French sorrel	Rumex scutatus	6	HP	○◐	Lf		Dye	Also *R. acetosa*
Garlic	Allium sativum	5	HP	○	Fl, Lf, Root		Nutr	
Garlic chives	Allium tuberosum	5	HP	○◐	Fl, Lf, Root		Nutr	
Garlic cress	Peltaria alliacea	6	HP	○◐	Fl, Lf			
Ginseng	Panax ginseng	6	HP	◐●	Root, Med			
Globe artichoke	Cynara scolymus	6	HP	○	Fl, Lf	Ins		
Goldenberry	Physalis peruviana	8	HP	○	Fr			
Good King Henry	Chenopodium bonus-henricus	5	HP	○	Fl, Lf, Med	Ins	Nutr, Dye	
Greek oregano	Origanum vulgare hirtum	5	HP	○◐	Lf, Seas	Ins		
Groundnut	Apios americana	3	HP	○◐	Sd, Root		N-fixer	
Groundplum milkvetch	Astragalus crassicarpus	4	HP	○	Seedpod	Ins	N-fixer	
Harebell	Campanula persicifolia	3	HP	○◐	Fl, Lf, Root	Ins, For		
Indian water lotus	Nelumbo nucifera	5	HP	○	Fl, Lf, Root			Water plant
Jerusalem artichoke	Helianthus tuberosus	4	HP	○◐	Root	Ins, Hab	Hr, Biomass	
Kale, curly	Brassica oleracea sabellica	6	HP	○◐	Fl, Lf	Hab		
Kale, perennial	Brassica oleracea ramosa	6	HP	○◐	Fl, Lf	Hab		
King's spear	Asphodeline lutea	7	HP	○◐	Fl, Lf, Root			
Lupine	Lupinus spp.	5	HP	○	Sd, Med	Ins	N-fixer	

Common name	Scientific name	No.	Type	Sun/Shade	Parts	Wildlife	Uses	Notes
Maca or Peruvian ginseng	*Lepidium meyenii*	6	HP	○◐	Root, Med	Ins		
Maximilian sunflower	*Helianthus maximilianii*	4	HP	○	Root, Sht	Ins		
Mexican tarragon	*Tagetes lucida*	9	HP	○	Tea		Dye, Repellent	Grown as annual
Mitsuba	*Cryptotaenia japonica*	5	HP	◐●	Lf	Ins		
Musk mallow	*Malva moschata*	3	HP	○◐	Fl, Lf, Sd	Ins	Fiber	
Nasturtium	*Tropaeolum minus*	9	HP	○	Fl, Lf, Sd		Repellent	Grown as annual
Nine-star perennial broccoli	*Brassica oleracea botrytis aparagoides*	6	HP	○◐	Fl, Lf	Ins		
Oca	*Oxalis tuberosa*	7	HP	○◐	Fl, Lf, Root			Can be grown as annual
Painted milkvetch	*Astragalus pictus-filifolius*	5	HP	○	Root	Ins	N-fixer	
Peppermint	*Mentha × piperita vulgaris*	3	HP	◐●	Lf, Tea	Ins		
Perennial buckwheat	*Fagopyrum dibotrys*	5	HP	○◐	Lf, Sd	Ins, Hab, Chk		
Pig nut	*Bunium bulbocastanum*	5	HP	○◐	Lf, Root	Ins		
Pink purslane	*Claytonia sibirica*	3	HP	◐●	Lf	Ins, For		
Pleurisy root	*Asclepias tuberosa*	3	HP	○	Fl, Lf	Ins	Fiber	
Pokeweed	*Phytolacca americana*	4	HP	○	Lf, Med	Hab	Dye	Leaves toxic unless cooked and rinsed well
Potato	*Solanum tuberosum*	8	HP	○	Root		Biomass	Grown as annual
Reed	*Phragmites australis*	5	HP	○◐	Lf, Root	Hab	Dye, Fiber, Bskt	Bog plant
Rhubarb	*Rheum rhabarbarum*	3	HP	○◐	Stem		Dye	Leaves are toxic
Russian sage	*Perovskia atriplicifolia*	6	E Sh	○	Lf	Ins, Hum	Wbr, Hr	
Salad burnet	*Sanguisorba minor*	5	HP	○◐	Lf		Soil stab	
Sarsaparilla	*Aralia nudicaulis*	4	HP	○◐	Fr, Lf	Ins		
Scorzonera	*Scorzonera hispanica*	6	HP	○◐	Fl, Lf, Root			
Seakale	*Crambe maritima*	5	HP	○◐	Fl, Lf			
Showy milkweed	*Asclepias speciosa*	2	HP	○	Fl, Lf	Ins	Dye, Fiber	

Useful Plants for the Herb Layer (continued)

Common Name	Botanical Name	Hardy to USDA Zone	Type	Light	Edible part or use	Animal use	Other use	Comments
Spearmint	Mentha spicata	3	HP	◐●	Lf, Tea	Ins	Nutr, Dye, Fiber, Biomass	
Stinging nettle	Urtica dioica	6	HP	○●	Lf			
Stonecrop	Sedum spp.	5	HP	○●	Lf, Med	Ins		
Strawberry	Fragaria spp.	3	HP	○●	Fr, Lf,	Ins	Nutr	
Sweet cicely	Myrrhis odorata	5	HP	◐●	Lf, Sd, Root	Ins	Polish	
Sweet flag	Acorus calamus	3	HP	○●	Lf, Root		Fiber	
Sweet vetch	Hedysarum boreale	3	HP	○	Root	Ins	N-fixer	
Sweet violet	Viola odorata	5	HP	○●	Fl, Lf	Ins		
Tarragon	Artemisia dracunculus	6	HP	○●	Lf (seas)	Ins		
Thrift	Phlox subulata	4	HP	○●		Ins	Ground cover	
Trailing bellflower	Campanula poscharskyana	3	HP	○●	Fl, Lf	Ins, For		
Tuberous water lily	Nymphaea tuberosa	5	HP	○	Root, Sd			Water plant
Turkish rocket	Bunias orientalis	7	HP	○●	Fl, Lf	Ins		
Wapato	Sagittaria latifolia	6	HP	○●	Root			Also *S. sagittifolia*
Water chestnut	Trapa natans	5	HP	○	Sd			Water plant
Watercress	Nasturtium officinale	6	HP	●○	Lf, Sd	Ins	Nutr	Water plant
Welsh onion	Allium fistulosum	6	HP	○	Fl, Lf, Root		Nutr, Repellent	
Wild ginger	Asarum caudatum	2	HP	○	Seas			
Winter savory	Satureia montana	6	E Sh	○	Lf	Ins		
Yacon	Polymnia edulis	8	HP	○●	Root			Can be grown as annual
Yampah	Perideridia gairdneri	7	HP	○●	Lf, Root			
Yarrow	Achillea millefolium	2	HP	○	Lf, Tea, Med	Ins	Nutr, Dye	

Useful Vines and Climbing Plants

Common Name	Botanical Name	Hardy to USDA Zone	Type	Light	Edible part or use	Animal use	Other use	Comments
Akebia	Akebia quinata	5	D Cl	○◐	Fr		Bskt	Also A. trifoliata
Clematis	Clematis spp.	5	D Cl	○◐		Ins		
Cucumber	Cucumis sativus	9	D Cl	○	Fr, Fl	Ins		Grown as annual
Grape	Vitis vinifera	6	D Cl	○	Fr, Lf	Hab, Food	Dye	
Hardy kiwi	Actinidia arguta	4	D Cl	○	Fr			
He Shou Wu	Polygonum multiflorum	7	D Cl	○◐	Fr, Lf, Med			
Honeysuckle	Lonicera spp.	4	D Cl	○◐	Fl, Tea	Ins, Hab	Bskt	
Hops	Humulus lupulus	5	D Cl	○	Fl, Lf, Med	Ins, Hab	Fiber, Dye	
Jasmine	Jasminum officinale	6	D Cl	○◐	Fl	Ins, Hab	Fragrance	Also J. beesianum, J. humile, J. nudiflorum
Kiwi	Actinidia deliciosa	7	D Cl	○	Fr			
Mashua	Tropaeolum tuberosum	8	D Cl	○	Fl, Lf, Root			Can be grown as annual
Maypop	Passiflora incarnata	6	E Cl	○	Fr, Fl, Lf, Med	Ins		Also P. edulis, P. mollisima
Melon	Cucumis melo	9	D Cl	○	Fr, Fl	Ins		Grown as annual
Mountain yam	Dioscorea batatas	4	D Cl	○●	Rt			
Nasturtium	Tropaeolum majis	9	A/P Cl	○	Fl, Lf	Ins, Hab		Grown as annual
Passionflower	Passiflora caerulea	7	E Cl	○	Fr, Fl	Ins		
Pea	Pisum sativum	Annual	A Cl	○	Fr, Fl	Ins	N-fixer	
Perennial pea	Lathyrus latifolius	6	D Cl	○●	YLf	Ins	N-fixer	
Sarsaparilla	Smilax aspera	8	E Cl	○◐	Sht, Root, Med		Wbr, Hr, dye	
Scarlet runner bean	Phaseolus coccineus	9	D Cl	○	Fr, Fl	Ins	N-fixer	Grown as annual
Squash	Cucurbita spp.	9	D Cl	○	Fr, Fl	Ins	Gourd	Grown as annual
Wisteria	Wisteria floribunda	6	D Cl	○		Ins	Bskt, N-fixer	

Glossary

allelopaths Plants that secrete a toxic substance that suppresses competing plants.

biodiversity The variety of organisms present, considered from many levels: cultivar, species, genus, family, and on up to include all five kingdoms, as well as the diversity of habitats and ecosystems.

buffer plants Plants placed between guilds or between allelopathic species. They should be compatible with the trees in each guild and should have a positive effect on one or both of the guilds to be linked.

chaperone plants Species that protect seedlings from harm until the juveniles are ready for life on their own.

companion planting Placing two or more plant species in a way that at least one species benefits the other(s) by deterring pests, attracting pollinators, and so on.

compost The rich, humusy end product of decomposition, made by piling surplus organic matter into a mound or bin and letting it rot.

cover crops Crops planted specifically to build soil, reduce erosion, and smother weeds.

drip line The invisible boundary under a tree's outermost leaves.

edge effect The increase in diversity that occurs where two systems meet, creating conditions favorable to inhabitants of both sides of the edge as well as new conditions at the edge itself that support new inhabitants (as when a river flows into the sea or a pond meets its shore).

forest garden A multistoried, food- and habitat-producing landscape that acts like a natural woodland.

Gaia Greek goddess of the Earth, and the origin of the word root *geo-*, as in geography and geology. Also, as in Gaia theory, James Lovelock's idea that many of Earth's processes are self-regulating.

graywater The household water from sink, shower, tub, and laundry drains.

guild A harmoniously interwoven group of plants and animals, often centered around one major species, that benefits humans while creating habitat.

hardscaping The term designers use for wood, stone, concrete, and other constructed elements such as walls, sheds, paths, fences, and the like.

humus A fairly stable, complex group of nutrient-storing molecules created by microbes and other forces of decomposition by the conversion of organic matter.

interplanting Combining plant varieties in ways that avoid competition for light, space, or nutrients and that often discourage pests.

microclimate gardening Arranging plants in a manner that will take advantage of variations in microclimate (such as placing a frost-tender plant against a warm, south-facing wall) or in ways that will create favorable microclimates (such as using a tree to shade a house from hot sun).

mineralization The process of converting organic carbon-containing compounds into inorganic plant food.

monopodial Forming shoots from a central axis; in this book the term refers to bamboo species that are often described as "running" (and thus potentially invasive).

narcissistic Plants that thrive on the leaf litter of members of their own family, such as the Solanaceae, or nightshade family.

niche The role or function within an ecosystem played by a particular organism. Think of a niche as a profession and habitat as the workspace for performing the job.

nitrogen fixers Plants that host symbiotic micro-organisms in nodules among their roots that "fix" nitrogen gas from the air by combining it with carbon to make amino acids and related molecules. Includes most members of the pea or bean family (Fabaceae), plus certain other species.

nurse plants Species that create shelter and other favorable conditions in which more delicate plants can get a start.

opportunistic plant Species that, when introduced to a new environment, use resources more effectively than existing plants and reproduce more quickly. A less loaded term than "invasive."

parasitoids Small wasps and flies that lay their eggs inside other insects or insect eggs.

permaculture A set of techniques and principles for designing sustainable human settlements.

pioneer plants Certain fast-growing annual grasses, herbs, and flowers that are the first florae to arrive after a disturbance.

plant communities Groupings of trees, shrubs, and nonwoody plants that naturally occur together and seem to be connected as a whole.

pollinators Beneficial insects that transport pollen for fruit and seed set.

polycultures Dynamic, self-organizing plant communities composed of several to many species.

predator insects Beneficial insects that consume pest insect species.

primary decomposers Invertebrates, bacteria, algae, fungi, and actinomycetes that are the first to consume organic matter.

scaffold plants Species whose physical presence lets young or otherwise vulnerable plants get established.

secondary decomposers Mold mites, springtails, certain beetles, and other organisms that feed on primary decomposers.

sectors Areas where outside energies such as wind, sun, fire, and so forth enter a site. These energies can be mitigated, captured, or otherwise influenced by placement of elements in the design.

sheet mulching Composting in place to eradicate weeds and build soil without the need for herbicides or tilling.

standing biomass The part of an ecosystem that is permanent, such as branches and large roots, as opposed to seasonal, such as fruit or deciduous leaves.

succession Change in composition of organisms in an ecosystem, often progressing from pioneer species to shrubs to trees.

swale A shallow trench laid out dead level along the land's contours to allow water to enter the soil.

sympodial Forming main shoots from secondary ones; in this book the term refers to "clumping" bamboo species, which are usually not invasive.

tertiary decomposers Soil organisms that feed on the secondary (and some primary) decomposers.

tilth The loose, crumbly structure of microbially rich soil, created by certain soil bacteria that secrete gums, waxes, and gels that hold tiny particles of earth together.

weeds A highly subjective category of maligned plants that even the United States Department of Agriculture admits are simply "plants that interfere with human activities."

zones A permaculture design method in which elements are placed according to how often they are used or need attention. The more an element is used, the closer to the house it is located.

Bibliography

Albrecht, William A. *The Albrecht Papers*. Acres USA, 1996. Somewhat quirky collection of papers by a soil scientist with vision.

Alexander, Christopher. *A Pattern Language*. Oxford, 1977. A classic on human-scale design.

Angier, Bradford. *One Acre & Security: How to Live off the Earth without Ruining It*. Willow Creek, 2000. A useful and broad-ranging resource for homesteading and small animal care.

Bell, Graham. *The Permaculture Garden*. Thorson's, 1994. A British-oriented introduction to permaculture gardening techniques.

Bennett, Bob. *Raising Rabbits the Modern Way*. Garden Way, 1980. Good introduction to rabbits in the backyard.

Brady, Nyle C. *The Nature and Properties of Soils*. Prentice-Hall, 1996. This major textbook on soils covers the whole subject in depth.

Brickell, Christopher. *American Horticultural Society Encyclopedia of Garden Plants*. Macmillan, 1990. An illustrated guide to most common landscape plants, with thousands of photos.

Brookes, John. *The Book of Garden Design*. Macmillan, 1991. A general guide by a well-known conventional landscape designer.

Buchanan, Rita. *Taylor's Master Guide to Landscaping*. Houghton Mifflin, 2000. A good, comprehensive introduction to landscape design techniques for the home owner.

Buchmann, Stephen L., and Gary Paul Nabhan. *The Forgotten Pollinators*. Island, 1996. An informative, well-written account of the role of helpful but endangered insects.

Campbell, Stu, and Donna Moore. *The Mulch Book: A Complete Guide for Gardeners*. Storey Books, 1991. A good introduction to mulching.

Capra, Fritjof. *The Web of Life*. Doubleday, 1996. An engaging account of how the new sciences of complexity and self-organization are affecting our understanding of living systems.

Cocannouer, Joseph. *Weeds: Guardians of the Soil*. Devin-Adair, 1950. Describes the role of weeds useful crops and as indicators of fertility, with much historical lore.

Coleman, Eliot. *Four-Season Harvest*. Chelsea Green, 1999. How to extend the growing season to the whole year, even in northern climates.

Conrad, Ross. *Natural Beekeeping: Organic Approaches to Modern Apiculture*. Chelsea Green, 2007. Natural methods for raising bees and keeping them healthy.

Creasy, Rosalind. *Organic Gardener's Edible Plants*. Van Patten, 1993. Descriptions of over 130 edible ornamental plants.

———. *The Complete Book of Edible Landscaping*. Sierra Club, 1982. The foundation book that brought vegetables into the front yard.

Dennis, John V. *The Wildlife Gardener*. Knopf, 1985. A good introduction to creating gardens for wildlife habitat.

Deppe, Carol. *Breed Your Own Vegetable Varieties: The Gardener's and Farmer's Guide.* Chelsea Green, 2000. A practical and in-depth guide, one of the best on the subject for gardeners.

Douglas, J. Sholto, and Robert Hart. *Forest Farming.* Rodale, 1985. A strong argument for growing trees for food and fodder, with descriptions of many species.

Druse, Ken. *The Natural Habitat Garden.* Potter, 1994. How to create prairie, meadow, woodland, and wetland gardens using native plants.

Facciola, Stephen. *Cornucopia II: A Source Book of Edible Plants.* Kampong, 1998. A comprehensive list and description of edible flora.

Farrelly, David. *The Book of Bamboo.* Sierra Club, 1984. A thoughtful and thorough investigation into the culture, varieties, and uses of bamboo.

Fern, Ken. *Plants for a Future: Edible and Useful Plants for a Healthier World.* Permanent Publications, 1997. Distributed in the United States by Chelsea Green Publishing. A British book covering a wide range of multifunctional plants.

Florea, J. H. *ABC of Poultry Raising: A Complete Guide for the Beginner or Expert.* Dover, 1977. A standard work on small-scale poultry care.

Flores, Heather C. *Food Not Lawns.* Chelsea Green, 2006. Permaculture gardening and community organizing with an urban focus.

Fukuoka, Masanobu. *The One Straw Revolution.* Rodale, 1978. Nature as a model for agriculture.

Gaddie, Ronald, and Donald Douglas. *Earthworms for Ecology and Profit.* Bookworm, 1977. One of the best books on worm composting and worm beds.

Gershuny, Grace. *Start with the Soil.* Rodale, 1993. A superb handbook on the how and why of creating great soil.

Gessert, Kate Rogers. *The Beautiful Food Garden Encyclopedia of Attractive Food Plants.* Van Nostrand Reinhold, 1983. How to landscape with good-looking vegetables.

Haggard, Ben. *Living Community.* Center for the Study of Community, 1993. The evolution of a premier permaculture site, written by a master designer.

Hart, Robert. *Forest Gardening: Cultivating an Edible Landscape.* Chelsea Green, 1996. A personal account of forest garden design by one of the originators of the field.

Hobhouse, Penelope. *Flower Gardens.* Little, Brown and Co., 1991. A well-illustrated volume by one of the experts on arranging plants by color and form.

Holmes, Roger. *Home Landscaping* (series). Creative Homeowner Press, 1998. A series of books, divided by geographic region of the United States, that covers landscaping basics and lists suitable regional plants.

Holmgren, David. *Hepburn Permaculture Gardens.* Holmgren Design Services, 1995. One of the few case studies of a complete permaculture design, covering David's home site in Australia.

———. *Permaculture: Pathways and Principles Beyond Sustainability.* Holmgren Design Services, 2002. Permaculture's principles applied to sustainability and energy descent, by the field's cofounder.

Howard, Sir Albert. *The Soil and Health.* Rodale, 1976. The relationship between good soil and healthy people by one of the originators of organic farming.

Hunt, Marjorie. *High-Yield Gardening.* Rodale, 1986. A superb guide to extending the growing season, high-density planting, and getting more from the garden.

Jacke, David, and Eric Toensmeier. *Edible Forest Gardens.* Chelsea Green, 2005. The new bible on forest gardening, highly recommended.

Jeavons, John. *How to Grow More Vegetables (Than You Ever Thought Possible on Less Land Than You Can Imagine).* Ten Speed, 1991. Biointensive (and labor-intensive) techniques that boost production; excellent for small spaces.

Jekyll, Gertrude. *Colour Schemes for the Flower Garden.* Ayer, 1983. One of several classic books by Jekyll on garden design.

Kauffman, Stuart. *At Home in the Universe.* Oxford, 1995. Kauffman shows how life inevitably will emerge when there is sufficient complexity.

———. *The Origins of Order.* Oxford, 1994. A dense and scholarly treatment of the ideas expressed in *At Home in the Universe.*

Kelly, Kevin. *Out of Control.* Addison Wesley, 1994. How our new understanding of biology is transforming both ecology and economics.

Kourik, Robert. *Designing and Maintaining Your Edible Landscape—Naturally.* Metamorphic, 1986. A comprehensive, well-researched book with great reference lists and tables.

Kress, Stephen M. *National Audubon Society Bird Garden.* DK, 1995. Designs and plants for gardens that provide food, water, cover, and nesting sites for birds.

Lanza, Patricia. *Lasagna Gardening.* Rodale, 1998. An entire book on sheet mulching, combined with growing suggestions for this method.

Lee, Andy, Pat Foreman, and Patricia L. Foreman. *Chicken Tractor: The Permaculture Guide to Happy Hens and Healthy Soil.* Good Earth, 1998. Using mobile chicken pens, with plenty of information on poultry raising in general.

Lowenfels, Jeff, and Wayne Lewis. *Teaming with Microbes.* Timber, 2006. A science-based but reader-friendly guide to the soil food web.

Ludwig, Art. *Create an Oasis with Greywater: Your Complete Guide to Choosing, Building and Using Greywater Systems.* Oasis Design, 2000. The best practical guide to graywater systems.

Luttmann, Rick, and Gail Luttmann. *Chickens in Your Backyard: A Beginner's Guide.* Rodale, 1976. A good book on small-scale chicken raising for the homeowner.

Mandelbrot, Benoit. *The Fractal Geometry of Nature.* W. H. Freeman & Co, 1983. Key insights into natural patterns by the developer of the fractal concept.

Matson, Tim. *Earth Ponds.* Countryman, 1998. The lore and constructions of earth-dam ponds.

McHarg, Ian. *Design with Nature.* Wiley, 1992. Innovative techniques for appropriate landscape design using map overlays.

McKinley, Michael. *How to Attract Birds.* Ortho Books, 1999. Instructions for attracting specific birds with plants and feeders.

Mollison, Bill, and Reny Slay. *An Introduction to Permaculture.* Tagari, 1991. Concise coverage of permaculture's basic principles.

Mollison, Bill. *Permaculture: A Designers' Manual.* Tagari, 1988. The fat bible on permaculture, worth many rereadings and perusings.

Morrow, Rosemary. *Earth User's Guide to Permaculture.* Simon & Schuster, 2000. An informal introduction to permaculture by an experienced teacher.

Neill, William, and Pat Murphy. *By Nature's Design.* Chronicle, 1993. Stunning photographs and clear explanations of nature's patterns.

O'Neill, R. V. *A Hierarchical View of Ecosystems.* Princeton, 1986. An advanced look at how ecosystems function.

Odum, Eugene P. *Fundamentals of Ecology.* W. B. Saunders, 1971. An early textbook that covers the basics of ecology in depth.

Pacey, Arnold, and Adrian Cullis. *Rainwater Harvesting.* Intermediate Technology, 1996. Many techniques for using rainwater.

Pfeiffer, Ehrenfried. *Weeds and What They Tell.* Bio-Dynamic Farming & Garden Association, 1981. How to use weeds to assess the type and fertility of the local soil.

Reich, Lee. Uncommon Fruits for Every Garden. Timber, 2004. A comprehensive guide to many of the plants used in permaculture design.

Reid, Grant W. *Landscape Graphics.* Whitney Library of Design, 1987. Excellent introduction to professional landscape drawing.

Romanowski, Nick. *Farming in Ponds and Dams.* Lothian, 1994. An Australian book on aquaculture and pond construction.

Seidenberg, Charlotte. *The Wildlife Garden.* University of Mississippi, 1995. An introduction to wildlife habitat gardening with examples of garden designs.

Smith, J. Russell. *Tree Crops: A Permanent Agriculture.* Devin-Adair, 1987. One of the inspirations for the permaculture concept, showing how trees are key to sustainable agriculture.

Stein, Sara. *Noah's Garden: Restoring the Ecology of Our Own Back Yards.* Houghton Mifflin, 1995. A well-written and compelling plea for allowing nature back into our yards, full of natural history.

Stevens, Peter S. *Patterns in Nature.* Little, Brown, 1974. A review of the common classes of patterns found in nature.

Stout, Ruth. *The Ruth Stout No-Work Garden Book.* Rodale, 1975. Using deep mulches to reduce labor and improve fertility.

Tekulsky, Mathew. *The Hummingbird Garden.* Crown, 1986. A guide to cultivating plants that attract these flying jewels; one of the best on the subject.

Thompson, D'arcy Wentworth. *On Growth and Form.* Dover, 1992. A magisterial text on how the shapes and patterns in nature are formed; a classic in the field.

Tilth. *The Future Is Abundant.* Tilth, 1982. An early book on sustainable gardening, still worth reading.

Toensmeier, Eric. *Perennial Vegetables.* Chelsea Green, 2007. The best book on growing perennial vegetables, covering most known species for temperate climates.

Tufts, Craig, and Peter Loewer. *The National Wildlife Federation's Guide to Gardening for Wildlife.* Rodale, 1995. How to provide garden habitat for birds, insects, and nocturnal animals.

United States Department of Agriculture. *Common Weeds of the United States.* Dover, 1971. A good technical guide to 224 species of weeds, with clear drawings. Organized by plant family, so it requires a little botanical knowledge.

Van der Ryn, Sim, and Stuart Cowan. *Ecological Design.* Island, 1995. The essential concepts of ecological design.

Verey, Rosemary. *The Art of Planting.* Little, Brown, 1990. A good coffee-table guide to placing plants by color, texture, and form.

Whitefield, Patrick. *The Earthcare Manual.* Permanent Publications, 1997. Whitefield's comprehensive, unique, and British vision of permaculture.

Whitefield, Patrick. *How to Make a Forest Garden.* Permanent Publications, 1997. Distributed in the United States by Chelsea Green. Instructions and ideas for forest gardens, with a British focus but usable in North America.

Yeomans, P. A., and K. A. Yeomans. *Water for Every Farm.* Keyline Designs, 1993. An inspirational view of how to store water in the soil.

Yepsen, Roger, ed. *Encyclopedia of Natural Insect and Disease Control.* Rodale, 1984. Natural pest control, with clear drawings and photos for identifying insects.

Resources

Magazines

Permaculture Activist
PO Box 5516, Bloomington, IN 47407
www.permacultureactivist.net/
$23/year, 4 issues.

Permaculture Magazine (England)
www.permaculture.co.uk
In the United States, contact *Permaculture Activist*
(above) for subscription information.
$29/year, 4 issues.

Permaculture Teaching and Consulting Organizations

Barking Frogs Permaculture Center
PO Box 52, Sparr, FL
32192-0052
www.barkingfrogspermaculture.org/

Culture's Edge
1025 Camp Elliot Rd.,
Black Mountain, NC 28711
828-669-3937
pcactiv@metalab.unc.edu

Central Rocky Mountain Permaculture Institute
PO Box 631, Basalt, CO 81621
970-927-4158
www.crmpi.org/
jerome@crmpi.org

Earthflow Design Works
739A E. Foothill Blvd. #130
San Luis Obispo, CA 93405
310-383-5495
www.earthflow.com/

The Farm Ecovillage Training Center
PO Box 90, Summertown, TN 38483-0090
615-954-3574
www.thefarm.org/etc/

Finger Lakes Permaculture Institute
PO Box 54, Ithaca, NY 14851
(607) 227-0316
www.fingerlakespermaculture.org/

Lost Valley Educational Center
81868 Lost Valley Lane, Dexter, OR 97431
541-937-3351
www.lostvalley.org
permaculture@lostvalley.org

Occidental Arts and Ecology Center
15290 Coleman Valley Rd., Occidental, CA 95465
707-874-1557
www.oaec.org/
oaec@oaec.org

Patterns for Abundance
5421 E. King's Rd, Bloomington, IN 47408
812-335-0383
permacultureactivist.net/design/Designconsult
.html

Regenerative Design Institute (Permaculture
Institute of Northern California)
PO Box 923, Bolinas, CA 94924
415-868 9681
www.regenerativedesign.org

Permaculture Institute USA
PO Box 3702, Pojoaque, NM 87501

505-455-0270
pci@permaculture-inst.org

Plant Databases on the Internet

The Ethnobotany Database
www.ars-grin.gov/duke
A database developed by James A. Duke and Stephen M. Beckstrom-Sternberg housed at the National Germplasm Resources Laboratory (NGRL). It contains 80,000 records of plants and their uses worldwide.

GRIN Taxonomy
www.ars-grin.gov/npgs/tax/
The USDA's Germplasm Resources Information Network database, with brief descriptions of over 34,000 plant species and links to further information. The focus is mostly on useful plants.

Plants for a Future
www.pfaf.org
Over 7,000 useful plants are described, with their uses, culture, and much other information in a well-designed searchable website. My favorite source of data on useful plants.

USDA PLANTS Database
http://plants.usda.gov/plants/index.html
This database includes names, checklists, automated tools, identification information, species abstracts, and other plant information on a large number of plants grown in the United States.

Seeds, Live Plants, and Garden Supplies

Abundant Life Seed Foundation
PO Box 772, Port Townsend, WA 98368
360-385-5660
www.abundantlifeseeds.com/
Nonprofit growers and collectors of nonhybrid seeds. Catalog $2.

Ames' Orchard and Nursery
Rt. 5, Box 194, Fayetteville, AR 72701
501-443-0282

Specializes in disease-resistant apple, pear, grape, raspberry, and other trees and small fruits for the South. Catalog for two first-class stamps.

The Banana Tree, Inc.
715 Northampton St., Easton, PA 18042
610-253-9589
www.banana-tree.com
faban@enter.net
Thousands of tropical seeds and bulbs.

Bountiful Gardens
Shafer Ranch Rd., Willits, CA 95490-9626
707-459-6410
www.bountifulgardens.org/
bountiful@sonic.net
A nonprofit research organization with a wide selection, including many heirloom cultivars.

Burnt Ridge Nursery
432 Burnt Ridge Rd., Onalaska, WA 98570
350-985-2873
www.burntridgenursery
Many nut and fruit trees varieties.

The Cook's Garden
PO Box 5010, Hodges, SC 29653-5010
802-824-3400
www.cooksgarden.com/
Retail and wholesale seeds with many heirlooms.

DeGiorgi Seed Co.
6011 N St., Omaha, NE 68117-1634
www.degiorgiseed.com
Over 1,500 varieties, including perennials, vegetables, and grasses.

Deep Diversity
Box 190, Gila, NM 88038
www.one-garden.org/deep.htm
The brilliant Alan Kapuler's delightful and esoteric seed collection.

Edible Landscaping Nursery
PO Box 77, Afton, VA 22920
804-361-9134
www.eat-it.com/
el@cstone.net
A wide selection of fruits, nuts, kiwis, and edible shrubs.

Fedco Trees
PO Box 520,Waterville, ME 04903-0520
207-873-7333
www.fedcoseed.com/trees.html/
Hardy tree fruits and nuts, small fruits, and berries as well as ornamentals.

Fern Hill Nursery
78703 Echo Hollow Lane
Cottage Grove, OR 97424
541-942-3118
fernhillnursery.com
Small but useful selection of multifunctional species and West Coast natives.

Forestfarm Nursery
990 Tetherow Rd., Williams, OR 97544-9599
541-846-7269
www.forestfarm.com
This may be the most extensive supply of useful plants in the United States—over 3,000 varieties. Catalog $5 and worth it.

Garden City Seeds
778 Hwy. 93 North Hamilton, MT 59840
406-961-4837
www.gardencityseeds.com/
A nonprofit carrying over 500 cultivars and green manures.

Greenmantle Nursery
3010 Ettersburg Rd., Garberville, CA 95542
707-986-7504
www.greenmantlenursery.com
Specializes in fruit and nut trees for homesteaders.

Harmony Farm Supply
PO Box 450, Graton, CA 95444
707-823-9125
www.harmonyfarm.com/
Seeds, irrigation supplies, fertilizer, and more for farm and garden.

Hidden Springs Nursery
Rt. 14, Box 159, Cookeville, TN 38501
615-268-9889
www.hiddenspringsnursery.com/
Unusual fruits and the like, including medlar, autumn olive, and other permacultural plants.

J. L. Hudson, Seedsman
PO Box 1058, Redwood, CA 94064
 www.jlhudsonseeds.net/
Sells open-pollinated varieties from all over the world. A wide array of useful food and medicinal species. Catalog $1.

Native Seeds/SEARCH
525 N. 4th Ave., Tucson AZ 85705-8450
520-327-9123
www.nativeseeds.org/
Specializes in heirloom varieties from Mexico and the Southwest. Catalog $1.

Nichols Garden Nursery
190 N. Pacific Hwy., Albany, OR 97321-4580
541-928-9280
www.gardennursery.com/index.html
info@gardennursery.com
A wide assortment of herbs and vegetables.

Oikos Tree Crops
PO Box 19425, Kalamazoo, MI 49019-0425
616-624-6233
Edible native fruits, nuts, tubers, and perennials.

One Green World
28696 S. Cramer Rd., Molalla, OR 97038
www.onegreenworld.com/

Large selection of multifunctional fruits, nuts, shrubs, bamboos, and more.

Oregon Exotics Rare Fruit Nursery
1055 Messinger Rd., Grants Pass, OR 97527
541-846-7578
www.exoticfruit.com/
Mouth-watering selection of exotic tubers and fruits, though a small inventory at present.

Ornamental Edibles
3522 Weedlin Court, San Jose, CA 95132
408-946-7333
www.ornamentaledibles.com/
Over 400 varieties of gourmet and edible flowers for urban landscapes.

Peace Seeds
2385 S.E.Thompson St., Corvallis, OR 97333
http://peaceseeds.com
An extensive selection of heirloom varieties and high-nutrition vegetables, maintained by the brilliant Alan Kapuler.

Peaceful Valley Farm Supply
PO Box 2209, Grass Valley, CA 95945
530-272-4769
www.groworganic.com
Seeds, irrigation, and natural pest-management supplies, and a very educational catalog.

Permaculture Seed and Plant Exchange
3020 Whiteoak Creek Rd., Burnsville, NC 28714
704-675-5664
An annual catalog that links growers and collectors with buyers.

Plants of the Southwest
Agua Fria Rd., Rt. 5 Box 11A,
Santa Fe, NM 87501
800-788-7333
www.plantsofthesouthwest.com/
Native plants and seeds from the Southwest.

Redwood City Seed Co.
PO Box 351, Redwood City, CA 94064
www.ecoseeds.com/
An early leader in untreated heirloom seeds; specializes in hot peppers.

Sandy Bar Nursery
PO Box 347, Orleans, CA 95556
530-627-3379
www.sandybarnursery.com/
Heirloom and unusual fruit trees, wide selection of vigorous, healthy stock.

Seed Savers Exchange
RR 3, Box 239, Decorah, Iowa 52101
www.seedsavers.org
Now offering its own retail seed catalog, Seed Savers is a nonprofit grassroots organization of gardeners who grow and preserve thousands of rare, nonhybrid plant varieties. Members receive an annual Yearbook from which they can order seeds from other listed seed savers.

Seeds of Change
521 Old Santa Fe Trail, #10,
Santa Fe, NM 87501
Open-pollinated, organically grown, non-GMO seeds selected for nutrition, drought tolerance, and genetic diversity.

Shepherd's Garden Seeds
30 Irene St., Torrington, CT 06790
203-482-3638
www.shepherdseeds.com/
Large collection of heirloom vegetable, herb, and flower seeds.

St. Lawrence Nurseries
325 State Hwy. 345, Potsdam, NY 13575
315-265-6739
www.sln.potsdam.ny.us
Specializes in fruits and nut trees for northern climates, managed organically.

Index

About the Author

Toby Hemenway is the author of the first major North American book on permaculture, *Gaia's Garden: A Guide to Home-Scale Permaculture*, and an adjunct assistant professor at Portland State University. He wrote the foreword for Heather C. Flores's *Food Not Lawns*.

After obtaining a degree in biology from Tufts University, Toby worked for many years as a researcher in genetics and immunology, first in academic laboratories including Harvard and the University of Washington in Seattle, and then at Immunex, a major medical biotech company. At about the time he was growing dissatisfied with the direction biotechnology was taking, he discovered permaculture, a design approach based on ecological principles that creates sustainable landscapes, homes, and workplaces. A career change followed, and Toby and his wife spent ten years creating a rural permaculture site in southern Oregon. He was associate editor of *Permaculture Activist*, a journal of ecological design and sustainable culture, from 1999 to 2004. His current project is developing urban sustainability resources in Portland, Oregon, where he now lives. He teaches permaculture and consults and lectures on ecological design throughout the country. His writing has appeared in magazines such as *Whole Earth Review*, *Natural Home*, and *Kitchen Gardener*. He is available for workshops, lectures, and consulting in ecological design.

Visit his Web site at www.patternliteracy.com.